RECKONING WITH SLAVERY

RECKONING
with
SLAVERY

*A Critical Study
in the Quantitative History of
American Negro Slavery*

**PAUL A. DAVID
HERBERT G. GUTMAN
RICHARD SUTCH
PETER TEMIN
GAVIN WRIGHT**

With an Introduction by
KENNETH M. STAMPP

New York

OXFORD UNIVERSITY PRESS

1976

Chapter 1 is reprinted with alterations from *The Journal of Interdisciplinary History*, v. (1975), 445–457, by permission of *The Journal of Interdisciplinary History* and the M.I.T. Press, Cambridge, Massachusetts.

AUTHORS' PREFACE

It is now little more than a century since slavery was abolished in the United States. Just as the "peculiar institution" posed a moral problem for antebellum Americans, the history of slavery poses a problem for present-day Americans who care to think about their country's past. The inability of historians (and others) to resolve fully the historical and ethical questions raised by the existence of slavery has resulted in a vast and continuous outpouring of scholarly work devoted to this facet of American history.

This is a book about one recent attempt to come to grips with the nature and meaning of slavery in America: the provocative and much discussed work *Time on the Cross* by Robert William Fogel and Stanley L. Engerman. The authors of *Time on the Cross* present an arresting new view of American Negro slavery, a view constructed around their reappraisal of its economic aspects. They argue that the slave economy of the South was unqualifiedly capitalistic, dynamic, and more efficient than the contemporary agricultural system based upon the labor of free men. As a result, slavery provided a high rate of economic growth for the South and a high standard of living for all Southerners—the enslaved as well as the free. According to *Time on the Cross*, the comparatively good treatment accorded to the slaves secured their willing cooperation in the productive activities in which they were deployed, and particularly in the running of southern plantations. Plantation slaves, the book asserts, were ambitious and worked harder and more efficiently than free farm laborers. They identified with their masters and adopted both a style of family life and a work ethic that neatly fitted into the dominant Victorian mode of middle-class behavior.

It has been a long time since a scholarly work of history (not to mention of economic history) has attracted so much attention, both inside and outside of academic circles. The immediate excitement and the welter of publicity which attended the publication of Fogel and Engerman's book in the spring of 1974 has, by now, largely abated. Yet the inherent interest of the subject treated in *Time on the Cross*, the striking novelty of many of the conclusions reached in its pages, and the sweeping claims made on behalf of the new historical methods which its authors champion, all remain. These now invite a closer and more reflective examination than they initially received.

In an early review, C. Vann Woodward hailed the rhetorical force and novelty of the thesis advanced in *Time on the Cross*, but voiced skepticism about its validity and ended by calling for "the most thorough and unsparing criticism" of its data, methods, and findings by qualified historians. All of the authors of the present volume have published technical review-articles dealing with *Time on the Cross*. Those reviews appeared in scholarly journals and were directed to a readership composed of professional economic and social historians; each sought to treat extensively one or another aspect of the book.[1] It is only in this volume that we offer the integrated and comprehensive critique called for by Woodward. Without sacrificing accuracy or unduly oversimplifying what are unavoidably complex questions, we nevertheless hope that we have managed in this book to present the results of our critical studies in terms which make them accessible to a wider audience.

Our book is not a polemic on the meaning of the Afro-American experience of slavery. We trust it will not be thought pretentious for us to say that we offer it instead as a scientific contribution to the writing of American history in general, and the history of antebellum southern society in particular.

[1] See David and Temin [1974]; David and Temin [1975]; Gutman [1975]; Sutch [1975a]; Wright [1975].

This wording of our purpose directs notice to an important distinction. A "scientific contribution to the writing of history" and a "contribution to writing scientific history" are not one and the same. The latter phrase evokes visions of a discipline aspiring to uncover durable "laws" that govern the workings of historical processes, objective truths somehow resembling the generalizations of physics or chemistry regarding the structure of the material world. None among us has either much hope or much sympathy for enterprises dedicated to realizing such visions. All of us, on the other hand, believe that there are many aspects of historical experience that can be more fully illuminated by applications of analytical approaches and statistical methods borrowed from the quantitative social sciences. More fundamental than this shared methodological bent is our subscription to the broader canons of empirical verification. This is the essence of scientific discipline, and it should unite professional historians of all methodological persuasions.

First among those canons is the one which insists upon replicability. Would-be scientific investigators are enjoined to present their data, to describe their sources, and to recapitulate their reasoning, in order to facilitate replication of their findings by skeptics. Such faith as is evinced in the organization of scientific disciplines reposes not with the intuitions and insights of gifted individuals but rather with science conceived of as an open, collaborative enterprise. From this vantage point it counts for little that claims for the truth of a particular conclusion may be ultimately vindicated, so long as the details of its derivation remain mysterious. A scientific conclusion, however inherently plausible or ideologically palatable it may be, is made scientific only by the condition that the specific methods employed in reaching it conform to the standards established in the discipline.

This is the context in which the present volume may be seen as a scientific contribution to the writing of history. It is concerned with the delineation and preservation of existing scientific norms. What has been undertaken here essentially is a study in replication: we have tried to assess a particularly arresting piece of historical writing against the recognized methodological standards of the discipline from which it claims to derive, the discipline of "historians and economists who are trained in the application of quantitative methods to historical problems." The undertaking of such an assessment as a *collaborative* responsibility, by people who have identified themselves with that discipline, seems to us to be particularly appropriate.

In a reasonably well ordered scientific discipline, the results of studies aimed at replicating findings reported by others seldom assume notoriety. Unfortunately, this seems to be one of those rare occasions. We would not have brought such a long and detailed critique of the sources, data, and techniques employed in *Time on the Cross* to the attention of our fellow historians and the public had we not found so much in the book that was methodologically objectionable. The manifold nature of these deficiencies warrants an open discussion of the validity of both the approach taken and the empirical findings reported in that book. We have sought to initiate such a discussion here, not in pursuit of methodological perfectionism but, rather, to expose the weak foundations upon which Fogel and Engerman have erected what appears to us to be a misleading interpretation of antebellum southern society and its relationship to the economy of the region.

Not every feature of the picture of life in the antebellum South that *Time on the Cross* projects is unfamiliar to professional historians or even to lay students of American history. But we have been forced to conclude that it is precisely the *novel* features of the book's argument that fail to withstand scientific scrutiny.

The function of scientific criticism of the kind undertaken here is to avert the repetition of procedural errors. Throughout this volume the subjects of foremost concern are not the lessons offered by *Time on the Cross* for "the understanding of contemporary issues," but the reasoning, the procedures, and the character of the empirical evidence that underlie the historical assertions made in that book. To those who would say that our treatment of *Time on the Cross* as more than a tentative and preliminary report is unfair, or at least uncalled for, because that book did not pretend to be a definitive statement of its authors' views, we must reply that it was neither publicly presented nor publicly received as mere speculation. *Time on the Cross* announces itself as the embodiment of the findings of "almost a decade and a half" of intensive and sophisticated research by a large body of scholars, from which "the main features of the actual operation of the slave economy are now clear." Surely any historical work which makes such claims deserves nothing less than to be taken seriously and to be judged on its own merits.

Our book is divided into three parts, which follow an Introduction by Kenneth M. Stampp. Part One deals with the *personae* of the historical drama, the individuals who participated in the system of slavery. It is addressed, in particular, to the reinterpretation which *Time on the Cross* presents of the motives and actions of the masters and the slaves. The opening chapter discusses the logical pitfalls that await historians or others who try to reason from a knowledge of the outcomes of social and market processes in order to arrive at conclusions about the personalities and the conduct of the individuals who participated in them. Three successive chapters then re-examine first, the evidence regarding masters' choices among, and slaves' responses to, different incentive structures, and the way these affected labor discipline and the work ethic among plantation slaves; second, the impact upon black slave families of the slave trade and the transfer of human chattel; and last, the relationships between masters and slaves that influenced the sexual mores and behavior of the members of the slave community.

Part Two of the book approaches slavery as an economic institution and re-examines the attempt in *Time on the Cross* to appraise the functioning of the system from a somewhat abstract, impersonal level, that is, by evaluating its overall material consequences. The opening chapter of this part analyzes the problematic aspects of applying the concepts of "economic exploitation" and "economic efficiency" to a mode of production based upon involuntary servitude. The next chapter evaluates the material consequences of the system based on slavery by considering it from a particular vantage point, that of the class that occupied the least favored position in the socioeconomic order—the slaves. This chapter corrects the factually misleading picture that *Time on the Cross* paints of the typical slave's economic condition. The last chapter of this part appraises the functioning of the antebellum southern economy from a different perspective, focusing upon the sources of the slave plantations' prosperity, and the bearing this had upon the capacities of the region's economy for long-term growth and development.

The third and concluding part offers a critical judgment of *Time on the Cross* as a work of history, and indicates an alternative direction in which future research on slavery and the economic and social history of the antebellum South might more usefully proceed.

The individual chapters forming the book's first and second parts each carry attributions to specific authors among our company, but the concluding part, like this preface, represents a collaborative statement to which we all have made some contribution and for which we equally share responsibility.

Although the individual chapter attributions apportion responsibility among us, they do not convey the mutual obligations we have contracted in the course of this collaborative effort. In any listing of acknowledgments then, our first acknowledgment must be made to each other. The independent reviews of *Time on the Cross* which we have published elsewhere record important debts of gratitude which were accumulated in connection with the preparation of those articles. We have not thought it necessary to reiterate any previous acknowledgments on this occasion, save for one: Stanley Engerman and Robert Fogel generously answered numerous questions and provided raw data which greatly facilitated some of the work upon which the following chapters report. To *Explorations in Economic History* and Academic Press, *The Journal of Economic History*, *The Journal of Interdisciplinary History* and M.I.T. Press, *The Journal of Negro History*, and the University of Illinois Press, we are obliged for permission freely to draw upon material we previously published in their pages.

We are much indebted to Carl Degler for encouraging this project at an early stage; to Nathan Rosenberg for supplying invariably useful editorial suggestions; to Sheldon Meyer of Oxford University Press, for sharing our views about the importance of the undertaking and displaying extraordinary toleration of the extra delays and complications attending works of multiple authorship; to Edward Steinmueller, Susan Steinmueller and Thomas Ulen for lending indispensable hands in the editing of the manuscript and the preparation of the index and concordance.

Finally, we must express our gratitude to Kenneth Stampp for the Introduction he has furnished for our book. His essay gracefully and durably bridges the deep chasm of methodological misapprehension and distrust that too often has threatened to leave historians who work in the differing traditions of the humanities and the social sciences permanently isolated from each other.

January 1976   P.A.D.
                                                                     H.G.G.
                                                                     R.S.
                                                                     P.T.
                                                                     G.W.

CONTENTS

Part Three: A Judgment

RECKONING WITH SLAVERY

INTRODUCTION

A Humanistic Perspective

Kenneth M. Stampp

Robert William Fogel and Stanley L. Engerman, in *Time on the Cross*, attempt a "radical reinterpretation" of slavery in the antebellum South.[1] As a revisionist work their book exemplifies a common historiographical phenomenon: the recurrent revolts against familiar ways of viewing institutions, social movements, and major events of the past. Even the cliché that every generation rewrites history is an understatement, for many an exciting fresh interpretation—occasionally one that some naïve reviewer hails as "definitive"—has not had time to find its way into the textbooks before it in turn is significantly revised. No doubt the process is both endless and inevitable. Discoveries of new data, experiments with new methodologies, varying perceptions of individual and group behavior, and an ever changing world which modifies our needs and our perspectives—all these evoke the novel conceptualizations which are the impelling force behind the rewriting of history.

History is not an exact science—not even the "New Economic History" with its immensely valuable methods of quantification and data analysis. Ultimately the most meticulously weighed and finely measured data, both numerical and literary, must be subjectively interpreted by the historian, for historical facts do

---

[1] Robert William Fogel and Stanley L. Engerman, *Time on the Cross*, Vol. I: *The Economics of American Negro Slavery*; Vol. II: *Evidence and Methods—A Supplement* (Boston, 1974). Hereafter cited FE, I, and FE, II.

not speak for themselves. Rather, as Edward H. Carr observes, "The facts speak only when the historian calls on them: it is he who decides to which facts to give the floor, and in what order or context." [2] How the historian decides these matters depends in part upon his own experiences and his perception of the world in which he lives. Between past and present, Marc Bloch reminds us, "the lines of connection work both ways. . . . In the last analysis, whether consciously or no, it is always by borrowing from our daily experiences and by shading them, where necessary, with new tints that we derive the elements which help us to restore the past." [3]

Historians react to this reality in different ways. Some simply get on with their research, adapt their procedures to the problem at hand, and refuse to be distracted by philosophical questions concerning the nature and meaning of history. Others, more keenly aware of the limitations of even the best historical work, still accept their mortality without despair, and are content to offer such revisionist insights as they have with full knowledge that one day a new revisionism will overtake them. Eugene Genovese, in a recent revaluation of slave culture, offers his reading of the sources "as one historian's considered judgment," warning nonspecialists "that all the sources are treacherous and that no 'definitive' study has been or ever will be written," for "the writing of history is a process of constant revision and debate." [4]

However, a few historians dream of immortality. Lee Benson, for one, deplores the "recurrent cycles of wheel-spinning revisionism" and insists that a more durable history can be written by replacing the "established historiographic system" with the analytical tools of modern social science. Thanks to data banks and computers, he argues, history can now be studied scientifically, and historians should be concerned with "discovering and developing general laws of human behavior." [5] Douglass C. North, for another, believes that history can be "something

[2] Carr [1962], p. 5.
[3] Bloch [1953], pp. 43–44.
[4] Genovese [1974], p. 676.
[5] Benson [1972], pp. 307–26.

more than a subjective reordering of the facts of the past as man's perspective changes with each generation." He, too, finds in the social sciences and in the methods of scientific research the tools for "a basic restructuring of historical inquiry." North suggests that the New Economic History, with its "well articulated body of theory and . . . abundance of relevant quantitative data," is the discipline best equipped to accomplish the restructuring he thinks is needed.[6]

Fogel and Engerman are prominent practitioners of the New Economic History, often called cliometrics, and *Time on the Cross* is an attempt at the kind of methodological restructuring for which present-day believers in the scientific study of history have called. Nowhere, Fogel and Engerman believe, "has the passion for numbers been more vigorously pursued than in the study of the economics of slavery." Cliometricians, they claim, in searching for quantifiable material, have ransacked "every conceivable source of information bearing on the operation of the slave system," including the manuscript census returns of 1850 and 1860, the family papers and business records of numerous planters, and the wills, probate records, and other legal documents deposited in county courthouses and now available on microfilm. As a result, "the cliometricians have amassed a more complete body of information on the operation of the slave system than has been available to anyone interested in the subject either during the antebellum era or since then."

According to Fogel and Engerman, great masses of quantifiable data were beyond the reach of "traditional" historians, because they lacked mathematical and statistical training and were therefore limited to the impressionistic use of "fragmentary" literary sources. The exploitation of the new data had to await the appearance of historians and economists "trained in the application of quantitative methods to historical problems." After World War II "a series of rapid advances in economics, statistics, and applied mathematics, together with the availability of high-speed computers, put information long locked in obscure archives at the disposal of a new generation of scholars" (FE, I, pp. 4, 7–8).

[6] North [1966], pp. v–vi.

What has been the result? A long-established "traditional interpretation" of slavery, incorporated in a "vast literature" written by "hundreds of historians" and "taught in most high school and college classes across the nation," has been contradicted in many of its essential aspects. "As significant as the correction of past errors," Fogel and Engerman report, "is the new information brought to light on the conditions of black bondage."

> Some of the discoveries [they explain] were at one time as unbelievable to the cliometricians as they will be to the readers of [*Time on the Cross*]. Indeed, many of the findings . . . were initially discounted, even rejected out of hand. But when persistent efforts to contradict the unexpected discoveries failed, these scholars were forced into a wide-ranging and radical reinterpretation of American slavery.

Accordingly, Fogel and Engerman warn their readers that *Time on the Cross* "will be a disturbing book" and ask them to show forbearance and to recognize that the book "represents the honest efforts of scholars whose central aim has been the discovery of what really happened" (FE, I, pp. 3–4, 8). The authors assure readers that forbearance will be rewarded, and, in explaining how, they execute a sudden and rather startling transition from cliometrics to presentist polemics: "For the finding we discuss not only expose many myths that have served to corrode and poison relations between the races, but also help to put into a new perspective some of the most urgent issues of our day" (FE, I, pp. 8–9).

This polemical style appears frequently in the text and supplement and becomes quite strident in the Epilogue, where the purveyors of the traditional interpretation of slavery are castigated for their "perversion of the history of blacks." Here Fogel and Engerman make clear the full significance of their title, *Time on the Cross*—an unlikely title for an ordinary work of cliometrics. In their rich metaphor, the spikes that still hold blacks on the cross after three hundred and fifty years "are fashioned of myths [about slavery] that turned diligent and efficient workers into lazy loafers and bunglers, that turned love of family into a disregard for it, that turned those who struggled for self-improvement in the only way they could into 'Uncle Toms.' . . . It's time to reveal not only to blacks but to

whites as well, that part of American history which has been
kept from them—the record of black achievement under adversity" (FE, I, pp. 258–64). So ends the book that, in the opening
pages of the Prologue, is soberly introduced as "part of a more
ambitious effort to reconstruct the entire history of American economic development on a sound quantitative basis" (FE, I, p. 6).

   Time on the Cross is clearly a blend of several ingredients.
One consists of findings based on "systematic data," defined as
quantifiable data that can be subject to "systematic statistical
tests." Another consists of findings based on "fragmentary,
impressionistic evidence" from literary sources, which Fogel and
Engerman regard as "on a relatively low level of reliability."
For example, they report that systematic data on the quality of
slave family life is lacking, and that "it has been impossible thus
far, to devise a meaningful index of the effect of slavery on the
personality or psychology of blacks." They base four of their ten
"principal corrections" of the traditional interpretation of slavery wholly or in large part on evidence that, by their definition,
is fragmentary and impressionistic. The third ingredient consists of interpretation, which often turns rather polemical and
which is sometimes based on fragmentary data (literary or
numerical) or on "assumptions which, though they are plausible,
cannot be verified at present" (FE, I, pp. 9–11).

   In commenting on *Time on the Cross* after publication, Fogel
explains that in attempting "to weave the findings of the
cliometricians into a wide-ranging reinterpretation of the slave
economy we passed over from social science to traditional
history. Appendix B [in the supplement] is social science; volume
I is not. Volume I is traditional history." Fogel does not claim
that *Time on the Cross* is "more scientific" than earlier works on
slavery—only that it draws more heavily "on the findings of
social science." [7] Yet, when Fogel and Engerman ask "how those
who framed the traditional interpretation of the slave system
could have been so wrong," and, presumably, why Fogel and
Engerman have been able to make their "radical reinterpretation," their explanation is entirely cliometrical. The differences
hinge "on the role of mathematics and statistics in historical

analysis," often on "technical mathematical points," and on "thousands" of computer hours (FE, I, pp. 9–11).

Fogel and Engerman are well-known American cliometricians, and *Time on the Cross* must be judged, above all, as a product of their methodology, as it is by the authors of this volume, all of whom (except the author of this introduction) are themselves quantitative historians. But the combination of three sometimes incongruous ingredients—cliometrics, traditional history, and a blend of speculation, interpretation, and polemics—leaves readers somewhat uncertain about what they are reading. Large parts of the book hardly conform to Benson's and North's model for the scientific study of history; its structural eccentricities, on the other hand, will puzzle traditional historians who have been trained to expect a great deal less.

However, about the general thrust of *Time on the Cross* there is no ambiguity. Fogel and Engerman reject an alleged traditional view that plantation agriculture was inefficient and that slavery was "so cruel, the exploitation so severe, the repression so complete, that blacks were thoroughly demoralized by it." In a flight of hyperbole (the handmaiden of polemics) they express their scorn for traditional notions, "contained in many current histories of the antebellum South," that black slaves were "cultural ciphers," lazy and careless workers, undernourished "if not starved," capable of only "routine tasks," sexually promiscuous, indifferent to family ties, and typically Sambos in their personalities. In short, their purpose is to disprove a tradition in which "masters and slaves are painted as degraded brutes. Masters are vile because they are the perpetrators of unbridled exploitation; slaves are vile because they are the victims of it" (FE, I, pp. 108–9).

In the historiography of antebellum southern slavery, *Time on the Cross* now stands unchallenged as the most favorable assessment of the impact of slavery on the southern economy, and the most cheerful portrayal of virtually all aspects of slave life, including income, conditions of labor, occupational mobility, marriage and child rearing, family life, cultural advancement, master-slave relationships, and, inferentially, the psychic impact of bondage on black people. Before the publication of this book, Ulrich B. Phillips, a Southerner noted for his sentimental view of life on antebellum plantations (though not of their efficiency), had written the classic account of slavery as a benign institution.[8] Fogel and Engerman are not sentimental about slavery or about planter entrepreneurs, and they are by no means members of the Phillips "school." Nevertheless, as to the conditions of life among slaves, Phillips in some respects portrays the system as slightly less benign than they, and he acknowledges more fully and explicitly its harsher side. As one reviewer, an economist, observes, Fogel and Engerman "are rather like prosecuting attorneys with a fine case who are . . . unwilling to cloud the jurors' minds with ambiguity." [9] Without qualification, slavery as an economic institution was efficient; with hardly a qualification, slavery as a social institution was benign.

The impact of *Time on the Cross* both on the popular media and on scholars was quite extraordinary. Unquestionably it was the most highly publicized and widely discussed work of history published in 1974, receiving much space in the metropolitan press, in weekly news magazines, and in literary periodicals. *Readers's Digest*, to illustrate the "startling . . . new findings" about the benign character of slavery "discovered by a new generation of unbiased historians," summarized most of Fogel and Engerman's generalizations. The "new insights" of these economists, said *Reader's Digest*, are based upon "computers, massive research, and sophisticated mathematical techniques"— techniques through which they learned that black people had found in slavery "room for opportunity and achievement. . . . [The] story is a triumph of the human spirit over adversity that [blacks] should be proud to have recorded." [10] Various personal appearances of the authors on television and before academic audiences culminated in a conference in October 1974 at the University of Rochester, where a large body of quantitative and humanistic historians spent three days appraising *Time on the*

[8] Phillips [1918]. See also Phillips [1929].
[9] Passell [1974], p. 4.
[10] Fleming [1975], pp. 127–28.

Cross. The Rochester conference had exceptional press coverage for a gathering of scholars whose papers and formal discussions turned only occasionally to the subject of sex.[11]

Professional historians and economists have reviewed *Time on the Cross* with a good deal less enthusiasm than the popular media. C. Vann Woodward, in one of the more restrained and noncommittal reviews, while leaving detailed criticism of Fogel and Engerman to those "who speak their own language," noted that in his reading of the book "the promptings of skepticism are not rare."[12] Other historians were not intimidated by the alleged mountains of data or the echo of computers, and they have challenged most of the claims of *Time on the Cross* and many of its "principal corrections" of the traditional interpretation. The five quantitative historians who contribute essays to this volume wrote some of the longest critical reviews; they undertake here the comprehensive evaluation that *Time on the Cross* deserves in view of its sensational claims and the remarkable publicity it received.

The authors of these essays find *Time on the Cross* to be a seriously flawed book—one that is likely to mislead readers as often as it enlightens them. They criticize Fogel and Engerman for inadequate use of the masses of quantifiable data available to them; for failing to fulfill their claim to have examined "every conceivable source of information"; and for careless or misleading use of sources, both numerical and literary. They question many of Fogel and Engerman's procedures, as well as inferences derived from them, and note their neglect, through documentation, "to provide readers with a basis for exercising critical judgments about the methods, evidence and reasoning that underlie the text."[13] Finally, they raise a host of questions about the book as a study both of the southern economy and of slavery as a social institution.

My view of *Time on the Cross* is from the perspective of a

[11] Other historical conferences on the book include one at the University of South Carolina, Columbia, in November 1974, and a session at the annual convention of the American Historical Association in Chicago in December 1974.
[12] Woodward [1974], pp. 3–6.
[13] See David and Temin in Chapter 1, below p. 35.

humanistic historian familiar with the literary and most of the numerical sources on slavery. I do not doubt the value of applying methods from the quantitative social sciences to the study of social and political as well as economic history, and I believe that my own study of slavery (Stampp [1956]) would have benefited from a computer analysis of some of my data. At the very least I would have saved many hours of "hand-made" computations and reduced the amount of impressionistic quantifying that is both implicitly and explicitly part of my methodology. Therefore, I do not react to *Time on the Cross* as a historian who views quantification as a "Bitch-goddess" to be spurned at all costs.[14] Besides, as we have seen, much of the book is derived from literary sources, is impressionistic in its quantitative procedures,[15] builds on assumptions and hypotheses that cannot be verified, and is polemical in its rhetoric. These are facets on which I can comment with some confidence, leaving technical cliometric problems to the other contributors.[16]

Perhaps the most common scholarly criticism of Fogel and Engerman is their failure (abundantly illustrated in this volume) to annotate their arguments in order to permit readers easily to examine their sources or determine the manner in which they arrive at conclusions. The text provides neither footnotes nor numbered citations to the supplement. To consult the supplement while reading the text is always difficult, often baffling, and sometimes futile. Fogel and Engerman repeatedly

[14] Bridenbaugh [1963], p. 326.
[15] For example, in fourteen pages of printed text (pp. 109–26) devoted to food, shelter, clothing, and medical care, Fogel and Engerman resort to vague, impressionistic quantitative measurements 63 times, or 4.5 times per page. They use the quantitative term "usually" 14 times, "many" 10 times, "most" 6 times, "generally" 6 times, "some" 5 times, and "much," "occasionally," "frequently," "sometimes," "often," "few," "virtually all," "time after time," "not uncommon," and "quite common" one to four times each. These impressionistic measurements are not always used with care, for they write "some" or "many" on occasions when they would have been more accurate to write "a few" or "hardly any."
[16] The difference between the work of quantitative and conventional historians is not always as sharp and clear as Fogel and Engerman make it appear to be; consequently, the chapters of this book written by quantitative historians deal with various non-quantitative matters as well.

quote from primary and secondary sources without citations in either the text or supplement, and one often searches both volumes in vain for evidence to support an important generalization. In their apparent concern not to put off readers with footnotes or other technical matters, they have discouraged all but the most persevering reader from tracing their steps. One quantitative economic historian justly complains that they have thereby failed to respect a cardinal "criterion of science: that experiments should be described so as to be reproducible by an unbeliever," [17] and this failure is no less disturbing to a humanistic historian.

If, in spite of all obstacles, one does examine Fogel and Engerman's sources, one discovers that their claim to have based their findings, to a significant degree, on "hitherto neglected sources" is not well founded. Other scholars have used all of their sources, often more thoroughly than they. Similarly their assertion that they accepted their "unbelievable" discoveries only after checking and rechecking their data, is not supported by a reading of their sources, which they have in fact used carelessly.[18]

Fogel and Engerman suggest, erroneously I believe, that some absolute measure exists by which a historian can distinguish qualitatively between the two kinds of evidence they claim to have used: "systematic evidence subject to rigorous statistical tests" and "informal and fragmentary evidence." At the risk of ignoring the technical meaning of these terms, I suggest that, for certain purposes, "systematic evidence," such as census returns, can be fragmentary, and that for many purposes the census returns of 1850 and 1860 are unreliable. On the other hand, literary evidence, which Fogel and Engerman classify as "informal and fragmentary," can be quite "formal"— when, for example, it consists of a systematic government report based on public hearings. Nor is it necessarily fragmentary: it may consist of every speech and official letter written by a public officeholder. For the public career of this person the

[17] Parker [1974], pp. 472–73.
[18] For illustrations, see especially the chapters (2–4) by Gutman and Sutch, below.

literary evidence may be complete and, in some aspects, even quantifiable. It is therefore misleading to pretend that "systematic evidence" is for all purposes and in every respect superior to, or more reliable than, evidence that Fogel and Engerman label as "informal and fragmentary." One needs only to read the essay on the shortcomings of the Seventh Census [1850], written by Superintendent J. B. D. DeBow as an appendix to the printed returns, to grasp the weakness of their claim. No statistical procedures for the processing of "biased" data can remedy the defects in systematic evidence accumulated by untrained, negligent, or incompetent census takers.

Turning from the problem of evidence to the argument of *Time on the Cross,* a common complaint of reviewers is that the authors are engaged much of the time in battles with straw men. They distort the work of other scholars through exaggeration or by quoting out of context, they refute myths discredited long ago, and they attack misconceptions of which no responsible scholar was ever guilty, thus encouraging readers unfamiliar with the literature to think that their book is far more revolutionary than it is in fact. With disturbing frequency they fail to acknowledge the contributions of earlier historians, or refer to them so unspecifically as to amount to no acknowledgment at all. Commenting on practices such as these in a broader context, Charlotte Erickson protests that "to play this game in academic literature . . . may indeed rob students of insights into the way in which scholars build upon each other's work in extending knowledge even with the most exciting new techniques." [19]

According to Fogel and Engerman, the "traditional interpretation" of slavery consists of five fundamental generalizations: (1) that, except on new land, capital investments in slaves were generally unprofitable, unless the owner supplied surplus slaves to the interstate slave trade; (2) that slavery in the late antebellum period was a dying institution; (3) that slave labor and the agricultural economy that exploited it were "economically inefficient"; (4) that slavery produced a stagnant, or retarded, southern economy; and (5) "that slavery provided

[19] Erickson [1975], pp. 359–60.

extremely harsh material conditions of life for the typical slave"
(FE, I, p. 226). Though an occasional "conventional" historian
may have rejected one or another of these generalizations, the
burden of the argument of *Time on the Cross* is that all five of
them are demonstrably incorrect.

In their Prologue, Fogel and Engerman list ten "principal
corrections" of the traditional interpretation of the southern
slave economy: (1) Slavery was a rational labor system that
survived because it was profitable. The return on investments in
slaves compared favorably with the return on other available
forms of investment. (2) On the eve of the Civil War, slavery
was still flourishing and gave no indication of an imminent
collapse for economic reasons. (3) During the 1850s slaveholders
were optimistic about the future of their labor system and
anticipated continued economic prosperity. (4) Slave agriculture
was efficient—indeed, 35 percent more efficient than the family
farms of the North. (5) The slave field hand was typically a
diligent laborer—"harder working and more efficient than his
white counterpart." (6) Slave labor was adaptable to an industrial economy, and the demand for slaves was rising more
rapidly in southern cities than in rural, agricultural areas. (7)
The slave family was not undermined by the interstate slave
trade or by sexual exploitation; rather, the family was "the
basic unit of social organization." Slaveholders encouraged
stable family life, because it was to their economic advantage to
do so. (8) The standard of living of southern slaves "compared
favorably with [that] . . . of free industrial workers." (9) "Over
the course of his lifetime, the typical slave field hand received
about 90 percent of the income he produced." (10) Between 1840
and 1860 the southern economy was characterized by rapid
growth and by an increase in per capita income that exceeded
the rate of increase in the rest of the country. "By 1860 the
South attained a level of per capita income which was high by
the standards of the time" (FE, I, pp. 4–6).

Among the straw men who march through the pages of *Time
on the Cross*, the most imposing is the "traditional interpretation
of slavery," which Fogel and Engerman themselves create and
which they fail to identify with any twentieth-century historian.
Most historians of the southern economy accepted the first four

of Fogel and Engerman's ten "principal corrections" long ago. Here their only innovation is the assertion that southern slave agriculture was 35 percent *more* efficient than northern family farms, an assertion whose validity this volume questions, especially in Chapters 5 and 7. The third of their "corrections," concerning the sanguinity of slaveholders, is a rather exaggerated statement based on a dubious quantitative exercise and bolstered by a superficial, unsystematic examination of literary sources. Credit for the sixth, regarding the adaptability of slavery to industrial activities, belongs to a book by Robert Starobin [1970] published four years before *Time on the Cross*. As for the seventh "correction," I know of no historian who argues that "slave breeding, sexual exploitation, and promiscuity destroyed the black family." None to my knowledge has ever denied that slaves lived characteristically in families, though some believe that the black family played a rather truncated role in the community life of southern plantations. Indeed, numerous black and white scholars have been arguing Fogel and Engerman's case for more than a decade. The essential point of the tenth "correction," relating to southern economic growth, antedates *Time on the Cross* by fourteen years.[20] The remaining three "corrections"—numbers 5, 8, and 9—represent novel assertions of substantive content, not assaults upon straw men. Whether Fogel and Engerman have proved that slaves worked more efficiently than free laborers, that their standard of living compared favorably with free industrial workers, and that they received about 90 percent of the income they produced are major questions critically examined in this volume. In each instance it is found that either the underlying reasoning, or the quantitative evidence, or both, fail to justify the novel assertions set down in the Prologue to *Time on the Cross*.

Contrary to Fogel and Engerman, there are in fact *two* traditional interpretations of the slave economy, one rooted in the antebellum northern abolitionist movement, the other in the antebellum southern defense of slavery. The abolitionist attack was overwhelmingly moral and religious, emphasizing the

[20] Easterlin [1960], pp. 73–140. In Chapter 7, below, Wright questions Fogel and Engerman's interpretation of Easterlin's findings.

secular American commitment to freedom and equality and the Christian doctrine that all men are equal in the sight of God. Unquestionably the moral judgments against slavery, implicit or explicit, found in the writings of twentieth-century historians stem from the abolitionist tradition; and in this sense Fogel and Engerman are neo-abolitionists themselves. Though abolitionists never argued that the physical treatment of slaves had any decisive bearing on the issue of the morality of slavery, their propaganda emphasized (and doubtless exaggerated) cruelties and atrocities for the purpose of winning converts.

Abolitionist publications devoted relatively little attention to the economics of slavery, but their occasional comments reveal a belief that the southern economy was backward, the slave labor system inefficient, and capital investments in slaves unprofitable. Fogel and Engerman correctly link the tradition of inefficiency and unprofitability to the abolitionists, but in explaining that tradition they make a serious error. They write as follows:

> That the quality of slaves, both as ordinary workers and as managers, could have been so completely misrepresented by the antebellum critics of slavery is testimony to the extent of their racist myopia. What bitter irony it is that the false stereotype of black labor, a stereotype which still plagues blacks today, was fashioned not primarily by the oppressors who strove to keep their chattel wrapped in the chains of bondage, but by the most ardent opponents of slavery, by those who worked most diligently to destroy the chains of bondage. [FE, I, p. 215]

That abolitionists were not free of racism is true enough—hardly any white Americans were. However, as a group they were decidedly less afflicted with it than the rest of their countrymen. Moreover, many of them were self-conscious and guilt ridden about their surviving prejudice and struggled to overcome it. Abolitionist societies campaigned against injustice to northern free blacks as well as to southern slaves.

Did the abolitionists, who were "the most ardent opponents of slavery," stress the inefficiency of *black* labor? [21] Almost never!

[21] In another passage, Fogel and Engerman assign equal responsibility to antislavery and proslavery writers for the false stereotype: "[N]either side ever called the alleged natural incompetence of the Negro into question. Quite the

The emphasis in their publications was on the inefficiency of *slave* labor. Abolitionists were characteristically environmentalists who argued that in the South blacks were what slavery had made them; in the North, what prejudice had made them. An essay by a Garrisonian abolitionist, Charles C. Burleigh, entitled "Slavery and the North" (1855), was typical of countless other antislavery pamphlets:

> What if the black man is inferior to the white? It does not follow that he always must be. Excel him where his chances are equal, before you boast yourself above him. Give him his liberty, and as strong a motive to exertion as you have;—a prospect of reward as sure and ample; not only wages for his toil, but respect and honor and social standing according to his worth, and see what he can then become. . . . His powers have never yet been fairly tried, for he has always had to struggle against difficulties and discouragements which white men do not meet. When free in name, he is denied a freeman's rights and hope and prospects, and open field of competition, and success to match his merit.

An argument such as this hardly suggests that abolitionists were led to their low opinion of slave labor by "racist myopia." [22] Rather, it suggests that they were misled by one of the naïve assumptions of classical economists—the intellectual ancestors of Fogel and Engerman—namely, that unfree labor is necessarily inefficient and its employment unprofitable.

Time on the Cross exposes the "racist myopia" of Frederick Law Olmsted, a Northerner who traveled extensively in the South in the 1850s and wrote three books on southern life,[23] to illustrate the contribution of antebellum critics of slavery to "the false stereotype of black labor." However, it fails to inform

---

contrary—each new round of debate served to raise the proposition of natural incompetence to the status of an axiomatic truth" (FE, I, pp. 216–17).
[22] I have not overlooked the fact that there was a soft and benevolent side to antebellum racism, which many abolitionists expressed in their writings. This was evident in their frequent portrayals of blacks as innately gentle and Christian people. See, for example, Fredrickson [1971], pp. 101–2. But these notions did not ordinarily lead abolitionists to negative judgments about the potential efficiency of free black labor.
[23] Frederick Law Olmsted, *The Cotton Kingdom* (New York, 1861), is an abridgment of *A Journey in the Seaboard Slave States* (New York, 1856), *A Journey Through Texas* (New York, 1857), and *A Journey in the Back Country* (New York, 1860). It is available in a modern edition (New York, 1953) edited by Arthur M. Schlesinger.

readers that Olmsted was not an abolitionist and that his opinions should not be confused with theirs.[24] His writings provide evidence for almost any interpretation of the southern economy—evidence of the efficiency and inefficiency of slave labor, of the profitability and unprofitability of investments in slaves, and of the productivity and unproductivity of the plantations. In some passages Olmsted accepts the current stereotype of the innate inferiority of blacks; however, more commonly he attributes the deficiencies of black labor to its enslavement. The issue here is not the accuracy of his comments on slave inefficiency, but how he explains it; and the crucial point is that the great majority of his comments on the southern labor system refer not to *black* labor but to *slave* labor. Though Olmsted's racism is obvious enough, he never explicitly argues that free black labor would be inferior to free white labor. Therefore, it would be more accurate to say that he was somewhat ambiguous on the issue rather than that he was a major contributor to the "false stereotype of black labor."

Occasionally Olmsted invites misunderstanding when, like so many others, he uses the terms "slave labor" and "black labor" interchangeably, simply because slave labor happened to *be* black labor. The resulting ambiguity is one for which Fogel and Engerman should show some tolerance, for they are guilty of it themselves. For example, on page 209 of the text, they refer to the "superior quality of black labor." Surely they do not intend the inverted racism implicit in this phrase but mean to argue for the superior quality of *slave* labor. Indeed, in the next sentence, they switch phrases and refer to the "high quality of slave labor," as if both meant the same thing. Again, on page 231,

<hr />

[24] Two southern critics of slavery, Cassius M. Clay and Hinton R. Helper, described in *Time on the Cross* (FE, I, p. 170) as "militant southern abolitionists," were decided racists and felt little sympathy for the slaves or desire for justice for free blacks. Neither Clay nor Helper had any connection with the northern abolitionist movement. Fogel and Engerman (FE, I, pp. 180–81) concede that Olmsted was not as much a racist as the two Southerners, that he was a liberal in his day, and that he felt goodwill for Negroes. But they add: "Olmsted's obvious goodwill toward Negroes has served to distract attention from the extent to which his biases led him to belittle the quality of black labor."

they declare that "blacks were better workers than whites," but on the same page they also assert the "superior quality of slave labor." In short, Fogel and Engerman, like Olmsted, sometimes confuse their readers.

The second traditional interpretation of slavery was a product of southern proslavery writers, and this interpretation has had an interesting history. Portions of it are evident in the writings of Ulrich B. Phillips, in those of other southern and some northern historians of the early twentieth century, and now in *Time on the Cross.* Of course, the extreme defense of slavery as a positive good is dead—it was seldom heard after Appomattox. However, one part of this positive-good tradition, rather than the abolitionist tradition, bears much of the responsibility for the "false stereotype of black labor" that Fogel and Engerman so passionately condemn. The southern defense of slavery, though utilizing historical, religious, sociological, and philosophical arguments, was primarily racial; and a crucial part of the racial argument was that blacks were innately lazy and incompetent and would work only under compulsion. Slavery, the argument ran, transformed a potentially vicious and idle population into disciplined and reasonably efficient workers. In this tradition it was the *free* blacks who were inefficient, not well-managed black *slaves!*

The portion of the proslavery interpretation that lives on in the writings of the Phillips school and in *Time on the Cross* is that which stresses mild treatment, moderate discipline, wholesome and comfortable living conditions, and minimal sexual exploitation. Proslavery writers attributed the generally good treatment of slaves partly to the masters' benevolence and partly to their self-interest as practical businessmen. "When slaves are worth near a thousand dollars a head," argued George Fitzhugh, "they will be carefully and well provided for." [25] Thomas R. Dew, Professor of History, Metaphysics, and Political Law at William and Mary College, was the first Southerner to develop this line of argument in an extended and systematic essay.[26] In fact, Dew's essay, published in 1832, though borrow-

[25] Fitzhugh [1857], p. 31.
[26] Dew [1832], reprinted in Washington, D.C., *Political Register*, Oct. 16, 1833.

ing heavily from earlier writers, was probably the first book-length defense of slavery ever written anywhere. If I were to locate *Time on the Cross* in the historiography of slavery, I would identify it with this second traditional interpretation; if I were looking for a label, I would be tempted to call it Neo-Dewism. Needless to say, the book is not a defense of slavery, and its argument is not racist, as was Dew's; but its highly favorable assessment of life in bondage originates in the traditional proslavery interpretation nonetheless.

Even the economic argument in *Time on the Cross* concerning the rationality, profitability, and viability of slavery, the efficiency of slave agriculture, and the relative wealth and prosperity of the antebellum South might be labeled, without undue exaggeration, Neo-Dewism. Proslavery writers, like the abolitionists, paid relatively little attention to the economics of slavery;[27] a few, when they did address the problem, conceded to their northern critics that free labor was cheaper and more efficient and defended their system in other ways. More often they advanced an economic defense as well. Dew argued that the productivity of slave labor was proven by the fact that slavery existed; had it not been profitable, it would have been abolished. In Virginia, he claimed, "slave labor . . . gives value to her soil . . . ; take away this, and you pull down the atlas that upholds the whole system." [28] Thorton Stringfellow presented evidence that the five Atlantic slave states during the previous two hundred years had accumulated wealth substantially greater than that of the New England States. Therefore, he asked, "Is it possible . . . to believe that slavery tends to poverty[?]" On the contrary, "slavery, as an agricultural investment, is more profitable than an investment in commerce and manufactures." [29]

Thus it is plausible to argue that Fogel and Engerman do not so much destroy a traditional interpretation of slavery as elaborate upon and reinforce one whose source runs back to

---

[27] Jenkins [1935], an analytical study of proslavery writings, did not find enough economic material to devote a chapter to it.
[28] Washington, D.C., *Political Register*, Oct. 16, 1833, p. 790.
[29] Elliott [1860], p. 538.

southern proslavery writers. In a way, Ulrich B. Phillips is more of a maverick than they, for he builds his case from a combination of the economic arguments of slavery's critics with the racial and sociological arguments of its defenders. On the other hand, the Neo-Dewists, Fogel and Engerman, reject only the racism and positive-good doctrines of proslavery writers, while preserving their economic and sociological arguments almost intact.

The so-called traditional interpretation of slavery is the largest straw man of *Time on the Cross*, but the book is well populated with lesser figures made of the same stuff. Because of the rather breathless claim in the Prologue that the book is replete with "unbelievable" discoveries, readers may easily assume that as each straw man topples the history of slavery is being rewritten in some fundamental way. For example, Fogel and Engerman report that "the common belief that all slaves were menials is false" (FE, I, p. 40). Among whom this belief is common they do not say. The statement is at best misleading, for no historian of slavery has ever believed this, and all of them, at the very least, have offered evidence that substantial numbers of slaves were not field hands. One finds no acknowledgment in either the text or the supplemental volume that Fogel and Engerman were not the discoverers of this well-known fact.

The passive voice sometimes enables the authors to avoid telling their readers precisely who are the believers in the myths they appear to be exploding. On page 24 they write: "It has been frequently asserted that slavery was dying in the United States from the end of the Revolution to 1810. . . ." Again, Fogel and Engerman do not name those who have asserted this, or when, or where; nor do they give citations in the supplement. Some historians once did argue that in the early national period slavery was a dying institution, and the myth is by no means dead. But this has not been the prevailing opinion in recent years, and Robert McColley [1964] published a book (not cited in *Time on the Cross*) effectively disputing the notion that slavery was moribund even in post-Revolutionary Virginia. Fogel and Engerman would have stated the case more accurately, though less dramatically, if they had described an old myth no longer

accepted by most modern historians, thus eliminating the straw
man and crediting the work of other historians.

A survey of the books on slavery and of general histories of
the antebellum South written by historians in the last twenty-
five years provides no evidence of many of the myths that Fogel
and Engerman claim to disprove. The following are examples of
these straw men, each of which is undocumented in either the
text or supplement:

1. Page 41: "The notion that slaveowners relied on the lash
alone to promote discipline and efficiency is a highly misleading
myth." Every twentieth-century historian of slavery describes
the variety of positive incentives planters used to promote
diligent labor.

2. Pages 53–54: Fogel and Engerman dispute "the notion that
speculative purchases and sales of slaves were common among
southern planters, that slaves were frequently bought and sold
to take advantage of temporary aberrations of price, in much
the same way as planters sought to profit from daily, weekly, or
monthly gyrations in the prices of cotton or railroad bonds."
Their explanation of why it would not have been practicable to
speculate in slaves in this manner is rather pointless, because
they are arguing with no one but the straw man of their own
creation.

3. Page 55: "While historians have been well aware of slave
renting, it has received insufficient attention in their writings."
Having lodged this complaint, Fogel and Engerman devote a
page and a half to the subject, adding nothing to what earlier
historians have said. Frederic Bancroft, in his study of slave
trading, gives an entire chapter to slave hiring practices, and
Robert Starobin treats the subject at length.[30] *Time on the Cross*
fails to acknowledge the contribution of either historian.

4. Page 75: "The frequent contention that slaveowners
preferred to work slaves to death at early ages, in order to avoid
the burden of maintenance at late ages is unfounded." This was
an old staple of nineteenth-century abolitionist propaganda, but
no twentieth-century historian of slavery or of the Old South
makes such a claim.

[30] Bancroft [1931], pp. 145–64; Starobin [1970], pp. 128–37.

5. Page 78: "The thesis that the *systematic* breeding of slaves for sale in the *market* accounted for a major share of the net income or profit of slaveholders, especially in the Old South, is espoused in one degree or another by most members of the anti-Phillips school." Fogel and Engerman define breeding for the market as "1, interference in the normal sexual habits of slaves to maximize female fertility through such devices as mating women with especially potent men, in much the same way as exists in breeding livestock; 2, the raising of slaves with sale as the main object, in much the same way as cattle or horses are raised." This was another common charge of nineteenth-century abolitionists, but no conventional historian of the past generation claims that slaves were bred in the Old South in the manner here described. Moreover, Fogel and Engerman distort the way in which the subject of slave rearing has been treated recently by several quantitative historians. (See Chapter 4 by Gutman and Sutch.)

6. Page 79: Fogel and Engerman claim that in spite of "many thousands of hours of research," historians "have failed to produce a single authenticated case of the 'stud' plantations alleged in abolitionist literature." They do not identify the historians who invested all that time in such an enterprise, nor do they explain what they mean by a stud plantation. There is scattered evidence that an occasional slaveholder took an unusually active interest in slave breeding; but, as historians know, evidence of slave plantations that were managed in a way analogous to stud farms is rare indeed.

7. Page 126: Fogel and Engerman question "the widely asserted contention that slaves were always feigning illness." No historian of slavery has made so absurd an assertion. What many have contended is precisely what *Time on the Cross* admits on page 119: that "planters worried about slaves who feigned illness."

8. Page 133: Fogel and Engerman challenge "the contention that a large proportion of slave children must have been fathered by white men." They do not define the vague quantitative term "large proportion," but if one were to assume that it means at least 20 percent, no historian has come anywhere near such a contention.

9. Page 133: *Time on the Cross* disputes "the widespread assumption that because the law permitted masters to ravish their slave women, they must have exercised that right." In this case it quotes, but does not identify, "one scholar" who made the following rather curious statement: "Almost every [white] mother and wife connected with the institution [of slavery] either actually or potentially shared the males in her family with slave women." There is not much to be said for this statement, except that it is indisputably true! The book does not explain among whom this assumption exists, what proportion of the masters are assumed to have ravished slave women, or what proportion of slave women are assumed to have been ravished. Since the term "ravish" is a common synonym for rape, it is important to know that the law of *no* southern state "permitted masters to ravish slave women"—or, for that matter, to have sexual relations even with consenting slave women. In this case, *Time on the Cross* creates a two-headed straw man, suggesting, first, that slaveholders had a legal right to ravish slave women, and, second, that a "widespread assumption" exists that masters exercised their right in numbers significantly larger than they actually did.

In another paragraph on the same page, Fogel and Engerman give a variation of their statement in the passive voice: "it has been presumed that masters and overseers must have ravished black women frequently. . . ." Again, they do not say *who* has presumed this; nor do they explain how often ravishing must have occurred to justify the use of the impressionistically quantitative term "frequently." Gutman and Sutch (Chapter 4), in examining the subject of sexual relations between white men and slave women, suggest an answer to this question.

10. Page 139: "also fallacious is the contention that slave marriages, since they were arbitrarily dictated by masters, frequently produced odd age combinations—young men married to old women and vice versa." The authors of this contention are not identified; but whoever they are, they clearly are at odds with the mythmakers who advanced the thesis that slaves were bred systematically for the market.

In addition to the straw men of *Time on the Cross*, several other characteristics require attention here. Quantitative historians criticize conventional historians, quite justifiably, for failing to quantify their data and for resorting instead to needlessly vague and imprecise quantitative terms. They also criticize conventional historians for presenting exceptional data as typical and attribute this fault to their impressionistic methodology. Therefore, it is surprising to discover that *Time on the Cross* amply illustrates both of these shortcomings. The most striking example is the manner in which it treats the subject of incentives to encourage field hands to labor diligently. Neither the census returns nor other systematic data furnish information on gifts or other pecuniary rewards to slaves; all available evidence comes from literary sources such as plantation records, travelers' accounts, and southern agricultural journals. These "fragmentary" sources provide the foundation for the book's generalizations about slave incentives.

Among the incentives that Fogel and Engerman mention are year-end bonuses, which they claim were "frequently quite substantial." The only example they give (FE, I, p. 148) is that of a Louisiana planter, Bennet H. Barrow, who "distributed gifts averaging between $15 and $20 per slave family in both 1839 and 1840." They do not report that gifts were distributed in only one of the remaining eight years of the Barrow record. Another incentive they discuss is the awarding of patches of land on which slaves grew marketable crops. They cite four cases (FE, I, pp. 148–52): 1. On the Texas plantation of Julian S. Devereaux, "in a good year some of the slaves earned in excess of $100 per annum for their families." Fogel and Engerman do not reveal what proportion of the Devereaux slaves had incomes of this or any other size, or how frequently the good years occurred. 2. On "several" Texas plantations "the leading hands . . . frequently earned between $40 and $110 per year. . . ." The plantations are unidentified; the ratio of "leading hands" to the total labor force is not given; and how frequently these earnings occurred is unclear. 3. On an unnamed Alabama plantation eight hands "produced cotton that earned them an average of $71 each." Again, Fogel and Engerman do not say how many hands were employed, or in how many years these amounts were earned. 4. "On still another [unnamed] plantation the average earnings of the thirteen top hands was $77." The authors provide no additional information.

While plantation records are fragmentary, they are abundant enough to present a much fuller picture of slave incentives—indeed Fogel and Engerman quantify smaller amounts of data on other subjects. In view of their commitment to quantification and their strictures against using atypical data as if it were typical, there is no reason why they should not have based their generalizations about incentives on the quantified records of a wide sample of those available. From such a sample they could have obtained the percentages of slaves who received "quite substantial" year-end bonuses or cash incomes from marketing their own crops. Instead Fogel and Engerman make the errors they attribute to conventional historians: they fail to quantify the quantifiable, and they use atypical cases to bolster their argument. The sources on which they depend do not suggest that year-end bonuses were "frequently quite substantial"; rather, a sounder impressionistic statement would be that gifts as large as those distributed by Barrow in 1839 and 1840 were not only exceptional on his plantation but on all others for which records survive. These sources also indicate that cash incomes of the size given in Fogel and Engerman's four illustrations were highly exceptional among field hands, indeed, almost unheard of, and that the majority of those for whom records exist had little or no cash income. On the other hand, there was scarcely a plantation on which punishment, or the threat of it, was negligible as an incentive. Therefore it is quite correct to say that force was the "principal basis" for obtaining labor from slaves, and incorrect to say, as Fogel and Engerman do (FE, I, pp. 241–42), that "pecuniary rewards were as integral a part of slavery as punishment." [31]

Another example of placing undue emphasis on atypical data

[31] In the supplement (FE, II, p. 118) Fogel and Engerman seem to reverse their position and concede that punishment, or the threat of it, was the "principal basis" of the slave labor system after all: "[W]e did not mean to suggest that all, or that even a majority, of slaves necessarily received such additional income." For a discussion of this problem, see Gutman and Sutch in Chapter 2.

appears in a discussion of slave housing, a subject analyzed by
Sutch in Chapter 6 of this volume. The census returns provide no
data on slave housing, and Fogel and Engerman therefore rely
on plantation records and travelers' accounts. In their description (FE, I, pp. 115–16) they note that there was "a considerable
range in the quality of housing." "The best," they write, "were
three- or four-room cottages . . . with up to eight hundred
square feet of space on the inside, and large porches on the
outside. . . . At the other pole were single-room log cabins
without windows." From this description one might expect to
find about as many examples of the first kind of housing as of
the second. But available data indicate that housing of the first
kind was quite rare, while that of the second was very common.
Thus by giving equal emphasis to two sets of data whose
relative importance is vastly different, Fogel and Engerman
have achieved a considerable distortion of the facts about slave
housing.

One of the more extravagant claims of *Time on the Cross* (FE,
I, pp. 263–64) is that it is the first book to tell black Americans
the truth about their years in bondage—the first to reveal the
history that "has been kept from them—the record of black
achievement under adversity." It portrays the "myths" that
question the diligence and efficiency of slave labor, the cohesive-
ness of slave families, and the work ethic of blacks who
"struggled for self-improvement" within the slave system, as
major forces that kept them suffering "the agony of racial
discrimination" after their emancipation from bondage. Fogel
and Engerman accuse all previous historians of slavery of
disseminating one or another of these "myths" and of the racial
slurs they find implicit in each of them. However, if there are
racial implications in these earlier interpretations—and there
may be, for racism manifests itself in many subtle ways—*Time
on the Cross* has by no means managed to escape them, for there
are significant racial implications in some of its interpretations
as well. In fact, the very shrillness of its antiracist rhetoric is
transparently patronizing and thus impedes the cause it attempts to serve.

The "myths" about slave labor and the alleged corrections in
Time on the Cross are examined in Chapters 1, 2, and 5 of this

volume, but certain matters relevant to racism are worth
considering here. To destroy the "myth" (believed by no
historian of slavery) that all slaves performed menial labor,
Fogel and Engerman report (FE, I, p. 40) "that over 25 percent
of males were managers, professionals, craftsmen, and semiskilled workers.[32] However, it is the approximately three-
fourths of the slaves whom Fogel and Engerman identify as
menial laborers who deserve further consideration. In the
planting, cultivating, and harvesting of southern staples and
food crops, field hands performed numerous tasks that ought to
be classified as skilled or semiskilled—in fact merit such
classification more than some tasks that *Time on the Cross* lists
in these categories. The problem is how to classify workers who
at different times performed skilled, semiskilled, and unskilled
tasks. At one point (FE, I, p. 41) the authors state that
agricultural workers engaged in tasks that involved the "accumulation of skills"; elsewhere (FE, I, p. 43; II, p. 42) they
concede that "field hands acquired a wide variety of farm

---

[32] Fogel and Engerman state (FE, I, p. 39) that 80 percent of slave women
worked in the fields and that "virtually all" of the remaining 20 percent were in
domestic or quasi-domestic occupations. Since women were not housewives
but part of the labor force, it is curious that Fogel and Engerman give their
percentages of non-menial slave labor for males only. When women are
counted, the proportion of non-menials declines to 23.2 percent, of whom
only 9.5 percent fall into their categories of managers and skilled craftsmen.

In breaking down these categories, Fogel and Engerman give no percentage for professionals, whom they identify (FE, I, p. 38) as architects and
engineers, because they numbered a mere handful. Oddly enough, they
ignore the largest and most influential group of slave "professionals":
preachers and exhorters. They greatly exaggerate the number of slave
overseers (see Chapter 2 of this volume) and the power and influence of
drivers in the cultural and community life of slaves, while they overlook the
crucial role of religious leaders. They are quite mistaken in their belief (FE, I,
p. 40) that foremen and craftsmen "led in establishing and enforcing codes of
behavior . . . as well as in shaping patterns of black culture." All in all, Fogel
and Engerman do not seem to be well informed about the sociology of slave
communities.

They do not appear to be better informed about the sexual mores of the Old
South. Fogel and Engerman offer the highly implausible suggestion (FE, I, p.
134) that, rather than having sexual relations with his own slave women, a
wealthy planter could have maintained a mistress in town, "where his
relationship could have been . . . more discreet."

skills." Yet their occupational classification lists field hands as unskilled "menial laborers"—hardly an accurate description of workers who performed various tasks that involved considerable skill. Contrary to Fogel and Engerman, the overwhelming majority of black slaves deserves to be counted among those performing skilled or semiskilled tasks either full-time or part-time. In spite of their desire to destroy racist myths, they help to perpetuate one by accepting the descriptively inaccurate occupational categories of the census takers.

Fogel and Engerman place particularly heavy responsibility for the survival of racism on those who question the efficiency of slave labor. Whether the inefficiency argument is racial or non-racial, they contend that the result is the same: it contributes to the "false stereotype . . . which still plagues blacks today." However, it is not altogether clear how *Time on the Cross* provides black Americans with a better historic image. We must remember that the abolitionist tradition denigrates *slave* labor not *black* labor. *Time on the Cross* contributes little to the destruction of myths or false stereotypes by replacing the racist caricatures of free black workers with cooperative, diligent, success-oriented slaves, "imbued like their masters" with the values of a Victorian bourgeois class.

One of the astonishing oversights of *Time on the Cross* is the existence of black resistance to bondage—a subject highly relevant to the question of slave efficiency and productivity. Tension always existed in the relations of masters and slaves; discipline was never perfect and sometimes broke down altogether; runaways, malingering, and other forms of day-to-day resistance were problems that plagued every planter. The effects of these problems on the productivity of slave labor are not easy to isolate and quantify; but Fogel and Engerman consider many other non-quantifiable aspects of slavery, and by ignoring resistance in their discussions of slave efficiency they are guilty of a major distortion. Evidence of resistance is overwhelming in the sources on slavery, and the failure of Fogel and Engerman to deal with it suggests either a severe case of myopia or, in their words (FE, I, p. 215), "the power of ideology to obliterate reality." They seem to think that to give malingering significance in a discussion of slave labor is somehow to stigmatize blacks as "lazy loafers," whereas to portray slaves as responsive to the punishments, rewards, and blandishments of their masters is to give blacks a more honorable history of "achievement under adversity." As David and Temin observe in Chapter 1, the authors of *Time on the Cross* seem oblivious to the moral issues raised by this attitude. Whatever the reason, Fogel and Engerman simply return to a very old-fashioned concept of the acquiescent slave, and to all of its potentially racist implications.

They resurrect the myth of acquiescence in still another way. The burden of their argument is that all the conditions of slave life—the standard of living, the amount of labor performed, the incentives offered, and the punishments inflicted—were determined by the careful calculations of rational slaveowners seeking maximum efficiency and profitability. However, by ignoring resistance, or the threat of it, Fogel and Engerman overlook the fact that slaves themselves played a vital role in determining the conditions of their lives. They describe slave foremen as mediators between masters and slaves (FE, I, p. 40), for which there is little evidence, but they fail to consider the far more important point that a community of slaves had ways of letting masters know when labor demands exceeded the slaves' own notions of what was reasonable. *Time on the Cross* takes from blacks a crucial part of their history when it erroneously portrays slaves as the passive recipients of their masters' benevolence, or the mere beneficiaries of a regime entirely defined by the economic calculations of efficient capitalist entrepreneurs. Again Fogel and Engerman revert to an old-fashioned, thoroughly discredited interpretation in which black slaves were mere instruments—persons acted upon but never acting in their own behalf.

My final comment concerns a general characteristic of *Time on the Cross* as a study of slavery and as a work of history—a characteristic that should disturb social scientists as much as humanists. In my opinion, the pages of this book seldom give readers a glimpse of real slaves and masters, only of disembodied abstractions and statistical averages. The book is written with little imagination and without a feeling for nuance or ambiguity—and, contrary to the opinion of one reviewer, history without ambiguity is not "the way good history has always been written." [33] The rich and varied texture of life in the Old South, the great range of black and white experience, the varieties of relationships among slaves and masters have all been averaged out and depersonalized, with the result that *Time on the Cross*, for the most part, concerns two characters: (1) the rational slaveholder, a man without passion or other frailties, who pursues relentlessly, and with complete understanding, his economic self-interest, and (2) the black slave, who is the beneficiary of his master's rational efficiency; who therefore lives in comfort, enjoying a secure family life, a rich community life, and a relatively high degree of social mobility; who, in consequence, willingly cooperates with his master to maximize profits and to make the Old South thrive.

This is not the story of slavery that has been hidden all these years in obscure documents, numerical and literary, waiting for some cliometrician to tell. It is not what the quantitative historians who contribute to this volume perceive. Fogel and Engerman assure their readers that they were at first unable to believe their own findings, that they tried repeatedly to refute them, and that they were literally forced into their "radical reinterpretation." Perhaps this is the way it really happened— perhaps these scenes of astonished incredulity did occur at the headquarters of this ambitious enterprise. I have no sure basis for disputing them, but I am a little skeptical nonetheless—first, because the sources on slavery are full of ambiguities and contradictions, presenting masters and slaves in immense variety and making *any* account of slavery without ambiguity false; second, because Fogel and Engerman themselves made many crucial and questionable decisions about the choice and use of evidence; and, last, because the authors of the present volume not only manage repeatedly to expose errors and systematic biases in the quantitative material presented by *Time on the Cross* but also question the logic of many of the inferences Fogel and Engerman have drawn from their "statistical findings."

[33] Passell [1974], p. 4. I do not mean to suggest that quantification results inevitably in an unnuanced and dehumanized history. Properly used, it should improve our comprehension of the great variety of human experience. I am suggesting only that this shortcoming is characteristic of *Time on the Cross*.

Why Fogel and Engerman present so cheerful a view of slavery as a benign institution, how they could miss the perplexing mixture of rational and irrational behavior of white masters and black slaves, is an interesting question. No doubt the reasons are as complex as slavery itself. As a sheer guess, their view of slavery may stem in part from a desire to make everything fit comfortably in a neo-classical behavioral model. The slave-plantation system was potentially profitable—Fogel and Engerman and many of their predecessors prove that beyond a doubt—and this fact may have fathered the wish to find it totally rational as well. Whatever the reason, there is no place in their schema for masters who behaved irrationally— who, for status purposes, owned more slaves than they could employ efficiently; who neglected or abused slave property; who punished in passion; who broke up slave marriages; and who "ravished" or simply made love to slave women at the risk of upsetting "the labor discipline on which economic success depended" (FE, I, p. 134).

In summary, Fogel and Engerman appear to be so preoccupied with the efficiency of slave agriculture that they disregard irrationality, friction, and conflict. As a result, two cliometricians who want to restore to blacks their true history in slavery have written a book which deprives them of their voice, their initiative, and their humanity. *Time on the Cross* replaces the untidy world of reality, in which masters and slaves, with their rational and irrational perceptions and their human passions, survived as best they could, with a model of a tidy, rational world that never was.

PART ONE

Masters and Slaves

CHAPTER ONE

Capitalist Masters, Bourgeois Slaves

Paul A. David
and
Peter Temin

Time on the Cross[1] is an ambitious, complex, and imposing book. Read at one level it offers a re-evaluation of chattel slavery in America as an economic institution. The focus here is macro-economic, attempting to appraise the functioning of the system by considering its material consequences. Although anathematizing the subjection of men to the will of other men as a categorically immoral arrangement, Fogel and Engerman simultaneously depict the capitalistic form of slavery found in North America in terms which make it appear economically functional and even socially benign. It was conducive, they say, to the efficient organization of agriculture, to rapid economic growth in the antebellum South, and to material treatment of the enslaved which was not only humane, but which compared favorably with the conditions afforded free workers during the nineteenth century.

Read at another level, *Time on the Cross* presents a bold reinterpretation of the motivations and behavior of the personae of a drama which many generations of historians and readers of American history have found compelling and disturbing. In quest of "an accurate historical image of the black man," the

[1] Robert William Fogel and Stanley L. Engerman, *Time on the Cross*, Vol. I: *The Economics of American Negro Slavery*, 286 pp. Boston, 1974; Vol. II: *Evidence and Methods—A Supplement*, 267 pp. Boston, 1974. The following text refers to these volumes, respectively, as FE, I, and FE, II.

authors challenge previous portrayals, rejecting most forcefully
the dual view of the masters as "vile" because they were
perpetrators of unbridled exploitation, and of the slaves as
"vile" because they were its victims (FE, I, pp. 108, 109). Gone is
Simon Legree, and with him the serio-comic figure of Sambo,
whom Stanley Elkins [1959] saw as a distorted personality, a
psychologically infantilized "inmate" of the plantation. But
gone also is the patriarchal Cavalier so fondly drawn by U. B.
Phillips [1918] and his school, and the uncompliant yet not
openly rebellious black who, in Kenneth Stampp's [1956] narrative, remained "a troublesome property."

In keeping with their account of the system as functionally
benign, Fogel and Engerman present characters who appear
animated by those simple interests and impulses which the
forces of the market are readily able to render harmonious.
Slaveowners, they say, were not "Cavalier fops" but "hard,
calculating businessmen"; "shrewd capitalistic businessmen"
who treated slaves with "paternalism" only when it made good
business sense to do so. And "the superior management of
planters" was matched by "the superior quality of black labor"
as shown by "slave teamwork, coordination, and intensity of
effort" as well as by "the responsiveness of the [slave] workers"
who "competed for [skilled] jobs." Slaves were, in short,
"diligent and efficient workers," who, being "imbued like their
masters with a Protestant ethic," strove "to develop and
improve themselves in the only way that was open to them"
(FE, I, pp. 73, 150, 201, 205, 210, 231–32, 263).

An unprepared reader may well find himself being swept
along by the sheer boldness of the authors' revisionism, by the
intimidating fervor with which the claims on behalf of their
quantitative methodology are advanced and the limitations of
conventional history are derided, and by the righteous passion
with which it is argued that their account—having been derived
by social science and purified of the racist ideology that taints
most previous historical writing—reveals at last "the true
nature of the slave system" (FE, I, p. 232). In the end, however,
Time on the Cross will be remembered as an unsatisfactory and
profoundly disappointing book.

As a work of technical economic history, the undocumented

and unannotated "primary volume" is unsatisfactory in that it fails to provide readers with a basis for exercising critical judgments about the methods, evidence, and reasoning that underlie the text. On close inspection of the supporting second volume it is found that the authors' most novel and notable assertions regarding the *consequences* of slavery (in terms of the material treatment of the slaves and the efficiency of the productive activities in which they were engaged) do not have a solid, scientifically incontrovertible basis in "fact." Curiously, and rather paradoxically, in order to evaluate the "performance" of the economic system based on this peculiar institution, the authors adopt a framework of analysis that leads them systematically to overlook the economic essence of slavery, namely, that the slaves had lost the freedom to exercise choices as producers and consumers. These criticisms are fully spelled out elsewhere, and there is no need to enter into them more explicitly at this point.[2]

But what of the second level of reinterpretation which the book has advanced? Taken as a more general historical account of the experience of slavery at the microcosmic level, *Time on the Cross* must be said to have pressed behaviorist social science to its natural limits, and then beyond. There are two distinguishable aspects of Fogel and Engerman's reportrayal of the masters and slaves of the antebellum South: the factual description and the moral judgment. Although these tend to run together in the authors' prose, the description of the way people acted and the imputation of motives consistent with those actions can be assessed as historical statements; they should stand quite independently of the implicit and explicit ethical judgments the authors' express about the propriety of the modes of behavior they see as characterizing the various players in this drama.

[2] Part II of this book provides a critical examination of the account of slavery's macroeconomic consequences which is presented in *Time on the Cross*. The chapters by David and Temin (Chap. 5), Sutch (Chap. 6), and Wright (Chap. 7) focus particularly on the evidence and methods that underlie Fogel and Engerman's assertions about the productive efficiency of slave agriculture, the material well-being of the Negro slave population, and the compatibility of slavery with the rapid economic growth and modernization of the South.

In their recasting, slaveholders appear as indistinguishable from pure economic men.[3] If they acted benevolently, even compassionately toward their human chattel, it was not out of patriarchal commitment but because the workings of capitalism in a highly competitive industry happened to make such behavior profitable, and because "the market" would have punished those owners who indulged in, or failed to prevent, the abusive treatment of their slaves. This conception has by now acquired a patina of familiarity among economic historians if not among historians in general.[4] Fogel and Engerman, however, do not stop with the bourgeoisification of the southern slavocracy. They hold that the slaves, too, learned to respond to a range of economic incentives that was created for them, seeking extra income, leisure, and occupational advance through cooperation and identification with the economic interests of their masters. In the underlying motivation of its members, then, the black slave community portrayed by Fogel and Engerman was thoroughly bourgeois, as much a part of capitalist society as was the white slave-owning class. The picture extends to the slaves' pattern of sexual conduct and child rearing, suggesting that their putative diligence in the cotton fields was part of a consistent mode of behavior—not simply a result of detailed supervision by overseers and slave drivers.

This new conception of the slave community is central to Fogel and Engerman's announced purpose in writing the book. In the Epilogue they say:

> We have attacked the traditional interpretation of the economics of slavery . . . in order to strike down the view that black Americans were without culture, without achievement, and without develoment for their first two hundred years on American soil. [FE, I, p. 258]

But *Time on the Cross* is not concerned with works of black writers and preachers of religion. It does not comment on the

---

[3] "Homo economicus" is a completely rational, well-informed individual who pursues his goals in a single-minded, internally consistent fashion.

[4] For a sampling of uses economic historians have made of this conception of the antebellum southern slaveowner as a profit-maximizing capitalist in a competitive industry, see Aitken [1971]. A critical discussion of the literature on this and closely related issues is provided by Wright [1973].

developments under slavery that led to the black tradition of work songs and to the evolution of jazz. Although the word "culture" is used, it is used in a very limited sense. The major part of "the record of black achievement under adversity," which the book claims to reveal (FE, I, p. 264), consists simply in the alleged ability of black slaves to internalize fully the Protestant work ethic and the mores of Victorian family life, to assimilate and function within a market-oriented society, and— even though largely confined to the lowest levels of the socioeconomic hierarchy—to strive successfully to make a profit for the enterprises that depended upon their exertions.

This remarkable behavioral account, if it is accepted, must raise for social historians a host of difficult problems concerning the integrity of the slave personality and of black culture in America, as well as some questions about the relation between the inner motives and outward mores of the slave-owning southern gentry. And then there are the obtrusive ethical problems, which become only more acute when all the actors in the tragedy are portrayed as creatures of rational volition. Can one say what is fit and proper behavior for individuals caught up within a coercive institutional situation? Or should we simply be content to struggle to comprehend the fragility of the human personality and to articulate the nature of the dilemmas continually created by the lordship-bondage relationship? [5]

A historical work, and certainly a work of economic history, might be readily forgiven having left unresolved the question of what is meant by the statement of a man that he was a "good" master, or of another that he was a "good" slave. *Time on the Cross*, however, lies at the opposite pole. Far from leaving the moral issues unresolved, Fogel and Engerman unhesitatingly pronounce judgments that reflect a particular viewpoint. The morality of individual behavior within the context of American slavery is for them seemingly a straightforward matter. The actions of slaveowners were economically self-serving, and however paternal or compassionate some masters (or all) might have appeared, they remain "mean" and unworthy of moral

[5] This last emerges as the central preoccupation in the recent work by Genovese [1974].

approval as a group. (See, for example, FE, I, p. 108.) Yet the active cooperation they supposedly managed to elicit from slaves who sought material self-improvement in "the only way that was open to them" is treated as a fitting subject for modern *black* pride.

The moral issues, however, are rather more complex than this. We shall shortly see that there is a close connection between one's perceptions of the objective conditions of bondage and the ethical standards one might wish to apply in judging what is "good" and "bad" behavior in masters and slaves. But before taking up these vexed questions, it is necessary to indicate that as a piece of descriptive history Fogel and Engerman's account of the motivation and behavior of masters and slaves is itself none too firmly based.

For the most part the picture of individual behavior and the characterization of individual motivation presented in *Time on the Cross* rest on little direct evidence. The authors are strict behaviorists in eschewing the personal testimony of masters and narratives of former slaves on such matters, except to cite the occasional illustrative anecdote. That such "anecdotal" material is not always handled in *Time on the Cross* with the scrupulous care that one might expect from professional historians may reflect nothing more than the authors' view that their case rests not on such embellishments as a few direct quotes can provide, but rather on an altogether weightier evidentiary basis.[6] Behaviorists, however, might be expected to identify statistically representative patterns of *individual* action before advancing models designed to rationalize them. Fogel and Engerman make no systematic use of observations on individual slaveowners, or slaves in this connection; instead, they venture to infer representative modes of action from their observations concerning the outcomes of market and nonmarket processes in which the individuals participated. Thus it is their "findings" about the

---

[6] A particularly flagrant case of distortion by removal from context is the use to which the authors have put (FE, I, p. 147) Bennet H. Barrow's exasperated and ironical diary entry, "My negroes have their name up in the neighborhood. . . ." For a full discussion of what "the evidence" actually reveals in this instance (and others involving the Barrow diary edited by Davis [1943]) see Chapter 4, below.

profitability, the comparative productive efficiency, and the
relatively favorable economic condition of the workers under
slavery which are used to project the image of plantations as
"factories" manned by industrious, self-improving blacks under
the direction of profit-maximizing captains of agriculture. The
microcosmic level at which Fogel and Engerman dispute previous ("traditional") interpretations of slavery is, in other words,
arrived at by extended inferences from the macrocosmic level.

On Masters

Even if one were prepared to accept on faith the latter body of
"findings," doubts would remain about the methodological
legitimacy of the use to which they are put. As a case in point,
take the profitability evidence. Since the path-breaking work of
Conrad and Myer [1958], there has been general agreement
among economic historians on the private profitability of
investment in the acquisition of Negro slaves in the antebellum
South. There are, of course, no comprehensive tax or census
statistics to disclose the aggregative flow of profits received by
the class of slaveowners from their human chattels. Nor have
samples of plantation records proved reliable as an immediate
source of information about the representative historical experience of "profit" defined in modern economic terms. Rather, by
piecing together fragmentary data (much of which does relate
to large plantation operations), economic historians have made a
variety of illustrative, hypothetical calculations to show the
"rate of return opportunities" confronting potential purchasers
of slaves. These reveal that purchase prices of prime-age slaves
were such that (for either males or females) the flow of net
revenues (reckoned as gross earnings less maintenance costs)
that could be anticipated over the remainder of the slave's life
would represent a normal market rate of yield on the investment in his (or her) purchase.[7] In treating the behavior of

[7] E. Saraydar [1964] offered the only serious challenge to Conrad and Meyer's
[1958] empirical conclusions offered by an economic historian. The criticisms
raised by Saraydar were, in turn, disposed of by R. Sutch [1965]. A helpful

slaveowners, however, Fogel and Engerman venture beyond these findings. Not only are we told that the individual owner's quest for greater profit almost invariably was the central motive explaining the observed employment of slaves in such profitable modes of production, but the hypothesis of profit maximization is taken as a basis for inferring that practices which would *not* have been most profitable were neither countenanced nor generally engaged in by slaveowners.

As Harold Woodman [1972] has pointed out in his penetrating review of earlier work on slavery by Fogel and Engerman, it simply is not legitimate to infer the motivations of individuals from evidence about the outcome of a market process as a whole. Given information about the motivation of individuals or behavioral rules, the shape of the market's equilibrium can be deduced. But it is not valid to reverse the direction of the logical inference because there are in general many other sets of individual behavioral rules that would be consistent with the same equilibrium configuration.

Consider the situation of the "agricultural capitalist" envisaged by Fogel and Engerman (FE, I, p. 232). He viewed slaves as just another productive asset and sought to use all his assets in ways that would be most profitable. For any given price of slaves, there were some uses in which they could be employed profitably and others in which they could not. As the price of slaves rose, the former group of uses shrank in relation to the latter group, and therefore the number of slaves demanded by him fell. At any given price of slaves our agricultural capitalist would continue to acquire slaves up to the point at which the profit rate from owning slaves had been forced into equality with the prevailing rate of return on other (equally risky) assets.

The demand curve for the services of slave labor thus defined did not, however, determine the price of slaves; prices are determined by the intersection of supply and demand curves.[8]

---

review of this literature was provided by Fogel and Engerman [1971]. Although their most recent technical survey (FE, II, pp. 64–79) brings things up to date and adds material based on their own researches, it is rather harder going.

[8] Demand curves show the number of units (slaves in this case) that potential purchasers or owners would buy at different prices. "Supply curves" show the number of units (slaves) available for sale at different prices.

What was the supply curve facing the class of agricultural capitalists? If no one who was not of that disposition held slaves, the supply curve would be completely inelastic and simply would indicate the number of slaves in the South at the given point in time.[9] On the other hand, if there were people who held slaves with reasons other than profit maximization in mind—whether they were "Cavalier fops," drunken sadists, or masters who loved their mulatto offspring more tham money—then the number of slaves available to the agricultural capitalist type of owner would be restricted to those not already-reserved for the diverse purposes of other groups. Yet even "Cavalier fops" must face the harsh realities of a limited budget. Having finite financial resources, the would-be patrician who is ready to live up to (if not for a time beyond) his means will be responsive to the prices of slaves in the following sense: *on average* he would hold more slaves were slaves cheap (vis-á-vis other things) than he would were slaves relatively dear. The supply of slaves facing the "agricultural capitalist" class of owner therefore may be thought of as varying in the normal way, positively with the price of slaves.[10]

If the market for slaves was in equilibrium, the allocation of the slave population between "agricultural capitalists" and "Cavalier fops" represented a point that simultaneously was on the slave-demand and the slave-supply curves just discussed. To describe that allocation one needs to know the shapes and positions of this pair of curves, not just the price at which they intersected. By itself, the observation that owners of slaves could earn a market rate of return on their investment at the prevailing price tells us only that the "agricultural capitalists"

[9] In other words, the quantity of slaves supplied would be the same at all prices. This is what is meant by complete "price inelasticity" of supply.

[10] This is equivalent to saying that the number of slaves reserved for the use of "noncapitalistic" owners varied inversely with the price of slaves, tracing out the normal, downward-sloping demand curve. When the price of slaves rose relative to other goods, "noncapitalistic" owners as a group demanded less slaves. *It is not necessary to assume individual rational utility-maximizing behavior in order to conclude that the demand for slaves by the* class *of* noncapitalist slaveholders will exhibit the usual properties of a demand curve. Cf. Becker [1962], and more generally, Sanderson [1974]. The latter paper is rather heavily mathematical.

as a group were in equilibrium, that is to say, on their demand curve. It cannot tell us that the specific point on their demand curve was one that left no significant portion of the slave population in the hands of irrational, noneconomic men.[11] Fogel and Engerman may well be correct in their assertion: "The demand of those slaveowners who desired to hold slaves for conspicuous consumption was quite small relative to the total demand for slaves" (FE, I, p. 71). But the basis for this statement is not disclosed, and it cannot have been inferred simply from observations of profit rates. That slave prices were consistent with market rates of return being earned by owners of that asset tells us that the economy was operating at a point on the demand curve of the "agricultural capitalists," and that there were at least a few such holders of slaves in the market. It fails to illuminate the motives of the *typical* slaveholder.[12]

The illegitimate methodological device of arguing from infor-

---

[11] Fogel and Engerman say: "The discovery of a high and persistent rate of profit on slaves constitutes a serious, and probably irreparable, blow to the thesis that the price of slaves was largely attributable to conspicuous consumption" (FE, I, p. 70). In the context of the present discussion it is clear that this is a blow which misses the target. We have seen that the behavior of the group who held slaves for conspicuous consumption motives would establish the supply curve facing "agricultural capitalist" demanders of slaves. It does not make economic sense to speak of the price as having been determined *more* by one group (Cavalier fops concerned with conspicuous consumption) rather than the other (agricultural capitalist), when it is their interaction that establishes the price.

[12] From this failure it should be apparent that greater caution is warranted than Fogel and Engerman display in interpreting their ingenious "index of the sanguinity of slaveholders" (FE, I, pp. 103–6). Changes in the relationship between current slave earnings and market prices could, at best, be taken to reflect changes in the expectation held by *marginal* buyers (sellers) regarding future earnings prospects. (The "marginal buyer" is one who is almost indifferent between buying and not buying; who would not buy if the price was even a little bit higher.) But there is a difference between the marginal purchaser and the average purchaser in the market at any moment in time. The existence of substantial "transactions costs," which Fogel and Engerman say were entailed in the breakup of slave families by sale, implies that there is no compelling reason to believe that all actual and potential slaveowners (the "slaveholding class" to which they refer) must have shared the expectations of even the average member of the minority who were buying slaves at any moment in time.

mation about rates of return to conclusions about the behavior and motivation of representative individuals reappears throughout *Time on the Cross*. On occasion, furthermore, the authors reverse direction and suggest that because there was objectively no profit to be gained by altering the extent to which some activity was pursued, the activity in question would not have been undertaken at all. In advancing the latter form of argument they err doubly, in that they ignore *both* the existing scale of activity that had brought the rate of return down to the prevailing market level, and the possibility that nonpecuniary motives may have been widely indulged at the expense of private profits or even long-run survival in the industry.

The argument Fogel and Engerman develop to support their contention that there was no commercial slave-breeding provides a particularly striking instance of this compound logical fullacy. Slave-breeding involved decisions about particular *uses* of human chattel, distinct from the basic decision whether or not to own that type of property. Yet, Fogel and Engerman invoke the hypothesized dominance of profit-maximizing motives to generate empirical assertions about what was and was not representative behavior on the part of planters in this (and other) matters distinct from their basic investment portfolio choices.[13]

The notions that slaves were reared with a view to future sale and that the social arrangements of plantations (and even the sexual lives of the Negroes) were manipulated toward this end are described by Fogel and Engerman as deriving largely from "unverified charges made by abolitionists" (FE, I, p. 78). To explode this "myth" the authors report N. G. Butlin's [1971]

[13] In addition to the illustrative case of slave-breeding discussed in the text, one should compare the parallel uses of this style of argument in regard to the profit considerations supposedly militating against separations of slave families by sales or removals (FE, I, pp. 52, 126–30), against "sexual exploitation" of slave wenches by owners and overseers (FE, I, p. 134), against employment of female slaves in commercial prostitution (FE, I, p. 135; II, pp. 113–14), against applications of physical abuse such as whipping other than "with restraint and in a coolly calculated manner" (FE, I, pp. 146–47). Such quantitative evidence as has been advanced in *Time on the Cross* to support the authors' revisionist position on each of the foregoing issues is subjected to quite devastating criticisms in Chapters 3 and 4, below.

finding that in the Old South, the supposed "breeding region," "the rates of return on men and women [slaves] were approximately the same" (FE, I, p. 79). But in a competitive market, two assets of comparable riskiness should earn the same rate of profit regardless of the specific uses to which they are put. The finding therefore can only show that the slave market was in equilibrium; it cannot tell us whether or not the equilibrium was one in which women were extensively used in bearing children rather than in field work.[14] Fogel and Engerman go on to say that the "systematic" breeding thesis is implausible because the extra profit to be gotten from (further) increasing the fertility of female slaves was trivial, "less than a dollar per year per slave" (FE, I, p. 83). Again, if the market was in the neighborhood of a competitive equilibrium there would be little opportunity for making profits by altering prevailing practices.[15] This kind of evidence may be held to show that the market was near equilibrium, but it does not illuminate the practices of slaveowners which brought it into such a state, nor can it suffice to establish the absence of slave breeding.[16]

And Slaves

Similar defects flaw Fogel and Engerman's portrayal of the

[14] A market is "in equilibrium" when both buyers and sellers can buy and sell the full amount they wish to at the market price.

[15] A "competitive equilibrium" is a market equilibrium in which the competition among different sellers has forced the price down to the point where no profit can be gained from selling an additional unit.

[16] Fogel and Engerman also reject (without explicit reference or text discussion) the demographic data published by Sutch [1974] on the existence of slave plantations with unbalanced sex ratios (FE, I, pp. 78–79). Later they say that it would have been irrational for a planter to have a slave population with unbalanced sex ratios because fertility rates were lower on plantations with unbalanced sex ratios than on those with balanced ratios (FE, I, p. 83). But, in addition to depending upon the premise of rational profit-maximization, this argument confuses maximizing fertility with maximizing profits. There seems to have been a cost to having unbalanced sex ratios: fertility dropped. But there was also an obvious benefit: one needed to have fewer costly males. And if a slave breeder was located in the Old South, where cotton farming could not pay for the male slave, the benefit could be larger than the cost.

slaves, who are said to have responded reliably to pecuniary incentives (not the lash) in respect to work effort and job advancement. Much is made of the fact, itself scarcely novel, that within the plantation labor force as well as within the slave population as a whole there existed an occupational pyramid, and a complex corresponding social hierarchy.[17] What is new is the inference the authors have drawn from this in recognizing

> . . . the existence of a flexible and *exceedingly effective* incentive system that operated within the framework of slavery. . . . In slave, as in free society, positive incentives in the form of material rewards, were a powerful instrument of economic and social control. Although slavery restricted economic and social mobility for blacks, it did not eliminate it. [FE, I, pp. 40–41; emphasis added]

The theoretical argument behind this statement confuses cause and effect. While individual mobility in an open, meritocratic society typically will generate a socioeconomic hierarchy, the existence of the latter hardly implies the operation of processes of occupational selection having the characteristics of free-market competition. Selection based on ascriptive attributes equally can generate an occupational pyramid; the army too has its functional ranks and social hierarchy. Elsewhere in the work it is evident that the rules for occupational transitions within the matrix of the slave system may have diverged in important respects from those which characterized the rest of nineteenth-century American society.[18] But this does not suggest to Fogel

---

[17] The precise shape of that pyramid is not at issue here, but the description of it given in *Time on the Cross* happens to be quite misleading. See Chapter 4, below.

[18] It is reported that slave artisans, and others occupying jobs requiring some training beyond that acquired in field work, were considerably older than the working population of the plantations as a whole (FE, I, pp. 150; II, pp. 117–18). This may have reflected the practice of rewarding older slaves of proven loyalty by elevating them to prestigious and physically less onerous pursuits. (It may have reflected also the fact that the labor force make-up of the particular plantations studied had not settled down to anything resembling a self-perpetuating [steady-state] distribution. This latter possibility is not considered by Fogel and Engerman, but it should induce considerable caution in reaching for inferences about persisting selection practices on the basis of such evidence.) In any event, the attributes on the basis of which older slaves were selected for further training need not have been correlated

and Engerman that the incentives, and the slaveowners' presumptions about the responsiveness and dependability of potential candidates for "occupational advancement" which those incentives reflected, may have been quite different from those found where workers are free.

To press this point still further, the inference that slaves responded to proffered opportunities for job-training is subject to the objections of Woodman [1972] to the use made of profitability findings. Aggregate data can indicate that there were indeed *some* slaves who rose to positions of skill and responsibility, perhaps stimulated by material incentives. But data on the composition of the labor force cannot show how numerous were the "highly responsive" compared with the rest; one must be told something about the supply of job slots with specified performance standards, and the strength of the existing inducements—material and other—to escape the lot of the ordinary field hand. And as for the new evidence Fogel and Engerman offer to support their assertion about the revealed diligence and efficiency of slave labor in plantation tasks, it is all indirect inference from their questionable calculation of the overall productivity of slave agriculture compared with free farming.[19]

Manifestly, diligent slave workers who go forth into the world "imbued like their master with Protestant ethic" must come from good homes, from families patterned on those of the middle class they emulate. *Time on the Cross* (FE, I, pp. 124–44) rounds out its portrayal of the slave community by peopling it with black fathers and mothers who (in that order of dominance) headed stable and secure families, who were solicitous of the normal physical, emotional, and moral needs of young children, and who—as a rule, and within the bounds set by the medical knowledge of their day—were able to protect and nurture their offspring in much the same way as did free people. This assessment goes well beyond recognizing that the slave

---

with the criteria generally used in screening young free workers who present themselves for training so that they may derive its benefits over a greater part of their life span.

[19] As is noted above, we have subjected these relative productivity calculations to critical examination in Chapter 5, below.

family had much greater power than historians formerly believed. It goes well beyond rejecting the now widely disputed notions embraced by the Moynihan Report, according to which slavery succeeded in emasculating black men, fashioned a matriarchy, and repressed the emergence of a strong sense of family among the American Negro people.

The positive case for family life under slavery, it will be appreciated, is not an easy one to document from the conventional sources available to historians of the antebellum South. The correspondence and diaries of slaveowners, and the accounts left by visitors, convey no such picture of family life within the slave quarters. Quite the contrary, on the question of parental affection and solicitousness these sources touch recurringly upon the stolid, impassive way in which black mothers and fathers faced the deaths of their infants and children; they express perplexity and exasperation at the contrast between the deep devotion of black "mammies" to their masters' children and the seeming indifference to the needs of their own offspring which slave wenches too often exhibited.

During the 1940s and 1950s American historians who tackled the delicate and emotion-laden question of black motherhood in bondage were concerned largely to reject racial slanders against "the Negro character"; they advanced essentially environmental rationalizations for the behavior chronicled by white observers.[20] More recently, Blassingame has used the evidence of slave narratives to argue that, although a distinctive set of family arrangements evolved among the slaves, individuals were nonetheless able to find in that family structure companionship, love, sexual gratification, instruction in avoiding punishment, and sympathy for sufferings endured.[21] Fogel and Engerman do not re-evaluate the family life of slaves in terms of its ability to fulfill these needs. In their account, the conditions of plantation life and labor appear so benign that it would have been awkward to have made much of the functional value of the slave's family life in creating a "zone of safety" within an otherwise hostile environment. To appreciate success in this

[20] Cf., e.g. Frazier [1948], Chap. 3; Stampp [1956], p. 346.
[21] J. W. Blassingame [1972], Chap. 3, esp. pp. 78–79.

dimension as a truly remarkable achievement, one first has to acknowledge the extraordinary and terrible countervailing pressures upon the slave family.[22] For the same reason, they could not consistently have entertained the "environmentalist" rationalizations which Frazier and Stampp offered for the sort of parental behavior that is described in the writings of white observers.[23]

Instead of examining the functions fulfilled by slave families, *Time on the Cross* concentrates on revising our notions about its form: family life in the slave quarters, as portrayed, did not differ radically from that among free Negroes and whites. Bits of contrary testimony from ex-slaves and their children are ignored, while testimony from white contemporaries is simply dismissed as too distorted to be worthy of efforts at rationalization—"perhaps because of a veil of racial and class biases which obscured [white observers'] vision and prevented them from seeing the real context of black family life" (FE, I, p. 144).

There is a close parallel here with Fogel and Engerman's rejection of direct testimony of white observers on slaves' performance as workers, and with their disregard for the slave narratives and songs as sources of information about attitudes toward work, cooperation, and discipline. And once again, rather than using qualitative, "literary" documents to support their account of sexual behavior, family structure and child care in the slave quarters, the authors offer preliminary "findings" inferred from new quantitative evidence. In this instance their

---

[22] Cf. the more cautious position assumed by Eugene Genovese [1974], pp. 451–52. Genovese's treatment of the slave family admits to having been influenced, if not entirely persuaded, by Fogel and Engerman's "impressive econometric work"—particularly their published findings concerning the frequency of separation of wives from husbands and children (ibid., pp. 457, 759). But the latter "findings" are grossly misleading, as is shown in Chapter 3, below.

[23] Ironically, because Fogel and Engerman (erroneously) maintain that forced separations of family members were not commonplace events in the lives of slaves, they must make rather restrained and qualified use of the abundant evidence on the anguished reactions produced by such partings. "During the relative infrequent instances when economic forces led the planter to destroy, rather than to maintain slave families, the *independent* striving of slaves to maintain their families came into sharp focus" (FE, I, p. 143).

line of inference about individual attitudes, motives, and behavior among the slaves is spun out from demographic data relating to aggregated fertility and mortality experience (FE, I, pp. 124, 136–39).

Our purpose at this point, it should be stressed, is not to argue the inherent truth or falsity of the novel vision of child care and slave family life projected by *Time on the Cross*. Rather, we mean only to indicate that, however implausible or compelling it may be found to be on *other* grounds, Fogel and Engerman's vision is not one to which any substance has been lent by the methodology that they invoke so stridently, the methodology of the quantitative social sciences.[24]

The piece of demographic evidence which Fogel and Engerman introduce as "most revealing" of the behavior of slave mothers in regard to the care of their offspring, is an estimate that the average time interval between successive births (for women who had a child that survived the first year of life) was "somewhat over" 24 months. "This," they say, "is the pattern of child spacing that one would expect to find in a noncontraceptive population in which mothers engaged in breast feeding for the first year of the children's lives" (FE, I, pp. 136, 137). Within a paragraph this inference is transformed into an established datum, suitable for incorporation into the broad fabric of the authors' argument:

> This finding hardly supports the charge that slave mothers were indifferent to their children, generally neglected them, and were widely engaged in infanticide. Quite the contrary, the ubiquity of the year-long pattern of breast feeding, combined with the nearly identical rate of infant mortality among slaves and southern whites, and with the rare occurrences of suffocation and other accidents as the cause of death of infant slave, suggests that for the most part, black mothers cared quite well for their children. [FE, I, p. 137]

Here, the pattern whose ubiquity is alleged is not the 28-month birth interval, but the year-long period of breast-feeding that Fogel and Engerman infer from it.[25] This is a permissible

[24] For a critical discussion of the principal factual assertions Fogel and Engerman make concerning child care and its effects on infant mortality, see Chapter 6.
[25] Although the unpublished paper by Steckel [1973], which is cited as the source for this birth interval in *Time on the Cross* (FE, II, p. 114), indicates that

inference, but by no means a necessary inference. It rests on the empirical validity of three premises which the authors have left unstated and therefore unexamined. Were it established that the slaves were not practicing contraception, and were it also the case that slave couples enjoyed regular and frequent intercourse throughout the woman's mid-month, and were there no basis for suspecting a prolonged sequence of postpartum anovulatory cycles, *then* an inference of an extended interval of amenorrhea induced by continuing lactation would be rather compelling. There is no cogent basis not to stipulate that the first and the third of the foregoing premises are satisfied in the case at hand. Yet, inasmuch as the facts concerning regularity and frequency of intercourse among couples remain in doubt, and as the couples in many instances were not resident on the same plantation,[26] and as there is ample cause here to consider the effects of fatigue upon the desire for regular and frequent coitus, it seems quite admissible to believe that the observed birth spacing could arise even though the average period of lactation was much shorter than one year. The point that frequency of intercourse is a variable which, like the duration of lactation, can materially alter birth intervals in noncontraceptive populations, is a quite general one, and familiar in modern demographic theory.[27]

---

120 observations were available on the interval between the first and second births to a given slave woman, and somewhat fewer observations were found pertaining to the next two birth intervals, the sources and nature of this particular set of underlying data are not specifically described in Steckel's paper. Inspection of the average number of slaves, and the lengths of time covered by the various plantation records that Steckel reports having consulted, suggest that the birth spacing estimates Fogel and Engerman refer to as indicating a "ubiquitous" pattern actually relate largely to the experience of several generations of slave women on only one or two plantations. Unfortunately, it has not been possible to settle this question directly. According to Steckel (telephone conversation, July 15, 1975), the necessary information on the distribution of observations was contained on original worksheets of his, but these no longer can be found.

[26] Chapter 3, below, cites data from an 1866 military census of Princess Anne County, Virginia, to support the assertion that slave husbands and wives not infrequently were owned by different planters in the same neighborhood.

[27] Cf. Keyfitz [1971]. Heuristic computations show that a reduction of coital frequency from 12 days in a 24-day (available) month, to 3 days—say, every

In other words, Fogel and Engerman's demographic inference is predicated on the belief that the marital and physiological circumstances of slave lives were essentially similar to those of the free couples for whom—as demographers have been led to surmise—24- to 30-month birth intervals are explained by an established custom of breast-feeding infants for more or less the first year of their lives. But that initial premise regarding the circumstances of marital life in the *slave* quarters is the very point at issue, and therefore it is hardly legitimate for Fogel and Engerman implicitly to assume it in order to make their case.

And what if the 28-month birth interval was in fact due to extended breast feeding, is this to be attributed to the care that black mothers aspired to give their children or to the concerns of slaveowners for valuable property? The separation of evidence on actions from that on motives is particularly difficult here— where the only direct evidence Fogel and Engerman adduce on the duration of nursing seems to derive from *published* advice on the management of slave plantations,[28] and the indirect

Sunday—would have the same effect upon expected intervals between birth as an additional 9-month period of non-fecundability due to the prolongation of lactation. Obviously the same average birth interval could result from many intermediate combinations, involving intercourse with greater frequency than 3 days in 24, and lactation lasting less than 12 months but longer than 3 months. We are grateful to Warren C. Sanderson for suggesting some appropriate parameter values enabling us to make these calculations using a simple model of reproduction as a renewal process.

[28] The plantation regimen described as prevalent in Fogel and Engerman's text (FE, I, pp. 123) provides for babies to be nursed 4 times per day during working hours until 6 or 8 months after birth and twice a day thereafter (FE, I, p. 123). No citations are provided for this generalization in Appendix B of Volume II, but the description appears to combine the best features of the two sets of instructions for estate management mentioned in this connection by Postell [1951], p. 120. It is relevant to note that both sets of instructions were *published* in contemporary southern periodicals and do not necessarily represent private communications between planters and their overseers. There seems to be more agreement on the recommended frequency of daily nursing (3 or 4 times in the working day), than on when weaning should occur. Cf. Genovese [1974], pp. 498–99.

Fogel and Engerman make no effort to balance their description of model plantation rules with former slaves' accounts of the reality of overseers' conduct. Even if the testimony of Moses Grandy, a former slave, is not "representative," it is instructive to hear him on this point: "On the estates I

demographic evidence as to actual practice turns out to be quite inconclusive.

Some Situational Ethics

The way the slaves are supposed to have responded to the *positive* incentives their masters devised for maintaining nuclear families, caring for their young, and working diligently was responsible (we are told) for the smooth and profitable operation of the system of slavery in the antebellum South. This is seen by Fogel and Engerman as the main "achievement" of the American Negro people in bondage. This is the view which distinguishes their book from every other major study of slavery published during the past three decades; Fogel and Engerman reject not only the Sambo image but also the conception that it was appropriate for the slaves to have resisted their bondage.

Time on the Cross thus raises a profound moral issue without treating it as such. We can approach the question by considering the choice faced by a prisoner whose captor has offered him a positive incentive to cooperate in a project of interest to "the authorities." He is asked to put at their disposal some physical or intellectual skill, and he must decide whether to cooperate on their terms or to refuse the proffered incentives. The authorities can punish recalcitrant prisoners, but the choice is still the prisoner's. By not revealing the full range of his abilities, even under duress, he may be able to preserve some uncertainty as to the extent to which he is actively cooperating. And the more his captor depends *upon him* to disclose such unique talents as he may possess, the more discretion he may feel able to exercise in setting some limits on his compliance. What should he do?

There is no general answer to this question. The essential issue arises in many different contexts, and different points of view may well exist about any particular situation. The story of

---

am speaking of, those women who had sucking infants suffered much from their breasts becoming full of milk, the infants being left at home; they therefore could not keep up with the other hands: I have seen the overseer beat them with rawhide, so that the blood and milk flew mingled from their breasts" (M. Grandy [1844], p. 18; quoted in Frazier [1948], p. 36).

the wartime building of a railway bridge on the River Kwai poses the problem in one form. The captive's dilemma is explored in quite different terms by Aleksandr Solzhenitsyn in *The First Circle*. Both these stories deal with choices faced by actual prisoners. But members of some radical working-class movements have held that the workers are prisoners within the capitalist system ("wage slaves" they used to say), and that rebellion therefore is the more appropriate response to this condition than wage bargaining and cooperation with the bosses. It is not hard to multiply examples, some of which engender agreement about the "proper" course of action and some of which pose painful dilemmas.

Some broad principles, however, can be extracted from consideration of the general issue. In any given situation involving interaction between people, the choice of noncooperation and resistance is more appropriate the more the circumstances resemble those of a prison. The choice of compliance and cooperation is more appropriate when the aims of the controlling powers, or even the unintended consequences of their undertakings, correspond to a goal sanctioned by the controlled individuals—or the historian who sits in judgment upon them. But if the rewards for cooperation are recognizably attractive to normal men, while the punishments for resistance are horrible, then empathy urges us to suspend judgments on individuals who have been brought to cooperate in *acts* which are thought to be morally repugnant.

Vague as these general ethical principles may be, they suffice to suggest that Fogel and Engerman's factual assertions—including those regarding the nature of slave family life and the material level at which plantation slaves were maintained—do have a bearing upon their moral evaluation of slaves' performance within the capitalist system as an "achievement under adversity." According to the authors, the conditions of life under slavery were not so bad, and the benefits from revolt, or northward flight into what was for black people a tightly controlled racist society, were small indeed. And as a social organization, Fogel and Engerman say, plantation slavery promoted the desirable goal of economic efficiency. This much seems to suggest that it was more appropriate for the slaves to have sought to work cooperatively within the system rather than to attempt to resist or flee it. But, on the other hand, if slaveowners were as constrained in their behavior by considerations of wealth-maximization, and treated slave workers and their children as well as Fogel and Engerman assert, then there were few risks to the slave who temporarily withheld his cooperation or adopted a pattern of behavior that denied his master access to the best of his talents.

While the inducement to revolt may have been minimal, it is possible that on most plantations only mild penalties were meted out for subtly insisting upon the nonidentity between one's self-interests and the interests of one's owner—by ploughing shallow, picking trashy cotton, leaving gates open, and the like. The moral issue involved in opting to cooperate fully, which is the characterization of slave behavior which Fogel and Engerman seek to put in place of the "day-to-day resistance" envisaged by Stampp, remains difficult to resolve under the objective circumstances of slavery as these are described by *Time on the Cross*.

The experience of slavery in America is not so far removed from us in time and space that we can dissect it without personal involvement. It is not like an atom of hydrogen whose "true nature" can be sought and "discovered" as an abstract intellectual exercise. Historians will see reflected in the peculiar institution the social problems and moral dilemmas of their day. And, as Marc Bloch [1953] said, this is appropriate for serious history. We can confidently expect that no definitive view will emerge concerning the nature of the "black achievement" under slavery, even when the motives and behavior of the historical participants and the material conditions of plantation life have been established more firmly than they are in *Time on the Cross*.

CHAPTER TWO

Sambo Makes Good, or Were Slaves Imbued with the Protestant Work Ethic?

Herbert Gutman
and
Richard Sutch

"The typical slave field hand," assert Fogel and Engerman, "was not lazy, inept, and unproductive. On average he was harder-working and more efficient than his white counterpart" (FE, I, p. 5). Enslaved blacks were "diligent," "devoted," "responsible slaves who identified their fortunes with the fortunes of their masters" (FE, I, pp. 231 and 147). This positive attitude was "elicited" from the slaves by their owners, characterized by Fogel and Engerman as "shrewd capitalistic businessmen" (FE, I, pp. 147 and 232). The masters motivated their slaves not so much with the whip as with positive incentives, primarily by establishing a "wide-ranging system of rewards" (FE, I, p. 148).

Masters also used force, according to *Time on the Cross*, but applied it "judiciously" (FE, I, p. 237). Whipping was "used with restraint and in a coolly calculated manner" (FE, I, p. 146). The slaveowners "generally used force for exactly the same purpose as they used positive incentives—to achieve the largest product at the lowest cost. Like everything else, they strove to use force not cruelly, but optimally" (FE, I, p. 232).

This view of the relationship between masters and slaves lies behind Fogel and Engerman's conception of how the slave economy worked. Masters were capitalist businessmen, and themselves imbued with the "Protestant work ethic." Their pursuit of profit did not lead them to mete out harsh treatment, frequent physical punishment, and meager provisions. In fact, the reverse was true. According to Fogel and Engerman, the masters found it easier and more profitable to socialize the slaves so that they came to share their owners' work ethic and interests. This was accomplished by good treatment and generous rations as rewards for the majority, and infrequent punishment for the troublesome few. The masters as portrayed in *Time on the Cross* were more like modern rational personnel managers than paternalistic but sorely vexed Cavalier gentlemen, and bore no resemblance at all to Simon Legree.

Time on the Cross's depiction of the slaves is even more startling than its portrayal of masters. The slaves were receptive to the master's manipulation. According to Fogel and Engerman, slaves responded to the owner's offer of rewards, and in the process they internalized the Protestant work ethic—so that work itself became its own reward—and they came to identify their master's interests with their own. There is no room in this model of slave socialization (for that is what it is) for a *slave* culture, or a *slave* work ethic, or *slave* interests other than those adopted from the slave-owning whites. It is as if the slave personality was perfectly malleable and as if the slaves were passive, waiting to be molded into their master's image. According to *Time on the Cross*, the slaves' master transformed them into calculating "economic" men and women; Sambo is portrayed as a success-oriented character who might belong in a novel by Horatio Alger—but with black skin.

Evidence supporting the view that such a transformation took place is not found in *Time on the Cross*. No evidence is offered to support the characterization of masters as rational personnel managers. No evidence is offered to demonstrate that masters were themselves imbued with the Protestant work ethic, although this is a crucial assumption of their model. No evidence is presented that masters deliberately attempted to socialize their slaves. Nor does the work offer evidence that slaves were successfully transformed, that they were passive recipients of their masters' values, that they actually were imbued with the Protestant work ethic. Rather, the evidence provided in *Time on the Cross* on these points is all indirect.[1]

[1] David and Temin, in Chapter 1, above, discuss the general question of the extent to which rational, profit-maximizing behavior can be said to have

Fogel and Engerman attempt to establish only the existence of the apparatus called for by their model of slave socialization. They seek to demonstrate that masters relied upon positive incentives such as cash payments or the promise of an opportunity to pursue a favored occupation, and they attempt to show that slaves were rarely whipped. But even the evidence offered on these points is unimpressive. Much of it is circumstantial, none of it is conclusive. Most of it is quite traditional. Hardly any of it comes from new sources. Often their sources are imprecisely summarized. Occasionally, the material is taken out of context. Important evidence is so misused as to cast considerable and disturbing doubt upon the entire argument. Moreover, even if one were to grant that Fogel and Engerman have established that the use of rewards was prevalent and the use of force was moderate, they have nonetheless failed to demonstrate the relevance of such findings to their argument. A case in point is their treatment of whippings.

The Frequency of and the Effectiveness of Whipping

The only systematic record of whipping now available for an extended period comes from the diary of Bennet Barrow, a Louisiana planter who believed that to spare the rod was to spoil the slave. His plantation

---

characterized the actions of planters, and the bearing upon this question of evidence concerning the profitability of slave ownership. The present chapter deals more specifically with Fogel and Engerman's assertions about the management of the plantation labor force and its relationship to the work ethic that had developed among the slaves. Nor can we take up here the complex of issues raised by Fogel and Engerman's implied conclusion that the planter class was not only "capitalistic" but was itself imbued with attitudes toward work associated with the Protestant ethic. It should be remarked, however, that neither the text nor the supplement to *Time on the Cross* gives any hint that among American historians this is a far from settled question. David Bertelson [1967] has asserted that although Southerners worked hard, they did not share the commitment to the virtues of work that distinguished their contemporaries in the North. C. Vann Woodward [1968] criticized Bertelson's book but nevertheless argued for recognition of important differences between northern and southern attitudes. Puritan attitudes in the South and attitudes toward work have been examined by Edmund S. Morgan [1967], [1971], and Babette M. Levy [1960]. None of these references appear in the bibliography of *Time on the Cross*.

numbered about 200 slaves, of whom about 120 were in the labor force.
The record shows that over the course of two years a total of 160
whippings were administered, an average of 0.7 whippings per hand per
year. About half of the hands were not whipped at all during the period.
[FE, I, p. 145]

Several questions come to mind. Is "0.7" a useful "average"?
Have the appropriate historical questions been asked of the
data? Assume for the moment that the numbers of slaves,
workers, and whippings are accurate. If so, then Fogel and
Engerman's report of "an average of 0.7 whippings per hand per
year" would be accurate. But that is not the significant average.
That statistic answers the wrong question. It is known, for
example, that "on average" 135 blacks were lynched every year
between 1889 and 1899.[2] How does one assess that average? Six
million blacks lived in the United States in 1889; 127 of them
were lynched. Is it useful to learn that the record shows an
average of 0.00002 lynchings per black per year, so that about
99.998 percent of blacks were not lynched in 1889? An accurate
average, that is a banal statistic. The frequency with which a
punishment is administered is a poor measure of its effectiveness
in curbing errant behavior. Presumably, it is the *fear* of
eventual punishment, not the *ex post* administration of punishment, which motivates or deters behavior. But there is no
obvious correlation between the number of times an individual
is punished and his fear of being punished. A slave need never
have felt the lash to know the consequences of disobedience.
Indeed, the execution of a punishment is an indication of the
failure of the punitive system. A successful system of physical
discipline would experience few lapses of behavior and exhibit a
low incidence of actual punishment. A high incidence might
simply indicate that the prescribed punishment was not a strong
deterrent.[3]

Southern law permitted slaveowners to punish their chattel,

[2] Woodward [1951], pp. 351–52.

[3] As economists, Fogel and Engerman might be forgiven for their confusion of
the frequency and incidence of punishment with its effectiveness, a point
more within the expertise of sociologists and criminologists. However, this
error is analogous to a famous pitfall in the economics of tariff protection: the
attempt to measure the effectiveness of a tariff or prohibitive tax by the
magnitude of the revenue which it raises.

and most historians agree that whipping them was the most common form of *physical* punishment, figuring as a central device in imposing order over troublesome slaves and in asserting the source of authority in a slave society. The essential statistic therefore is not the average number of whippings per hand per year. Such an "average" does not measure the utility of the whip as an instrument of social and economic discipline. It is much more relevant to know how often the whip and its use were brought to the attention of a plantation's labor force. The appendix table in Edwin Davis's edition of the Barrow diary records 175 individual whippings during a 23-month period.[4] One hundred and seventy-five whippings administered during a 23-month period means that, "on average," a slave was whipped every 4 days. Among them, 60 were females. A male was whipped every 6 days, and a female once every 12 days.[5] Are these averages "small" or "large"? If a whipping is viewed primarily as an instrument of labor discipline, a whipping every 4 days means that this instrument of physical discipline had a quite adequate social visibility among the enslaved. Since the whippings were publicly administered in the slave quarters on Barrow's plantation, the lash must have been an ever-present threat.

The relevant historical questions which should have been asked of the Barrow's plantation records seem to us to have been missed by Fogel and Engerman. How were the punishments administered? Were they public or private? Were the other slaves required to be present? Were the punishments clearly related to incidents of individual malfeasance or were they indiscriminately applied? Were slaves with special skills or

---

[4] Fogel and Engerman apparently miscounted this number, since they report 160, not 175, whippings over a two-year, not 23-month, period (FE, I, p. 145). Barrow's diary has been published under the editorship of Edwin Davis [1943]. It is this published version which Fogel and Engerman cite as their source (FE, II, pp. 116 and 252).

[5] Since a number of the whipping incidences recorded in Barrow's diary involved the whipping of several slaves, the number of separate occasions on which one or more slaves were whipped would be somewhat less than the number given by the simple average. Unfortunately, the tabulated incidents are not dated, making it impossible to count the number of days during which one or more whippings took place.

favored occupations treated differently? Were men and women treated differently? Young and old?

In the context of the answers to such questions the "0.7 whippings per hand per year" would take on meaning. It would have a place. Standing alone, it is more misleading than helpful. Moreover, even this lone statistic is in error. Fogel and Engerman have inaccurately used the sole document they cite on this question.

The Frequency of Whipping: A View from the Barrow Plantation

The record of whippings referred to by Fogel and Engerman iş based upon tabulations made by Barrow and scattered throughout his diary. These the editor of the diary, Edwin Davis, assembled and relegated to an appendix. With one exception all of the incidents recorded occurred between December 1839 and October 1841, a period of one year and eleven months.[6] Fogel and Engerman erroneously label their whipping statistics as referring to a "Two-Year Period Beginning in December, 1840" (FE, I, p. 145).[7] They also miscounted the number of whippings

[6] The appendix is entitled "Misconduct and Punishments: 1840–1841" (Davis, [1943], pp. 431–440 and xi). The specific listings are not dated. However, a number of the incidents are also referred to in the diary, allowing one to be reasonably certain about the period of time covered by the tabulations. Compare the diary entries for Dec. 25, 1839; Feb. 18, 1840; March 13 and 20, April 18, June 23, and July 30, 1840; Aug. 16, 1841; and Oct. 1, 1841 (pp. 175, 181, 185, 186–87, 191, 200, 205, 239, and 244) with the appendix entries at pp. 431, 432, 433, 433, 433, 434, 439–40, and 440 respectively. The one exception referred to in the text is the last entry (p. 440), which refers to an incident in January 1844 (p. 315).

[7] Fogel and Engerman were apparently misled by a statement in the second listing of the Appendix which reads: "Anica   Filthiness, in the milk and butter. Her and Darcas alike. December 10, 1840 improved very much" (Davis [1943], p. 431). It Is not clear from this entry, nor from the diary, whether the reference to December 1840 was a later amendment recording the improvement of Anica and Darcas or an error in listing the date of the original misconduct of the two slaves. In any case, the fourth entry in the Appendix clearly refers to an incident which occurred on Christmas Day 1839 (p. 175), and the third entry reads: "Peter   Told me several lies Christmas." The other entries are, it is obvious, arranged chronologically.

recorded. There were 175, not 160. Fogel and Engerman's statistic on the frequency of whipping per slave and the statement that "[a]bout half the hands were not whipped at all during the period" are both based upon an erroneous estimate of the labor force (p. 145). They put that force at "about 120" (p. 145). Although the reader is not told how this estimate was made,[8] it is considerably larger than the one made by Barrow's editor Davis:

> [There is a] lack of accurate information as to the number of field hands used from year to year. In 1836 he [Barrow] kept from fifty to sixty workers in the field. Three years later the average was about the same, and the number evidently did not increase much during the years which followed, although by mustering all forces as many as seventy pickers could be put in the field at one time.[9]

Even after making a generous allowance for nonfield hands (based on Fogel and Engerman's estimate that 15.4 percent of plantation slaves were in nonfield occupations (FE, II, p. 37)), there would only be between 59 and 71 hands implied by Davis's estimate of the number of field hands. This is approximately 50 to 60 percent of Fogel and Engerman's own estimate. Barrow himself noted in a diary entry for September 26, 1839, that he had only 51 pickers and 6 "sick or pretending." On August 12, 1842, he counted his labor force at 65 hands, and on September 10, 1842, he had 72 slaves picking cotton. Among the 72 were at least 11 children.[10]

Barrow's plantation, Fogel and Engerman write, "numbered

---

[8] Fogel and Engerman state that the Barrow plantation had "about 200 slaves" (FE, I, p. 145). This number is apparently based upon the estate inventory taken in June of 1854, thirteen years after the whipping statistics and eight years after the last diary entry (Davis [1943], pp. 39 and 392–406). However, as the estate inventory clearly indicates, the holdings of Barrow were increased in 1843 (pp. 399, 14, and 281–82) and again in 1852 (pp. 401–2 and 14). In 1843 we also know that he bought seven slaves, and in 1850 he purchased one more (p. 39). Birth (1835–46) and death (1831–45) lists (pp. 427–31) show that slightly more than twice as many slaves were born as died in these years. At least 22 slaves who were over the age of seven in 1840 and who did not reside on the plantation in 1839–41 were included in the estate inventory of 1854.

[9] Davis [1943], p. 29.

[10] Davis [1943], pp. 163, 268, and 422.

about 200 slaves." On the contrary, in 1840 Bennet Barrow reported to the Assistant United States Marshal who was enumerating the census of that year that he owned only 129 slaves.[11] Fogel and Engerman exaggerated the number of slaves owned by Barrow in that year by 55 percent. This error probably explains how they exaggerated the number of workers. Fogel and Engerman set the ratio of the labor force to the population on Barrow's plantation at 60 percent. If we accept this ratio, the 129 slaves Barrow owned would imply that he had approximately 77 hands.

Sixty of Barrow's hands were recorded as having been whipped during the 23-month period.[12] Of the approximately seventeen slaves who were not whipped, eight were 14 years old or younger.[13] Five others who escaped the lash were women who were pregnant during the period under consideration.

By seriously overestimating the number of hands, Fogel and Engerman underestimated the extent of whipping as a form of punishment on Barrow's plantation. About 22 percent of the working slaves were not whipped. Fogel and Engerman placed this proportion at "[a]bout half" (FE, I, p. 145).

Using their *inaccurate* count of the number of whippings, their *greatly exaggerated* estimate of the number of hands, and their *erroneous* measurement of the length of time covered, Fogel and Engerman estimated that Barrow's slaves received "an average of 0.7 whippings per hand per year." This statistic is also wrong. Each of their errors contributed to the substantial

---

[11] This number was communicated to us in private correspondence by William Scarborough, who examined the manuscript returns of the 1840 Census, which are retained in the National Archives.

[12] This number was calculated from Davis [1943], pp. 431–40 and 239. Ambiguous cases were always counted as separate hands. For example, Dave Bartley (pp. 432, 434–38, and 440) was considered a different person than Bartley (p. 433) and Jenny (or Jeny or Jenney) (pp. 432, 433, and 437) and Old Jenney (Jenny O.) (p. 439) were kept distinct. However, plausible variant spellings of the same name were combined (Betsy and Betsey; Little Cato and L. Catto, Josh and Joshua, etc.), and a number of typographical errors or misreadings were corrected (L. Dare for L. Dave, Kiah for Kish).

[13] The youngest slave to be whipped was 11-year-old July (Davis [1943], p. 432). His age is established on p. 404. The second youngest was 15-year-old Grace (3 whippings (pp. 395, 433, and 435)).

underestimate of the correct average of 1.19 whippings per hand per year, a figure 69 percent larger than that reported by Fogel and Engerman.

In their concentration on whipping, Fogel and Engerman failed to note that Barrow's punishment was not confined to the use of the lash. During the two-year period under consideration, Barrow jailed, chained, beat with a stick, threatened with death, shot with a gun, raked the heads of, and humiliated his slaves. In the use of humiliation, Barrow seems to have been particularly ingenious. His diary notes the following:

December 24, 1839:
intend Exhibiting Dennis during Christmas on a scaffold in the middle of the Quarter & with a red Flannel Cap on.

July 5, 1840:
. . . had the Jack [mule] rigged out this evening with red flanel on his years [ears] & a Feather in them & sheet on, "in the Quarter." . . . Made Alfred and Betsy ride him round the Quarter dismount and take a kiss, for quarreling, Jack & Lize   Frank & Fanney the same.[14]

At other times Barrow assigned unpleasant tasks or forced slaves to work late as punishment. He apparently sold two slaves who displeased him. He had one young man "ware womens cloths" for running away and was apparently pleased with the results since he repeated the tactic the following year. On another occasion he put men to washing clothes "as punishment." [15]

Fogel and Engerman rely entirely upon the records of a single plantation for evidence on the masters' use of punishment, evidence which is later generalized to produce a picture for the entire slave South. The danger in this procedure is so self-evident, that we shall not dwell upon the point. Instead, we ask why they failed to weigh the full punishment record reported in Barrow's diary.

The Role of Physical Punishment: An Alternative View of the Barrow Plantation

Barrow's unusual diligence in recording the floggings of his slaves has provided modern historians with a rare opportunity to

[14] Davis [1943], pp. 175, 219, 434, 239, 178, 175, and 202. Also see p. 433.
[15] Davis [1943], pp. 78, 163, 91, 84, 112, 151, and 164.

Table 1:
Comparison of Fogel and Engerman's Estimate Relating to the
Barrow Plantation circa 1840 with the Actual Values

Number of:	Fogel and Engerman	Actual	Source
Slaves	"about 200"	129	Manuscript Census, 1840
Working slaves	"about 120"	57–72	Barrow Diary
		59–71	Implied Estimate by Davis
		77	Estimate by Gutman-Sutch
Slaves whipped	54[a]	60	Barrow Diary
Percent of:			
Slaves who worked	60.0	44.2–60.0	
Workers who were whipped	45.0	77.9	

Source: FE, I, p. 145.

[a] Calculated by applying the "percentage of hands" who were not whipped according to our reading of Fogel and Engerman's Figure 40 (p. 145), to their estimate of the number of hands.

examine the relations between whipping and slave labor efficiency. Had Fogel and Engerman delved into this record more deeply, they might have learned that Barrow's field hands had not internalized the Protestant work ethic and, at least according to Barrow, did not "identify" their fortunes with the fortunes of their owner.[16]

[16] Whether or not Barrow's response to the behavior of his cotton field hands was "typical" is a difficult question to answer. He was born in 1811, and, according to his biographer Davis, his "mode of living was that of a well-to-do planter." "A substantial and respected man in his community," observed Kenneth Stampp, "Barrow inherited lands and slaves from his father; he was in no sense a crude parvenu" (Stampp [1956], p. 186). There are other hints that Barrow was not unusual among Louisiana cotton planters. At least one

To substantiate this we need consider only the whippings listed in the appendix of the Davis volume. Other methods of labor discipline will be put aside and in what follows it will be assumed that the whippings list is a full and accurate record. Slave misconduct and whippings then may be examined for those 66 slaves who are listed as cotton pickers by Barrow in other appendixes published by Davis (the two cotton-picking lists are dated Nov. 3, 1838, and Sept. 10, 1842).

Table 2 indicates the frequency with which Barrow whipped his cotton pickers. Eighty percent of the men were whipped at least once during the 23-month period. Seventy percent of the women felt the lash at least once. In all, 50 of 66 male and female cotton pickers were whipped at least once during this period. These 50 slaves together were whipped no fewer than 130 times. If we compare the list of cotton pickers with the names of women who gave birth to children during the 23-month period (they were listed in a separate appendix), it is learned that 12 female cotton pickers gave birth to 14 children during these years. Seven of the mothers were whipped in this period (two of them twice, and a third no fewer than four times).

The same appendix in which Davis listed whippings also includes evidence indicating the varieties of slave "misconduct" detected by Barrow, the misconduct which had led to physical punishment but not necessarily whipping. It is hardly a complete list of incidents of slave misconduct during the 23-month period but serves nevertheless as a useful document bearing

---

planter nearby copied Barrow's plantation "rules." Bobby Jones points out that Barrow's plantation rules, reprinted as an appendix in the Davis volume, were not original to this Louisiana planter. He had copied them verbatim from a "restrictive" system of plantation management advocated by the *Southern Agriculturalist* and then reprinted in the March 1846 *Southern Cultivator* (Jones [1965]). His biographer, Davis, insists that in his "general outlook on the institution of slavery" Barrow was "typical of his time and section." Davis adds:

In general Barrow treated his slaves better and took more time in the organization of his labor system than did many of the neighboring planters. He was in the planting business for the sole purpose of making money and evidently believed that a contented black would work far better than one who was dissatisfied with his surroundings.

Table 2:
Frequency of Whippings of Barrow's
Male and Female Cotton Pickers

Number of times whipped	Males		Females		Total	
	Number	Percent	Number	Percent	Number	Percent
0	7	19.4	9	30.0	16	24.3
1	8	22.2	5	16.7	13	19.7
2	10	27.8	6	20.0	16	24.3
3-4	8	22.2	8	26.7	16	24.3
5+	3	8.3	2	6.7	5	7.6
Total	36	100.0	30	100.0	66	100.0

Source: Davis [1943].

directly on the thesis that slaveowners had successfully transformed the "work ethic" of their slaves. Barrow sometimes
listed a disorderly slave but failed to describe the particular
"disorder." Nevertheless 267 identified disorderly acts were
described, over 80 percent of all those listed. Women committed
slightly more than two in five (43 percent). A variety of
"disorderly" acts were recorded including family quarrels, child
neglect, theft, "impudence," visiting town, and running away.
Failure to keep the evening curfew fixed by Barrow was a
frequent infraction. But most significantly, 73 percent of the
acts listed related directly to *inefficient labor:* "for not picking as
well as he can"; "not picking cotton"; "very trashy cotton";
"covering up cotton limbs with ploughs"; "for not bringing her
cotton up"; and so forth. In other words, most of Barrow's slaves
were disciplined for not conforming to the Protestant work
ethic.

In all, the 66 cotton pickers engaged in no fewer than 181
disorderly acts. Only 12 had unblemished records. The average
per hand did not differ between men (4.3) and women (4.2).
Among those with disorderly records, 80 percent committed

three or more acts which merited their masters' chastisement. More than 3 in 10 were listed seven or more times on Barrow's list.[17]

It would take some effort to reconcile these numbers with the notion that Barrow's cotton pickers were members of a well-disciplined, orderly, and efficient laboring class. Either we must conclude that Barrow was a "psychological pervert who gloried in the exercise of unlimited force for its own sake"—an explanation that Fogel and Engerman would surely reject (see FE, I, p. 232)—or that his workers were *not* socialized to a positive "work ethic." Either conclusion undercuts Fogel and Engerman's reliance upon this single plantation as an illustration of the moderate use made of force by rational personnel managers who had successfully imbued their slaves with a "Protestant work ethic."

In 1838 and 1842 the picking lists also give the amount of cotton picked by individual slaves, and the relationships between the most productive cotton pickers, whippings, and acts of recorded misconduct in 1839–41 are most interesting. Twelve men and twelve women counted as Barrow's best field laborers. In Table 3 we compare them with the least productive cotton pickers. The more productive cotton pickers—both the male and female pickers but especially the females—were significantly more "disorderly" and were more frequently whipped than the less productive cotton pickers. If the main thrust in the arguments of Fogel and Engerman is sound, the least productive workers should have received more frequent whippings.

The Barrow slaves, of course, did not have to read their owner's diary to know how frequently and why he used the whip. They surely had enough familiarity with Barrow and his whip to realize how their owner defined slave misconduct. And yet their acts of misconduct over the 23-month period were by any measure numerous. Those acts of misconduct—mostly variants on the theme of not working "hard enough"—provoked their owner to violence. These same cotton pickers, moreover, were members of the last generation of adult Afro-American

[17] See Gutman [1975], Tables 3 and 4, pp. 27–28.

slaves. Upon emancipation, some were grandparents, and most were in their middle forties.[18] Surely if any generation of enslaved blacks had internalized the work ethic prized by their owners, it had to be this one. It was not. Barrow himself knew why. On April 16, 1840, he wrote in his diary: "am directing them to make a slow & sure lick in one place & to cut the full width of the hoe every time—unless reminded of it they would stand & make 4 or 5 licks in one place, tire themselves & do no work, have several grown ones that work harder & do less than any in the field." He added disgustedly two days later: "there never was a more rascally set of old negroes about any lot than this. Big Lucy   Anica   Center & cook Jane.   the better you treat them the worse they are, Big Lucy the leader, corrupts every young negro in her power." [19]

If what Fogel and Engerman call the Protestant work ethic had been successfully internalized by the Barrow slaves, the values associated with it would have passed along from slave generation to slave generation. But, according to Barrow, the opposite happened. Too many of the "young" slaves listened to Big Lucy, and her message quite obviously differed from that emphasized by Barrow. Barrow therefore had an unusually difficult task and was kept busy "transforming" different generations of enslaved blacks. That fact may explain the frequency with which he used the whip.

Fogel and Engerman rest their entire argument about the use of punishment upon a single source describing a brief period of time upon a single plantation. That is surprising. Given that they chose to do so, the casual selection with which they extracted material from that source is shocking. In more ways

[18] The approximate ages of 14 male and 16 female cotton pickers in 1840 can be learned from the 1854 inventory. All but three of the males whipped were between the ages of 19 and 26. The others were older, the oldest among them aged 37. Betsey was 45, and another of the female cotton pickers was a 13-year-old, but nine of the other eleven women whipped were between the ages of 15 and 26. The median age of cotton pickers whipped was nearly the same for men (23.8) and women (23.2). That means that these men and women had grandparents probably born in the eighteenth century and great-grandparents who probably were native Africans. These men and women were a few generations removed from initial enslavement.

[19] Davis [1943], pp. 191–93.

Table 3:
Productivity and Chastisement on Barrow's Plantation

	Average Number of Disorderly Acts		Average Number of Whippings		Number of Slaves	
	Males	*Females*	*Males*	*Females*	*Males*	*Females*
Most Productive Pickers	5.3	5.7	2.4	2.7	12	12
Least Productive Pickers	3.7	3.1	1.9	1.1	24	18

Source: Davis [1943]. Also see Gutman [1975], Table 5, pp. 29–30.

than one Barrow's diary directly contradicts the central theme of Fogel and Engerman's argument.

Rewards and the Protestant Work Ethic

Rewards were as much a part of slavery as punishment. No modern historian denies that the hands who picked the most cotton or the "breeding wenches" who bore the most children were frequently rewarded with extra food or clothing rations, assignment to choice tasks, or occasionally a small amount of money which could be used to purchase tobacco, jewelry, or trinkets from peddlers who catered to this demand. Such incentives become, in Fogel and Engerman's view, the primary means of motivating labor and imbuing the Protestant work ethic. Slaveowners, they assert, "developed a wide-rangeing system of rewards." They categorize these positive labor incentives into three types: "short-run" rewards, rewards "over periods of intermediate duration," and rewards of "a long-term nature, often requiring the lapse of a decade or more before they paid off" (FE, I, pp. 148–49).

The only evidence offered on short-run rewards is a brief paragraph (apparently based on Stampp's discussion[20]) indicating some of the ways in which diverse planters sought to spur productivity:

> Included in this category were prizes for the individual or the gang with the best picking record on a given day or during a given week. The prizes were such items as clothing, tobacco, and whiskey; sometimes the prize was cash. Good immediate performance was also rewarded with unscheduled holidays or with trips to town on weekends. When slaves worked at times normally set aside for rest, they received extra pay—usually in cash and at the rate prevailing in the region for hired labor. Slaves who were performing well were permitted to work on their own account after normal hours at such tasks as making shingles or weaving baskets, articles which they could sell either to their masters or to farmers in the neighborhood. [FE, I, p. 148]

Such examples hardly show that planters *developed* ("caused to evolve," "brought into being," "generated") a *system* ("a coordinated body of methods or a complex scheme or plan of procedure") of positive labor incentives. It needs first to be known how many planters used such devices and then how regularly they were used. But there is no hint in *Time on the Cross* that the authors have examined planter practices in order to uncover such regularities. Second, it must be established that the rewards offered slaves were provided selectively as *incentives*, not just as a matter of custom which would entitle every slave regardless of past or promised performance to a share. Yet on this crucial issue no evidence is offered.[21]

Fogel and Engerman's treatment of intermediate-term "positive labor incentives" is flawed by much more than a failure to provide adequate documentation. The evidence that is offered is misinterpreted, and the sources they draw upon are misused. Only three examples of intermediate incentives are described: a profit-sharing scheme by the Alabama planter William Jemi-

[20] Stampp [1956], pp. 164–70.
[21] Interestingly, the former slave Solomon Northup described as a "custom" the practice of Louisiana owners "to allow the slave to retain whatever compensation he may obtain for services performed on Sundays." If viewed that way by slaves and their owners, this arrangement would not count as a short-term positive incentive (Osofsky [1969], p. 331).

son[22]; the arrangements by which the Texas planter Julian L. Devereaux marketed the crop that slaves grew on separate plots allotted to them crediting the proceeds to individual families; and finally year-end bonuses "given either in goods or cash" and "frequently quite substantial" [FE, I, p. 148]. The last of these three illustrations deserves attention. Once again, Bennet Barrow serves the purposes of Fogel and Engerman but once again in curious ways. They write:

> Bennet Barrow, for example, distributed gifts averaging between $15 and $20 per slave family in both 1839 and 1840. The amounts received by particular slaves were porportional to their performance. [FE, I, p. 148]

Unless Fogel and Engerman had access to materials not included in the Davis volume, these numbers are wrong. There is no way to tell from that work how many slave families lived on the Barrow plantation in 1839 and 1840. The statement that gifts averaged "between $15 and $20 per slave family" is therefore at best an estimate. The diary records cash Christmas gifts only in 1838 ($500 in total) and in 1840 ($700). Barrow's financial records (reproduced in another appendix by Davis) recorded the expenditure of $700 in 1839 for gifts and put the cash amount in 1840 as $720. No other year-end bonuses were recorded in the diary for the ten-year period during which it was kept save the exception of 1845 (the last year of the diary) when a total expenditure for Christmas gifts was only $60.[23] Thus the two years selected by Fogel and Engerman from the ten-year diary were two years out of three in which substantial gifts were provided, and they were the two years of the three in which Barrow was most generous. These facts cast grave doubts on whether or not a *system* of short-run or intermediate positive incentives existed on the Barrow plantation. Barrow's diary

[22] The same example is cited by Stampp in *The Peculiar Institution* [1956], pp. 167–68.
[23] Davis [1943], pp. 139, 218, 412, 414, and 419. There is also an ambiguous entry for 1841. Barrow's financial account book reads: "New Orleans for negros [$] 1,055.00" (p. 415). This could be interpreted as an expenditure on gifts in light of the entry in Barrow's diary for Dec. 26, 1841: "gave the negros articles purchased for them in N. Orleans" (p. 248). Barrow's editor, however, interpreted the account entry as representing money paid for the purchase of new slaves (p. 39).

entries at the holiday season tell a different story from the one
suggested by Fogel and Engerman:[24]

1836
Dec 24   negros went to Town for Christmas
Dec 26   House Jerry & Isreal chained during Christmas Jerry for
         general bad conduct—for a year and better—Isreal bad
         conduct during cotten picking season
Dec 29   gave the negros a dinner

1837
Dec 26   negros went to Town
Dec 29   negros preparing for a dinner
Dec 31   negros seemed to enjoy Christmas verry much ran two of
         Uncle Bats negros off last night—for making a disturbance—
         no pass—broke my sword Cane over one of their skulls

1838
Dec 24   hands went to Town payed them last night over $500
Dec 30   the negros behaved badly last night at their supper

1839
Dec 23   negros went to Town to day Turnbulls Overseer Bailey caught
         Dennis yesterday
Dec 24   intend exhibiting Dennis during Christmas on a scaffold in the
         middle of the Quarter & with a red Flannel Cap on
Dec 25   negros appeared in fine spirits yesterday Let Darcas out of
         Jail—Dennis confined in Jail
Dec 26   had quit a Dance yesterday—some of the old negros &c.
Dec 28   negros preparing for a dinner
Dec 29   negros had quit a fine supper last night

1840
Dec 24   Gave the negros money last night $700. all went to Town to
         day
Dec 29   negros preparing for a Dinner
Jan 3   Gave the negros a verry fine dinner yesterday evening at the
         House and afterwards inspected their manners in the Ball-
         room several acted very rude as usual. put them in Jail

1841
Dec 22   Making up pants for men as Christmas presents
Dec 26   *gave the negros articles* purchased for them in N. Orleans

1842
Dec 28   Gave the negros as much of Evry thing to eat & *drink* during
         the Hollidays as they Wanted times so hard no able to give
         them any thing more

1843 and 1844
[No diary record of any celebration or gift-giving]

[24] Davis [1943], pp. 85, 104, 139, 175, 218–19, 247–48, and 313–14. See page
412 for evidence of the 1839 bonus.

1845
  Dec 25   negros seem quite Lively
  Dec 29   getting tired of Hollidays, negroes want too much, Human
           nature.

Reading these entries together makes it difficult to accept
that Barrow's behavior indicates that he had developed a system
of positive rewards meant to motivate the labor of his slaves.
There is no evidence that the "amounts received by particular
slaves were proportional to their performance."

Why did Barrow fail to pay his slaves cash bonuses after 1840?
Was it because business conditions had deteriorated and made
cash short? That is hinted at in the 1842 entry. Or was it because
Barrow's slaves had performed inefficiently by his standards? Or
was it simply because Barrow was "getting tired of Hollidays"?

The three examples presented by Fogel and Engerman
neither support nor refute the thesis that labor productivity
increased following the introduction of such schemes. Even
assuming that they were common, a mere listing tells us nothing
about their effectiveness. Did slave productivity increase as a
consequence of such schemes? It is hard to tell just what such
"examples" mean. By way of introducing the Devereux example, Fogel and Engerman write "Masters also rewarded slaves
who performed well with patches of land ranging up to a few
acres for each family" [FE, I, p. 148]. It is well known that
slaves over the entire South worked such patches of land. But
were these bits of land given to slaves as "rewards" for efficient
labor or as "stimuli" to more efficient labor? Fogel and Engerman assume it happened for one of these reasons. Yet, no
evidence is offered which sustains either connection. "It was the
universal custom in Georgia," explained Ralph Flanders in
Plantation Slavery in Georgia, "to allow slaves the privilege of
raising small crops of their own, for which the master paid cash,
or which could be exchanged at the storeroom for anything they
chose to buy." [25] There is a great difference between a "universal
custom" and a selective labor incentive. A custom is a habitual
practice, an established way of doing things. If it happened this
way, the garden patch hardly served as a positive labor
incentive. That does not mean, of course, that such patches
failed to create other satisfactions among the enslaved.

[25] Flanders [1933], p. 146. Emphasis supplied.

Occupations as Rewards

According to Fogel and Engerman, the most important "long-run positive incentive" used to inspire the willing co-operation of slaves was offering the possibility that they would be allowed to advance to "occupations" above that of field hand. Household staff positions, for example, were regarded as superior to field jobs. Slaves worked hard in the field, suggest Fogel and Engerman, to earn assignments as house servants, gardeners, grooms, and coach drivers. Management positions and skilled trades were also open to slaves. Plantations with 25 working hands or more (that is, approximately 50 slaves) would have need of one or more "drivers," slave foremen who directed and were responsible for the work of fellow bondsmen. Fogel and Engerman even claim that over one-half of the overseers were slaves. Other deserving slaves were allowed to acquire the skills of a carpenter, blacksmith, or other artisan craft.

As a result of this incentive system, according to *Time on the Cross,* "over 25 percent [26.3 percent] of males were managers, professionals, craftsmen, and semiskilled workers." For the slave, "[c]limbing the economic ladder brought not only social status . . . it also had significant payoffs in better housing, better clothing, and cash bonuses." [26] For the masters this system produced "devoted, hard-working, responsible slaves" (FE, I, pp. 40, 149, and 147).

The trouble with this picture is that Fogel and Engerman have no direct evidence to support it. The plantation guide quoted to support the suggestion that occupations were used as "prizes for performance" was written for Jamaica in 1823 and says nothing about typical practice in the United States (FE, II, pp. 117–18 and 262). Fogel and Engerman also believe they have found evidence of the prevalent use of occupations as rewards in the age structure of slave "artisans." Young slaves were rarely found in skilled or semiskilled jobs, while those over forty were

[26] There is no evidence in *Time on the Cross* to support this claim that slaves with superior occupations received better housing and clothing or cash bonuses. However, Fogel and Engerman offer a conjectural argument that the "earnings" of skilled slaves "must have been" higher than that of the field hand (FE, I, p. 152).

disproportionately represented (FE, I, p. 150; and FE, II, Table B.18, p. 118). Fogel and Engerman's interpretation of this finding is that the young bondsmen competed among themselves for the privilege of becoming carpenters, blacksmiths, grooms, coach drivers, and house servants in their later years.[27] While the "skewed age distribution of artisans" observed by Fogel and Engerman (FE, II, p. 117) is consistent with the notion of an occupational incentive system, it is not firm evidence that such a system was widely adopted. It is also possible that skilled occupations were assigned to slaves who were too old for heavy work or who had been maimed or were otherwise unsuited for field work. Such a policy would also result in a skewed distribution of skilled workers.

A second alternative explanation for the relative shortage of young artisans is that the relative demand for trained slaves may have been declining over time. If fewer slaves were trained during the last few decades of slavery than had been the practice earlier, then there would have been a disproportionate number of older artisans on the eve of the Civil War. This possibility is consistent with Fogel and Engerman's explanation of the decline of urban slavery during the 1850s. They argue that, despite the fact that the demand for slaves in the cities was increasing, it did not increase as fast as the demand for slaves in the rural districts. At the same time, they argue, "there were no close substitutes for slave labor" in the rural areas. "In the cities, however, free labor, particularly immigrant labor, proved to be a very effective substitute." Consequently, Fogel and Engerman assert, "as the competition of the cities and the countryside forced the price of slaves up relative to the price of free labor, the cities shifted toward the relatively cheaper form of labor" (FE, I, p. 102). Exactly the same mechanism would explain a shift away from the training of skilled slaves. It would not necessarily be because the demand for skilled slaves was declining, but simply that free labor, particularly immigrant

[27] The list of occupations defined by Fogel and Engerman as "artisan" in this context includes, in addition to those listed in the text: sawyer, shoemaker, wheelwright, engineer, bricklayer, cooper, mason, carriage driver, and gardener (letter from Engerman, July 15, 1974).

labor, was a better substitute for skilled slaves than for field hands. In fact, since many city slaves were artisans and most rural slaves were field hands, the conclusion that the tradition of artisan skills among slaves was being eroded by the cotton boom of the 1850s is nearly unavoidable.

In any case it seems that the age-distribution of artisan slaves cannot by itself be used to support the Fogel-Engerman hypothesis that skilled occupations were offered as rewards. Their case is left only with the evidence on the proportion of slaves who were engaged in managerial, professional, artisan, domestic, and semiskilled occupations. These estimates (apart from their discussion of the age-structure of artisans) represent the only *new* evidence on owner-sponsored positive work incentives offered in *Time on the Cross*. It is upon this evidence that they must rest their case that masters developed a "system of rewards," since their discussion of the short-run and intermediate-term rewards supplied no information which would sustain their reinterpretation of the significance of these widely known practices.

That is why the claim made by Fogel and Engerman that 26.3 percent of the male slaves held occupations other than field hand takes on so much significance for their thesis that slaves were imbued with the Protestant work ethic. "Neglect of [this] fact," according to Fogel and Engerman, is partially responsible for

> the failure to recognize the existence of a flexible and exceedingly effective incentive system that operated within the framework of slavery. The notion that slaveowners relied on the lash alone to promote discipline and efficiency is a highly misleading myth. In slave, as in free society, positive incentives, in the form of material rewards, were a powerful instrument of economic and social control. [FE, I, pp. 40–41]

Yet even if Fogel and Engerman's estimate that over one-quarter of the adult male slaves "held preferred occupational positions" were correct (FE, I, p. 40), the figure by itself would say nothing about the Protestant work ethic or the master's objectives in manipulating the occupational status of his bondsmen. However, we shall set this objection aside, since, as we shall see, Fogel and Engerman's estimate of the proportion of slaves with preferred occupations is not correct. Thus their

Protestant-ethic thesis, along with their characterization of masters as rational personnel managers, is left totally without support.

The Occupational Hierarchy of Slavery: A View from Plaquemines Parish[28]

How many slaves advanced above the level of field hand? Fogel and Engerman's estimate is that

> Within the agricultural sector, about 7.0 percent of the men held managerial posts and 11.9 percent were skilled craftsmen (blacksmiths, carpenters, coopers, etc.). Another 7.4 percent were engaged in semi-skilled and domestic or quasi-domestic jobs: teamsters, coachmen, gardeners, stewards, and house servants. [FE, I, p. 39]

How were these numbers obtained? According to Volume II of *Time on the Cross*

> The share of skilled and semiskilled laborers in nonfield occupations on plantations was determined from a sample of 33 estates, ranging in size from 3 to 98 slaves, retrieved from the probate records. [FE, II, p. 37]

Time on the Cross does not say how these estates were chosen or where they were located. After publication the authors reported that *all* of the estates (and they reported there were only 30, not 33) were located in Plaquemines Parish, Louisiana. Fogel and Engerman collected probate records from 54 counties in 8 Southern states (FE, II, p. 24) but rest their argument on a single Louisiana Parish. Plaquemines Parish, however, was atypical. It was a sugar parish, many of its slaveowners were Creole French, their holdings were uncharacteristically large, and the age distribution of the slaves was heavily skewed toward males over 14 years of age.[29]

[28] See Gutman ([1975], pp. 48–61) for a discussion of Fogel and Engerman's treatment of the skill distribution among urban slaves.

[29] According to the published Census Reports for 1860, no cotton was grown in the Parish (U.S. Census, 1860, Agriculture, p. 67). Sugar was the predominant, almost exclusive, staple crop grown. (The published report of rice production for Plaquemines Parish is apparently in error (Menn [1964], p. 68).) The population was 63.4 percent slave (U.S. Census, 1860, Population, p. 194). Slaveholdings with fifty or more slaves accounted for 13.4 percent of

It is not even clear how Fogel and Engerman chose the 30 slaveholdings from the 65 probate records collected from this parish. While many of the omitted inventories did not record the occupations of the slaves (suggesting to fogel and Engerman, perhaps, that the trouble had not been taken to list the skills possessed), it is also the case that among the holdings included in their sample, as well, there were many slaves without recorded occupations. Such slaves were counted by Fogel and Engerman as field hands. Our presumption is that the slaves on the omitted slave holdings just mentioned were also field hands, since it would follow that slaves with no special skills recorded in the probate inventories had no skills to record. This presumption is strengthened by the observation that the omitted farms were much smaller than those included. The median size of farm omitted for this reason had only 2 adult males. The median size of included farms was 12. The average sizes were 5 and 17, respectively. Fogel and Engerman also inexplicably excluded seven slave holdings in Plaquemines Parish which did list the occupation of every male slave over 14. The 13 male hands on these 7 holdings were all specifically listed as field hands. There were 6 other holdings excluded which listed skills for some slaves but recorded nothing for the others. Again our presumption would have been that the slaves with no recorded skills were field hands.

The 30 selected probate records "revealed" to Fogel and Engerman that 15.4 percent of the male slaves 15 years old and older possessed skills (FE, II, p. 37). Even this figure is in error. Our recomputation based on the same 30 holdings and accepting the same definitions gives 14.8 percent.[30] If the entire 65

Plaquemines' slaveowners while only 5.7 percent of the slave farms in the Parker-Gallman sample were of this size (U.S. Census, 1860, Agriculture, p. 230; and Foust [1967], Table 6, p. 46). Among the slaves 15 years of age and over, the sex ratio was 134 males for every 100 females (U.S. Census, 1860, Population, pp. 192–93). For the proportion of Creole masters among the large slaveholders, see Menn (1964, Table 10, p. 86).

[30] We have been unable to identify the cause of this discrepancy. The definition of "skilled" slaves in this context is *any* slave with a designated occupation other than a field hand or driver. Fogel and Engerman report that only 11.9 percent of the male slaves 15 years old and older on the 30

slaveholdings from the Plaquemines court records are included rather than just the 30 employed by Fogel and Engerman, the percentage of skilled and semiskilled male slaves falls from 14.8 percent to 11.4 percent, less than 75 percent of the figure reported in *Time on the Cross*.

When Fogel and Engerman attempted to project their findings from this single county to the entire South their calculations were flawed by a serious error. Based upon the assertion that the "percentage of skilled slaves was fairly constant over plantation size," they applied a constant skill ratio (15.4 percent) to all size classes of farms in the *cotton* South (FE, II, pp. 37 and 40). Actually the percentage of adult males with skills was *not* constant across the four size classes of farms used by Fogel and Engerman within either the Fogel-Engerman sample or the entire Plaquemines sample.[31] We present the comparisons in Table 4.

Had they used the fraction of males over 14 who were skilled based on *their own sample* to weight each of the four size classes, Fogel and Engerman would have found only 12.7 percent of the slaves in the cotton South were "skilled." Had they used the full Plaquemines Parish sample, the fraction would have fallen to 10.2 percent. This last figure is only two-thirds of the figure reported in *Time on the Cross*. Fogel and Engerman exaggerated the percentage of "skilled" slaves by over 50 percent. Our correction brings the percentage of male slaves with occupations other than field hand from 26.3 percent down to 21.1 percent. Had Fogel and Engerman used the Plaquemines sample properly and had they recognized that the skill ratio was not invariant with the size of farm, their own procedure would have revealed a significantly less skilled slave

---

Plaquemines estates were "nonfield craftsmen." This category was defined in the same way as the "artisans" discussed in note 27. Our recomputation found 11.6 percent of the slaves were "craftsmen."

[31] Fogel and Engerman's conclusion that the skill ratio was constant was apparently based upon the results of a poorly designed linear regression of the number of skilled slaves on the number of males over the age of 14 from each of the 30 estates (FE, II, p. 37). Had it been calculated using an appropriate statistical procedure, Fogel and Engerman would have avoided their erroneous interpretation.

population than they describe in *Time on the Cross*. In this case, it is also important to note that the procedure adopted is highly suspect. It is based upon the assumption that the distribution of occupations on estates in a Louisiana sugar parish can be applied to the size distribution of farms drawn from the *cotton* counties of the South and that the final result can be interpreted as being applicable to the entire "agricultural sector" of the slave south [FE, I, p. 39; II, p. 40].[32] This procedure is questionable in any case owing to the very different technologies required for sugar and cotton. At least one major difference which appears strikingly in this case is that sugar plantations, unlike cotton farms, had need of coopers to manufacture the hogsheads in which the sugar was packed for shipment. Twenty percent of the skilled slaves in the Plaquemines sample were coopers. If we decrease the percentage of skilled slaves by 20 percent, it would fall to 8.2 percent and the percentage of male slaves with nonfield-hand occupations would fall to 19.1 percent.

Black Slave Drivers

Fogel and Engerman apparently were not content to rely upon the Plaquemines Parish sample to estimate the number of slaves who were slave drivers and "assistant" slave drivers. Had they done so, they would have found that 3.7 percent of the slaves in their sample (or 3.3 percent of the full Plaquemines sample) were drivers. This figure apparently struck Fogel and Engerman as too low, since they say:

> The probate records thus far processed do not provide an adequate basis for determining the proportion of slaves on each plantation who were drivers. Our estimate of the share of males over 10 [*sic*, read 14] who were

[32] See Table 4, footnote b. Even if Fogel and Engerman were to expand their investigation of the probate records to provide a more representative sample, they would have to take into account the upward bias in probate listings of slave artisans. By themselves and without correction, probate records record too high a percentage of slave artisans in the *general* male population. Fogel and Engerman point out, that as a group slave artisans tended to be older men (FE, I, p. 150; FE, II, pp. 117–18). But probate records usually undercount younger adult slaves and therefore exaggerate the number of slave artisans. Illustrations of this tendency are provided in Gutman [1975], pp. 75–77.

drivers is based on the conventional ratio of one driver to every 30 slaves. [FE, II, pp. 38–39] [33]

Table 4:
Percent of Skilled Adult Male Slaves on Farms, Plaquemines Parish, Louisiana

	Percent on each size plantation who were "skilled"	
Slaves per Plantation[a]	Fogel/Engerman Sample	Entire Probate Sample
1–10	0.0	0.0
11–30	9.6	7.5
31–50	22.5	16.8
51 or more	15.1	13.2
Average, Sample	14.8	11.4
Weighted Average, Cotton South[b]	12.7	10.2

[a] These are the size classifications used by Fogel and Engerman (II, Table B.5, p. 40).

[b] The weighted average is computed using the weights reported in FE,II, Table B.5, p. 40. These weights were based upon a sample of farms selected from the cotton-growing countries of the South. The sample was drawn from the enumerators' manuscripts of the 1860 Agricultural Census and was originally collected by William Parker and Robert Gallman for use in an unrelated project. For details on the Parker-Gallman sample, see Parker [1970], Wright [1970], and Foust [1967].

[33] If it is Fogel and Engerman's contention that the skill of a driver was too minor to be noted by the court appraisers when determining his market value, then it throws into contention their claim that these slave foremen should be considered as part of the "managerial and professional class" (FE, I, p. 39; II, pp. 39–40) and that they deserve a share of the credit for the efficiency and productivity of slave agriculture (FE, I, p. 210). Our own review of the Plaquemines sample suggests that drivers *were* conscientiously noted in the probate inventories. With only 4 exceptions every one of the 18 inventories with 30 or more slaves recorded drivers, and all but one of the plantations with drivers had at least 20 slaves.

To support this "conventional ratio" they cite Flanders's *Plantation Slavery in Georgia.* However, Flanders was discussing the "seacoast" region where rice was the predominant crop, and his ratio was "one driver to every thirty *working hands,*" not every 30 *slaves.*[34] Since there were approximately 2 slaves for every working hand, Fogel and Engerman's misquotation of Flanders had the effect of doubling the numbers of drivers required on a given plantation. Even if they had not erroneously doubled the number of drivers, it would hardly be appropriate to label a single observation from a Georgia rice plantation as a "conventional ratio" applicable to cotton farms.[35] The task system of organizing labor was common among rice planters, and it is too facile to assume that the gang system of labor—common on cotton plantations—had the same "ratio" of drivers as the task system. Nevertheless, for illustrative purposes, we have corrected Fogel and Engerman's calculations so that the ratio of 30 *hands* per driver, rather than 30 *slaves*, is the basis of the estimate for drivers. The result is that 8.25 percent of the adult males over 14 on large farms would have been drivers, not 12.2 percent as reported in *Time on the Cross.*[36]

---

[34] Flanders [1933], p. 143. Emphasis supplied.

[35] *Time on the Cross* also notes in apparent support of this "conventional" ratio discussions by Gray and Scarborough of the ratio of hands to *overseers.* Gray [1933], I, p. 546. Scarborough [1966], p. 8. The figure of 30 laboring slaves per overseer is given by Gray for rice plantations in the colonial period. He cites a figure of 50 *hands* per overseer for cotton and asserts that even more slaves per overseer could be optimally handled on sugar estates (Gray [1933], I, p. 546). Scarborough cites both of Gray's sources for the colonial rice plantation and also Kenneth Stampp, Charles Sydnor, and Thomas Carroll (Scarborough [1966], pp. 8 and 204–5). Stampp's source is Sydnor (Stampp [1956], p. 38). Sydnor's source is Carroll (Sydnor [1933], p. 67). Carroll, according to Sydnor, "estimated that in Oktibbeha County [Mississippi] most of the owners of thirty or more slaves had overseers" (p. 67). In any case the ratio of hands or slaves to overseers is irrelevant to the ratio of hands to drivers.

[36] Fogel and Engerman claim that all slaves over age 10 were hands, and that 68 percent of the slave population was over 10 (FE, II, p. 39). Thus on a plantation with n slaves, .68n would be hands requiring $.68n/30 = .022667n$ drivers. Fogel and Engerman also say that 55 percent of all males were 15 or over (ibid.) and presumably one-half of the typical slave force would be male. Therefore, .275n slaves would be adult males, and the fraction of this number

Fogel and Engerman applied their incorrect percentage to all plantations with 11 or more slaves (approximately 7 or more hands) (FE, II, p. 40). They identify this proportion, however, as "assistant drivers" on farms with 11 to 30 slaves (FE, II, p. 39).[37] This procedure produced their estimate that 10.4 percent of *all* male slaves over 14 were drivers or "assistant drivers." Applying our corrected estimate to all farms in the cotton sample with 11 or more slaves lowers this to 7.0 percent. But even this is probably still too high. If we accept the 3.3 percent figure obtained from the Plaquemines Parish sample, we would probably be closer to the truth.

Correcting the percentage of adult males with nonfield-hand occupations to remove the exaggeration of the number of drivers brings the figure down to 12 percent, from the original 26.4 percent.

Black Overseers

Finally, and most incredibly of all, Fogel and Engerman estimate that 1.6 percent of all adult males on plantations with 51 or more slaves were overseers (FE, II, pp. 39–40, and 151–52; and I, pp. 200–201 and 210–12).[38] This result is obtained by

---

who were drivers would be .0226667n/.275n = .0825 or 8¼ percent. Fogel and Engerman erroneously obtained 12.2 percent by taking the conventional ratio to be 30 *slaves* per driver. This would require .03333n drivers and .03333n/.275n = .1212, very close to 12.2 percent.

[37] These assistant drivers were added to the semiskilled class by Fogel and Engerman (FE, II, p. 39). According to their estimates 3.9 percent of all males over 14 were semiskilled assistant drivers. Recomputing this percentage using the correct driver ratio lowers it to 2.6 percent. When added to the 11.4 percent of skilled or semiskilled slaves found in the full Plaquemines sample, then that class contains 14.0 percent. Fogel and Engerman estimated 19.3 percent.

[38] Once again Fogel and Engerman neglect the Plaquemines data. Had they used these inventories they would have found only 2 slaves out of 706 males inventoried who might plausibly be identified as "overseers." Both of these slaves were on plantations included in the Fogel-Engerman subsample (518 males over 14 were included in their sample). One on a farm with 65 slaves was identified as a "commandeur," the other on a holding of 76 slaves was titled "maitre." French terms were used, of course, because Plaquemines had a substantial French-speaking population.

assuming that the farms included in the Parker-Gallman sample which had no free overseers must have had overseers and that these overseers must have been slaves. "On large slaveholdings [over 50 slaves]," Fogel and Engerman have found, "only one out of every four owners used white overseers," and "[o]nly 30 percent of plantations with one hundred or more slaves employed white overseers" (FE, I, pp. 200 and 211). Despite the fact, which Fogel and Engerman note themselves, that 25 percent of the remaining plantations might have been overseen by sons or other male relatives of the planter (FE, I, p. 212), and despite the fact, which they overlook, that almost all of the remaining plantations potentially could have been overseen by the planter himself, Fogel and Engerman jump to the remarkable conclusion that 72 percent of the large plantations were directed by slave overseers (FE, II, p. 41).

This conclusion is not warranted. Not only do they neglect the possibility that the slaveowner or his relative might have managed without a paid overseer, but, far more seriously, they neglect the fact that the Parker-Gallman sampling procedure only counted those members of the free population who lived in the same *house* as the farm-owner.[39] Since many overseers obviously were provided their own homes, it is not surprising that only a fraction of the large farms in the Parker-Gallman sample had an overseer recorded.[40]

[39] Unless the census enumerator took the unrequested effort to note the relation of the separate dwellings to the farm-owner's, it would not even be possible to determine which overseers were attached to which farms. This overzealousness on the part of the assistant marshals who enumerated the population was extremely rare, and in the cases where the enumerator did note the connection the Parker-Gallman sample did not count the neighboring overseer or his family (Gallman [1965], p. 9; and comparison of the Parker-Gallman data with census manuscripts).

[40] It is easy to show that Fogel and Engerman by their procedure have undercounted the number of free overseers in the South. In the Parker-Gallman sample there were only 39 farms with 100 or more slaves (Foust [1967], p. 46). Of these apparently 12 had overseers since Fogel and Engerman report that "just 30 percent" were so equipped (FE, I, p. 200). There were approximately 29 overseers on the 109 farms with 51 to 99 slaves (Foust [1967], p. 46; and a reading by eye of FE, I, Fig. 46, p. 201). Farms with 16 to 50 slaves contributed 103 overseers, and the smallest class of farms had 52

The antebellum South had slave overseers, but their number
was insignificant.[41] They deserve study, but their place in the
southern slave occupational structure and plantation managerial system needs to be measured more carefully first. Fogel and
Engerman have produced no valid evidence at all to support
their "startling" assertion that on "a majority of the large
plantations, the top nonownership management was black." Yet
they scorn historians for using "a biased sample of evidence, on

---

additional overseers (FE, II, p. 151, and Foust [1967], p. 461). Thus the entire
Parker-Gallman sample had only 196 overseers for a total of 40,576 slaves
(Sutch [1975], p. 187), or 207 slaves per overseer. In the 1860 census the five
leading cotton states (South Carolina, Georgia, Alabama, Mississippi, and
Louisiana) reported 18,717 overseers [U.S. Census, 1860, Population, pp.
670–71) and 2.07 million slaves, 110 slaves per overseer. The Parker-Gallman
sample underenumerated overseers by 50 percent. It strains credulity to
suggest that these missing overseers all were on free farms or managing
southern factories (FE, II, p. 152). Fogel and Engerman use the following
calculation to lend credence to their reliance upon the Parker-Gallman
sample to estimate the number of free overseers:

> Analysis of the data . . . shows that 14.5 percent of the medium
> plantations (16 to 50 slaves) had free overseers, that 3.0 percent of the
> small plantations (1 to 15 slaves) had free overseers. . . . [If] these
> figures . . . are applied to the size distribution of slaveholdings for 1850,
> they account for 13,739 overseers out of the national total of 18,859.
> Another 1,887 overseers were employed in the North. Thus the residual
> number of overseers left for large slave plantations could not exceed
> 3,233. . . . [O]nly 40 percent of these large estates would have had white
> overseers. [FE, II, pp. 151–52]

This calculation is flawed by the fact that the 3.0 percent proportion for the
small farms is based on a sample of 1860 *farms* but is applied to the number
of *slaveholdings* in 1850 [not 1860!]. Since a very significant number of
holdings with just one or two slaves employed them as domestic servants in
urban areas, it is inadmissible to apply the proportion of overseers on *farms* to
this group. Compare the percentage of slaveholdings contained in the
Parker-Gallman sample and in the 1850 and 1860 censuses (Foust [1967], p.
46; and U.S. Census, 1860, Agriculture, pp. 247–48):

Size of holding	Parker-Gallman Sample	1850 Census	1860 Census
1 slave	11.4%	19.8%	20.1%
2–4 slaves	20.4	30.4	28.6
5–9 slaves	22.0	23.2	23.3

[41] Starobin [1971], pp. 59–65.

a relatively small group of plantations which were unrepresentative of the whole" to support the "traditional" conclusion that the "white overseer [was] . . . a ubiquitous figure, present on virtually all plantations of one hundred or more slaves and on the majority of those with fifty to one hundred slaves" (FE, I, pp. 212 and 211).

No calculation, no piece of evidence presented in *Time on the Cross* is more important to Fogel and Engerman's contention that slaves were imbued with a positive work ethic than their estimate that "over 25 percent of [slave] males were managers, professionals, craftsmen, and semiskilled workers." It is the only piece of systematic evidence they offer. Yet, as we have seen, arithmetic errors and flawed procedure have conspired to overrepresent the frequency with which slaves became managers (read: overseers) and professionals (read: drivers?). Furthermore, *Time on the Cross* relies upon a small, unrepresentative, and improperly handled sample of slaveholdings to estimate the percentage of males who became skilled craftsmen and semiskilled workers. The result is a greatly exaggerated estimate of the percentage of slaves with privileged occupations. Table 5 collects all of the corrections we have made to show their cumulative impact on the occupational share estimated in *Time on the Cross*. Using Fogel and Engerman's sources and methods —but correcting their mistakes and distortions—we find that the percentage of male slaves over 14 who had nonfield occupations was 11.46 percent, not 26.30 percent as claimed in *Time on the Cross*.

The Occupational Hierarchy of Slavery: A View from Kentucky's Union Army

> It was on the talented, the upper crust of slave society, that deprivations of the peculiar institution hung most heavy. This, perhaps, explains why it was that the first to flee to northern lines as Yankee advances corroded the Rebel positions were not the ordinary field hands, but the drivers and the artisans. [FE, I, p. 153]

If this view is correct then the occupations of ex-slaves recruited by the Union Army in Kentucky during the war

Table 5:
Percentage of Male Slaves 15 Years Old and Older with Non-field-hand Occupations

	Percentage of the Male Slave Population 15 Years Old and Older
FOGEL AND ENGERMAN'S ESTIMATE	26.30
Less:	
Exaggeration in Estimate of "skilled" slaves, Plaquemines, La.	5.20
Fraction of Coopers in Plaquemines sample	2.04
Exaggeration in Estimate of Drivers	4.45
Exaggeration in Estimate of "Assistant Drivers"	2.63
Exaggeration in Estimate of Black Overseers	0.52
CORRECTED ESTIMATE	11.46
Artisans and Other Nonfield Occupations	8.16
Drivers and "Assistant Drivers"	3.30

Source: See text.

should show a preponderance of artisans. In fact, substantially more than 25 percent of these men should have held occupations other than that of field hand, since the latter figure is alleged by Fogel and Engerman to have been the proportion characterizing the population from which they came.

Kentucky Union Army recruitment records have been collected by Leslie Rowland.[42] She has examined records for 20,905 black Kentucky soldiers. Occupations are listed for all but 329 of

[42] This information has been generously made available to us by Rowland, who collected the data as part of her ongoing study of Kentucky blacks during the Civil War.

these men (98.4 percent).[43] This evidence gives a markedly different distribution of slave skills from the one Fogel and Engerman constructed by sampling the probate records of Plaquemines Parish.[44] Of the twenty thousand men with listed occupations, all but 527—that is, 97.4 percent—gave as their occupations "farmer" and "laborer." The occupational distribution of these soldiers is presented in Table 6, which also includes for comparison the distribution estimated by Fogel and Engerman.

Two possible interpretations of the discrepancy between the occupational distribution of Kentucky's black soldiers and Fogel and Engerman's occupational distribution suggest themselves. It is possible that Fogel and Engerman were wrong in their assertions about who fled first from bondage, and that the population of slaves with high skill levels—artisans, drivers, and overseers—were vastly underrepresented among Kentucky blacks who took up arms against the Confederacy. Such men may have retained a loyalty to their owners, a reward their owners gained by allowing them to hold privileged slave status. Another alternative is that Fogel and Engerman were wrong about the fraction of male slaves in the upper echelons of the

[43] There were 114 men who did not have an occupation next to their names, and another 215 were simply described as "slaves."
[44] The rolls make no distinction between slaves and free blacks, but the vast majority listed must have been slaves. Regiments (and the companies therein) were used for those units known by Rowland to have been recruited primarily in Kentucky. The descriptive rolls do not give a place of residence, but Rowland assumed that recruitment at a Kentucky point indicated that the slave or free black had been a Kentucky resident in 1860. Because her work focuses on Kentucky blacks, Rowland, correctly, counted only volunteers and drafted men at Kentucky points. No substitutes—wherever they entered the army—were counted. To be accepted as a substitute, a black had to be ineligible for the Kentucky draft. That meant he had to be under the age of 21 (aged 17 to 20) or from another state which had no draft (that is, a state in rebellion). Large numbers of substitutes were contraband blacks from the Confederate states. The resultant undercount of 17- to 20-year-olds biases the occupational distribution of the *soldiers* upward. Men under 20 were less likely to have skills than men over 20. That means that the percentage of unskilled Kentucky soldiers was greater than that given in the table printed in this text.

Table 6:
Occupational Distribution of Kentucky Black Union Army
Soldiers Compared with the Occupational Structure of Adult
Male Slaves on Farms in *Time on the Cross*

Occupation	Kentucky Black Soldiers		Fogel and Engerman Percent
	Number	Percent	
Farmer or Laborer	20,049	97.44	73.7
Artisan	331	1.61	11.9
Servant	99	.48	
Drayman, Waggoner, or Teamster	86	.42	7.4
High Status[a]	11	.05	7.0
Total	20,576	100.0	100.0

[a] Among these eleven Kentucky soldiers were five clergymen and three clerks.

Sources: Letter from Leslie Rowland; FE,II, Table B.5, p. 40.

occupational distribution. If the Kentucky military occupational
distribution is an accurate reflection of the Kentucky slave
occupational distribution (by the war's end about one-half of
Kentucky's adult male slaves were in the Union Army), there
would be reason to doubt that the positive reinforcement
provided by realization of opportunities to rise within the
occupational structure could have nurtured ambition and elicted
hard work from the typical slave.

New Myths for Old

Fogel and Engerman claim that slaves worked hard, resource-
fully, diligently, efficiently. They claim that rewards were more
characteristic of slavery's incentive system than was punishment. They claim that slaves were imbued with the Protestant
work ethic. They claim that slaves were commonly the top

nonownership management of plantations. They claim that occupational mobility was an important feature of slavery.

After making all of these startling claims, they acknowledge that the "question that begs to be explained is how so many previous scholars could have been so badly misled . . . ?" (FE, I, p. 212). Their answer is almost as startling as their "findings": previous historians of slavery erred in accepting the "almost indestructible image of black incompetence" (FE, I, p. 215). "The principal cause of the persistence of the myth of black incompetence in American historiography," we are told, "is racism" (FE, I, p. 223). It was racism that blinded previous historians to the "superior quality of black labor" and the relative satisfactions that emerged from the relatively decent "material conditions" of slave life. According to *Time on the Cross,* historians did not see that the economic successes of the planters rested upon a transformed and positive slave work ethic.

The slaves, Fogel and Engerman write in summarizing the historians' traditional argument, "did not succumb; they resisted" (FE, I, p. 230). Their resistance expressed itself in the quality of their everyday labor. It took a "subtle form" (FE, I, p. 231). Kenneth Stampp explains:

> They were not reckless rebels who risked their lives for freedom . . . [W]hen they could, they protested by shirking their duties, injuring the crops, feigning illness, and disrupting the routine. These acts were, in part, an unspectacular kind of "day to day resistance to slavery." [45]

Fogel and Engerman vigorously dispute this point. Stampp erred because he "overestimated the cruelty of the slave system." He misjudged the work habits of ordinary slaves. "The logic of his position," insist Fogel and Engerman, "made it difficult to acknowledge that ordinary slaves could be diligent workers, imbued like their masters with a Protestant ethic, or that, even though they longed for freedom, slaves could strive to develop and improve themselves in the only way that was open to them" (FE, I, pp. 231–32).

[45] Stampp [1956], pp. 108–109.

We wonder what Bennet Barrow might have thought of this debate. Could it be that "rascally" Big Lucy "corrupt[ed] every young negro in her power" as a form of "day-to-day resistance"? Is that why Barrow whipped so many, so often? Or was she imbued "like Barrow" with the Protestant work ethic?

It was a study of Barrow's whipping, it will be recalled, that led Fogel and Engerman to conclude:

> While whipping was an integral part of the system of punishment and rewards, it was not the totality of the system. What planters wanted was not sullen and discontented slaves who did just enough to keep from getting whipped. They wanted devoted, hard-working, responsible slaves who identified their fortunes with the fortunes of their masters. Planters sought to imbue slaves with a "Protestant" work ethic and to transform that ethic from a state of mind into a high level of production. "My negroes have their name up in the neighbourhood," wrote Bennet Barrow, "for making more than any one else & they think Whatever they do is better than any body Else." Such an attitude could not be beaten into slaves. It had to be elicited. [FE, I, p. 147]

Barrow entered that sentence in his diary on October 15, 1840. Fogel and Engerman extracted the sentence from the full diary entry, and in the process completely distorted its meaning. Barrow was not praising his slaves for identifying their "fortunes" with his "fortunes," as is made clear in the *full* diary entry together with the entries that preceded it:

October 1 Made all hands stop & trash cotten this morning. . . .
October 2 . . . Women trashing cotten men doing little of every thing, *not much of any thing*
October 5 . . . the trashyiest stuff I ever saw, some of my young Hands are doing verry Badly Ralph Wash E. Nat E. Jim Jim T. Henry Israel Harriet Sam & Maria Lewis & Randal
October 6 . . . bad news from the Cotten market
October 9 . . . never saw more cotten open to the Acre. & verry trashy . . .
October 11 . . . Gave the negros shoes. . . .
October 13 . . . I think my hands have Picked cotten worse this year than in several years picked it verry trashy & not better weights nor as good as *common*, intend Whipping them *straght*
October 15 Clear verry pleasant, Never have been more dissatisfied with my hands all Excepting 'Lize I [L?] Hannah Jensey Atean & Margaret, am sattisfied the best plan is to give them every

thing they require for their comfort and never that they will do without Whipping or some punishment. **My negroes have their name up in the neighborhood for making more than any one else & they think Whatever they do is better than any body Else.**[46]

Read in the context of the diary, it is quite clear that Barrow's single sentence is meant to scorn the self-image that his slaves had of themselves and the image that others, including perhaps whites nearby, had of them. Barrow knew otherwise.

We wonder what Frederick Law Olmsted might have thought of Fogel and Engerman's analysis of the Protestant work ethic? According to *Time on the Cross* it was superior slave labor which underlay the high efficiency of southern agriculture. Yet when Olmsted toured the South and investigated these precise issues he found neither superior labor nor high efficiency. Why not? According to Fogel and Engerman, he too was a victim of the "myth of black incompetence."

> Even on those few occasions when Olmsted actually witnessed gangs working in the field, he failed to appreciate the significance of slave teamwork, coordination, and intensity of effort, although he faithfully recorded these features of their work. The hoe gang, he reported on one of these instances, "numbered nearly two hundred hands (for the force of two plantations was working together), moving across the field in parallel lines, with a considerable degree of precision. I repeatedly rode through the lines at a canter, with other horsemen, often coming upon them suddenly, without producing the smallest change or interruption in the dogged action of the labourers, or causing one of them, so far as I could see, to lift an eye from the ground." What conclusion did Olmsted draw from this experience? Did he view it as a remarkable demonstration of teamwork of black laborers and of the intensity of their concentration on the task at hand? The "stupid, plodding, machine-like manner in which they labour," said Olmsted, "is painful to witness." [FE, I, p. 205]

What conclusion did Fogel and Engerman draw from Olmsted's experience? That it was "a remarkable demonstration of the teamwork of black laborers and of the intensity of their concentration on the task at hand." What explains this remarkable teamwork and intense concentration? Olmsted tells us in his next sentence, a sentence omitted by Fogel and Engerman:

[46] Davis [1943], pp. 212–14. Boldface supplied for emphasis.

A very tall and powerful negro walked to and fro in the rear of the line, frequently cracking his whip, and calling out, in the surliest manner, to one and another, "Shove your hoe, there! Shove your hoe." [47]

Were these slaves imbued with the Protestant work ethic? Like Barrow, Olmsted knew otherwise.

[47] Olmsted [1860], p. 82.

CHAPTER THREE

The Slave Family:
Protected Agent of Capitalist Masters or
Victim of the Slave Trade?

Herbert Gutman
and
Richard Sutch

An appreciation of the status of the slave family is essential to
the central thesis of *Time on the Cross*. Fogel and Engerman
insist that slave workers were highly efficient and productive
laborers because they had been imbued with a "Protestant work
ethic." The master "sought" to produce this "state of mind" to
achieve "a high level of production" (FE, I, p. 147), but it must
have been the slave family which transmitted these values from
generation to generation. This view presents the slave family as
the main instrument by which the master socialized his workers
and servants. But the slave family was made to serve the
master's interest in other ways as well. According to *Time on
the Cross*, the master used the slave family as a primary basis of
plantation organization: it "was the administrative unit for the
distribution of food and clothing and the provision of shelter."
The slave family was "an important instrument for maintaining
labor discipline." And it "was also the main instrument for
promoting the increase of the slave population." For the
successful working of the peculiar institution the slave family
was thus "of central importance" (FE, I, p. 127).

It is a basic premise of this discussion that the slave
population was grouped in family units. But for Fogel and
Engerman's argument it is also essential that enslaved blacks
lived in *stable* families. If they were unstable or insecure, slave
parents would have had little reason (or opportunity) to socialize

their children to work hard. Weak and shifting family relationships could hardly be the primary instrument for the administration of plantations. Fogel and Engerman therefore could not rest their economic argument without venturing into the social history of slavery in an attempt to establish that slave masters respected the "sanctity of the slave family" (FE, I, p. 129).

In order for the slave family to maintain its stability, it was necessary for it to resist successfully two forces which, it is traditionally argued, were continually operating to destroy it. On the one side, the slaveowners have been portrayed as interfering in the sexual lives of slaves, motivated both by their desire to accelerate the rate of population growth and by their own lust for black women. On the other side, the contingencies of the market and the workings of the slave trade have been depicted as an ever-present threat, continually breaking families by sale, separating children from their parents and husbands from their wives.

To support the contention in *Time on the Cross* that slave families were stable and secure, Fogel and Engerman reject as unfounded abolitionist propaganda the view of the slave family as the victim of these two destructive forces. They argue that "slave breeding" and "sexual exploitation" are "myths" and they claim that relatively few slave families actually were separated by owners for economic (or other) reasons. They list their conclusions on these points as one of their "principal corrections of the traditional characterization of the slave economy":

> The belief that slave-breeding, sexual exploitation, and promiscuity destroyed the black family is a myth. The family was the basic unit of social organization under slavery. It was to the economic interest of planters to encourage the stability of slave families and most of them did so. Most slave sales were either of whole families or of individuals who were at an age when it would have been normal for them to have left the family. [FE, I, pp. 4–5].

In Fogel and Engerman's view, the stability of the slave family was promoted by the master by "exhortations" and by "a system of rewards and sanctions" (FE, I, p. 128). The master depicted in *Time on the Cross* also sought to protect the slave family by avoiding both "sexual exploitation" and participation in the slave trade. In this chapter our focus is upon Fogel and Engerman's treatment of the slave trade. The issues concerning sexual conduct are taken up in the following chapter.

In short, Fogel and Engerman's thesis is that the slave economy was efficient because slaves were imbued with the Protestant work ethic inculcated through the agency of the stable slave family, which in turn was protected by the masters' reluctance to engage in the slave trade. In the preceding chapter we have demonstrated how little evidence Fogel and Engerman have offered to establish that slaves actually *were* imbued with the Protestant work ethic. We also provided some evidence of our own that suggests that slaves had not internalized such values. If our view of the matter is accepted, Fogel and Engerman's argument that the economic interest of planters led them to encourage the stability of slave families collapses as a consequence. We cannot, however, dismiss the topic of the slave family with this logical observation. In the course of their own argument, Fogel and Engerman have presented a misleading portrait of the slave trade and have greatly exaggerated the stability of slave families. Because these issues are of great importance in and of themselves, a critique of Fogel and Engerman's case is called for, regardless of the outcome of the debate on work incentives and punishment.

Furthermore, Fogel and Engerman's use of quantitative methods and qualitative assumptions in their treatment of the slave family points up—perhaps more clearly than anywhere else in the book—the failure of quantitative methods to provide historical evidence when divorced from the qualitative methods of history. We can draw two lessons from a close study of the failure of *Time on the Cross* in this regard: First, statistics can be of enormous aid to the historian, and, second, no amount of sophisticated "cliometrics" can overcome uninformed and erroneous assumptions about historical situations.[1] "Quantitative history," as Philip Curtin has noted, "is no substitute for nonquantitative history, it simply goes on where the other leaves off."

[1] These two points have also been made in another context by Philip D. Curtin [1975], p. 108.

The evidence offered in *Time on the Cross* for Fogel and Engerman's assertions about the slave family is not drawn from conventional historical sources. Fogel and Engerman have not cited the diaries and letters of planters to produce evidence on their motivations. They have not used the narratives of slaves or ex-slaves to obtain evidence concerning the slave family. Fogel and Engerman support their portrayal of the masters' motivation and behavior toward their slaves and the slave family with indirect evidence only. They rest their entire case upon the statistics of slave sales, which are used to infer the frequency with which slave marriages were disrupted. Such evidence is not only indirect with respect to Fogel and Engerman's argument that planters respected the slave family, but it is even farther removed from their attempt to establish the intentions of slaveowners.

Fogel and Engerman's apparent reliance upon strictly quantitative evidence to write the history of the slave family conceals the fact that the statistical findings they present rest heavily upon assumptions about nonquantitative history. These assumptions are critical to their quantitative manipulations. If we alter the assumptions, we alter the statistical conclusions. Yet despite their importance, these assumptions are treated very casually in *Time on the Cross*. Often they are left unstated. Rarely are they documented.

Nonquantitative evidence is also employed in *Time on the Cross* in another way. Assertions about the motivations and attitudes of slaveowners are combined with the statistical findings to form the chain of inferences that leads to Fogel and Engerman's conclusion: American slaves lived in stable families. These assertions are also essential to the conclusions, yet in *Time on the Cross* they are offered as no more than unsupported assumptions. A few paragraphs drawn from Volume I illustrate these points. We have supplied emphasis to the pertinent words:

> *[M]ost* planters shunned direct interference in the sexual practices of slaves, and attempted to influence fertility patterns through a system of positive economic incentives, incentives that are akin to those practiced by various governments today. . . .

> First and foremost, planters promoted family formation both through exhortation and through economic inducements. "Marriage is to be

encouraged," wrote James H. Hammond to his overseer, "as it adds to the comfort, happiness and health of those entering upon it, besides insuring a greater increase." The economic inducements for marriages *generally* included a house, a private plot of land which the family could work on its own, and, *frequently*, a bounty either in cash or in household goods. The *primary* inducements for childbearing were the lighter work load and the special care given to expectant and new mothers. [FE, I, pp. 84–85]

And later in the same volume:

To promote the stability of slave families, planters *often* combined exhortations with a system of rewards and sanctions. The rewards included such subsidies as separate houses for married couples, gifts of household goods, and cash bonuses. They *often* sought to make the marriage a solemn event by embedding it in a well-defined ritual. *Some* marriage ceremonies were performed in churches, *others* by the planter in the "big house." In either case, marriages were *often* accompanied by feasts and *sometimes* made the occasion for a general holiday. The sanctions were directed against adultery and divorce. For *many* planters, adultery was an offense which required whippings for the guilty parties. *Some* planters also used the threat of the whip to discourage divorce. [FE, I, p. 128]

It should be noted that Fogel and Engerman are describing *regularities* in planter behavior: That is what words such as "most," "generally," "often," and "frequently" convey. Here, as elsewhere, it remains a central task for social historians to describe—and then to explain as best they can—the *regularities* that appear in social behavior. It is also important to explain how such historical evidence has been used to *establish* a regularity ("most," "generally," "often," and "frequently"). Not one of the suggested regularities described in the passages reprinted here rests on evidence reported in either volume of *Time on the Cross*. While the authors give the impression that literary evidence or conventional scholarship support these assertions, no references are supplied by either the text or the supplement. The only "evidence" reported in *Time on the Cross* is quantitative data.[2]

[2] This is not to say that quantitive evidence on such matters is unobtainable. Let us consider, as an illustration, the "ritual" of slave marriage. Did planters often make slave marriage "a solemn event by embedding it in a well-defined ritual?" In 1866 and 1867, a District of Columbia clergyman remarried 875 former slave couples. All were asked who had first married them. Some could not remember. A small number said a clergyman. A yet larger number replied:

The source of Fogel and Engerman's misleading characterizations of the slave family and the slave trade, however, lies not in their use or neglect of quantitative data but rather in their failure to question crucial nonquantitative assumptions underlying their argument. Closer examination shows these assumptions to be demonstrably incorrect.

The Forced Relocation of Slave Labor

The interstate migration of slaves is known to have been enormous. Sutch has estimated that during the decade of the 1850s over a quarter of a million slaves were moved across state lines, nearly one slave in fifteen.[3] Using the same estimating procedure, we calculate that more than a million slaves entered into the interstate migration between 1790 and 1860. This flow of enslaved Afro-Americans must count as one of the greatest *forced* migrations in world history.

This forced migration was essential to the maintenance of the economic efficiency of slavery. A relocation of the labor force was required by the westward expansion of cotton production. The expansion was pushed by the spectacular increase in the world demand for cotton, and the westward movement was facilitated by improved transportation networks. Since the external slave trade had been abolished early in the nineteenth

---

"joined by permission of master" and "ceremony read by their master." Is this the "well-defined ritual" Fogel and Engerman refer to? Nearly half (48 percent) replied: "No marriage ceremony" (Gutman [1972], pp. 1197–1218).
[3] Sutch [1975], p. 178. It should be noted that Goldin's estimates of the interstate migration of slaves which are reported by Fogel and Engerman (FE, I, Fig. 12, p. 46; and FE, II, pp. 43–48) and are used in their calculations are considerably below Sutch's estimates, despite the contention in *Time on the Cross* that the two sets of figures "differ only trivially" (FE, II, p. 45). The bulk of the difference is explained by the fact that Goldin made no estimate of the migration of children under 10, who constitute nearly 18 percent of Sutch's estimate [Sutch [1975], Table 3, p. 179). Despite the importance of children in the migration, *Time on the Cross* merely asserts that this omission "introduces a small downward bias in the estimates" (FE, II, p. 44). Goldin also neglects the slaves who were transported to other states during the 1850s but who died before 1860 (letter from Goldin, June 6, 1974). According to Sutch's estimate these migrations were approximately 10 percent of the total moves made by slaves 10 years of age or over.

century, the opening of the new lands depended upon transporting slaves from the Old to the New South. Sutch has estimated that Delaware, Maryland, Virginia, North Carolina and South Carolina supplied 68 percent of these migrants in the 1850s, and that Mississippi, Louisiana, Arkansas, and Texas received 89 percent of them.[4] Had the migration been small, it is doubtful that high productivity could have been maintained upon the relatively poor eastern soils, given the rapidly increasing population.

The relocation of slave labor had to occur either by the internal slave trade or by the migration of slaves and owners together. Fogel and Engerman claim that the efficiency of the slave labor market and the maintenance of Southern prosperity did not imperil the slave family. Therefore, they began their argument with the assertion that the internal slave trade was small. "About 84 percent of the slaves engaged in the westward movement," they say, "migrated with their owners," families intact (FE, I, p. 48).

This estimate is one of the half-dozen most significant new "findings" reported in *Time on the Cross*. The importance of this percentage to Fogel and Engerman's entire argument about the "slave family" cannot be exaggerated. It serves, for example, as the numerical underpinning for their rejection of "the contention that the interregional slave migration resulted in the widespread division of marriages, with husbands wrung from wives and children from both" (FE, I, p. 49).[5] Despite its clear importance, Fogel and Engerman surprisingly do not inform readers of how the statistic "84 percent" was derived. Although it was not made clear in either volume of *Time on the Cross*, the figure for the percentage of slaves sold from among those in the interstate migration was obtained by comparing William Calderhead's estimates of the number of slaves sold from Maryland

---

[4] Sutch [1975], pp. 177–78.

[5] In this sentence, incidentally, Fogel and Engerman confuse a slave marriage with a slave family. A husband sold from his wife resulted in the breakup of both a slave marriage and family. But a child sold from its parents resulted only in the breakup of a slave family. That distinction is of great importance. Most slave sales reported by Fogel and Engerman involved young men and women and therefore broke up families, not marriages.

between 1830 and 1860 with Claudia Goldin's estimates of the
net migration out of that state over the same period. By this
procedure Fogel and Engerman estimate that 16.2 percent of
the slaves who entered into the interstate migration of slaves
exchanged masters (FE, II, p. 53).[6]

Leaving aside the obvious question of the propriety of
applying an estimate for Maryland to the entire South, a check
of these sources reveals that Fogel and Engerman must have a
made a serious error in division. Calderhead says: "In the thirty
years before the Civil War, Maryland's contribution was about
18,500 slaves." [7] Goldin has given us her estimate of net
out-migration for Maryland over the same period as 55,948.
Thus according to this estimating procedure, 33 percent, not 16.2
percent, of the slaves migrating from Maryland were sold.[8]

---

[6] Fogel and Engerman "confirm" their estimate that 16 percent of the slaves
who entered the interstate migration were sold by comparing the percentage
of males in the interstate trade (estimated by Goldin) with the percentage of
males among slaves sold in New Orleans. Making the assumption that 50
percent of the slaves who moved as part of a complete plantation across state
lines were male, Fogel and Engerman compute that if 15.7 percent of the total
migration were produced by sales and the balance by the migration of
plantations, the weighted average of the two sex ratios would just give
Goldin's aggregate estimate (FE, II, p. 53). Stanley Lebergott reminds us,
although Fogel and Engerman do not, that had they assumed that 49 percent,
rather than 50 percent, of the slaves who moved with their masters were male,
the percentage of sales estimated by the Fogel and Engerman procedure
would rise from 15.7 percent to 26.3 percent (Lebergott [1975]). If 48 percent
were male, the percentage rises to 34 percent. If Claudia Goldin's estimate of
the percentage of males in the interstate migration was only 5 percent too
low, the Fogel-Engerman estimate of the percentage of sales would be three
times greater than they estimate. "Such sensitivity to initial assumptions,"
suggests Lebergott, "must create unease among those who would use
[these] estimates" ([1975], p. 699).

[7] Calderhead [1972], p. 53.

[8] Engerman has written that he and Fogel obtained the numerator for their
calculation by taking one-half of Calderhead's estimated 18,500 sales, "which
is," explains Engerman, "*our* interpretation of sales" (letter from Engerman,
Nov. 4, 1974, emphasis supplied). He did not explain how they might defend
the halving of Calderhead's estimate. (There is also an unexplained discrepancy between the 16.2 percent reported in *Time on the Cross* [FE, II, p. 53]
and the 16.5 percent one obtains by dividing one-half of Calderhead's number
by Goldin's migration estimate.

The estimating procedure itself, however, is internally inconsistent. Calderhead *assumed* that 50 percent of the slaves migrating from Maryland were sold. That assumption and his own estimate of the total migration are the basis for nearly one-half of his total estimate of sales. Yet Calderhead's estimates of the total migration are much too low[9] and, in any case, are inconsistent with Goldin's. If we use Calderhead's implicit out-migration estimates, rather than Goldin's, to compare with his out-of-state sales or, alternatively, if we correct Calderhead's sales estimate to be consistent with Goldin's migration estimates (or, for that matter, with any other estimate of migration which is also consistently used in the denominator), we simply retrieve the assumed 50-percent figure. Any consistent procedure based on the assumption that 50 percent of the interstate migration was sold will produce the conclusion that 50 percent of the slaves were sold, and 50 percent migrated with their owners. It can be no other way. Fogel and Engerman's 16 percent results in part from an error of division. But even when the error is corrected, the result is still a totally baseless number produced by a faulty procedure.

Without more research it is not possible to establish accurately the percentage of the slaves crossing state boundaries who were sold. The exactitude of Calderhead's 50 percent figure is illusory, as it is nothing more than a rough guess based on no less arbitrary figures ranging from 30 to 80 percent.[10] There is

[9] This point is discussed in more detail below. Incidentally, it is likely that Calderhead's estimate of the slaves "sold south" from Maryland is too low. The determination of whether a given sale involved a transfer out of state was made on the basis either of the state of residence of the purchaser or the fact that a Maryland purchaser was a known professional slave trader (Calderhead [1972], p. 49). There is no assurance, however, that Calderhead was able to establish the names of all professional traders and their local agents. Local agents and assistant traders were, according to Bancroft [1931] quite common (pp. 29–30). Nor is it known whether all slaves purchased by traders were "sold south," some might have been resold to Maryland residents. This last point, of course, helps to counter the downward bias in Calderhead's estimate but it probably does not eliminate it.

[10] Calderhead based his 50 percent assumption on estimates by Collins (40 percent sold) and Bancroft (70 percent sold). The American Anti-Slavery Society [1841] put the proportion at "four-fifths [80 percent] or more" (p. 13).

nothing to be gained by pretending that we know more, in fact, than we do. Cliometrics cannot turn assumption into fact.

Owner-Accompanied Migrants and the Threat to Slave Families

For the sake of argument, let us accept Fogel and Engerman's "finding" that of the slaves engaged in the "westward movement" 84 percent migrated with their owners. Is this evidence that slaves moving with their owners failed to experience the breakup of a family or a marriage? That depends. Fogel and Engerman *assume* that all members of Upper South slave families involved in the great migration belonged to the same owner. This assumption is essential to their argument that 84 percent of the slaves involved in the migration moved in *family units* with their owner. Fogel and Engerman claim that slave husbands and wives among these owner-accompanied "migrants" did not experience marital separations when their owners moved "the plantation" from (say) Virginia to Mississippi. Their subsequent analysis of the impact of the interregional redistribution of the slave population on the slave family gives no attention to the marital and familial arrangements of these 84 percent of the "migrant" slaves, whose family status might have been disrupted by the interregional transfer. *Time on the Cross* reveals nothing about the relationship between slave marriage and family and the patterns of slave ownership among Upper South slaves, which would sustain the assumption that the members of most slave families—and especially the husband and wife—belonged to the same owner. Yet this assumption is the essential precondition for accepting their argument.

The only published data indicating the relationship between

The lowest estimate seems to be the oft-cited quotation from a Wheeling newspaper, the *Virginia Times* (probably in 1835), that "not more than one-third had been sold." This estimate is quoted by the American Anti-Slavery Society ([1841], p. 13), Collins ([1904], p. 62), and Bancroft ([1931], pp. 385 and 397). Bancroft cites *Niles' Register*, 51 (Oct. 8, 1836), p. 83, as his source. However, this estimate (for the state of Virginia) only includes those sold in the state of origin and excludes those sold in the state of destination.

slave ownership and the Upper South slave family comes from an 1866 military census of former slaves living in Princess Anne County, Virginia. These blacks gave the names of their owners in 1863, and from this information we may learn about the relationship between ownership and slave family structure. In two of three families that were composed of either a husband and wife, a husband, wife, and their children, or a father and his children, at least two members of the slave family had different owners. Most commonly (and not surprisingly), the husband or father had a different owner from the wife, mother, and children.[11]

Unless a spouse was *purchased* by a migrating owner, Upper South slave families were frequently broken simply by the movement of an owner with his resident slaves to the Lower South. No sale need have been involved. The notion of the sale as a measure of the ways in which interregional migration broke up slave marriages and slave families is thoroughly inadequate. Sales could unite families as well as rend them asunder. Indeed, there are some indications that, prior to migration, owners purchased slaves in order to keep families together. But the evidence which has come to light thus far remains scanty and is not free of contradictions. "In my neighborhood," said a South Carolina planter of the pre-1835 period, "every planter agreed that, if he has a negro married to a negro woman belonging to another, and he wishes to get rid of the negro or quit the vicinity, he will either offer the slave to the proprietor of the negro woman, or will himself purchase the latter; in this case, the price is regulated by the other planters." [12] An advertisement in the *Augusta Chronicle and Sentinel* in 1859 explained that a local Georgian planned to sell his farm and real estate as well as several house servants. He was moving to Cherokee, Georgia. "They are negroes of excellent character," said the notice of these house servants, "and as the object of the owner in selling, is to avoid the necessity of separating husbands and wives, they will not be sold out of the city or its immediate neighborhood." [13] Some of this man's slaves had spouses who

[11] Gutman [1972], pp. 1197–1218.
[12] Calhoun [1917–19], II, p. 268.
[13] Bancroft [1931], pp. 217–18.

belonged to other whites in or near Augusta, and he obviously respected their unions. But the former Pittsylvania County, Virginia, slave, Lorenzo Ivy, recollected an experience quite different from that which the foregoing advertisement would suggest:

> Ole Marsa caught de "cotton fever." Ev'ybody was dyin' to git down South an' raise cotton to sell. So dat ole man separated families right an' lef'. He took two of my ants an' lef' der husban's up here, an' he separated seven husban's an' wives. One 'oman had twelve chillun. Yes sir! Separated 'em all an' took 'em wid him to Georgy and Alabamy.[14]

The separation of Ivy's two aunts from their husbands and of seven more "husban's an' wives" would never have been recorded in an interregional sales record.

The Frequency of Slave Sales: A View from Anne Arundel County

Not all slave sales were cases of slaves "sold down South." Many were local transactions. Fogel and Engerman again draw upon Calderhead's study of Maryland in their attempt to estimate the frequency of all slave sales.

> A study of slave trading in Maryland over the decade from 1830 to 1840 revealed that total sales (local and interstate) amounted to 1.92 percent of the slave population each year. If that ratio is projected to the national level, total slave sales over the period 1820–1860 averaged about fifty thousand per year. [FE, I, p. 53]

This estimate, however, presents far too sanguine a view of the matter. The impression is given that the figure is based upon data for the state of Maryland. This is not the case. For the decade of the 1830s Calderhead has estimated that 3141 slaves were sold in Maryland, and then shipped out of state (excluding slaves convicted of crimes and sold out of state by the courts). He also reports that the ratio of total sales to out-of-state sales recorded in the registered bills of sale which he examined was 6.22 (cf. FE, II, p. 52). This suggests that 16,391 additional slaves were sold locally. When combined with Calderhead's estimate of

14 WPA [1940], p. 173.

460 sales of criminals, these figures give 19,992 sales within the state. To this must be added the number of slaves transported out of state and sold upon arriving at their destination. Calderhead estimates this number at 3600. As a result, his estimate of the total dicennial sales of Maryland's slaves is 23,592.[15] Now, in 1830 there were 102,994 slaves enumerated in the State; by 1840 the number of slaves had fallen to 89,495.[16] The average population (96,245) suggests an annual sales rate for Maryland of 2.45 percent, nearly one-third larger than Fogel and Engerman's figure of 1.92 percent.

After publication Stanley Engerman explained how he and Fogel calculated the frequency of sales:

> The 1.92 is based upon Anne Arundel [County, Maryland]. We checked with Calderhead and got total sales from holdings and estates, since this is the county with most complete data. We then divided by the average [slave population] of 1830 and 1840 [for] Anne Arundel County. The same number, approximately, would come from [Calderhead's published estimates of the within-state sales for Maryland] and the average state population [that would be 2.08 percent]. The reason for the big discrepancy [between 1.92 and 2.45 percent] rests on one key assumption—the treatment of what happens in [the] state of inflow to those slaves who migrated, we have zero, [Calderhead has] fifty percent [of the migrating slaves sold upon arrival at their destination].[17]

The explanation is important for two reasons. First, the estimates on the frequency of slave sale reported in *Time on the Cross* are based upon the experience of a single county in the decade of the 1830s, generalized (without adjustment or qualification) to cover the entire slave South and the entire forty-year period extending from 1820 to 1860. The second point of importance is that the "big discrepancy" to which Engerman refers arises from Fogel and Engerman's exclusion of the slaves who were transported by their owners out of Maryland and immediately sold in other states. Since they were interested in the frequency of sale as a measure of the extent to which

[15] Calderhead [1972], pp. 51–52. As we shall show below, Calderhead's estimate of the number of slaves sold out of state is too low because he based it upon an inaccurate estimate of the total out-migration of slaves from the state.

[16] U.S. Census, 1830, p. 83 and U.S. Census, 1840, p. 201.

[17] Letter from Engerman, November 4, 1974.

slaveowners avoided disposing of their property through sale, the omission of any known sales of Maryland slaves—regardless of where the sales occurred—cannot be justified.

While it is not permissible to neglect the out-of-state sales entirely, one can certainly quarrel with Calderhead's estimate of the number. He cites Winfield Collins and Frederic Bancroft as his authority for the assumption that 50 percent of the slaves moved out of Maryland were sold either within the state or upon reaching their destination.[18] Collins, on the basis of rather slim (and hearsay) evidence, concluded that "at least three-fifths of the removals of slaves from the border slave States to those farther South from 1820 to 1850 were due to emigration" and not to sale. After criticizing the quality of the evidence used by Collins and others (but supplying no new evidence), Bancroft made his own guess that "fully 70 per cent of the slaves removed from the Atlantic and the border slave States to the south-west were taken after purchase or with a view to sale." Calderhead states that his 50 percent figure is "taken as a compromise" between Collins's 40 percent and Bancroft's 70 percent.[19] Clearly, this can be regarded as no more than a very rough approximation.

Our quarrel, however, is not with Calderhead's estimate of the proportion of the out-of-state migration of slaves who were sold. Poorly supported as his estimate is, there is as yet no firmer basis for offering another figure. It is rather Calderhead's estimate of the total migration which is clearly incorrect. His estimates imply a net out-migration from Maryland of 14,402 slaves during the decade of the 1830s.[20] Our own estimate of the

[18] Calderhead is less than clear about this assumption. An alternative interpretation of Calderhead's procedure is that he assumed that of the number of migrant slaves remaining after subtracting his estimate of those sold within the state into the interstate trade (3601), 50 percent were sold upon arriving at their destination. This seems to be what the text of his article states [1972], p. 53). However, his footnote and the references to Collins and Bancroft suggest the reading we give in the text. We have chosen to interpret Calderhead in this fashion because doing so tends to minimize the estimate of the percentage of Maryland's slaves that were sold.

[19] See Collins [1904], p. 62; Bancroft [1931], pp. 397–98; and Calderhead [1972], p. 53.

[20] Calderhead estimated that 3141 slaves were sold in Maryland and shipped south, 460 were criminals deported by the state, and 3600 were removed from

net exportation of slaves in that decade is 33,729, or more than twice Calderhead's implicit figure.[21] The 50 percent estimate suggests that 16,864 slaves were sold after being moved out of Maryland. When combined with Calderhead's estimate of slaves sold locally, this gives a grand total of 33,255 of Maryland's bondsmen sold during the decade of the 1830s. This represents 3.46 percent of the Maryland slave population.

Fogel and Engerman do not estimate how many slaves, in all, were sold into the internal slave trade of the United States. Indeed, they do not estimate how many of Maryland's slaves were sold. None of their quantitative sources allow them to estimate directly these numbers. Instead they draw upon Calderhead's study of the Maryland slave sales for data relating to Anne Arundel County in the 1830s.[22] Their estimates for this single county in a single decade are then inflated proportionately to obtain an estimate of the total number of sales in the slave South for the period 1820–60. Leaving aside their omission of out-of-state sales, this is, at best, a very dubious procedure. What basis does one have for supposing that Anne Arundel County in the 1830s—or the state of Maryland for that matter—was typical of the antebellum South in this respect? None is presented by Fogel and Engerman, and readers of *Time on the Cross* are not told that this critical estimate is based upon the experience of a single county.

Anne Arundel County lies between Baltimore and Washington, D.C., less than twenty-five miles from either city. Calderhead's study relies upon the bills of sale (for slaves) recorded

the state and sold upon reaching their destination. The total is 7201, which is 50 percent of the number given in the text.

[21] This calculation is based upon the censuses of the slave population of Maryland (U.S. Census, 1830, p. 83; and U.S. Census, 1840, p. 201) and uses procedures developed elsewhere (Sutch [1975], Appendix, specifically equation 10, p. 202) and survival ratios calculated by Goldin (FE, II, p. 46).

[22] Fogel and Engerman's explanation that Anne Arundel had the most complete data does not agree with Calderhead's comment that eight counties have complete bill-of-sale records for the period 1829–62 (Calderhead [1972], p. 48) and that five counties had "fairly complete records" of estate sales (p. 51). Since the percentage of the slaves sold in Anne Arundel (1.92 percent per year) was less than the eight-county average (2.08 percent per year), it cannot be argued that that one county exaggerated the extent of the trade.

in that county's records. A slave sale would be recorded in the Anne Arundel records only if the sale took place within that county (and only if the participants chose to fulfill their obligation to record the sale). It is quite probable that a good number of the sales of Anne Arundel slaves did *not* take place locally. Baltimore and Washington were both established seats of a large slave trade, where a number of professional slave traders kept permanent offices. There is no doubt that many slaves were brought from the rural counties of Maryland to be sold in these urban markets.[23] Presumably such sales were recorded not in Anne Arundel County's records but in Baltimore's. If the slaves were sold in Washington, the sales went unrecorded in Anne Arundel.

The problem is not overcome by relying upon the estimates of sales Calderhead gives for the entire state of Maryland, as we have done. Calderhead's study of the 1830s is based upon the sales of slaves in only seven of Maryland's 19 counties. Baltimore is not among them, and the District of Columbia, of course, is not part of Maryland.[24] Yet when Calderhead inflated the number of sales recorded in the seven counties to produce an estimate for Maryland, he did so *solely* upon the basis of the ratio of the population of the state to that of the seven counties examined. This procedure obviously underestimates the sales for

[23] Bancroft [1931], pp. 45–66 and 120–23.
[24] Calderhead [1972], p. 48. Baltimore was not included in Calderhead's study because the 111 volumes recording the bills of slave sale before 1852 have been destroyed (p. 48). The figures for Baltimore County presented in Calderhead's table (p. 51) are based upon the post-1852 data contained in just three volumes extrapolated backward "to give an approximation of the totals for the earlier decade [the 1830s]" (p. 50). This is probably an inappropriate procedure since Bancroft notes "[t]here seems to have been less slave-trading in Maryland during the 'fifties than during the 'thirties" (Bancroft [1931], p. 120). Moreover, it is not even clear that Calderhead's post-1852 Baltimore County figures include Baltimore City which was administratively distinct from the county. Comments made by Calderhead suggest that they do not [Calderhead [1972], pp. 48 and 50–51]. In any case, Calderhead's estimate that only 131 slaves were sold south from Baltimore County in the 1830s is discredited as an estimate for Baltimore City by the fact that in the single year of 1836, 208 slaves were shipped from Baltimore to New Orleans (p. 45).

the entire state.[25] It is evident that Fogel and Engerman's estimate of 1.92 percent for the annual incidence of slave sales lacks solid foundation.

The Frequency of Slave Sales: Implications for the Slave Family

Fogel and Engerman assert that all slave sales "amounted to 1.92 percent of the slave population each year," a sales rate they later describe as "low" (FE, I, p. 53). The next two sentences in *Time on the Cross* read:

> If that ratio is projected to the national level, total slave sales over the period 1820–1860 averaged about fifty thousand per year. In other words, on average, only one slaveholder out of every twenty-two sold a slave in any given year, and roughly one third of these were estates of deceased persons. [FE, I, p. 53]

Numbers such as these might have a place in an effort to discredit "the notion that speculative purchases and sales of slaves were common among Southern planters." But in the context of a discussion of the security of the slave family, this interpretation of the 1.92 percent rate of sales is unsatisfactory. The foregoing averages tell us about the behavior of slaveholders, not about the slaves' view of the slave trade. Rather than demonstrating the trivial magnitude of slave sales, Fogel and Engerman's own estimate provides evidence that the threat of sale touched every American slave family. Accepting for the sake of argument Fogel and Engerman's estimate that 1.92 percent of the slaves were sold in any given year, we compute that a slave would have had a 49.3 percent chance of being sold

[25] Calderhead [1972], pp. 50 and 52–53. Even Calderhead's estimate of sales within those parts of Maryland he studied may be biased downward since it includes only those sold legally (p. 47). Illegal sales in violation of a law prohibiting the out-of-state sale of slaves who had been promised delayed manumission (p. 54) or in violation of covenants in previous slave deeds (p. 53) would not be recorded in the county's "Accounts of Sales." The carelessness of out-of-state buyers might also have meant that some bills of sale went unregistered. Calderhead also omitted all slaves who were sold along with the land they worked whenever a plantation changed hands (p. 48).

at least once in the course of a 35-year lifetime.[26] Application of
this same 1.92 percent sale rate to a typical slave family
suggests that, on the average, an individual would witness 11.4
sales of members of his family of origin and of his own
immediate family during his lifetime.[27]

Of course, the probability of a family disruption through sale
varied widely from owner to owner, from region to region, and
over time. Some slaves were under much less risk than average,
others much more. The point of these simple calculations is to
demonstrate that, even when employing Fogel and Engerman's
own estimate, the threat of sale was sufficiently large to affect
the life of every slave.

These are striking implications, and if we use the higher
estimate which we derive from Calderhead's study of Maryland
(that 3.46 percent of the slaves were sold each year) the
implications are even more startling. Our estimate implies a 70.8
percent risk of sale in a 35-year period and over 20 expected
sales of a slave's family members during his lifetime.

Even these revised estimates should not be considered to be of
high reliability. They too are based upon a number of unsupported assumptions. Three underlying assumptions deserve
further attention and could well be made subjects of further
research. First, the assumption that Maryland can be taken as

---

[26] If .0192 is the probability of being sold, then .9808 is the probability of *not*
being sold, in a given year. Start with 10,000 new-born slaves. During the first
year 192 will be sold and 9808 will remain. Of these remaining, 188 will be sold
in the second year (9808 $\times$ .0192 = 188) and 9620 will remain unsold (9808
$\times$ .9808 = 9620). At the end of the third year 9435 will remain (.9808^3 $\times$
10000 = 9435). The life expectancy of a male slave at birth, as given by
Evans, was 35 years ([1962], p. 212). After 35 years only 5074 slaves will not
yet have been sold (.9808^{35} $\times$ 10000 = 5074). Therefore 4926 will have been
sold at least once. The probability is computed as

$$1 - (.9808)^{35} = .4926$$

[27] We assume that a "typical" slave had a father aged 26 and a mother aged
24 at his birth; was preceded by 3 older siblings, aged 6, 4, and 2 at his birth;
and was followed by 3 younger siblings. We further assume the typical slave
married a spouse who was 20 years old and together produced 7 children.
Using figures based on Evans's table of life expectancies for slaves ([1962], p.
212) to estimate the expected number of years of life for each of the 17 family
members which would be witnessed during the typical individual's expected
lifetime gives 593 years at risk. Multiplying by .0192 we get 11.4.

representative of the South (while better than the assumption that Anne Arundel County is representative) is dubious. Studies of the frequency and cause of slave sales in other regions are clearly needed. Second, the assumption that one-half of all migrating slaves were sold is also highly suspect.[28] A study of the westward migration of slaves which explored the mechanisms by which the relocation of labor was accomplished would be most worthwhile. Finally, the simplifying assumption that the threat of sale touched all slaves equally clearly needs improvement. An estimate of the age and sex distribution of the slaves sold would add substantially to our understanding of this matter. Apparently there exists in both the New Orleans sale invoices and in the Maryland records information on these matters which awaits analysis. In short, what is needed is not an abandonment of a statistical approach to the problem of slave sales but rather a more careful one—an approach more sensitive to the assumptions—than has yet been offered.

The Destruction of Slave Marriages: A View from New Orleans

After belittling the extent of the slave trade, *Time on the Cross* takes up the threat posed to the integrity of slave marriages by the sale of slaves to the interstate market. On this point Fogel and Engerman find their "strongest" evidence in data recorded in the New Orleans slave sale invoices between 1804 and 1862. Their findings are described as follows:

> Data contained in sales records in New Orleans, by far the largest market in the interregional trade, sharply contradict the popular view that the destruction of slave marriages was at least a frequent, if not a universal, consequence of the slave trade. These records, which cover thousands of transactions during the years from 1804 to 1862, indicate that more than

---

[28] An accurate estimate of the fraction of Maryland's slaves who were moved out of state and then sold would by itself take us a long way. Yet, even with such a figure, we could not be confident that Maryland was typical of the entire slave exporting region of the South. The declining fortune of slavery in that state probably increased the out-migration of slaveowners with their slaves, thus reducing the proportion of within-state sales. Between 1850 and 1860 there was a 14 percent decline in the number of slaveowners, but only a 3 percent decline in the number of slaves (Sutch [1975], Table 1, p. 177).

84 percent of all sales over the age of fourteen involved unmarried individuals. Of those who were or had been married, 6 percent were sold with their mates; and probably at least one quarter of the remainder were widowed or voluntarily separated. Hence it is likely that 13 percent, or less, of interregional sales resulted in the destruction of marriages. And since sales were only 16 percent of the total interregional movement, it is probable that about 2 percent of the marriages of slaves involved in the westward trek were destroyed by the process of migration. [FE, I, p. 49]

The particular figures which Fogel and Engerman have extracted from the record of slave sales in New Orleans, the way they report these findings in their text, and the uses to which the findings are put in refuting the "conventional wisdom" on the destruction of slave marriages deserve our attention. But no less worthy of closer scrutiny are the New Orleans slave market records themselves. Unfortunately, Fogel and Engerman do not provide an adequate description of the data drawn from this source, or discuss the limitations of these records. A number of difficulties, nevertheless, limit the ways in which this source can be properly used.

The size of the initial data base from which a sample of "approximately 5,000 slave sales" has come is not revealed in *Time on the Cross* (FE, II, p. 24). Richard C. Wade examined some of these same records and found more than 4400 invoices in 1830, "over 4,000 in 1845–6, and less in 1834–5," and "over 3,000 . . . in the last ante-bellum year." Wade said that the figures "fluctuated annually." [29] If about 2000 such transactions occurred each year, the implication is that Fogel and Engerman have sampled about four percent of the total data (possibly an adequate sample). However, in view of the pattern of changes in the New Orleans slave population between 1820 and 1860 (indicated in Table 1), it is important to know whether the Fogel-Engerman sample covered the entire period. A "sample" drawn primarily from the years 1820–40 (when the New Orleans slave population greatly increased) promises to record more interregional sales than a "sample" that draws primarily from the years 1840 to 1860 (when the resident slave population greatly declined). The latter twenty years, of course, comprise the more important period. The domestic slave trade was at its

[29] Wade [1964], pp. 199 and 314.

height in those decades. Unless large numbers of Upper South slaves were shipped first to New Orleans and then sold into the interior sugar and cotton plantations, it is quite possible that a sample based primarily upon the two latter decades contains serious biases.[30]

Table 1:

The Slave Population of New Orleans 1820, 1840, and 1860

Year	Male Slaves	Female Slaves	Total Slaves
1820	2,709	4,646	7,355
1840	9,795	13,653	23,448
1860	5,382	8,003	13,385

Source: Wade [1964], p. 330.

There are several other questions concerning this inadequately described sample. We assume that in their demographic analysis of the slave sales in the New Orleans records, Fogel and Engerman did not include slaves involved in local sales. If they did include them, the entire analysis is flawed. It might well have been that local sales involved different sorts of slaves than interregional sales, and the figures produced are applied to draw conclusions about slaves sold in the interstate trade. If "local sales"—that is, sales between sellers and buyers who had Louisiana or other Deep South residences—are excluded, the sample is cut from 5000 to 1250, since Fogel and Engerman indicate that only 25 percent of the slaves sold in New Orleans were from exporting states (FE, I, p. 53).

Determining the residence of a New Orleans *seller* is a bit more complicated than Fogel and Engerman indicate. New Orleans, as is well known, had a large number of *resident* interregional slave traders. When such a resident Louisiana

[30] One finding derived by Fogel and Engerman from the sample, for example, is that an unusually large percentage of slaves traded in New Orleans belonged to Louisiana owners at the time of sale and that a smaller but still significant percentage had other Deep South owners (FE, I, p. 53). These findings would lose much of their meaning if the sample drew mostly on the 1840–60 period when the New Orleans slave population dropped significantly.

trader sold slaves purchased in the exporting states of the Upper South, were these sales counted as local or interregional sales? If Fogel and Engerman counted them as local sales—sales involving Louisiana "residents"—they greatly undercounted the number of Upper South slaves in their sample of 5000. It is possible, of course, that there were insignificant demographic differences between slaves involved in local and interregional sales, but that cannot be known until there are separate profiles of each group. *Time on the Cross* reports no such analysis.

With these reservations in mind, let us turn now to the way in which Fogel and Engerman have "exploited" the New Orleans records to support their view that the slave migration did not result in "the widespread division of marriages" (FE, II, pp. 49 and 51).

Time on the Cross makes a strong point of the fact that the records of the New Orleans slave market are a massive volume of "hard data." It is claimed that "modern statistical methods" have been mobilized to exploit this information and that the superiority of this approach over that available to "previous scholars" explains why their findings are so "far from accepted truth" (FE, I, pp. 50–51). Yet Fogel and Engerman actually used only three simple ratios from the New Orleans documents: the ratio of women sold together with children to all women sold; the fraction of children under 13 sold without their parents to the total sales; and the ratio of women sold with both their mate and children to all women of that age cohort sold with children. The computation of a ratio can hardly be termed a "modern statistical method" unavailable to conventional historians. Moreover, most of their conclusions are not based upon data but rather on assumptions which are unsupported, often unstated, and, in our opinion, of dubious validity. Moreover, in the course of their calculations, Fogel and Engerman made several errors. When corrected, the results from the New Orleans records do not seem "far from the accepted truth."

The procedures Fogel and Engerman use to move from three simple ratios to their conclusion are complicated—and are made to appear even more so by the cryptic descriptions which

Volume II supplies. But the issue is so important that it is worthwhile to look at them in detail.

The first of the three ratios Fogel and Engerman report was that "more than 84 percent of all sales over the age of fourteen involved unmarried individuals" (FE, I, p. 49). According to their "Technical Notes" in Volume II, however, the "84 percent" (actually 84.3 percent) of the New Orleans sample of slave sales which involved unmarried individuals does not refer to "all sales over the age of fourteen," as the text of Volume I would have readers believe. The figure in question is actually the estimate only for "women aged 20–24" (FE, II, p. 51). This fact is noteworthy in that it indicates how few sales must have been sampled to yield the reported results. We have already noted that perhaps only 1250 sales should properly have been included in the New Orleans sample. If we assume that roughly one-half were sales of female slaves then there were only 625 females sold in the sample. According to Fogel and Engerman approximately 66 percent of the New Orleans sales were of slaves 13 to 24 years of age (FE, I, Fig. 14, p. 50). Thus approximately 416 sampled sales were women 13 to 24. If we guess that roughly half were teenagers (13 to 19), then only about 208 sales form the basis of Fogel and Engerman's calculation. Of these only 33 had presumably been married (208 × 0.157 = 33). Note that one married slave more or less would change the percentage by approximately one-half a point. Fogel and Engerman's sample is too small for confidence in the precise magnitude of the estimates—references to "5,000 sales" notwithstanding.

Fogel and Engerman have based their conclusions on the *assumption* that the marital status of women, ages 20–24, who were sold in New Orleans followed the same pattern as the marital status of all women sold. Yet if Fogel and Engerman's data on the age of slave women at the birth of their first child is credited, then a substantial fraction of the women, ages 20–24, were not yet married. Fogel and Engerman claim—by their definition of marriage—that the average age of a slave woman at marriage was 22.5 (FE, I, p. 137). According to their Figure 14 (p. 50), over 26 percent of the slaves sold in New Orleans were over the age of 24. Yet they assume that the statistic concerning women, ages 20–24, can be used to give the marital status of both the men and women in this older group. Needless to say, this assumption is dubious, and undoubtedly contributes to a significant underestimate of the proportion of married slaves sold.

To make matters even worse, Fogel and Engerman do not even have information on the marital status of the women they did study. The New Orleans sale invoices do not describe the prior marital status of women (or men) in the New Orleans slave market. The only demographic data indicated for all slaves sold are age and sex.[31] How, then, does one estimate prior marital status for most slaves from just their age and sex? Fogel and Engerman explain:

> We consider as slave marriages all unions that the slaves involved intended, or expected, to be "stable" (for our purposes, this term need not be defined), regardless of what view others may have had of these unions. For the purpose of estimating the breakup rate, we take as evidence of such intent, the existence of a child. In other words, we consider every case of a slave woman who is sold with a child but without a husband to be a broken marriage. Since some women with children did not intend to have stable unions with the fathers, this assumption tends to exaggerate the degree to which the slave trade destroyed marriages. However, because we are attempting to show that the breakup rate was low, it is appropriate that we choose a criterion of marriage that biases the result against the case we are trying to make. [FE, II, pp. 48–49]

In other words, the "84 percent" of slave sales represents the proportion of females, ages 20–24, sold without children. This proportion represents unmarried women only if *all* married women had surviving children and *no* married woman was ever sold apart from her children.

Estimating in this way the number of marriages broken *prior* to the sale of slaves in the New Orleans market greatly underestimates the number of slave marriages broken by sale. Several hypothetical examples will suffice to demonstrate this bias:

[31] For a small number—those slaves sold in "complete families"—the sale invoices apparently indicate familial relationship. Fogel and Engerman, incidentally, do not define what they mean by "complete family." Does it mean only a husband, wife, and their children? Or does it include a husband and a wife, a mother and her children, and even a father and his children?

1. The slaves John and Mary were married but childless. Prior to their purchase by an interregional trader, they lived in Virginia. John and Mary were sold to different Louisiana buyers. Mary would count as a single woman in the Fogel-Engerman estimate. But her marriage had, in fact, been broken by sale.

2. The slave woman Tenah and her children lived with a North Carolina owner prior to sale. Her husband Sam belonged to a different owner. Tenah and her children were sold to an interregional trader. Her husband remained with his North Carolina owner. At the time of sale, Tenah was 45 years old, and her two children were aged sixteen and eighteen. Tenah was sold separately from her children. Tenah would count as a single woman in the Fogel-Engerman estimate. But her marriage had, in fact, been broken by sale.

3. The slaves Harriet and John were married and belonged to a Kentucky owner. So did their three children. The three children died. John and Harriet were sold to separate Louisiana purchasers. Harriet would count as a single woman in the Fogel-Engerman estimate. But her marriage had, in fact, been broken by sale.

Fogel and Engerman assert that "women with infants or young children were virtually always traded with their offspring." No evidence in *Time on the Cross* sustains this important generalization. In 1836, at the height of the interregional slave trade, Ethan Allen Andrews, a Yale College graduate who had spent some years teaching in the South, published *Slavery and the Domestic Slave Trade.* Andrews had returned to the South in 1835 to investigate the slave trade in Maryland, the District of Columbia, and Virginia. He described the behavior of slave traders quite differently from the portrayal offered by Fogel and Engerman. "The southwestern trader," said Andrews, "wants only those slaves who will be immediately serviceable upon the cotton and sugar plantations. Young children, therefore, are for his purposes of no value." Interstate traders often found young children "an encumbrance." A visit among a boatload of slaves headed for the Deep South convinced the former school teacher that "frequently . . . they sell the mother while they keep her children." Andrews told of one Virginia trader accused of "sending off a number of mothers without their little children, whom he had purchased with them. He had separated them, because the children were of no value in the market to which the mothers were sent." "It is difficult," Andrews admitted, ". . . in such reports to separate truth from falsehood." [32]

Historians share that difficulty with Andrews, but that is not sufficient reason for evidence to be ignored. It may, in fact, have happened, as Fogel and Engerman suggest, that most infant children were sold with their mothers. But what about older children, children aged, say, ten or twelve? Frederic Bancroft determined that "as a rule, the dividing line between children that were worth more with their mothers and those that were worth more without them was at about eight years of age." This historian insisted, furthermore, that "when women of ages 35 or 40" were sold in slave markets "without any children, or with only those of tender age, it was almost certain that there had been separations." [33] It is possible that some of the young children sold in the New Orleans slave market (9.3 percent of the sample was made up of children under the age of thirteen) were sold separately from their mothers. If so, Fogel and Engerman counted their mothers as "single" women.

It might, of course, be argued that Andrews was a biased contemporary observer, and that Bancroft was a biased twenti- eth-century "neo-abolitionist" historian. And it might be argued that the hypothetical examples provided above rarely occurred. But such arguments do not confront the essential fact that a document which records only the sex and age of a person cannot reveal much about that person's prior marital status. The data needed to estimate precisely the number of slave marriages broken by interregional (or local) sale are lacking. To assume facts not in evidence, as Fogel and Engerman have done, is to assume the conclusion to be derived from them. This is hardly an exemplary application of the "scientific method" to the writing of social history.

[32] Andrews [1836], pp. 49–50, 105–6, 146, 149, and 165.
[33] Bancroft [1931], pp. 197 and 202.

If 84 percent of the women, ages 20–24, were sold singly, then 16 percent were sold as part of some kind of family unit. Of the women who were sold along with their children or husband or both, only 6 percent were accompanied by their husbands. (This percentage is the second ratio drawn from the New Orleans records.) Fogel and Engerman assume that one-quarter of the remainder or another 23.5 percent were widowed or "voluntarily" separated (FE, I, p. 49; II, p. 52). Thus, even by their own curious method of reckoning a marriage, 70.6 percent of the "married" women sold in New Orleans were "involuntarily" separated from their husbands; wives wrung from their husbands, so to speak. In the place of the passages which *Time on the Cross* devotes to exploding the "myth" of husbands and wives separated by slave-trading, one must imagine reading the following:

> Data contained in the sales records in New Orleans, by far the largest market in the interregional trade, sharply contradict the popular view that the destruction of slave marriages was at least a frequent, if not a universal, consequence of the slave trade. After accounting for those sold with spouses or widowed or voluntarily separated from a husband prior to sale, it turns out that only 71 percent of the married women, 20–24, with children had been separated from their husbands.

Yet this is precisely what Fogel and Engerman computed, and these are the data upon which they rest the conclusion that "the New Orleans data show that slaveowners were averse to breaking up black families" (FE, I, p. 52).

The Interstate Slave Trade as a Threat to Slave Marriages: From Anne Arundel County to New Orleans

Fogel and Engerman claim that the New Orleans sale invoices establish that "13 percent, or less, of interregional sales resulted in the destruction of marriages." "And since sales were only 16 percent of the total interregional movement," an estimate Fogel and Engerman derived from their study of Anne Arundel

County, Maryland, "it is probable that about 2 percent of the marriages of slaves involved in the westward trek were destroyed by the process of migration" (FE, I, p. 49). So argue Fogel and Engerman. But their calculations are demonstrably incorrect. We have already seen that the "16 percent" is without foundation. Our interest here is in the calculation of the "13 percent."

A Technical Note reports this same figure more precisely as 13.1 percent (FE, II, p. 52). We have attempted to reconstruct in Table 2 the procedure for obtaining this estimate. Only two percentages are taken from the New Orleans Records: the percentage of women, aged 20–24, sold without their children or husband (84.3 percent); and the percentage of women sold with their husband (1.01 percent). The residual (14.7 percent) were women sold with children but without their husband. However, according to *Time on the Cross* only three-fourths of this group (11.03 percent of the total) were "involuntarily" separated from their husbands, since Fogel and Engerman assume that the rest were widows (or "voluntary" separations). In addition to the involuntary separations in the residual group, Fogel and Engerman estimate that 0.94 of 1 percent of the total were married but childless women who were involuntarily separated from their husbands. The two categories of involuntary separations taken together total 12.0 percent of all women aged 20 to 24. Fogel and Engerman report 13.1 percent—they have apparently made another computational error. Our main interest, however, is not in this error but rather in the procedures and the assumptions that underlie the calculation of the fraction of women whose marriages were involuntarily broken by the interstate slave trade. Fogel and Engerman's procedure rests upon two doubtful sets of assumptions; first, those assumptions used to infer the number of women sold as childless who had been separated from their husbands, and, second, those assumptions used to estimate the proportion of widows in the New Orleans sample.

Childless Wives: All but 1.5 percent of the women sold without children in New Orleans, according to Fogel and Engerman, were single. They assume that no mother was ever separated from her children and sold individually. Fogel and

Engerman then calculate that 7.65 percent of all slave women 20–24 were married but had no surviving children (FE, II, p. 52). Yet they take only one-sixth of this percentage for their New Orleans calculations on the presumption that slave buyers in that city "were *six times* more likely to buy an unmarried woman than a married one" because of their "strong preference for unmarried women," a preference that reflected "the influence of powerful economic and social forces which militated against the disruption of families" (FE, II, pp. 51–52).

The estimated six-to-one preference was obtained by comparing the overall proportion of "single" women to ever-married women in the New Orleans sample with the comparable proportion for all women 20–24 in the exporting states.[34] Not only is the presumption that slave buyers preferred unmarried to married women completely unsupported by direct evidence, its application in this instance amounts once again to assuming the point in contention. If we refuse to grant that Fogel and Engerman have established the six-to-one preference for unmarried women, then we could replace their low estimate of married women sold separately with a higher one. If we choose a number large enough, then the total of ever-married women sold in New Orleans would become great enough to refute the contention that New Orleans buyers preferred unmarried women.

[34] This procedure is described in over two pages of entirely unnecessary algebra (FE, II, pp. 38 and 49–51). However no space was devoted to describing the estimating procedure for the ratio of "single" women to ever-married women, 20–24, in the exporting states. Fogel and Engerman correctly explain that these estimates cannot be gotten directly from the New Orleans invoices but add: "They can, however, be estimated by combining information contained in the probate records with information contained in the census" (FE, II, p. 50). A page later, however, they point out that the ratio has been "estimated from census data." They must mean the manuscript slave census schedules, but they never describe just how such estimates were made. The census enumerators usually listed slaves by their age and sex. They were arranged in order of descending age without names or groupings to indicate family connections. How can one possibly estimate marital and family connections from such a listing? And how, especially, is it possible to use the slave manuscript census to separate out by specific age groupings women with children from childless women? That, after all, is what Fogel and Engerman mean by married and unmarried women.

Table 2: Women, 20–24, Sold in the New Orleans Slave Market Classified
Following Fogel and Engerman's Procedures

	Percentages based on New Orleans data	Percentages of Total	
		Percentages based on assumptions	NOTES
Sold Without Children	84.3		a
Single Women		83.04	e
Married, No Children†		1.26	b
Sold with Husband		0.01	c
Widowed		0.31	d
Involuntarily Separated*		0.94	e
Sold With Children, Without Husband†	14.7		e
Involuntarily Separated*		11.03	e
Widowed		3.68	d
Sold With Children and Husband†	1.0		c
Total	100.0		

Addenda:
* Total Involuntarily Separated — 12.0
† Total Ever Married — 17.0

ª The percentage reported is the value of "X" (FE, II, p. 51), which is defined
in terms of "U′ " and "M′ " (FE, II, p. 49), which are in turn defined in Table
B.4 (FE, II, p. 38).
ᵇ For Fogel and Engerman's discussion of this fraction, see (FE, II, p. 52). The
figure we give is equal to $10.2 \times 0.75 \times .165$, which is our interpretation of
their cryptically described procedure. If we understand it, this procedure will
give a slightly low estimate, since no allowance was made for women who had
been married 2 or more years without surviving offspring, only for women
married one year without children.
ᶜ "Of those who were or had been married," say Fogel and Engerman, "6
percent were sold with their mates" (FE, I, p. 49). Fogel and Engerman
interpret all women who were sold with children (15.7 percent) plus that
fraction of women sold without children who were new brides (1.26 percent)
as having once been married. Six percent of 16.96 percent is 1.018 percent.
Using the same procedure described in note b to distribute this total between
women with husbands but no children and women sold with both husband

Fogel and Engerman's entire procedure, in fact, produces answers built into it by assumptions that are unsupported by historical evidence. This can be illustrated by turning their assumptions around. Fogel and Engerman wished to demonstrate that slave buyers in New Orleans had "strong preferences for unmarried women" and they *assumed* children were never separated from their mothers (FE, II, pp. 51 and 49). Suppose, instead, that one wished to support Andrews's contention, quoted earlier, that slave buyers had strong preferences for women without children, and suppose it is assumed that slaveowners felt no compunction about separating mothers from their children. Then it could be argued that the proportion of women ages 20–24, with no surviving children, sold in New Orleans should reflect the proportion of childless women, ages 20–24, in the exporting states. The latter proportion is 47 percent, according to Fogel and Engerman (FE, II, p. 51). Thus 53 percent of the New Orleans women would have been mothers. But since only 15.7 percent were actually sold with their children, 37.3 percent of the women and 70.4 percent of the mothers would have had to have been separated from their offspring. We could also calculate (using Fogel and Engerman's formulas) that slave buyers were 2.4 times more likely to separate a mother from her children than to buy them along with her. This would demonstrate the "strong preference" for women unencumbered by children predicted by Andrews (indicating perhaps "the influence of powerful economic and social forces"). What this hypothetical calculation proves, of course, is not that Andrews was right but rather that Fogel and Enger-

---

and children, gives 0.013 in the first group and 1.005 in the second. The table records these numbers rounded to two places following the decimal point.
ᵈ According to Fogel and Engerman, "at least one quarter" of those "who were or had been married" but were not "sold with their mates" were "widowed or voluntarily separated" (FE, I, p. 49). Elsewhere, they contradictorally say, "approximately 25 percent of those women with children, but without husbands, were widows" (FE, II, p. 52). We have taken the second interpretation since that is associated with the technical, rather than the popular, discussion of the procedure. Had the first interpretation been taken the percentage of women sold who were widows with children would have been approximately 4 percent.
* Computed as a residual.

man's procedure produces conclusions built in by assumption. With such a procedure, one can establish almost anything.

Widows: How did Fogel and Engerman estimate the percentage of slave widows, ages 20–24, sold in New Orleans? Once again by assumption. Their critical assumption is that widowed mothers were nearly five times more frequent in New Orleans sales than they were in the general population. Fogel and Engerman apparently think this was "likely" because buyers "prefer[ed] widowed to married women" (FE, II, p. 52), but they offer no supporting evidence.[35] Considering their own insistence that cooperation and efficiency were promoted on slave plantations by fostering stable family life (FE, I, pp. 126–28), we do not see the logical consistency of their assumption that slave holders would prefer widowed women with children to complete family units (FE, II, p. 52). This "calculation" is little more than the expression of an unsupported impression of the authors.

The claim that only 2 percent of the *married* female slaves who were transported across state lines had their marriages forcibly dissolved is based on Fogel and Engerman's earlier estimates concerning percentage of interregional moves caused by sales (16.2); percentage of sales that involved ever-married women (15.7); and percentage of the married women whose marriages were destroyed (70.6). This calculation (.162 × .157 × .706 = .018) actually gives, if one accepts the ingredient estimates as valid, the percentage of *all female* migrants, not just ever-married ones, who were taken from their husbands. The correct calculation (using Fogel and Engerman's parameters) gives 11.4 percent of the *married* women (.162 × .706).

Even this corrected figure is not accurate. As we have already

---

[35] Fogel and Engerman use Evans's survivor table to estimate that 5.18 percent of the women aged 20–29 (not 20–24!) would be widows (FE, II, p. 52). This number is one-half of the death rate for males 20–29 over a 10-year period (Evans [1962], Table 15, p. 212). They next assert that widowed wives with children would be preferred to married women with children in the same proportion as unmarried women were "preferred" to married women (six to one). We suspect that the ratio of childless women to mothers overstates the predominance of single women in the New Orleans sales, therefore we also suspect that Fogel and Engerman seriously overstate the number of widows as well.

argued, Fogel and Engerman's estimate of the percentage of sales in the westward movement (16.2) is much too low. If we could accept Calderhead's estimate that 50 percent of the migrants were sold, we would conclude that 35.3 percent of the married women moving west were separated from their husbands (.5 × .706). Moreover, our 35.3 percent figure, like Fogel and Engerman's erroneous 2 percent one, is based upon the clearly incorrect assumption that marriages were destroyed only by sale, and never when owners or relatives of owners moved west with their bondsmen.

Calderhead estimated that approximately one-half as many slaves exchanged masters when estates were divided among heirs as did so when slaves were sold (FE, II, p. 115). Assuming that this ratio also applies to the interstate exports and that the propensity to destroy marriages was the same through such transfers as through sales (cf. FE, II, p. 115), an additional 17.6 percent of the marriages were broken in this manner, giving a total of 52.9 percent. Furthermore, if we were to reject Fogel and Engerman's contention that 25 percent of the women sold with children were widows and instead assume that the proportion of widows sold in New Orleans matched the national average, then our estimate of the marriage destruction rate would rise from 53 percent to 67 percent.[36] Fogel and Engerman have multiplied error by error and then misreported and misrepresented the result. They put the same figure at only 2 percent.

The Overall Rate of Marriage Destruction

Fogel and Engerman's estimate that only 13 percent of marriages were broken in the course of the interstate slave trade does not rest, as they claim, upon "hard data." It rests upon unsupported assumption. Nevertheless, this number, in turn, is

[36] It might also be noted that this figure applies only to women 20 to 24. Yet in this age group men predominated in the interstate migration (Sutch [1975], Table 3, p. 179), many of whom obviously left wives behind them. Furthermore, the marriage-destruction rate of older women and men was undoubtedly higher. The estimation of the number of marriages broken by sale from the perspective of young women minimizes the true number.

the basis of their calculation that "roughly 8.6 percent of all slave marriages were destroyed through economic transactions involving slaves" (FE, II, p. 116). By itself this statistic seems to us shockingly high. It does not, in our view, support the conclusion that slaves felt their marriages were secure from disruption through sale. What does this percentage mean? If, for example, 2 million slave marriages took place between 1820 and 1860, it follows that 172,000 slave marriages were "destroyed through economic transactions." (That is 172,000 more occurrences than among nonslaves.) If we assume that each couple so separated had ten blood relatives nearby, and twenty intimate slave friends, that means that *each year* 4300 marriages were broken by sale, affecting no fewer than 8600 husbands and wives and 129,000 blood kin and friends. That means that between 1820 and 1860 more than 5 million persons—all slaves—directly or indirectly experienced the psychological and social crisis that accompanied the breakup of a slave marriage by sale.

As shockingly large as the estimated 8.6 percent marriage destruction rate thus appears, it is still much below the truth. It is based upon estimates which we have already demonstrated to be in error. The proportion of the slave population of Maryland which was sold each year, according to our correction of Fogel and Engerman's estimate, is 3.46 percent. Thirteen percent of these sales broke a marriage, say Fogel and Engerman. Thus a married slave in that state would face a 0.453 percent chance of being sold in any given year. The spouse would face a similar risk. Therefore, 9.1 couples out of every 1000 would be separated by sale annually. Since a typical marriage might last 24 years before the death of one of the partners (FE, II, p. 115), the probability that a given marriage would be destroyed by sale is 19.6 percent. Multiplying the probability of annual destruction by 1.5 to account for marriages broken by division of estates after the death of slaveowners (as suggested by Fogel and Engerman (FE, II, p. 115) gives an estimate of 29 percent. Roughly three marriages in every ten would be broken involuntarily by an economic transaction conducted by the owner.

This estimate is based on the state of Maryland. It was derived using the same procedure and the same numbers (corrected only to eliminate their error in calculating the frequency of sale) employed by Fogel and Engerman. *Time on the Cross* seems to suggest that such a figure might plausibly be applied to the entire South (FE, II, pp. 115–16). But let us not go so far. It is likely that exporting states (such as Maryland) experienced higher marriage break-up rates than the states of the Lower South. Nevertheless, the slaves whose marriages were destroyed in Maryland frequently ended up in Mississippi and Louisiana. This makes it instructive to examine just what blacks residing in these states have recorded about their own slave marriages. The Freedman's Bureau issued marriage certificates to former slaves following emancipation. When these registers were made, each slave was asked if he or she had had an earlier marriage. If previously married, the ex-slave was asked if the union had been broken and, if so, how. Gutman and Blassingame have both examined these records. Significantly their estimates agree much more closely with our Maryland estimates than with those reported by Fogel and Engerman. The comparison is made in Table 3.

A full analysis of the Mississippi and Louisiana wartime marriages registers will appear in Gutman's forthcoming study ([1976], Chapter 3). But Gutman's figure, reported in Table 3, and Blassingame's study were both published in 1972, so that these findings were available to Fogel and Engerman.[37] It is surprising that they failed to consider the Freedman's Bureau data. At least the sharp differences between the Gutman-Blassingame figures and their own might have alerted Fogel and Engerman to the computational errors in their own work.

Whatever the future research on the sale of slaves may reveal, it will not change the fact that *Time on the Cross* presents inaccurate estimates of the proportion of slaves sold, the proportion of marriages destroyed, and the proportion of the interstate migration accounted for by the trade. The authors have misused their sources, failed to disclose important information on the representativeness of their data, and left readers with the misleading impression that the threat posed by sales to the slave marriages (implied by their estimate) is negligibly

[37] Both works are in fact cited in the bibliography of *Time on the Cross* (FE, II, pp. 250 and 257).

Table 3:
Comparison of Estimates of the Marriage-Destruction Rate

Observer	Source	Percentage of Marriages Broken by Force
Fogel and Engerman (FE, II, pp. 115–16)	Calderhead's study of Maryland	8.6
Gutman and Sutch	Calderhead's study of Maryland	29.0
Gutman ([1972], pp. 1197–1218)	All Mississippi and Louisiana slaves aged 30 and older registering marriages in 1864–65	22.7
Blassingame ([1972], Table 1, p. 90)	2888 ex-slave unions registered in Mississippi, Tennessee, and Louisiana in 1864–65	32.4

"low." Ultimately, *Time on the Cross* says nothing about either the motivations of masters who participated in the trade in human property or the motivations of those who avoided slave sales.

Separations of Children from Their Parents

In much of Fogel and Engerman's treatment of the slave trade there is a confusion between a slave family and a slave marriage. Throughout their discussion of family stability they use the two concepts interchangeably. Almost all of the evidence they present deals with slave marriages, yet it is essential for their conclusions that stability extend to the family, not just to the relationship between husband and wife. A young individual's being sold from his or her slave family and thereby separated from parents and siblings should be counted as evidence of a broken slave family. But because Fogel and Engerman deal with marriages, they implicitly discount such sales as unimportant. Their confusion of the matter greatly weakens their overall argument. Moreover, their brief discussion of the sale of children contains two serious and inexplicable distortions.

It was illegal to sell a child under 10 separately from his or her mother in New Orleans. But this was not the case outside of Louisiana.[38] Despite the law limiting the sale of young children, the records of the New Orleans slave market reveal that 9.3 percent of all slave sales were of children, 12 years old or younger, sold separately (FE, I, pp. 49–50). (This is the third ratio drawn from the New Orleans records.) Fogel and Engerman conclude:

> Projected to the national level, this implies that the total interregional sales of children amounted to just 234 per annum. This small number of child sales could easily have been explained by orphans, as U. B. Phillips and other southern historians have claimed. Because of the high death rates of the time, approximately 15.9 percent of children under thirteen were orphans. Thus there were approximately 190,000 orphans in the age category 0–12 in 1850. The interregional sale of just 1 out of every 810 orphans would account for the full extent of the trade in children. [FE, I, p. 50]

In this passage, Fogel and Engerman have seriously understated the magnitude of the interregional sales of children sold separately. According to Calderhead, 50 percent of the interstate trade in slaves was produced by sales. Roughly 270,000 slaves were exported from the selling states during the 1850s.[39] Therefore there were approximately 135,000 slaves sold in the interregional slave trade. Projecting the New Orleans ratio of child sales to the national level gives 12,555 slave children sold into the interstate trade during the decade. This is over 1200 children per year—not 234 children, as reported by Fogel and Engerman. Even if we used Fogel and Engerman's erroneous estimate of the percentage of interstate migrants who were sold, the number of parentless-child sales would be over 400, some 1.7 times Fogel and Engerman's estimate.

[38] Stampp [1956], p. 152.
[39] Sutch [1975], Table 3, p. 179.

There is another error in the quoted passage: Fogel and Engerman wildly exaggerate the percentage of orphaned slave children. They say that 15.9 percent of all slaves under 13 were orphans. They do not say from what source this figure was obtained. In any case, it is incorrect. For a slave to have been an orphan when sold, both of the child's parents would have to be deceased. The probability that a male and a female in their twenties would both die within the course of 12 years (according to Evans's survivor table) is 1.65 percent. If they were in their thirties the probability would rise to 2.15 percent.[40] We can see no reason why the percentage of 13-year-olds who were orphaned should exceed 2.2 percent. Younger children would be even less likely to be orphans, since their parents would have had fewer years at risk. For example, less than one-half of 1 percent of five-year-olds whose parents were in their thirties at the child's birth would be orphans. In spite of the "high death rate of the time," a weighted average suggests that only about 1 percent, not 15.9 percent as *Time on the Cross* claims, of all slave children under 13 were orphans.[41]

In 1860 there were 775,000 slave children under 10 who had been born in the exporting states.[42] Adding 16 percent to account for 10-, 11-, and 12-year-olds, and applying our estimate of the percentage of children orphaned, yields at the outside 9000 children orphaned during the decade. This is an insufficient number to explain the 12,500 children exported without their parents from these states over the decade of the 1850s.

Fogel and Engerman complain that Bancroft and other historians dealing with the slave trade used mostly "the accounts of firsthand observers," contemporaries who "lacked the hard data needed to actually determine the scope and nature of this trade" and who therefore "could only convey their impressions." Historians like Bancroft chose "between . . . conflicting and contradictory tracts" and the "conventional view

[40] Evans [1962], Table 15, p. 212.
[41] This estimate is based upon an assumed death rate among parents of 14 per thousand, which exceeds Evans's estimates for 30- to 39-year-olds. The weights were based on a hypothetical age distribution of children under 13 also computed from Evans ([1962], Table 15, p. 212).
[42] Sutch [1975], Appendix Table 3, p. 206.

of the slave trade" which was "fashioned" by historians who "uniformly rejected the impressions of southern writers as apologetics and accepted the views of northern or European critics as accurate" (FE, I, p. 51). Fogel and Engerman, however, have not used the New Orleans records to confront Bancroft's essential point. We leave aside the volume of local and interregional sales. "The fact," Bancroft insisted, that "all but a small percentage of the slaves had for sale were 'single,' or young mothers with children, is conclusive evidence that it was common to divide families." [43] In other words, the predominance in the New Orleans sales of single individuals, far from being evidence of the security of the slave family, is evidence that slave sales typically broke up slave *families*, since, as Bancroft knew, nearly every slave belonged to a family. The evidence in the New Orleans slave sale invoices presented by Fogel and Engerman does no more than confirm Bancroft's conclusion that it was "common to divide families." Bancroft, however, dealt with families, not with marriages. And Fogel and Engerman never consider the impact of slave sales on the *slave family*. Any child, including an unmarried teenager, sold from his parents counts as evidence of the breakup of a *slave family*. There is no other way to read such evidence.

To suggest, as Fogel and Engerman do, that the removal of such persons "occurred at an age when it would have been normal for them to have left the family" not only obscures the significant fact that the slave family was *involuntarily* broken by such sales, but it overlooks an important distinction. The decision by a white teen-age youth to quit his Virginia or Maryland home for Georgia or Alabama cannot be equated with the sale of a black teen-age youth from his Virginia or Maryland slave family. No one has described the difference more precisely than Frederick Douglass:[44]

> The people of the north, and free people generally, I think, have less attachment to the places where they are born and brought up, than have the slaves. Their freedom to go and come, to be here and there, as they list, prevents any extravagant attachment to any one particular place, in their case. On the other hand, the slave is a fixture; he has no choice, no

43 Bancroft [1931], p. 199.
44 Douglass [1855], pp. 176–77.

goal, no destination; but is pegged down to a single spot, and must take
root here, or nowhere. The idea of removal elsewhere, comes, generally, in
the shape of a threat, and in punishment of crime. It is, therefore,
attended with fear and dread. A slave seldom thinks of bettering his
condition by being sold, and hence he looks upon separation from his
native place, with none of the enthusiasm which animates the bosoms of
young freemen, when they contemplate a life in the far west, or in some
distant country where they intend to rise to wealth and distinction. Nor
can those from whom they separate, give them up with that cheerfulness
with which friends and relations yield each other up, when they feel that
it is for the good of the departing one that he is removed from his native
place. Then, too, there is correspondence, and there is, at least, the hope of
reunion, because reunion is *possible*. But, with the slave, all these
mitigating circumstances are wanting. There is no improvement in his
condition *probable*,—no correspondence *possible*,—no reunion attainable.
His going out into the world, is like a living man going into the tomb,
who, with open eyes, sees himself buried out of sight and hearing of wife,
children and friends of kindred tie.

It was as if Douglass had foreseen the failure of historical
imagination which, in another century, could produce the bland
observation that most of the slaves sold away "were at an age
when it would have been normal for them to have left the
family." The reasons for regarding such abuses of the method of
comparative social history with grave suspicion are apparent
from the very terms in which Douglass chose to phrase his
response. The casual equating of the experiences of free men
and slaves, which is implicit in the comparison offered by *Time
on the Cross*, ought not to be dismissed as an innocent lapse.
Rather, it panders to an impulse to deny that the condition of
bondage could have totally transformed the social and psychological meaning of family separations for the blacks who
experienced them, giving the legendary geographical mobility
of nineteenth-century Americans a profoundly different significance for Afro-American people than it had for other
members of our society.

CHAPTER FOUR

Victorians All?
The Sexual Mores and Conduct
of Slaves and Their Masters

Herbert Gutman
and
Richard Sutch

Throughout *Time on the Cross* slaveowners are depicted as profit-maximizing capitalists engaged in business and motivated primarily by economic considerations. A natural implication of this view of the American slave economy—one drawn equally by the nineteenth-century English economist J. E. Cairnes (1862) and the American economists Alfred Conrad and John Meyer (1958)—is that slaveholders would find it in their interest to increase the fecundity of slave women beyond that rate of birth which the slaves would have established if left to arrange their own lives. To accomplish this the slaveowner would have to have interfered in some way in the sex lives of his slaves. This interference might range from offering rewards to women who conceived children to more direct practices such as arranged matings and encouragement of sexual intercourse on the part of young slave women soon after they became capable of bearing children. But whatever form the master's practices took, they would be calculated to increase his profits, and under the pressure of the competitive system humane gestures and social conventions which were incompatible with maximum economic efficiency would become a luxury that only a few owners could afford.

An alternative view of the motivation of slaveowners—one perhaps seen more in novels than in histories—is that masters were driven by passions baser than simple greed: cruelty and lust. Such masters would also interfere in the sex lives of their slaves, not for profit but to gratify their own sexual desires and compulsions. While these are extreme characterizations, both stereotypes imply that the integrity of the slave family would have been threatened by outside sexual interference. This point has been made by a number of historians and sociologists who have gone on to argue that these sexual intrusions (coupled with the constant threat of involuntary family disruption posed by the slave trade) fundamentally distorted the structure of the black family under slavery, destroying its resemblance to the patterns of family life and organization shared by Americans whose heritage was one of freedom.

Fogel and Engerman, on the other hand, argue that the slave family was strong and stable. Moreover, they claim that the masters had an economic interest in fostering and protecting the nuclear slave family. While Fogel and Engerman appear to subscribe to the notion that owners had an interest in increasing the birth rate, they firmly reject the contention that masters directly interfered with "normal family life to increase fertility": slave breeding, they say, was a "myth" (FE, I, pp. 83 and 78).

The crux of the argument advanced in support of their position is that any attempt to interfere sexually in the lives of the slaves ultimately "might undermine slave morale and discipline." "Distraught and disgruntled slaves," we are told, "did not make good field hands" (FE, I, pp. 78 and 84). Sexual interference also would have deleterious effects upon slave discipline and morale in the longer run, by undermining the stability of the slave family. Supposedly this was a matter of great concern to the slaveowners because they had made the slave family the agency through which the "Protestant work ethic" was transmitted from slave generation to slave generation.

Indeed, Fogel and Engerman go beyond this to argue that because the "sanctity of the slave family" was so important to the owners, they sought to promote "prudish" sexual mores among the slaves and to imbue them with their own "Victorian" attitudes on the subject. According to *Time on the Cross*, slaveowners had unusual success in converting the enslaved to

their own standards of sexual and moral behavior. Ordinary
slaves lived in "stable and nuclear families," waited until
marriage to have sexual intercourse, and did not marry until
they were 20 (women) and 24 (men) years old. Rational profit
maximizers did more than imbue Sambo with the Protestant
work ethic. They also created the conditions that made his wife
and daughter into prudish women (FE, I, pp. 126–44). "Victorian
attitudes predominated in the planting class," and these beliefs
helped to protect slave women from "sexual exploitation." Fogel
and Engerman report that sexual intercourse, whether forced or
voluntary, between white men and slave women resulted in
"only a very small percentage of the slaves born in any given
year." They go on to claim that "racism" reduced the "demand
of white males for black sexual partners." This low demand in
addition helped to "limit the use of slaves as prostitutes" (FE, I,
pp. 129–35).

In presenting this view of sexual mores and practices of slaves
and their masters, Fogel and Engerman rely almost exclusively
upon conjecture and theoretical argument. They present very
little data, quantitative or otherwise. All of their claims about
Victorian and prudish slave sexual behavior, for example, rest
upon a set of observations which suggest to them that the
average age of slave women at the birth of a first child was 22.5
years of age and that the slaves did not practice contraception.
This "high average age," they argue, "suggests that the
prevailing sexual mores of slaves were not promiscuous but
prudish" (FE, I, p. 138). And the "prevalence of prudishness in
the conduct of [slave] family life" is the only "evidence" offered
to explain why slaves would become "distraught and disgruntled" as a result of overt efforts to manipulate their sexual
behavior (FE, I, pp. 138 and 84). Despite Fogel and Engerman's
total reliance upon their estimate of the *primapartum* age of
slave women, we shall see that they have grossly misused the
data upon which their estimate is based.

Nor does *Time on the Cross* offer evidence that slaveowners
actually did attempt to imbue slaves with Victorian sexual
attitudes. Their sole argument that the southern planters
themselves held such beliefs rests upon the assertion that there
was a low incidence of miscegenation. A low incidence of

interracial sexual intercourse might, of course, have been the result of racism rather than Victorianism, a possibility that *Time on the Cross* leaves open. But in any case, Fogel and Engerman's claim of a low incidence of miscegenation is contradicted by the evidence which they themselves present.

Their assertion that "white men who desired illicit sex had a strong preference for white women" (FE, I, p. 135) is supported only by a demonstrably irrelevant citation to a study of prostitutes residing in Nashville, Tennessee, in 1860.

Finally, Fogel and Engerman's contention that slave breeding was a figment of abolitionists' imaginations rests largely upon their assertions concerning the infrequency of slave sales, although an additional, essentially theoretical argument is developed to suggest that the rearing of slaves for future sale would not have been economically profitable. The dubious nature of the first claim, regarding the infrequency of slave sales, has already been exposed in the preceding chapter. Later in this chapter we will have occasion to point out the flaws which Fogel and Engerman add in the course of developing their theoretical argument.

The evidence presented in *Time on the Cross* concerning sexual mores and conduct is insubstantial, and as will be seen in more detail, what is presented is largely misleading. But more facts and better facts on the particular matters which receive Fogel and Engerman's attention, would not suffice to render logically more coherent the main line of the argument that they advance on this issue. At least the logical gaps should be noticed.

To begin with, if the alleged prudishness of the slaves is supposed to explain why they would become "distraught" as a result of interference with their "normal sexual habits" (FE, I, p. 78), we are left to wonder why rational and dominant masters would have constrained themselves by inculcating such habits and attitudes in their slaves.

Biological realities certainly did not require that slaveowners encourage stable slave families in order to ensure a high level of slave fertility. A labor force which reproduces itself does not need to depend upon the "nuclear family." Nor is there much evidence that slaveowners viewed the matter in this way.[1] Slave

[1] The only direct evidence offered in *Time on the Cross* to support these claims, and it is extremely weak, is a statement made by James H. Hammond

women were valued as breeders and mothers, but their value as
slave wives is rarely mentioned by contemporaries. The letters
between overseers and their employers are full of references to
slave births and to increases in the owner's stock of slaves. On
the other hand, John Spencer Bassett, who studied the letters
that passed between the family of James K. Polk and the
overseers they employed, reports:[2]

> not a reference to the marriage of slaves in all the 275 letters that have
> come into my hands. Within this long period [*ca.* 1833–*ca.* 1858] many such
> unions must have occurred on the plantation, but no overseer thought it
> worth his while to mention one. Also, there may have been divorces or
> separations of husband and wife. The letters contain no suggestion of
> such occurrences. The overseer wrote about the things that he thought
> the owner ought to know. He doubtless assumed that Polk had no concern
> with a negro marriage or a negro divorce.

Second, as no evidence is provided in *Time on the Cross* to
establish what behavioral norms planters were actively seeking
to establish in the slave quarters, we are asked by Fogel and
Engerman to infer both the masters' intentions and slaves'
attitudes from the factual premise that the slaves were a
"noncontraceptive population" in which the age of women at the
birth of their first child was "high." Such facts, if facts they be,
might be accepted as consistent with sexual prudishness and an
absence of promiscuity. But it does not follow automatically
from the observation of a high age of marriage that slaves
necessarily were prudish, nor that their "morale and discipline"
would be undermined by transgressions against the sexual
mores of Victorian family life.

The Primapartum Age of Slave Mothers

Even if slaves were prudish and masters Victorian, and even if
slaves had objected to overt interference in their sexual affairs,

---

in a letter to his overseer. "Marriage is to be encouraged," wrote Hammond,
"as it adds to the comfort, happiness and health of those entering upon it,
besides insuring a greater increase" (FE, I, p. 84).

[2] The quotation is taken from Bassett [1899], pp. 260–61. The same letters
regularly reported the birth of slave children. Bassett, by the way, was hardly a
detached student of slave morality. He believed that it was "the authority of
the master that taught [the slave] . . . to improve his ideas of morality" and
that "in many ways slavery instilled" in blacks "the fundamentals of
civilization" (pp. 21–22).

the encouragement of early marriage need not have clashed with these sexual mores. Slaveowners should have found it both good business *and* at least acceptable morality to encourage marriage at a young age. This would make available to the women more time during their lives to bear children and thus increase the size of the completed family.[3] To reject this awkward implication of the situation portrayed in *Time on the Cross* the authors present data purporting to establish the infrequency of early marriage. One would suppose from all this that the data thus introduced related to the ages of slave mothers at the birth of their first child. But that is not the case.

What *Time on the Cross* actually reports is "the distribution of the ages of mothers at the time of the birth of their first *surviving* child" (FE, I, p. 137, emphasis supplied). There is a vast difference between the age of a woman at the birth of her first child and the age of a woman at the birth of her first *surviving* child. But Fogel and Engerman gloss over this important distinction to argue that their data contradict

> the charge that black girls were frequently turned into mothers at such tender ages as twelve, thirteen, and fourteen. Not only was motherhood at age twelve virtually unknown, and motherhood in the early teens quite uncommon, but the average age at first birth was 22.5 (the median age was 20.8). . . . By far the great majority of slave children were borne by women who were not only quite mature, but who were already married. [FE, I, p. 137]

These estimates of the age of the mothers at the birth of their first surviving child are not even based upon direct observation of the women's ages at the child's birth. Rather, 20.8 years is the median difference between the age of slave women and the age of their oldest child at the time of a probate inventory.[4] For

[3] Even if the completed family size was not changed, early marriage would have increased the number of births in the population. Since mortality constantly thinned the ranks of women throughout their childbearing years and since the total population was growing, there were considerably more young women than old. As a simple demographic model can demonstrate, even when the total number of conceptions in a woman's lifetime remains unchanged, a lowering of the age of first birth can have a substantial effect upon the rate of population growth (Coale and Tye [1961]).

[4] A check of the probate inventories with the first-birth tabulations supplied to us by Stanley Engerman in a letter of July 15, 1974, shows that all children up

example, when an inventory recorded a woman of 24 with children aged 4 and 2, her age at first birth would have been computed as 20 years, which is the age of the mother, not necessarily at her first birth, but at the birth of the oldest child still surviving in her household. Death or sale might have removed the first-born.[5] Mortality among the children was high; therefore the Fogel-Engerman estimate of the age of the mother at first birth is biased significantly upward. A correction for mortality based upon an estimated risk of death could have been made but was not.[6]

The older the eldest surviving child at the time of the probate inventory, the more likely would there have been an older sibling who had previously died. For example, if the age of a second-born child was exactly 2 years, the probability that the elder sibling was still alive was only about 66 percent. The probability that a 4-year-8-month-old third-born was the eldest surviving child would have been 17.8 percent. The probability that a seventh-born child had no surviving siblings at birth would have been 0.5 percent. Infant and childhood mortality were that high.[7]

---

to the age of 13 whose mothers were identified were included in the calculation.

[5] Another problem with this procedure is that at some age, the probate assessors would value children separately from their mothers, thus precluding a positive identification of the eldest even when the child was living on the same holding as the mother. For example, the Poivre estate held nine slaves when it was inventoried in March 1847 in Plaquemines Parish. One of these slaves was a woman of 30 with a 10-year-old son priced together at $600. The holding also included an 11-year-old girl worth $300. Fogel and Engerman assume that the son was the first-born and set the age of the mother at first birth at 20 years. If the 11-year-old girl had been her daughter then they should have set the mother's age at the birth of the eldest surviving child at 19 years. Since Louisiana law prohibited the sale of children under 10 apart from their mothers, it would have been logical for the courts to set an independent value for the 11-year-old girl.

[6] The procedure followed by Fogel and Engerman which is described in this paragraph was related to us by Stanley Engerman on June 4 and July 15, 1974, and confirmed by a comparison of their estimates (FE, I, Fig. 37, p. 138) with the probate inventories which they collected.

[7] All of these calculations are based upon a population described as "Model West: Level 5" (Coale and Demeny [1966], pp. 42 and 6). This model

Assuming a typical child spacing of 28 months on the authority of Steckel, Fogel and Engerman could have lowered the *primapartum* age of the appropriate fraction of mothers by this length of time for each missing child.[8] Given the expected frequencies of children by birth order and assuming an average age of the eldest surviving child of only 56 months,[9] the median age of mothers at first birth would have to be lowered by approximately 1.5 years, to 19.3 years.[10]

Even if proper use of the probate records had yielded the figures for representative *primapartum* ages as high as those reported by *Time on the Cross*, a vast amount of contemporary evidence—quantitative as well as literary—would nevertheless still contradict such "findings" and the inferences Fogel and Engerman derive from them. In testimony before the American Freedman's Inquiry Commission in 1863 (and later ignored by the Commission in its published reports), black witnesses indicated to Yankee questioners their perception of the prevalence

---

population is deemed most appropriate to reflect the antebellum slave population (Coale and Rives [1973]; and Eblen [1974], p. 302). The fertility parameters were based upon Steckel [1973] (Table 2, p. 8). The probabilities estimated are probably too low since no adjustment was made for the fact that most high-fertility populations exhibit a higher infant-death rate among first-born than second-born (see, for example, Smith [1960], p. 121). For further discussion of slave infant mortality, see Chapter 6, below.

[8] Steckel [1973], Table 2, p. 8.

[9] In Plaquemines Parish, Louisiana, the average age of the eldest child in the records used by Fogel and Engerman, was 5.6 years (67 months) and the median age was 5 years (60 months). Our use of 56 months in the calculation reported in the text is intended to be a conservative estimate for the entire sample.

[10] Eighty-four percent of the Plaquemines mothers to whom Fogel and Engerman attribute a *primapartum* age of 30 or over had an eldest surviving child 5 years old or over, suggesting the possibility that there had been other children who were evaluated separately since they were older. If we exclude the mothers whose eldest surviving child was 5 or older, the median *primapartum* age computed by the Fogel-Engerman technique would fall by 2 years. It should be noted that this calculation takes into account the age distribution of mothers expected in a population growing at the rate of the U.S. slave population between 1850 and 1860. The age distribution is relevant since in a growing population there will be proportionately more young women. The first born of such women are more likely to have survived to be recorded than those of older mothers.

of prenuptial intercourse among the slave population. Then about 40 years old, Harry McMillan had been born a slave in Georgia and had grown up in Beaufort, South Carolina. "Colored women," he was asked, "have a great deal of sexual passion, have they not? They all go with men?" "Yes sir," McMillan responded, "there is a good deal of that. I do not think you will find four out of a hundred that do not; they begin at fifteen or sixteen." Robert Smalls, a black who had escaped dramatically from Charleston with his slave family and some friends by seizing a Confederate gunboat, was in his early twenties and able to testify from still-vivid recollections. His views did not differ from McMillan's views on the sexual passion exhibited by colored women. To his answer of a Commission member's question about "young women," Smalls added, "They are very wild and run around a good deal." "What proportion of the young women have sexual intercourse before marriage?" he was then asked. "The majority do," said Smalls, "but they do not consider this intercourse an evil thing." Smalls and McMillan, incidentally, were the only South Carolina slaves who testified before the Commission.[11]

We need not rely just upon the testimony of these two former slaves to learn about prenuptial sexual intercourse among slaves. Plantation records examined by Gutman indicate that at least one of five slave mothers had one or more children prior to settling into a monogamous and stable slave union. Even though most white observers never understood it, most slaves found prenuptial intercourse and even prenuptial pregnancy and childbirth compatible with subsequent monogamous marriage. Estimates of the median age of slave women at the birth of their first child based upon direct observation of those ages from plantation records we have examined are summarized in Table 1. These records can support a median age of birth of no more than 19 years. The age at which sexual intercourse began must have been somewhat earlier than 18 unless one wants to argue that pregnancy invariably followed from the first act of intercourse.

[11] Testimony of Harry McMillan and Robert Smalls, Freedman's Inquiry Commission [1863].

Table 1:
Median Age of Slave Women at the Birth of First Child

Name of Plantation	Location	Approximate Years Covered	Number of Women	Median Age
Cameron	North Carolina	1776–1841	24	18.9
Good Hope	South Carolina	1797–1856	31	18–19
Stirling	Louisiana	1828–1865	49	18.7
Watson	Alabama	1843–1865	32	19

Source: Gutman [1976], Chapters 2 and 3.

The median, however, conveys little about the shape of the distribution. On the South Carolina Good Hope plantation, for example, only two women were older than 25 at the birth of a first child. Two others were not yet 15. On the Cameron plantation, one of the twenty-four women was 14 and eleven others either 16 or 17. Four women were between 24 and 31. The median age at birth of first child among the Cameron slave women was 18.9; the average age, 17. Confirming data exist among other plantation women. A birth register covering the years between 1802 and 1860 on the St. Helena Island (South Carolina) Fripp plantation shows that of ten women five had a child at the age of 19, two at the age of 20, and the other three were aged 15, 16, and 17. The median age for these ten women was 18.3, and the average age about 19, but nearly one-third of them had a first child before their eighteenth birthday. Records also exist for a dozen slave women on the Virginia Cedar Vale plantation (1836–62), and two out of three of them were between 17 and 19 years old at the birth of their first child.[12]

In Volume II of *Time on the Cross* brief mention is made of the existence of data on the age of mother at first birth drawn from "plantation records." Although this is said to indicate a

[12] Except for the Fripp plantation records, the data summarized in this paragraph draw from Gutman's forthcoming study, Chapters 2 and 3. The Fripp information comes from Johnson [1930], p. 103.

somewhat younger "average age" for such women, that information does not prompt Fogel and Engerman to correct or qualify the average age reported so authoritatively in Volume I. It merely puzzles them.

> Data obtained from the plantation records indicates an average age of mothers at first birth which is approximately one year less than that indicated by the data in the larger sample from the probate records. We have not yet been able to determine whether this difference is due to some statistical artifact or whether it reflects a behavioral difference, such as a lower age of marriage on large plantations. [FE, II, p. 114]

We have been told that Richard Steckel [1973] was the source of this report (letter from Engerman, Nov. 4, 1974). Yet Steckel reports an average age of 19.4 years based upon "Plantation Records." [13] This is curious since "approximately one year less" than the probate-record average age reported in *Time on the Cross* is "approximately" 21.5 years, not 19.4 years. The difference between 22.5 years and 19.4 years is obviously a "statistical artifact," testimony to the biased procedure used by Fogel and Engerman to estimate the age of first birth from probate records, and a mis-citation of their own source. We need not look to "behavioral differences" to explain it away.

If one accepts an average age at first birth of 19.4 years, it does not follow that "slave parents closely guarded their daughters from sexual contact with men." Fogel and Engerman imply that only sexual abstinence could explain the low number of births among very young slave women, since they describe the slave population as "noncontraceptive." This argument neglects, however, the fact that the age of menarche (first menstruation), and by implication, the age of fertility, has declined substantially from what it was in the mid-nineteenth century.

The Decline in the Age of Menarche

Norwegian girls in the mid-1840s typically were older than 17 before they began menstruating. In the 1860s women of Germany and Finland averaged over 16.5 years at menarche.[14] A

[13] Steckel [1973], Table 2, p. 8.
[14] Tanner [1962], Figure 31, p. 153, and Tanner (1973), pp. 42–43.

southern medical journal reported in 1839 a distribution of the age of menarche among French women which indicates a modal age of 16.5 years. This report was treated by the editor as if it could be applied to southern white women. Today American girls experience their first menstrual period at a median age of 12.76 years.[15]

The cause of this marked secular trend toward younger ages of puberty is still open to debate. It seems to be statistically associated with the secular increase in the average height of adults. The most common explanations advanced for the phenomenon attribute the decline to improvements in diet (particularly, increased protein intake), hygiene, and general economic circumstances.[16] Although we have been unable to find a firm estimate of the age of menarche for slave women,[17] Sutch's study of their diet, in Chapter 6 of this volume, suggests that it is plausible that black women experienced their first menstruation at an age at least as high as that of contemporary Europeans.[18] In order to compare the age of a slave mother at the birth of her first child with a modern notion of the age of puberty, one should subtract approximately 2 or 3 years from the median *primapartum* age of the slave women. Judged then from a modern perspective, the probate inventories investigated by Fogel and Engerman suggest a pattern of behavior equivalent to one in which *half* of the women were already mothers by

[15] *Southern Medical and Surgical Journal*, III, May 1839, p. 507, and U.S. National Center for Health Statistics [1973], Table 3, p. 12.

[16] Tanner [1968] and Shorter [1974].

[17] Dr. Samuel Cartwright writing in the *New-Orleans Medical and Surgical Journal* in 1852 put the age of "maturity" of slave women at 18 years (Cartwright [1852], p. 197). In 1849 the *Southern Medical and Surgical Journal* reported the case of a 12-year-old mother in England with much amazement and commented upon the "extreme youth of the mother." This suggests that the editor expected puberty at higher ages (Eve [1849], p. 610).

[18] There does not appear to be any significant difference between white and Negro women in the age of menstruation after correction for income level. If anything southern black girls reach menarche at older ages than both whites and other Negroes (Michelson [1944]; and U.S. National Center for Health Statistics [1973], Table 3, p. 12). Physical maturation has also been shown to be slower in the American South than in the North (Mills [1937]; and Michelson [1944]).

their seventeenth birthday. Viewed in this way slave women would appear to have had a phenomenally low median age at first birth. If the median age for menarche of slave women was 15 or 16, then at least one-half of them would have become physically capable of childbirth by 17. Nearly one-fourth of all women gave birth *as measured by Fogel and Engerman* at or before the age of 17. Since menstruation is frequently irregular during the first year of menarche and fertility does not reach full potential until several years after, this is a spectacular rate of early motherhood; it would be hard to explain except by widespread practice of early sexual intercourse. This is exactly what the slaves McMillan and Smalls reported: "they begin at fifteen or sixteen."

Age Differences Between Slave Spouses

Fogel and Engerman's assertion that a narrow age spread separated slave wives and husbands is equally open to question. A bar chart accompanies the following paragraph:

> Also fallacious is the contention that slave marriages, since they were arbitrarily dictated by masters, frequently produced odd age combinations—young men married to old women and vice versa. Figure 39 shows that most marriages were contracted among partners quite close in age. The average age difference between husband and wife was just three years. In almost all cases, the man was the same age or older than the woman. Reversals in this pattern were quite uncommon. [FE, I, p. 139]

Our reading of Figure 39 is reproduced in Table 2. The number of slave marriages examined is not stated. We are not told whether these marriages involved rural or urban slaves, Upper or Lower South slaves, farm or plantation slaves. The ages of marital partners are not revealed. No source is cited for this data. It could not have come from manuscript censuses' schedules, and very few plantation owners recorded slave marriages, much less the ages of marital partners, in their business records. Other data that disclose the ages of slave husbands and wives shortly following their emancipation (1864–66) suggest that Fogel and Engerman's finding does not describe the *typical* slave marriage. Slave husbands were often a good many years older than their wives.

Table 2:
The Distribution of Age Differences Between Slave Husbands
and Wives

Husband's Age Minus Wife's Age	Estimated Percentage
Less than −3	2
−1 to −3	6
0	12
1–3	44
4–6	19
Over 6	17

Source: FE, I, Fig. 39, p. 140.

The 1864–65 Mississippi and Louisiana military marriage registers included information elicited from 18,904 slave men and women marrying for the first time or validating with the military clergy a settled slave marriage. All but a handful had been slaves. In the Davis Bend, Natchez, and Vicksburg marriage registers, between 20.5 percent (the husbands of wives at least 50 years old) and 39 percent (the husbands of wives aged 30 to 39) of all men registering marriages were at least 10 years older than their wives. A significant percentage of the husbands listed in the Montgomery County (1866) and York County (1865), Virginia, military population censuses also were much older than their wives. In slightly more than three in ten Montgomery County Black marriages, the husband was at least ten years older than his wife. York County black couples revealed an even greater percentage of marriages with that large an age spread. A similar pattern is found in the 1866 Goochland County and Louisa County, Virginia, marriage registers. Depending upon the age of the Goochland County wife, the percentage of husbands at least ten years older than their wives ranged from 30 to 42 percent. This pattern was repeated among Louisa County slave couples (see Table 3).

Table 3:
The Percentage Distribution of Age Differences Between
Black Husbands and Wives; Louisa Country, Virginia, 1866

| | Years Husband is Older than Wife | | | |
Age of Wife	Under Five (%)	5 to 9 (%)	10 and Over (%)	Number
15–19	29	45	26	58
20–29	44	23	33	427
30–39	38	23	39	346
40–49	42	25	33	198
50–59	52	16	32	114
60 plus	76	4	20	51
All ages	43	23	34	1,194

Source: See text, footnote 19

These three sets of data[19]—one describing Mississippi and Louisiana blacks, and the other two, Virginia blacks—raise grave doubts about the value of Fogel and Engerman's source for their demographic data about enslaved Afro-Americans. The ages in the three sets of data which we cite here were given by the former slaves themselves. Fogel and Engerman report that no more than 17 percent of slave husbands were more than six years older than their wives. But Louisa County blacks reported three times as many marriages involving men at least five years older than their wives. What explains this discrepancy? Possibly another statistical artifact.

Miscegenation

Since all American slaves were originally descendants of black

[19] The data reported here and in Table 3 are taken from Gutman's forthcoming work, Chapter 8, and are based upon unpublished Freedman's Bureau records.

Africans, since no whites were slaves, and since the number of free blacks who migrated to the United States before the Civil War was trivial,[20] the growth of a mulatto population has been taken as incontrovertible proof of sexual contact between the masters and the slaves. In 1860, according to the Census, 13.2 percent of the Afro-American population was reported as "mulatto" [21] It should be noted immediately that neither this designation nor the term "black" was officially defined by the Census Office and that the reports of the skin color of slaves were made by their owners, while the color of free blacks was determined from visual inspection by the census taker.[22]

A long, technical note in the supplementary volume of *Time on the Cross* is devoted to describing a computation of the fraction of slave births which would have had to have been fathered by white men in order to account for the number of mulatto births implied by the Census data on mulattos in the slave population (FE, II, pp. 101–11). Assuming the census enumerator and his informants employed the definition of mulatto as a person of one-eighth ancestry of another race, Fogel and Engerman estimate this fraction at between 6.05 and 13.87 percent (FE, I, p. 132; pp. 102 and 104–5).[23] If the Census

[20] Sutch [1975], p. 203.

[21] In 1850 the percentage was 11.2 (USBC [1918], Table 1, p. 208). The fraction of the *slave* population returned as mulatto was less: 7.7. percent for 1850, 10.4 percent for 1860 (FE, II, pp. 101–2). However, since the free-colored population's origins were largely from the manumission and escape of slaves and since it is alleged that the mulatto offspring of slaveowners were frequently given their freedom, a count of the mulatto slaves would minimize the extent of "sexual exploitation" of slave women.

[22] The fact that the sex ratio among mulattos in 1860 was 909 men per 1000 females while amongst blacks it was 1010 suggests that systematic biases probably exist in the data (USBC [1918], p. 207 and Table 5, p. 211).

[23] High as they are, Fogel and Engerman's estimates are biased downward by their use of Evans's survivor tables to estimate the number of births (FE, II, Table B.14, p. 103) rather than the Census survival-ratio method, which would automatically correct for systematic biases in the Census figures (Sutch [1975], Appendix). Using the Census survival-ratio method gives the percentage of mulattos among all slave births as 16.37 percent rather than 15.20 (FE, II, p. 102). This correction by itself increases the calculated lower bound of white fathers to 7.24 percent from 6.05. There are other biases in Fogel and Engerman's procedure as well. It assumes that the fraction of slave parents

Office defined mulattos as persons with white ancestry at some level greater than one-eighth, the figure would have to have been even higher.[24] Yet the authors of *Time on the Cross* characterize their estimate as not sustaining "the contention that a large proportion of slave children must have been fathered by white men" (FE, I, p. 133). How large is "large" in this context, we wonder?

Since the calculations produced by the technique that Fogel and Engerman have adopted are very sensitive to the assumptions made about the definition of mulattos and about the racial preferences of both slave and white men—not to mention the accuracy in the Census reports—this approach is probably not very reliable. More to the point is the report that 4.5 percent of the ex-slaves interviewed by the Federal Writers' Project had a white father (FE, I, p. 133). Since this is the fraction of those who could identify their fathers, since some ex-slaves interviewed did not know who their fathers were, and since elderly blacks being questioned by white interviewers in the 1930s may

---

who were mulatto was the same as the share of mulattos in the 1850 population (FE, II, Assumption 2, p. 102). The high rate of mulatto births which Fogel and Engerman compute for the decade of the 1850s (15.2 percent), when extrapolated backwards into the 1840s, suggests that a disproportionate share of the 1850 mulattos may have been children. In fact, if only 10 percent of the children in 1850 were mulatto (instead of 7.7 as assumed by Fogel and Engerman), then only 6.6 percent of the slaves over 10 would have been mulatto in 1850. In this case the proportion of births fathered by whites in the 1850s would have to have been higher to explain the number of mulattos born. Recalculation puts this proportion in the range of 7.38 to 14.07 percent. This recalculation ignores the fact that a higher death rate among children than in the entire population would mean that the estimated number of mulatto births upon which the calculation is based would also have to be revised upward (Evans [1962], p. 212; and FE, II, Table B.14, p. 102). Other assumptions made in formulating the model also tend to bias Fogel and Engerman's estimates downward. For example, if—contrary to Fogel and Engerman—mulatto slaves had a preference for mulatto mates, then the number of mulatto births attributable to slave unions would be small and the fraction of white-fathered mulattos would have to rise.

[24] For example, if one-fourth white blood was required for the mulatto designation, as was the official Census definition in 1890 (USBC [1918], p. 207), then the proportion of slave children fathered by whites would rise to between 7.9 and 24.6 percent (see FE, II, p. 105: $e = a = .5$).

well have been hesitant to say they had a white father, this figure is likely to be a lower bound.[25] Yet Fogel and Engerman dismiss this finding in favor of their calculation of 1 to 2 percent of white fathers, based upon the "admixture of 'Caucasian' and 'Negro' genes among southern rural blacks today" (FE, I, p. 133; II, pp. 110–13). The latter piece of evidence, however, contains a number of flaws. The measured frequency of "Caucasian" genes in Evans and Bullock counties, Georgia, was determined for "blacks," not for "mulattoes" or near-whites, and therefore would not give an accurate picture for the entire population descendant from slaves. Second, migration and selective economic advancement has reduced the proportion of mulattos in these rural counties and increased the proportion in northern urban areas. The fraction of white fathers estimated by Fogel and Engerman for the "black" populations of New York, Detroit, and Oakland ranged from 3.6 to 5.2 percent (FE, II, Table B.17, p. 111).

This is not all, for Fogel and Engerman's computation of the fraction of white fathers is based upon the assumption that this fraction was constant from 1640 to 1965 (FE, II, p. 112). Given the fact that a large portion of the slave population was imported to the American colonies *after* 1640, and indeed after 1720 (FE, I, Fig. 6, p. 25), it seems implausible to assume that the rate of gene transmission was constant from 1640 on. According to Fogel and Engerman's logic, whites would have had to have been impregnating black women in Africa at the same rate as in America from 1640 until 1807, when slave imports were prohibited. Had Fogel and Engerman assumed that gene transmission began in 1710, the stable proportion of white fathers would have been estimated at 2.5 percent for the rural Georgia blacks and 5.5 for Oakland, California, blacks. Glass and Li, Fogel and Engerman's authorities on this type of calculation, note that it is important to make a *minimum* estimate of the number of generations of intermixture when using the procedure adopted by Fogel and Engerman. Fogel and Engerman not only ignored this advice but they did not report

[25] For a criticism of the reliability of the ex-slave narratives, see Woodward [1974].

Glass and Li's own estimate that the rate of gene transmission was 3.58 percent per generation, suggesting that 7.16 percent of "negro" children had white fathers.[26]

These scraps of evidence pieced together suggest to us that the proportion of slave children who were fathered by white men was above 4 percent and perhaps as high as 8 percent during the 1850s. We take the 4 percent figure as a conservative guess. Fogel and Engerman suggest that such a fraction is not "large." But consider for a moment the implications of a 4 percent rate of miscegenation. It suggests, for example, that a slave mother of seven children would have had one chance in four of having had a child by a white man under the extreme and implausible assumption that white sexual contacts were randomly distributed among fertile slave women. A 4 percent miscegenation rate also implies that there was a minimum of 32,000 sexual contacts between whites and slaves each year, and this estimate attributes to white men and black women the rather spectacular impregnation rate of 25 percent.[27] On the assumption that white men's sexual attentions were directed randomly at women between the ages of 15 and 30, each such slave woman had a 5.6 percent chance of being sexually approached by a white man each year, and a 58 percent chance of being approached at least once during the 15-year period of her youth.

Of course, white men were not likely to have distributed their attentions so indiscriminately. They would have singled out the young and attractive. If a random selection gives over a 50

[26] Glass and Li [1953], pp. 11–12.

[27] This estimate is computed from the Parker-Gallman sample. The age distribution of women was converted to the number of prime-fertility equivalent women by using a procedure developed by Sutch [1975], Table 9, p. 189. This number was multiplied by the average prime-age fertility rate (294.7 per thousand [Table 10, p. 190]) to obtain the number of children born. This estimate was divided by the total number of slaves included in the Parker-Gallman sample to obtain the ratio of births to the enumerated population (5.1 percent) which was then multiplied by the slave population of the United States in 1860 to estimate the total number of births. Four percent of this number is the assumed number of white-fathered births and four times that number is the number of assumed sexual contacts.

percent risk of approach, selectivity must have meant that favored women were almost certainly the target of white men's lust. A planter in Louisiana informed Olmsted ([1861], p. 240):

> There is not a likely-looking black girl in this State that is not the concubine of a white man. There is not an old plantation in which the grandchildren of the owner are not whipped in the field by his overseer.

Slave Prostitutes:
A Non-Fact from Nashville

The suggestion that racism would have kept white men from an interest in black women is, of course, naïve. Equally uninformed is Fogel and Engerman's attempt to use information on Nashville's brothels to support this contention. They spend several paragraphs (FE, I, pp. 134–35; II, pp. 113–14) making the points that there were no slave prostitutes in Nashville, Tennessee, that only a tiny percentage of the nonslave prostitutes were Negroes, and that this small number were "light-skinned" mulattos. Their source for these "facts" is David Kaser.[28]

Kaser makes clear that his information comes from the manuscript Census of Population for 1860, which—as a check with the manuscripts confirms—recorded occupations for the *free* inhabitants only. Kaser's study could not have discovered slave prostitutes even if Nashville had been alive with them.[29] "The failure of Nashville's brothels to employ slave women" is a non-fact, and as such it is *not* "of special interest" as claimed by Fogel and Engerman (FE, I, p. 135). Nor is Fogel and Engerman's theoretical model of prostitution in Volume II (pp. 113–14) of value. It amounts to the conjecture that *if* there were no slave prostitutes it might have been because free prostitutes enjoyed their work (would "get positive nonpecuniary income") and were willing to work for less money on this account. Thus,

---

[28] Kaser [1964], p. 380, cited at FE, II, p. 113.
[29] It should be noted—as Kaser was careful to do ([1964], p. 380)—that the enumeration of prostitutes undoubtedly missed many who participated in this occupation. Those who were employed only part-time or who had legitimate "front" occupations might have been led by their honesty, politeness, shame, or fear to report an alternative as their major source of income.

Fogel and Engerman argue, a slaveowner who cared only about money and disregarded the "pleasure" obtained by his slave women would find too much competition from free women. Fogel and Engerman have neither shown that there were no slave prostitutes nor established that women who sell their sexual favors enjoy their work. Their model of the supply of, and demand for illicit sex is as superfluous as their facts are nonexistent, and is as naïve as are their assumptions about the "pleasure" experienced by prostitutes and the sexual preferences of white males.[30]

Slave Breeding: Business or Myth?

The issue of "slave breeding" has been somewhat confused because participants in the debate have failed to define the term adequately. One of the present writers has defined it rather broadly as any practice of the slave master intended to cause the fertility of the slave population to be higher than it would have been in the absence of such interference.[31] So defined, "breeding" includes the use of "rewards" for childbearing, the encouragement of early marriage and short lactation periods, and the provision of both pre- and post-natal medical care, as well as practices more reprehensible to modern as well as to many nineteenth-century sensibilities.

Fogel and Engerman assert that slave breeding "is more than the existence of general incentives for the encouragement of large slave families." They go on to add that it "involves two

---

[30] Kaser reports 9 free mulatto prostitutes in the city ([1964], p. 380). Since there were only 406 free Negro women in Nashville (U.S. Census [1860], Population, p. 467), the incidence of reported prostitution among free black women was 22.2 per thousand. This is below the frequency exhibited by the city's white women, 32.6 per thousand but this seems hardly enough evidence to demonstrate "that white men who desired illicit sex had a strong preference for white women" (FE, I, p. 135). If blacks had a stronger sense of morality than did whites, as Fogel and Engerman argue (FE, I, pp. 138–39), this—and not the white males' tastes—might explain the lower incidence of prostitution among free blacks than among whites. However, we would not be willing to turn a general argument of this nature on the existence of 9 free, colored, Nashville prostitutes.

[31] Sutch [1975].

interrelated concepts: 1, interference in the normal sexual habits of slaves . . . ; 2, the raising of slaves with sale as the main objective" (FE, I, p. 78). As it turns out, however, our differences with Fogel and Engerman do not turn upon a quibble over definitions but rather upon evidence and economic logic.[32]

Whatever the definitions of "breeding," demographic evidence contained in the 1850 and 1860 censuses provides strong circumstantial evidence of the prevalence of inducements to childbearing, particularly in the so-called "breeding" states of the Atlantic seaboard and along the northern border of legal slavery. Slave women in these states exhibited higher fertility than did those of the importing regions, and their fertility rates approached the upper bounds of human capacity. The sex ratios on slave farms (with at least one woman) in the Parker-Gallman sample show a *surplus* of 232 women per 1000 men. In the exporting states the excess reached 300 per 1000. The rate of fertility rose across farms as the women-to-man ratio increased, and the ratio of children to adults rose even more sharply.[33]

Fogel and Engerman ignore this type of evidence and instead conjecture that slave "breeding" would not have proven worthwhile. This argument is based upon two suppositions: that interferences with the sexual lives of slaves could have little effect upon the rate of population growth (FE, I, pp. 82–83); and that there existed high costs to slave breeding which would have eroded away all profit in the business (FE, I, pp. 83–86). Neither of these propositions is supported with evidence, with the exception of a claim that "[f]arms with high women-to-men slave ratios exhibit lower fertility rates than farms with equal

[32] Our quibbles are two: (1) Fogel and Engerman do not define what the *normal* sexual habits of slaves were, thus what does and what does not constitute "interference" is not clear; (2) whether slaves were raised for sale or for use by their owner does not seem to be relevant to the issue of breeding. Owners could be interested in fostering a high birth rate because they (or their children) would have had use for the labor. No sale need be intended.

[33] The information reported in this paragraph is drawn from Sutch [1975]. See also Engerman [1975] for a critique of Sutch's article. The criticism has not persuaded Sutch to alter his conclusions.

sex ratios" (FE, I, p. 83).[34] In fact, Sutch has shown that this is false.

Farms with women-to-men ratios between 1.1 and 3.0 exhibit significantly higher fertility than did farms with sex ratios between 1.0 and 1.1 and this was true in both the buying and the selling states. The peak fertility in the "breeding" states was reached at sex ratios in the range between 1.5 and 2.0 women per man and fell off somewhat on holdings with even more disproportionate ratios.[35] This decline may have been caused by the increased incidence of venereal disease (which can produce sterility) or by a form of passive resistance to the master's interference, as Fogel and Engerman suggest (FE, I, p. 84). But in any case, the fertility rate per *female* is not the relevant measure. The appropriate index to measure the impact of a sharply unequal sex balance on the economic return to the slaveholder is the ratio of children to *adults* of both sexes. The number of children per woman might decline at high women-to-men ratios, but yet the number of children produced for a given investment in adults could continue to increase. This seems to have been the case on the selling-state farms included in the Parker-Gallman sample. Table 4 reproduces the figures reported by Sutch.

Fogel and Engerman's conjecture that there were considerable costs to slave rearing which would offset the potential returns is no more than that, a conjecture. The risk of disease and the disruption of plantation discipline may have increased as ever-more-callous procedures were employed to increase the birth rate. However, Fogel and Engerman provide no estimate of the magnitude of these effects. In fact, their argument rests

[34] Fogel and Engerman do not cite their source, but clearly, it was Steckel ([1973], Chart I, p. 19), who shows a lower child-to-female ratio on Parker-Gallman farms where the women-to-men ratio exceeded 2 than on farms with ratios between 1.1 and 2. This measure is faulted by the absence of a correction for the age distribution of females (a 15-year-old girl is unlikely to have many children 5 or under), by the failure to compensate for the problems associated with the inclusion of farms with only one or two women (the women-to-men ratio on a farm with two women and one man is 2), and by the fact that the sex ratio was calculated for the entire population, including children, rather than solely for the adults.

[35] Sutch [1975], Table 12, p. 193.

Table 4:
The Ratio of Children, 0–14, to Adults, 15–44, in the Selling States,[a] by the Inverse Sex Ratio of Adults

Number of Women per Man, 15–44	Ratio of Children to adults[b]
greater than 3.0[c]	1.37
2.0 to 3.0	1.36
1.5 to 2.0	1.27
1.1 to 1.5	1.14
1.0 to 1.1	1.01
less than 1.0	0.99

[a] Maryland, Delaware, District of Columbia, Kentucky, South Carolina, Virginia, Tennessee, North Carolina, and Georgia.
[b] Based upon the Parker-Gallman sample of farms in 1860 with five or more female slaves, aged 15–44. Sample size: 248 farms.
[c] Includes farms with no men.

Source: Sutch [1975], Table 12, p. 193.

more on the small size of the estimated return to an increase in the birth rate than it does on the supposed costs.

> [N]et income from childbearing was only about 10 percent of the total net income earned by women during their childbearing years. Consequently, even if the fertility rates of females could have been raised by 25 percent, an increase that would have brought slave fertility above the level usually considered to be the biological maximum, the increase in annual net earnings per female slave would have been less than 2.5 percent, since not all income-earning *females* were in the childbearing ages. Furthermore, females accounted for only 40 percent of the net income attributable to slaves. Hence the maximum increase in net income per working slave, through attempts to manipulate fertility rates, would have been below one percent—or less than a dollar per year per slave (in dollars of 1850). This trivial increase in net income could easily have been offset by the effects of selective breeding on worker morale. [FE, I, pp. 83–84]

This argument is circular. It begins by assuming that *no* inducements to increased fertility were present and then hypothesizes an increase in fertility which would have taken it above "the biological maximum." In other words, it amounts to asserting that not much *more* profit could be earned from increasing the slaves' fertility because it was close to the biological maximum already. But suppose inducements to fertility were widespread; and, in fact, that "breeding" was the cause of the high birth rates observed. The appropriate question in that case would be: How much would the birth rate (and the profit rate) have fallen if breeding practices were stopped? Since the existence or nonexistence of widespread inducements to fertility is precisely the question at issue, the question should not be begged.

Not only is Fogel and Engerman's argument circular but also it is based upon an incorrect estimate of the fraction of a woman's earnings which are attributable to childbearing. The authors of *Time on the Cross* find that only 10 percent of the income of a slave woman was due to childbearing. This was based upon the value of a new-born infant computed from their study of slave prices (they rather curiously call this price the value of a "birthright") and the probability of a live birth in a given year taken from a stable population model (FE, II, pp. 83–84). They estimate the price of a new-born infant by extrapolating a "sixth order polynomial" fitted to paired observations on price and age of slaves culled from the probate inventories which they collected (FE, II, p. 80). This procedure, we suggest, greatly biased downward the value of a slave at birth.

In the first place, the observations on the value of infants which helped shape the polynomial in the neighborhood of age zero were primarily for children evaluated without their mother.[36] Since the absence of an infant's mother would greatly increase the risk of death, it would likely depress the value of the child.[37] In the second place, Fogel and Engerman adopted an

[36] Some of the children in the probate inventories had no mothers. Most small children were not assessed separately but included as a unit with their mother. In those few estates where separate values were set for children, the court's estimate was undoubtedly influenced by the sale price of infants sold without their mother, since no other ready means of estimating an infant's value was available.

[37] There is a related problem in evaluating women, 15–44. Since most women with children were assessed as a unit with their children, Fogel and

estimating procedure which did not weight all observations equally. All values for the price of slaves were first averaged for each age. Then the sixth-degree polynomial was fitted to the averages rather than to the original set of observations (FE, II, p. 80). Since there were many fewer price observations of very young slaves (FE, I, Fig. 15, p. 72), this procedure gives considerably more weight to those (biased) observations than they would have otherwise received. Third, the use of a sixth-degree polynomial to extrapolate the age-price profile to the zero-age axis also forced the estimated value of the new-born child below that which would have been obtained had a more flexible statistical technique been used. Examination of Fogel and Engerman's Figure 15 shows that the fitted curve falls below the *average* observations for the three lowest age groups (0, 1, and 2 years old) (FE, I, p. 72). The result is that the intercept computed falls considerably below the point that one might choose by eye. For example, we judge the average relative price of a new-born infant from the scatter of male-slave prices to have been close to 15 percent of the peak adult price. Fogel and Engerman's procedure gives only 3.5 percent. In terms of dollars, our reading suggests a price close to $150.00, not $30.60.[38]

Other estimates of the value of new-born infants are considerably higher than Fogel and Engerman's $30.60. For example, Olmsted reported the estimate of a Virginia planter that a child "was worth two hundred dollars . . . the moment it drew

---

Engerman's estimates of a slave woman's price in the prime childbearing years are based heavily upon women who, for some reason, were childless. Since such women would be worth less money, this procedure biases both the price and the net income estimates based on those prices downward. Fogel and Engerman estimate that women in their mid-twenties were worth only 80 percent of an average male of that age. Another major study of slave prices has found that prime-aged women were worth as much or more than men (Conrad and Meyer [1958], pp. 163–64, and Table 16, p. 165). Evans reported female prices ranging from 85 to 91 percent of male prices in the 1850s, though his comparison may be plagued by the same problem as Fogel and Engerman's (Evans [1962], Table 28, p. 225).

[38] The average of the male and female "birthright" for the Old South over the period 1846–55 is the figure given in the text (see Fogel and Engerman [1972], p. 9).

breath." Bancroft cites several sources to support his estimate that "each babe in arms added from $100 to $200 or more to the value of its slave mother." No less an authority than Lewis Gray noted: "In 1859 infants were valued at from $7 to $10 a pound," although "[s]ometimes the rule was to value an infant at a year's service of the mother." Since a slave woman could be hired for between $46 (in Virginia) and $120 (in Louisiana) and new-born infants weigh 6 to 10 pounds, Gray's rules suggest a value from 2 to 4 times that "computed" by Fogel and Engerman.[39]

Fogel and Engerman attempt further to discredit the "breeding hypothesis" by suggesting that the magnitude of the proceeds from interstate sales was unimportant relative to income derived from agriculture. They argue that slave sales "could hardly have been the margin between success and failure of plantation agriculture" (FE, I, p. 48). In this argument their economic logic is flawed. They compare their (incorrect) estimate of the net income derived from the interstate sale of slaves to the *gross* value of agricultural output. Since only a fraction of this gross output could be represented as net income, this comparison biases downward the importance of the interstate trade. A more appropriate estimate to make would be the fraction of the total profit derived from slave owning which could be attributed to out-of-state slave sales. Our calculations suggest that approximately 10 percent of the total return to slaveowners in the exporting states was derived from this source.[40] In Maryland the proportion would be about twice as large.

[39] Olmsted [1861], p. 53; Bancroft [1931], pp. 78, 55, and 79; Gray [1933], I, pp. 664–65; and USDA [1867], p. 416. Also see Weld [1839], p. 16.

[40] Fogel and Engerman's estimate of the annual rate of return earned by slaveowners is "about 10 percent on the market price of their bondsmen" (FE, I, p. 70; and II, p. 78). According to Sutch's estimates 1.08 percent of the slaves of the "selling" states were exported each year. In Maryland the proportion rose to twice that (Sutch [1975], Table 2, p. 178). Calderhead [1972] suggests that 50 percent of the exported slaves were sold (p. 53). Since slaves who were sold were predominately in the prime-age class, they were worth on average approximately 56 percent more than the average slave. This number is based upon the age distribution of slaves in 1860; estimated age distribution of slaves exported (Sutch [1975], Table 3, p. 179); and Fogel and Engerman's relative price of slaves by age and sex (see Sutch

Calderhead's Maryland data suggest that a typical sale in the 1830s involved 2.5 slaves. Using Sutch's estimate of the average value of a slave sold ($800) and Fogel and Engerman's estimate of a 25 percent profit margin, the average "profit" per slaveholder who participated in the interregional slave trade was $500 per sale, undoubtedly a significant contribution to his total net income.[41] It does not seem implausible to suggest that for many slaveowners such sales *did* make the difference between success and failure.[42]

"Time on the Cross" and Sexual History

Very few of the pieces of evidence presented in *Time on the Cross*, and scarcely any of the inferences drawn from them

---

[1975], p. 178; and Ransom and Sutch [1975], Table 2, p. 12). Thus approximately a one percent annual rate of return on the exporting states' stock was earned through out-of-state sales.

[41] See Calderhead [1972], unnumbered table, p. 51. It should be noted as well that this calculation leaves out capital gains. During the 1850s the price of slaves rose 72 percent or 68 percent after adjustment for inflation (Sutch [1965], p. 225). Had this important effect been taken into account the profit rate would rise to over 55 percent and the net return from a typical sale would more than double.

[42] Fogel and Engerman also argue that there was no greater incentive to breeding in the poor-soil states than on virgin land in the New South as is usually maintained (FE, I, pp. 80–81). Their argument compares an improperly measured and interpreted estimate of the "value" of the child-bearing capacity of a female in the New South with a similar measure for the Old South (see Chapter 5 below). Even if their numbers were correct, their logic is flawed. These figures demonstrate only that breeding was profitable in both regions but do nothing to establish which region had a comparative advantage in slave rearing. Neither the absolute value (as long as it is positive) nor the relative fraction of the slave's price accounted for by "childbearing capacity" is relevant. Likewise, neither the absolute value nor the relative fraction of an automobile's price accounted for by the cigarette lighter is relevant to explain why some lighters are used frequently and others not at all. What would be relevant to the slave-breeding issue is the impact on the rate of return of a change in the decision whether or not to breed children. Since we have already discussed the "profit" from the sale of slaves, we shall not dwell upon this point here, beyond reaffirming our own opinion that differential incentives to breed did exist and reflected the two regions' comparative advantages.

concerning the sexual life of slaves or the sexual practices of their masters are salvageable. Fogel and Engerman's new quantitative data are meager, hopelessly biased, contradicted by other sources, and frequently distorted or misinterpreted. Their arguments are confused, circular, and so unsubtle as to be naïve. Some of their conclusions can be disproved, while others remain unsupported conjectures, in some cases fanciful speculations.

PART TWO

Institution and Economy

CHAPTER FIVE

Slavery: The Progressive Institution?

Paul A. David
and
Peter Temin

Time on the Cross brings to a close an historiographic cycle that began with the publication of Ulrich Bonnell Phillips's *American Negro Slavery* [1918]. According to Fogel and Engerman, the material conditions under which plantation slaves lived and worked compared favorably with those of free workers in the agriculture and industry of the time. Slavery was not a physically harsh, labor-degrading regime. Nor was it an unprofitable system irrationally supported by paternalistic planters. It was good business practice in a highly competitive industry to care for and seek to make the most productive use of the competent and industrious workforce—particularly when abusive treatment of so valuable an asset would be at the economic expense of the slaveowners themselves. The system that had grown up around the holding of human chattels, in their view, was not riddled with "internal economic contradictions" nor was it verging upon "collapsing under its own weight." On the eve of the Civil War, slavery was a commercially vigorous and highly efficient mode of agricultural production, and the slave plantations formed the leading sector in the rapidly developing regional economy of the antebellum South.

Obviously, *Time on the Cross* is an ambitious and imposing book. Unlike most works of the new economic history it has been featured in *Time, Newsweek* and many other popular journals and newspapers. The broad argument has been well projected to reach the general public, but the specific details of the authors' historical research are presented in a way that precludes comprehension by that readership. Indeed, much of the underlying technical economic and statistical methodology has been made so unnecessarily difficult to follow that without further elucidation it will remain inaccessible to all but a tiny number of the book's readers.

It is obligatory upon our profession, therefore, to furnish general historians and other scholars with an appraisal of *Time on the Cross* as a technical work of economic history. This chapter is part of that process of evaluation. It contains four sections. The first undertakes to restate Fogel and Engerman's theses in the context of the recent literature on Negro slavery in America. Their arrestingly novel assertions about the material treatment of the slaves, and the relative efficiency of agriculture based on slave labor are shown to occupy a central place in the logical design, as well as in the rhetorical fabric of the book. The second and third sections of the review accordingly examine the evidence adduced in support of each of these assertions, taking them in turn. Although the authors' text forcefully argues that by comparison with free workers the plantation slaves were materially well-off and highly productive, both claims appear to lack adequate scientific foundation. This is not just a matter of undue literary license having been taken in restating esoteric technical findings for popular consumption. The seemingly "neutral" numbers generated by Fogel and Engerman's quantitative methods carry a persistent bias, portraying slaveowners, and the conditions and work performance of the blacks they held in bondage, in a more favorable light than would be cast by a more complete analysis.

The fourth and concluding section turns from technical criticism of the evidence actually adduced, and questions the basic conceptual approach Fogel and Engerman have followed in re-evaluating the economic performance of the peculiar institution. Paradoxically, the authors of *Time on the Cross* appear to have adopted a framework of analysis that leads them systematically to overlook the economic essence of slavery, namely, that the slaves lost the freedom to exercise choices as producers and consumers.

The Argument in Its Historiographic Context

Fogel and Engerman do not help the reader to place their work on the economics of American Negro slavery within its larger historiographic context. They do not suggest that many of the "corrections" they would make in the neo-abolitionist portrayal of the peculiar institution form part of the broader reinterpretive trend in recent contributions to black history. The authors are promoting a particular methodological approach which they fervently oppose to the conventional, "un-social-scientific" study of history. This mission leads them to gloss over the ebb and flow of debate in the historical literature of the last three decades, and to construct a fictitious protagonist against whom the arsenal of quantitative methods can be shown off as totally devastating, and hence having a "revolutionary" impact upon the interpretation of slavery. Even C. Vann Woodward [1974] has felt obliged to record, in an otherwise uncritical review, that no historian has ever simultaneously held all the positions in "the traditional interpretation" against which Fogel and Engerman inveigh. Yet it is only against the actual historiographic background that the nature of their achievement can be properly grasped and assessed.

The considerable scholarship of Phillips and his followers was devoted to rehabilitating the progressive image of white supremacist society in the antebellum South; it provided a generally sympathetic and sometimes blatantly apologetic portrayal of slaveholders as a paternalistic breed of men. These planters, it turned out, had borne the economic (and ultimately the military) burden of trying to maintain a commercially moribund but socially benign institution; they had contributed to the making of America the control and instruction that was required for the gradual cultural and industrial acclimatization of inherently incompetent African savages. Through the perfection of plantation slavery the masters had managed a difficult problem of racial adjustment which had been thrust upon them by historical circumstances.

The reaction of the late 1930s and 1940s against the sort of racial bigotry that drew support from Phillips's work effected a complete reversal of the moral light in which the question of slavery was viewed. The vantage point correspondingly shifted from that of the master to that of his slave. The reversal culminated in Kenneth M. Stampp's *The Peculiar Institution* [1956], which rejected both the characterization of blacks as a biologically and culturally inferior, childlike people and the depiction of the white planters as paternal Cavaliers coping with a vexing social problem that was not of their own making. The slaveholders, said Stampp, had built the system consciously, bit by bit, decision by decision. They had done so for profit, and they had been duly rewarded. Despite the unspeakable oppression to which the resulting regime had subjected the slaves held within it, American blacks somehow had remained uncrushed in spirit. Their resistance was not that of mass rebellion, of vain insurrection, but a day-to-day affair: the meek, smiling ones who many thought were "contented though irresponsible" had protested their bondage "by shirking their duties, injuring the crops, feigning illness, and disrupting the routine." In the end the slave had remained unbroken as a person, "a troublesome property."

In 1958 Alfred Conrad and John R. Meyer's now-renowned paper on the economics of slavery provided rigorous support for the assertion by Stampp (and before him by Gray [1933]) that ownership of slaves represented a profitable private investment in the antebellum South. But it was Stanley Elkins's *Slavery: A Problem in American Institutional and Intellectual Life* [1959] that carried the rejection of Phillips still further. The personal and societal consequences flowing from the trauma of enslavement and the deprivations of slavery could not be comprehended within the terms of a mere point-by-point response to Phillips's account of a fundamentally genial regime rather like a boarding school. Think instead, suggested Elkins, of the phenomenon of mass personality distortion produced by a total institution like the Nazi concentration camp. Unfettered capitalism had created on the mainland of North America a peculiarly harsh and hopeless system of slavery, which left the typical bondsman broken in spirit—a psychologically "infantilized" inmate described by the stereotype of "Sambo."

From this high-water mark reached in the late 1950s, the tide of the anti-Phillips reaction began to recede. Comparative studies of slavery in the New World contradicted Elkins's presupposition that the Sambo stereotype was a peculiarity of the North American historical experience.[1] Doubts were raised about his assertion that the system of slavery developed there was—in its actual operation, as distinct from its legal provisions and restraints—significantly more "closed," and correspondingly more harsh than that which had evolved in Latin America. The *a priori* plausibility of this last comparative proposition appeared to be still further reduced by the results of Phillip Curtin's [1969] meticulous examination of the available quantitative evidence relating to the Atlantic slave trade. Of the Africans carried to the New World, all but a small fraction were absorbed in the comparatively high mortality environments of the Caribbean sugar islands and Brazil; yet those brought to the northern mainland not only reproduced themselves, but grew in number at a rate not very different from the free, white population.

The emphasis given by Stampp and Elkins to the masters' systematic recourse to physical cruelty and unrelieved material deprivations—in pursuit of the related objectives of profit and psychological domination of the blacks—also came in for criticism from Eugene D. Genovese. In *The Political Economy of Slavery* [1965], he suggested that the former interpretive emphasis improperly deflected attention from the pre-capitalistic, aristocratic, patriarchal aspects of the southern slaveowning class, and obscured the many paternalistic features of plantation life. Subsequently, in a bold reversal of Elkins, Genovese [1974] has argued that paternalism constituted the more serious, more insidious mode of assault upon the autonomy of black culture and the slave's personality.

This broadening line of counter-argument indicated that Elkins, and perhaps also Stampp, had under-represented the extent of the psychological and cultural breathing space which had been allowed American Negro slaves. J. W. Blassingame's

---

[1] Cf., for example, the essays by Sidney W. Mintz, Marvin Harris, David Brion Davis, Arnold S. Sio, and others in Foner and Genovese [1969].

The Slave Community [1972], based largely on a cautious
re-examination of published slave narratives, portrays plantation life as holding out positive incentives as well as providing
negative inducements to cooperate in the ostensible commercial
undertakings of the organization. Within the structure of
controls, moreover, the slaves found it possible to maintain
greater stability of family life than has often been supposed, as
well as to create and preserve their own religion, folklore, and
music.

However much the vantage point and the moral tone diverged
from that of Phillips, the paternalistic aspects which were so
prominent in his description of plantation life had thus begun to
make their way back into the historical literature during the
1960s. Recognition of these outwardly more genial qualities of
the peculiar institution now was enlisted in the effort to retrieve
for American *blacks* some "usable past," some reconstruction of
history that would leave them more than victims of a social
tragedy, brutally infantilized, cut off from their cultural roots,
dependent upon white society.[2]

For this purpose, however, a full rehabilitation of the system
of slavery did not seem required. Indeed, Genovese's attention
to planter paternalism was initially coupled with his dismissal of
Stampp's and Conrad and Meyer's point about the private
profitability of slaveownership as unilluminating; in *The Political Economy of Slavery* he sought to recast in Marxian terms the
traditional Phillipsian representation of slavery as an economically dysfunctional system of production. In the resulting
account of southern "backwardness," the derived precapitalist
ideology of the ruling planter class, the unsuitability of the
mode of plantation organization for the conduct of diversified
farming, and slavery's distorting effects upon the distribution of
income and the structure of demand within the region, all
served to obstruct the economic modernization of the South. The
slaveholders made, and ultimately fought vainly to preserve, a
quasi-feudal political and social order based upon a distorted,
non-progressive economy; the era of the planters' hegemony and
tutelage hardly could have been expected to provide Afro-

[2] Cf. Davis [1974], pp. 9–10, for this imputation of purpose.

Americans with any useful preparation for assuming a place in modern urban-industrial society, even if it had allowed them some considerable decency and dignity in the terms of their bondage.

Time on the Cross has finished the work of up-ending Elkins and Stampp. It asserts that through the unseen operation of competitive market forces a private vice, the planter's greed for profit, became a (comparative) social virtue. Unfettered capital-ism in America thus led to a form of slavery which was peculiarly benign insofar as concerns the social and material circumstances of its human chattel. Equipped with this explanation for the manifestations of paternalism so central to Phillips's view of plantation life, the authors turn on Genovese and proceed to marshall the research of many other economic historians in order to contradict his representation of the antebellum southern economy as necessarily backward and stagnant.

Much of this second aspect of their thesis therefore should be familiar enough to professional readers. Richard Easterlin's [1961] compilation of regional income estimates for the United States had shown us that the economy of South as a whole was not falling behind the rest of the nation in the period 1840–60, and that within the region high levels of Gross National Product (GNP) per capita had been attained on the eve of the Civil War. Charles Wesley's [1927] work on the urban Negro labor force, Robert Evans's [1962] study of the slave hire market, and, more recently, Robert Starobin's *Industrial Slavery in the Old South* [1970] provided ample evidence that slaves could be and were utilized in non-agrarian pursuits. Studies of the distribution of income and wealth in the antebellum period by Robert Gallman [1969] and Lee Soltow [1971] suggested that the degree of inequality among the free population was not notably greater in the South than in the North. The effect of the presence of the planter class in the rural South was counterbalanced by the comparative smallness of the southern urban population, urban wealth-holding being typically more concentrated than rural, irrespective of region.

Although there is much room for disagreement and debate over the interpretation of this evidence, Fogel and Engerman adhere to the views enunciated in their earlier published works.[3] *Time on the Cross* comes down unequivocally in favor of the judgment that Southern prosperity in the 1850s, and the rapid growth of production recorded in the interval between the censuses of 1840 and 1860, not only typified the region's past course of development, but betokened also its capacity for sustained rapid growth and economic modernization.

To this sweeping revision of Genovese's picture of the slaveholders' economic milieu, *Time on the Cross* adds two arrestingly bold and essentially novel propositions. Both have a close connection with the authors' contention that the material conditions of life and labor were not especially harsh or degrading to the typical plantation slave. First, it is their view that the consumption standards at which slaves were maintained compared favorably with those of contemporaneous free agricultural labor in the South and, indeed, even approached the economic condition of urban industrial workers in the North during the latter half of the nineteenth century. Were this so, the direct transfer of income (to the free population as a whole) effected by slavery, itself could not have caused a very pronounced additional skewing of the overall distribution of income within the South.

The second novel proposition is that as an agricultural system plantation slavery was more efficient in its use of the factors of production than the free family farm typical of the North. Fogel and Engerman assign economies of scale only partial responsibility for the greater measured productivity of southern plantation agriculture. Instead they argue that the comparative industriousness and personal efficiency of the Afro-American laborers vis-à-vis the free work force must have been the principal cause underlying their findings on this score. The conclusion complements the proposition that the typical slave was a well-cared-for productive asset.

[3] Compare Fogel and Engerman [1971], Chap. 24 ("The Economics of Slavery"), esp. pp. 333–38, with FE, I, PP. 247–57. In dismissing the criticisms of their position on the growth of the southern economy advanced by "one scholar" (un-named), the authors (p. 252) appear to be referring to Woodman [1972], esp. pp. 338–39, although this article does not appear in Fogel and Engerman's bibliography. Woodman's criticism, in any case, has not been adequately answered in *Time on the Cross.*

Having stood both Elkins and Stampp on their heads as far as concerns the harshness of slavery under pure capitalism, and having concluded that black bondsmen must have been more efficient workers than free whites, Fogel and Engerman are thus in a position to dismiss the Sambo stereotype as utterly without objective basis in either the circumstances or behavior of the typical slave. They brand it as merely another pernicious myth, created as much by the latent prejudices of abolitionist propagandists as by the open bigotry of southern white supremacists. Even Frederick Law Olmsted gets some knocks here for "racial prejudices" and "northern chauvinism." Moreover, *Time on the Cross* is not above detecting subtle traces of lingering racism, or at best an insensitivity to the poisoning of race relations, in those neoabolitionist historians who would perpetuate the denigration of blacks' performance as slaves by attributing it not to biological inferiority but, alternatively, to mass infantilization or evasive non-collaboration.[4]

The paradox of *Time on the Cross* is that its laudable announced aim of rectifying a historiographic injustice and restoring to American Negroes today a source of justifiable pride in their cultural heritage has led the authors to the excesses of an utterly sanguine reappraisal of the peculiar institution. The commercial success of capitalistic slavery somehow emerges as the most fitting subject for modern black pride.

[4] "The principal cause of the persistence of the myth of black incompetence in American historiography is racism." Thus begins the section of the text headed "Toward an Explanation for the Persistence of the Myth of Black Incompetence," on page 223 of FE I. Eight pages later: "What, of course, is common to Stampp and Elkins is agreement on the characteristics of slave behavior: slaves lie, steal, feign illness, behave childishly, and shirk their duties. Indeed, this characterization has been one of the enduring constants in the literature on slavery." The innuendos carried by the wording of Fogel and Engerman's excruciatingly labored critique of Stampp's *Peculiar Institution*, in FE II, Appendix C, are especially unfortunate: "Stampp's inadequate definition of black accomplishments under slavery may have been related to his approach to the issue of racism. While Stampp unequivocally rejected the contention that Negroes were *biologically* inferior to whites, he did not consider how [racism] might have affected the views of both the "eyewitnesses" and the historians that he invoked as authorities. . . . Stampp reported as fact, untinged by racism, Olmsted's description of slaves as 'chronic' malingerers . . ." (FE, II, pp. 234–35. Emphasis added).

Few readers will miss the irony that this book, whose passionate title is meant to convey the depth of the authors' moral condemnation of slavery, in substance actually transcends even U. B. Phillips's rehabilitative intentions. Cool, detached social science, we are told, requires one to face up to the fact that Negro slavery in its time was a "vigorous, deeply entrenched, and rapidly growing economic system"—indeed, putting "purely moral" considerations aside, a comparatively benign institutional arrangement worthy of a progressive America (FE, II, p. 16). The revelation of what Fogel and Engerman construe to have been "the record of black achievement under adversity" seemingly demands nothing less than a historical work "which would," to quote David Brion Davis, "in most respects bring a smile of approval from the grim lips of John C. Calhoun." [5]

The keystones of this reinterpretive edifice, and the proximate sources of the rhetorical confusions which impart to the book a puzzling and paradoxical quality, are not hard to locate. They are found in the assertions Fogel and Engerman advance concerning the material conditions of the slaves' lives, and the latters' willing, industrious efficiency as workers. These two propositions, as we already have seen, underlie the truly novel arguments which *Time on the Cross* contributes to revising the macro-economic portrait of the antebellum South as a backward agrarian region. Further, taken in combination with Stampp's and Conrad and Meyer's point about the private profitability of slave-ownership, these same propositions form the empirical basis upon which Fogel and Engerman construct new characterizations for the *dramatis personae*. The patriarchal Cavalier has been turned into the shrewd master, an enlightened capitalistic manager of personnnel. And Sambo's place is now occupied by the keen, "achieving" slave who strives for some measure of self-improvement within the considerable breathing space allowed him by competitive capitalism.[6]

[5] Davis [1974], p. 11.
[6] The role of these new characterizations in the overall structure of *Time on the Cross*, and the use of economic arguments to support them, are discussed in Chapter 1, above. For discussion of the implicit models of slave socialization and master-slave relations embraced by Fogel and Engerman, and their use of demographic data and conventional historical sources on these questions, see also Chapters 2–4, above.

What evidence and arguments support these two tenets of Fogel and Engerman's bold reinterpretation? Are these, perhaps, the "most telling revisions" which "turn on technical mathematical points, points which despite their obscurity are vital to the correct description and interpretation of the slave economy"? Just how have they been derived from "the new techniques and hitherto neglected sources" which the authors rather dauntingly allude to in their opening chapter, "Slavery and the Cliometric Revolution"?

Alas, the full text of *Time on the Cross* may be studied endlessly without learning the answers to these questions. To understand how this could be, one first must grasp the format of the book. It is presented in two volumes, the first (FE, I) being the text and an index thereto, the other (FE, II) comprising a bibliography and various appendices—including, as Appendix B, an extended set of technical notes pertinent to assertions made in the text.

Although the reader of the text is initially cautioned to "keep in mind [the] distinction between the principal findings of the cliometricians and our attempt to interpret them" (FE I, p. 10), this is not so easily done when only "interpretations" are being presented. We do not allude here to the deep epistemological problems raised by Fogel and Engerman's desire to distinguish cleanly between findings of "fact" and their "interpretation." A more immediate difficulty is that the findings of other historians, as well as their new empirical results described in Appendix B, are not invariably reported in the same terms by the narrative discussion of the text. The "primary volume" of *Time on the Cross* offers a popularized account, which has only slightly more of a claim to represent faithfully the nature of the authors' own research contributions than were it to have been prepared by someone else altogether.

Fogel and Engerman's text itself is utterly unencumbered by documentation. Curiously, conventional historians who initially have reviewed the first volume seem to have been so unnerved by "the rattle of electronic equipment," and the tramping legions of research assistants "heard off stage," that they failed to complain of this omission. The absence of footnotes, bibliographic citations, discussion of sources, explicit mention of methodological problems, in short, of the standard critical apparatus of works of professional history is intended on this occasion "to encourage the widest possible discussion of the findings of the cliometricians" (FE, I, pp. 11–12). But a heavy burden thereby has been placed upon any scholar who undertakes to inform "popular" discussions by critically examining these findings and relating them to the authors' conclusions.

The problem is that the second volume, subtitled *Evidence and Methods*, does not simply set out the bushels of footnotes which, one might imagine, had studded an original, unpruned version of the text. The author's introductory essay (Appendix A) on the roles of ideology, humanism, and science in the historical study of slavery discloses that only as much as they have been able to learn about slavery using the method of the social sciences, and no more, has been set down in Appendix B. Yet, to produce the reinterpretation offered by their first volume, something more was needed:

> We were obliged to invoke assumptions which, though plausible, cannot be verified at present, and to rely on additional evidence which is too fragmentary to be subjected to systematic statistical tests. [FE, II, 4]

One has to turn to Appendix B remembering that it does not pretend to document the text in full, but only the portions (extensive as they are) for which Fogel and Engerman have felt themselves able to present a suitably social-scientific basis.

And on these, Appendix B proves to be tough going indeed. Throughout the appendices the authors deploy an elaborate, sometimes bewildering system of internal cross-references and numerical bibliographic citations whose general effect is accurately conveyed by the following item [FE, II, p. 120]:

> 4.11.1 The various points on the curve in Figure 41 are the values of the right-hand terms of equation 4.7 for each value of t from 9 to 75. The values of the variables entering equation 4.7 were estimated in the manner described in 3.4.9 and 4.10.1, except that an allowance of 26 per cent was added to basic income to cover the average amount of "extra" income received by slaves (see 6.7.1.2). The resulting figure ($42.99) was the average value of M. Atwater's weights [366, pp. 52–53] were used to convert the average value of M into age and sex specific values.

Quite obviously, Appendix B has not been written for anyone to sit down and read. It is neither a full set of conventional footnotes nor a self-contained technical monograph that can justly be evaluated on its own merits. It does not make available to other historians any of the original data from the probate records or the manuscript censuses upon which Fogel and Engerman have drawn. Far from undertaking to explain to conventional historians the cliometric methods which the authors espouse, the logic of their economic arguments (and their demographic analyses, about which we need say little in this chapter) is made unnecessarily hard to follow, and the descriptions of the actual quantitative methods employed oscillate between the extremes of frustrating imprecision and ostentatious overformalism.

But, the details of Fogel and Engerman's difficult second volume, and the mysteries of Appendix B in particular, must be our main preoccupation. For it is to these that one is directed by the sorts of questions which the professional historian—and, most of all, the methodologically threatened "conventional" historian—will rightly want to have answered before he goes on to consider the more subtle problems of historical interpretation posed by *Time on the Cross*.[7] Clearly it is important to know how seriously to take the authors' prefatory admonitions to keep in mind the difference between the cliometric "findings" discussed by the supporting technical volume, and their attempt in the text at a broader interpretation of the historical experience of American Negro slavery. But it is no less vital to determine whether the claim implied in this warning can be safely accepted. Has cliometrics really provided startling "findings of fact" about which there is little room for argument? Do the key empirical propositions advanced by Fogel and Engerman—those regarding the comparatively favorable material conditions of life, and the greater efficiency of slave labor—possess an

---

[7] C. Vann Woodward ([1974], pp. 3, 6), observing that Fogel and Engerman's second volume, *Evidence and Methods*, "is given over to documentation, defense of method, algebraic equations, tables and graphs, and computer language [of which we find none] beyond the comprehension of laymen," voices this hope; "Their findings, their data, and their methods should have the most thorough and unsparing criticism . . . , especially [by] those who speak their own language."

objective "scientific" status that derives from the methods employed in securing them?

The remainder of this chapter is geared to respond to these questions. From the detailed examination of the authors' evidence and methods on the material treatment and the productive efficiency of slaves, presented in the two following sections, we think it will become apparent just how unwarranted it is to accept their empirical "findings" as scientifically incontrovertible. But the closing section of the chapter takes up the still more fundamental point that many of the defects revealed by a close reading of the supporting, technical volume turn out to be conceptual rather than narrowly methodological. No greater degree of analytical rigor or meticulousness of scholarship on the authors' part could really have redeemed the claim to have arrived at an ethically neutral economic appraisal of the "performance" of a social institution, let alone the institution of chattel slavery. The entire conception of producing a "scientifically objective" or "value free" reappraisal of the economic welfare consequences of slavery seems to us to be peculiarly ill-founded. For the ethical and behavioral premises upon which modern economic welfare analysis rests are immediately inconsonant with the degree of personal involition which remains the defining attribute of the institution in question. In this respect, we shall argue, the strain of paradox and confusion which runs through *Time on the Cross* involves more than a mere problem of rhetoric.

Methods and Evidence on Material Treatment

The material side of the slaves' treatment is approached by Fogel and Engerman from three vantage points. First, indexes of the absolute standard of living are matched against those relating to free workers in other regions and periods during the nineteenth century. Second, the average income retained by slaves—which is to say, the value of their consumption—is compared to the income of free agricultural workers. Finally, the relationship between the value of slave consumption and slave production is considered, indicating what part of the fruits of their labor was taken from them. In taking up these points in turn, fullest and most careful attention will be reserved for the third. For it best illustrates the way that the text of *Time on the Cross* simplifies for "popular" presentation some intricate, novel, and far from uncontroversial quantitative analyses which the authors report in their "secondary" volume.

The material conditions under which Negro slaves lived are suggested by several indexes: dietary standards, clothing allotments, housing space, medical care, and rates of mortality.[8] The attempt at a systematic quantitative reappraisal is carried furthest in the case of the first of these, and the findings reported by Fogel and Engerman on this score are the most original as well as the most impressive. No serious historian of American Negro slavery has suggested that black bondsmen typically were kept at a starvation level. Stampp decided that instances "of deliberate stinting of rations were fortunately few; and the imbalance of the average slave's diet resulted from ignorance more often than penuriousness" on the masters' part.[9] Still, one may be surprised by Fogel and Engerman's conclusion that slaves in 1860 had excellent diets, surpassing the average diet of free Americans in 1879 by ten percent as far as concerns caloric content, and that typical slave diets were *nutritionally* adequate even by modern-day standards (FE, I, pp. 113–15).

Rather than relying on the information that can be culled from plantation records, instructions to overseers, or the southern agricultural press, the authors have developed figures for the food quantities comprising the average slave diet on a systematically selected sample of plantations, by making use of the so-called "disappearance method." In their variant of this statistical procedure, the total amount of each food item available for slave consumption is obtained as a residual from data on production and estimates of other utilization for the representative plantation, and the result is then divided by the representative number of resident plantation slaves. Thus "other utilization" should include not only what was set aside

---

[8] Chapter 6 of this volume presents a detailed critique which reveals a pervasive pattern of bias toward overstatement of the slaves' lot in respect to each of several indexes considered in *Time on the Cross*. We comment here only on the question of slave diets.

[9] Stampp [1956], p. 288.

for seed and livestock feed, and what was shipped from the plantation in processed or unprocessed form, but also some allowance for the "homegrown" foodstuffs retained for use at the table of the plantation's white residents. To deal with the difficult problems of estimating off-plantation sales of foodstuffs and non-slave consumption, Fogel and Engerman have selected (from the Parker-Gallman 1860 manuscript census sample[10] a sub-sample of plantations designed to minimize the quantitative importance of these non-slave consumption uses:

> In order to be able to separate free from slave consumption, we derived our estimates from a sample of large slave plantations (over 50 slaves). In order to separate consumption on these plantations from the sales of surpluses to cities, we further restricted the sample to plantations that were in counties at least 50 wagon miles away from the nearest cities. [FE, II, p. 94]

For good measure, however, they reduce the estimated production of beef and pork, which well might have been salted and barreled for shipment to more distant markets, and they deduct generous additional allowances for the consumption of meat and milk by the resident white population (Cf. FE, II, p. 95).

Two problems concerning this procedure come immediately to mind. First, the derived figures purport to show the average slave diet. Not all slaves would have consumed this diet, and the relationship between the average diet and the diet of any particular slave is unclear. The procedures used by Fogel and Engerman could easily be extended to provide an estimate of variance[11] in the average diet from one plantation to the next, but other methods would have to be employed to determine seasonal and longer temporal variations. Fogel and Engerman have followed Conrad and Meyer's [1958] methodological lead here, in concentrating on the slave *system* rather than individual slaves or plantations. Nonetheless, a little more attention to individual variations in the quality of slave life would have been illuminating.

[10] Data on a sample of southern farms compiled from the manuscript census by Professors William Parker and Robert Gallman using both the population and agricultural enumerations. For further details of this sample, cf. [1970] especially the articles by Gallman, Foust and Swan, and Wright.

[11] "Variance" is a statistical measure of the dispersion in the size of a variable around its average value.

Second, given that the authors make generous allowances for the food consumption of the resident whites, the rationale for restricting the sample to large plantations, holding more than 50 slaves, is not entirely persuasive. Less than one-fourth of all slaves lived on plantations in this size class, according to the statistics compiled by Lewis C. Gray (see FE, II, p. 144, for Gray's tabulations). Further work is needed to show that the average diet estimated by the disappearance method for this sample was typical of the standard at which the whole slave population lived. Since Fogel and Engerman find that there were considerable apparent economies of scale in plantation agriculture (i.e., that larger farms were more efficient than smaller ones) (FE, I, pp. 192–93), the suspicion may be entertained that slaves on large plantations ate better than some others.[12]

Such reservations notwithstanding, it would appear that the estimates Fogel and Engerman present for the caloric value of the diets of slaves in 1860 are considerably better grounded than the 1879 estimates for the free population with which they are compared. M. K. Bennett and R. H. Peirce, the authors of the study from which Fogel and Engerman obtained the latter figures, also employed the "disappearance method" in estimating per capita consumption of cereals and other vegetable foodstuffs from the United States. But 30 percent of estimated calorie consumption was derived from estimated consumption of "major animal products" about which Bennett and Peirce themselves express the most serious reservations.[18] In approximating per capita consumption of beef, lean pork, and bacon and salt side around 1879, they simply extrapolated their 1909/1911 estimates on the per capita ratios of hogs on farms and cattle on farms without making any adjustments for changes in livestock

---

[12] It may be noted that Fogel and Engerman's concentration on large plantations might have been suggested by Stampp's assertion that, in the quality or variety of food given, there were no "appreciable differences" in the practices of large and small slaveholders. But why take this for granted when all else is being cast into doubt?

[13] Cf. Bennett and Peirce [1962]. The methodological supplement is referred to in the published Bennett-Peirce [1961] study which Fogel and Engerman cite (FE, II, p. 98).

weights or slaughter/inventory ratios. And in the case of whole milk consumption, a more important source of calories than any other among the animal products group, Bennett and Peirce have said that their figures (reproduced without qualification or comment in FE, II, p. 94) represent "no more than reasoned conjectures" prepared "on the slenderest basis."

It is, therefore, somewhat unclear as to whether the figure of 4100 calories given as the energy value of the typical slave diet and the 3700 calories estimated for Americans in 1879 overstate or understate the actual average daily rates of food consumption. But the meaning one should attach to the results of this comparison—even if the true average calorie intakes of these two quite different populations had been established—is still less obvious than it might at first appear.

There is reason to suppose that on the average plantation slaves in every age- and sex-class (above age 10) were more active and consequently would have higher energy *requirements* than the corresponding groups in the free population.[14] This is so both because the age- and sex-specific labor for participation rates were higher for the slave population and because the kind of work in which rural, plantation slaves were engaged was physically more strenuous than that of the average member of the entire American workforce in 1879.[15] A modern textbook of physiology reports the following *occupational* differences in (adult male) energy requirements: 2000–2400 calories per day suffice for a shoemaker, 2700–3200 for a carpenter or mason, 3200–4100 for a (free) farm laborer, and so on, with over 5000 calories being required by a lumberman.[16] Thus, after due adjustment for differences in demographic and occupational

[14] Since we are not told anything about the age- and sex-composition of the slave population represented in the sample studied by Fogel and Engerman, we cannot say whether there were proportionately more adult males—whose calorie *requirements* exceed those of women and children—than was the case for the 1879 U.S. population as a whole.

[15] In this connection it would be interesting to know what proportion of the slave force (on the large isolated plantations comprising Fogel and Engerman's sample) were house servants rather than field hands.

[16] Cf. the data from Tigerstedt's *Textbook of Physiology* reproduced in Sherman ([1946], p. 190).

distributions, it might well turn out that the averages reported by Fogel and Engerman are consistent with members of the slave population having a *lower* caloric intake relative to their needs than comparable members of the free northern population.

Indeed, when caloric requirements are considered, it seems quite possible that southern slaves might have been suffering from some measure of food energy deprivation. Comparatively little seems to be known about the effect of food energy deprivation (calorie deficits) at levels which are neither drastic nor accompanied by serious shortage of essential nutrients. In some experiments made before World War I with healthy young male subjects, a gradual reduction of food energy intake to levels about a third below what they would have consumed resulted in the lowering of body weight and basal metabolism per unit of weight, combined with "perhaps a somewhat intangible saving of energy in the muscular activities of everyday life." [17] Adoption of more languid movements, perhaps. Taking place under unstressed conditions, these organic adaptations reportedly "seemed to involve no mental or physical cost except for *a somewhat vague lowering of animal spirits.*" At the risk of belaboring the point, it may be suggested that the "optimum" dietary standard for slaves which the rational southern planter is supposed to have sought to establish, would not be determined solely by considering the fuel *needs* of "the human engine." His slaves were also men, and setting their rations with a view to achieving some "lowering of animal spirits" could have effected a saving of supervisory and police costs—without entailing much loss in routine work performance.

These comparisons in terms of energy equivalents may be contrasted with Fogel and Engerman's comparison of the value of slave consumption with the value of free farm income. The difference is a substantive one, and we must be reminded that calories and welfare are only loosely related. It is well known that a nutritionally adquate diet can be secured today for far

[17] Sherman ([1946], pp. 195–96), reporting on the findings of G. F. Benedict and his co-investigators.

less than most of us spend on food. The extra expenses, we assume, are for satisfactions beyond calories and vitamins. Slaves, even if they were getting a nutritionally balanced diet, were not able to indulge these other food-related desires as were free men. Sweet potatoes and "pot-likker" may have been healthy, but were they the preferred diet of free men? More formally, free men allocated their food expenditures in accordance with their tastes. Since slaves were not able to reallocate their expenditures to the extent that free men could, the slave welfare represented by a calorie of food was less than the welfare represented by a calorie in a free man's diet. One might well have asked: At what (low) levels of real income does the preponderance of carbohydrates and fats in diets of free men approach that found in the average diet of southern Negro slaves? [18]

Using the value of consumption rather than nutritional equivalents does not completely remove this problem. But the ranking of foods reflected in market prices undoubtedly was closer to the tastes of slaves than the nutritional ranking, and the use of values gets closer to the question of slave welfare. Among the "Paradoxes of Forced Labor" presented by the final chapter of *Time on the Cross*, there appears the following puzzle:

> Odd as it may seem, the optimal combination [from the slaveholder's viewpoint] of force and pecuniary income was one that left slaves on large plantations with *more* pecuniary income per capita than they would have earned if they had been free small farmers. [FE, I, p. 239]

To support this, Fogel and Engerman immediately refer readers

> to appendix B, where it is shown that the average pecuniary income actually received by a *prime field hand* was roughly 15 per cent greater

[18] This point can be made more broadly. The relationship of the value of foodstuffs to that of the other consumption goods and services alloted to slaves is considerably higher than that observed among the poorest free families in nineteenth-century America. This difference in "budget structure" presumably reflected a choice on the part of the masters, rather than peculiar preference of slaves. According to Engel's Law, the proportion of income spent on food falls as income rises. Only free men poorer than the poorest free men in nineteenth-century America would have allocated their expenditures in the manner attributed to slaves by Fogel and Engerman.

> than the income he would have received for his labor as a free
> agricultural worker. [Emphasis added]

Appendix B however, says something else: "In other words, the
labor income of the slave *family* was 15 percent larger than the
labor income of the corresponding free *family*" (FE, II, p. 158,
emphasis added). What are we to make of the discrepancy?

What the authors have done is to construct a slave family of
the same size (6.48 persons) and demographic structure as the
typical free southern cotton belt farm represented in the
Parker-Gallman sample drawn from the 1860 manuscript census. The estimated total slave income (basic maintenance and
extra earnings from the produce of slave "patches") which a
group of this size and composition would receive was then
computed,[19] and compared with the estimated *labor* income of
the typical free southern farm in the cotton belt.

It is generally acknowledged that the rates of labor force
participation and the length of the hours worked per year were
significantly greater for the women and children of the slave
population than for corresponding members of free farm
households. From this it follows that the income earned *by a
(male) prime field slave* was certainly *not* greater than the labor
income of his free counterpart by as much as 15 percent—if
indeed it exceeded the latter at all.[20] Moreover, the labor income
of the free southern farm family to which Fogel and Engerman
refer represents only 58 percent of the total income of their

[19] Cf. FE, II, pp. 159–60. Using "Atwater's weights" (we presume), the authors
have adjusted their ($42.99) figure for per capita slave income slightly
upward, to allow for the difference between the age-sex composition of the
constructed family group and that of the representative plantation population
—to which the average maintenance and extra income allowances refer.
"Atwater's weights," to which cryptic reference is made by the section
(4.11.1) we have quoted from Appendix B (on p. 176 above), receive more
explicit attention below.
[20] See below, pp. 211–12, for discussion of the differences in hours worked by
the free and slave labor force. We reckon that a *minimum* adjustment on this
account would indicate that the slave work force put in 16 to 22 percent more
male equivalent manhours *per worker* than the free southern agricultural
labor force. In addition to this, one must consider the higher proportion of the
women and children in the rural slave population that were part of the work
force.

farm. The other 42 percent is imputed as a return to farm capital.[21] Yet, the dominant part of the free farm's capital represented the fruits of the past labor of its owners in activities such as land clearing, fencing, house- and barn-raising. Fogel and Engerman's imputation seriously understates the actual share of average gross income which a farm family might expect to derive from the acquisition and improvement of land.

The resolution of this "paradox of forced labor" is thus simple. When free southern farm folk refrained from volunteering for slavery, they were *not* sacrificing pecuniary income in order to avoid the unpleasantries of "gang labor," as the authors would have us believe. The puzzle which seemed to require the latter style of explanation is wholly of Fogel and Engerman's own manufacture. For their textual representation of the situation implicitly assumes that the women and children of free farm families were putting in the same labor effort as was exacted from their enslaved counterparts, and further supposes that under freedom it would not be possible for a man to acquire property by retaining the fruits of his labor—or to reap windfall capital gains on lands wrested at little non-labor cost from the American wilderness. True, racism and economic power relations in the Reconstruction South militated against the full participation of black freemen in this process. But that is a *different* tragedy. It provides no reason to implicitly depict the free (white) farm folk of the antebellum era as a landless agrarian proletariat whose pecuniary compensation was on average exceeded by that of slaves fortunate enough to find themselves working on large plantations.

We turn now to the ratio between slave consumption and slave production. This is discussed in terms of its complement, "the rate of expropriation," which is treated as a part of the total "exploitation" of slaves in the first volume (FE, I, pp. 5, 153), but is labeled "the rate of exploitation" in Appendix B (FE, II, p. 124). The way this concept is used can be seen from the

---

[21] This imputation is based on the results of statistically estimating a cross-section Cobb-Douglas production function (for all southern farms and plantations in the Parker-Gallman sample) in which there turned out to have been some significant scale economies. Cf. FE, II, pp. 133, 143.

ninth, and perhaps the most counter-intuitive of the revisionist conclusions listed in the Prologue to the text. We quote it in full:

> 9. Slaves were exploited in the sense that part of the income which they produced was expropriated by their owners. However, the rate of expropriation was much lower than has generally been presumed. Over the course of his lifetime, the typical slave field hand received about 90 percent of the income he produced. [FE, I, pp. 5–6]

The phrasing rather startlingly suggests that close to 10 percent (actually, 12 percent) of all the revenues that the typical slave produced would be taken by his master. This, however, is not the case.

Chapter 4, where this "finding" is discussed in more detail, introduces the concept of the "expected present value" (alternatively called the "average accumulated value") of the income expropriated. What is being taken by the masters appears in this context to be the *value at the time of the slave's birth* of the anticipated future revenues that he will produce, less the anticipated future cost of his maintenance. It is this amount, represented as a fraction of the value at birth of the anticipated future revenues which yields the 10–12 percent "rate of exploitation" (cf. FE, I, p. 153, and II, p. 124).

The quantities involved in the comparison, then, are less than the simple totals of the slave revenue and maintenance costs, because a dollar of income produced or expended in the future is worth less than that at present. The higher is the rate of interest which might be earned on an investment made in the present, and the further removed into the future is the anticipated dollar of receipts of disbursements, the smaller will be its value in the present—its present value. Thus, a dollar taken from a slave during his youth must count for more in the present value of all such expropriations than does a dollar taken still later in his life.

For the first decade or so of a slave's life, however, the costs of caring for him exceeded the value of the revenue he produced; only thereafter would he yield a positive net revenue. In reckoning the present value of net revenues anticipated at the time of birth, each dollar of *negative* net revenue (as it is incurred during the slave's childhood) counts more heavily than each dollar of the positive net revenue taken in his adulthood.

The importance of this discounting scheme may be gauged from the following fact, gleaned from Appendix B: Corresponding to the 10–12 percent exploitation rate referred to in Fogel and Engerman's text, the ratio of the simple (*un*discounted) sum of expected net revenues to the simple sum of expected total revenues is reported as 49 percent.[22]

Let us, for the moment, defer consideration of which of these two ratios is really conceptually the more appropriate measure of the degree to which the typical slave was economically "exploited." For it seems, both from the foregoing and from Fogel and Engerman's discussion, that before they could get to the stage of choosing whether or not to discount the net revenues, they first had to assemble historical estimates of the typical revenue and consumption expenditure streams throughout the full life cycle of a slave, and then appropriately reduce the net revenue at every age by the (declining) portion of a representative cohort of newborn slaves who could be expected to survive to each age. This, however, is not the case.

Instead, the authors argue that in a competitive market for slaves the equilibrium price of a newborn slave (which they call the "value of a birthright") could not be substantially different from the sum of discounted expected net revenues over his lifetime[23] (Cf. FE, II, pp. 58–59, 83). Thus, if we are prepared to grant their unverified assumption that the market for slaves was in competitive equilibrium, Fogel and Engerman have ingeniously managed to finesse a formidable research task by using the average market price of a newborn slave instead of

[22] Cf. FE, Vol. II, p. 125 (sect. 4.11.6.2). The 49 percent figure in question appears to be correct, despite the fact that the algebraic formula for it is confusingly given (incorrectly) as: $B/\sum \lambda_t R_{gt}$, where λ_t is the average survival rate to the t*th* year, R_{gt} is the gross revenue in the t*th* year and B is the "birthright." Instead of B, elsewhere defined as a *discounted* magnitude [B = $\sum \lambda_t (R_{gt} - M_t)/(1 + i)^t$], in this context Fogel and Engerman obviously meant to refer to $B° \equiv \sum \lambda_t (R_{gt} - M_t)$. Notice that, like the discounting factor $(1 + i)^{-t}$, the survival frequency (λ_t) declines with increasing t and therefore it too accords heaviest weight to the (early) negative entries in the net revenue stream. We return to this point later in the text, following explanation of the way Fogel and Engerman have estimated the net revenues, $(R_g - M)_t$.

[23] In the same way, the value of a plot of land equals the present value of the net income to be derived from it.

calculating the numerator of their ratio expression for the "exploitation" rate.[24] But two distinct qualifications must be noted.

In the first place, the estimate of the value of a birthright does not derive from *market* prices at which actual transactions in newborn infant slaves were concluded. It was, instead, obtained by extrapolation from a large body of information about the *appraisal* values placed on older (male) slaves. Although the text (FE, I, p. 73, and Fig. 15) describes an age-distribution of some 5000 slave valuations simply as "prices of males slaves in the Old South," Appendix B (FE, II, p. 79) speaks of the "age-price profile" in question as having been "developed from data in the probate records," without elaborating on the nature of that data. The precise geographical and temporal make-up of the sample of probated estates is not disclosed, nor is one told the number and size distribution of the estates involved. The latter might indicate that the number of independent *sets* of age-specific relative valuations lay well below 5000, since it is likely that large slaveholding units (upwards of 50) were disproportionately represented among the estates probated. Still more remarkable is the authors' total silence about the relationship between appraisal values and market prices of slaves.[25]

---

[24] The method of calculation outline here (i.e., replacing the present value of the expected net revenue stream by the value of the birthright) is not the one described in the relevant portions of Appendix B, specifically FE, II, pp. 119–20, including section 4.11.1 quoted here (p. 176 above) and the sections referred to therein. The method Fogel and Engerman *describe* is incorrect, but we have verified in private conversation with the authors that they followed the different procedure outlined here.

[25] Some students of the southern probate records casually assert that slave appraisals were usually low in relation to actual market prices. Cf., for example, Postell [1951], p. 52. The important question here, which remains unanswered, is whether there were significant disparities between the relative age-specific appraisal values and the relative age-specific transaction prices. More generally it is most plausible to think that the appraisers worked with conventional valuations which were both less subject than market prices to regional variations, and less sensitive to changing expectations about the future course of market values. Perhaps this is why the dispersion of relative values drawn from estates in a region as large as the Old South is not greater than it appears to be from Fogel and Engerman's Figure 15 (FE, I, p. 72). And

On the assumption that Fogel and Engerman have not been misled by substituting relative appraisal values for relative market prices, it is important to add a brief word about the derivation of the age profile of slave "prices." Their procedure was to average the relative values observed in the probate data for each age, and then fit a curve to the averages. This use of averages does not generate accurate statistical estimates of the margin of error surrounding the fitted age-profile. In view of the importance the authors attach to the intercept of this curve (the value at age zero is the estimated value of the birthright), the absence of a proper estimate of the standard error of this intercept is a serious omission in their quantitative work.[26]

Momentarily suspending these doubts, suppose that somehow the authors have come up with the right figure for the market price of a newborn infant slave. It remains to consider the theoretical legitimacy of their intended finesse. This brings us to the second necessary qualification. Rather surprisingly, the technical discussion of the purchase market for slaves (Appendix B, sect. 2.1.3) abstracts completely from the most elementary considerations of the modern theory of asset-pricing under

perhaps, too, this is why they are able to report that an "age-price profile" for male slaves computed from the probate data during a period of rapidly falling market prices of slaves (1838–43) "was quite similar to" the corresponding profile computed from data for the period 1850–60, when slave prices were rapidly rising. Fogel and Engerman (FE, II, p. 79) note this counter-theoretic "similarity," describing it as a puzzle for which no explanation has yet been suggested.

[26] According to Appendix B (FE, II, p. 80) the relative "price" observations for each age were first averaged, and a sixth-order polynomial (in age) was then fitted, by least squares regression, to the sample midpoint observations thus obtained. The estimated equation, however, is not reported.

Although the coefficients (including the intercept constant) estimated in this fashion can be said to be unbiased estimates of the "true" parameters of the curve, it is almost certain that they are not numerically identical to the estimates that would have been derived had the polynomial been fitted to the original (unaveraged) observations. Fogel and Engerman offer no justification in Appendix B for choosing to use their method instead of the other, more conventional econometric procedure—even though their choice entails sacrificing the ability to compute a correct statistical "confidence interval" for the age-profile of prices upon which they have relied in several different portions of their work.

uncertainty. When the yield of an asset is subject to random variation, only an individual who is utterly indifferent to risk ("risk neutral") would find the asset just worth buying when the present value of its *expected* yields (i.e., the expected stream of net revenues) was infinitesimally greater than the purchase price.[27] Thus, Fogel and Engerman's approach would be justifia-

---

[27] Readers familiar with portfolio theory will recognize that the following text attempts a simplified treatment of the problem of risk by assuming, in effect, that the acquisition of an individual slave would increase the absolute variance of the total revenue stream derived from the slaveholder's entire portfolio of assets. Although the text discusses the riskiness of individual slave property, strictly speaking it is not the variance of the yields on a particular asset that matters to a prospective purchaser, but rather the effect upon the overall riskiness (yield variation) of the portfolio to which it is added. Were one to imagine that variations in the net earnings derived from different slaves would be *uncorrelated,* very large slaveholders would benefit from the operation of the law of large numbers. Since individual variability of slave revenues would tend to cancel out in the aggregate, such large slaveholders could more or less forget about the variance around the expected profile of earnings from any particular slave. We should then have to inquire (a) how large a group of slaves a single owner would have to have held for such a situation to obtain, and (b) whether in southern slave markets the offer-price was in effect being set by the demands of such already large slaveholders. These constitute intriguing questions for future quantitative historians of slavery. But the premise that variations of the yields on individual slaves would be uncorrelated is also an empirical proposition, and one that should not be allowed to pass unchallenged.

Quite the contrary. There are several good reasons for thinking that (as the text discussion implicitly assumes) there would have been *positive* covariation of the yields derived from the individual slaves held by a single owner—at least over some very considerable range in the size of slaveholdings. First among these is the fact that *individual* slaveholdings tended to be quite concentrated geographically, and the slaves employed in one or two lines of business rather than distributed over a wide range of dissimilar economic activities. Second, the southern economy did not offer a wide array of economically independent pursuits in which slaves might be profitably engaged; in any sub-region the fortunes of slaveholders tended to rise and fall together with the changing market conditions for the dominant (export) staple crop. Third, slaves typically were employed jointly in production with the other, non-human assets that made up the owner's portfolio; rents derived on land and on slaves would rise and fall jointly, with the price of cotton. Lastly, slaves do not resemble stock certificates, bonds or other financial assets which may be lodged in a given investor's portfolio without exerting any influence upon one another; human chattel belonging to a single estate

ble only if those on the buying side of the (perfectly competitive) slave market treated the prospective returns on their investments as if these were foreseen with certainty.

This is a rather strong assumption to have left unstated. Most of the theoretical and applied economic analysis of decision-making under uncertainty proceeds on the different hypothesis that risk *aversion* is the dominant mode of behavior. For risk averse individuals the positive valuation placed upon a dollar of income (unexpectedly) gained is less than the negative valuation associated with a dollar of income (unexpectedly) lost.[28] Comparing the two net income streams, one whose present value was known with certainty, and a second whose present value remained uncertain but *on the average* was identical to that of the first, risk averse individuals would always offer less for the right to receive the uncertain net income stream. Moreover, the greater the range of variation around any given average (or

---

typically were held in close physical proximity and therefore were susceptible to a variety of biological and social forms of interaction. No one can read accounts of everyday life on the plantations of the antebellum South without acknowledging the concerns on the part of masters, mistresses, and overseers with the many ways in which such interactions might give rise to (what the modern economist would describe as) "the positive covariation in asset performance." An even-tempered, well-disposed servant could set "a good example to the others" and thus ease the running of the Big House; a willful, tempestuous personality could keep the slave quarters in a continual uproar, provoking a string of incidents requiring extra attention. Likewise in matters of health: an old slave woman might turn out to be "a treasure" in dispensing therapeutic herbal preparations to the sick, or she could set young mothers against medically sound practices in postpartum care. More simply still, the likelihood of one slave contracting a contagious disease was increased by the infection of another belonging to the same household or plantation. Since the likelihood of infection of the plantation's population increased with its size, and the consequent increase in opportunities for a contact with an infected member of the neighboring populations, this consideration alone would have tended to operate against the effect of the law of large numbers referred to above.

[28] This is tantamount to saying that the risk averse individual is one for whom the marginal utility derived from income (or wealth) is diminishing. The measures of risk aversion proposed by Arrow and Pratt make use of this property of the usual utility index, and thus incorporate the hypothesis that risk aversion increases with the level of income (or wealth). Cf., for example, Arrow [1965], Chap. 2.

expected) present value, the less the asset would be worth to a risk averter: the prospect of an outcome very far above the expected present value would be more-than-counterbalanced by the prospect of an outcome equally far below it.

Consider, then, the stream of net revenue from the ownership of a slave. Clearly it would not be known with certainty, and therefore the prevalence of risk aversion among those on the buying side of the market would imply that the competitive market price would always be a *lower bound* estimate of the sum of discounted expected net revenues. This is to say that—even in the best of circumstances, in which the market value of the birthright had not been understated—Fogel and Engerman's figure of 10–12 would represent a *lower bound* measure of "the rate of exploitation" that they wish us to consider.

The extent of downward bias deriving from the substitution of asset prices for expected present values in this connection is comparatively large when the asset in question is a very young slave, rather than an adult. In the case of a newborn infant there is a particularly wide dispersion in the *a priori* distribution of future physical and intellectual capacities, as well as of personality traits. In addition, the shape of the *a priori* distribution of survival rates would change with age and the accumulation of information about the individual's physical constitution and medical history. On balance there seems to be good reason to suppose that the variance of the *a priori* distribution of future net revenues would *diminish* as a male slave passed from infancy to youth, and would continue to do so as he entered the prime of adulthood.[29] Part of the rise in the

---

[29] What happens thereafter is considerably less clear, since the declining variance of the individual slave's survival may be offset by increased variance in the various dimensions of "performance" with the onset of senescence. The situation for females passing from adolescence into their reproductive years is more complex than that for males: decreased variance of the *a priori* distribution of fertility can be offset by increased "risk" due to childbearing. In the present state of knowledge all these statements must be regarded as conjectural, but they serve equally to suggest the implausibility of assuming that the variance of the future net revenue stream is independent of the slave's age. We are indebted to Professor Warren C. Sanderson for impressing upon us the fact that Fogel and Engerman must rely upon this implausible assumption in order to infer an age profile of average net

age-price profile of male slaves (to an apparent peak around age 27) therefore reflected progressively smaller asset-price discounts on account of risk.

Because Fogel and Engerman ignore the influence of attitudes toward risk upon the prices of assets, the complicated method they have devised for utilizing the information contained in their "age-price profiles" must lead them to draw erroneous inferences about the shape of the (unobserved) age-profile of average net earnings yielded by male and female slaves in the Old South.[30] Supposing risk aversion to have been the predominant investor attitude, the net revenues inferred by Fogel and Engerman for the years before the slave's peak level of net revenue will tend to be low *by comparison* with the peak net revenue.[31] As there is no strong basis for supposing that their net earnings profile is too high (relative to the peak) in the subsequent portion of the life cycle, the simple undiscounted sum of inferred net revenues up to and beyond the apparent "peak earnings" period of the slave's life will have been *understated* if Fogel and Engerman have managed to set the absolute peak level of net earning for males at a correct dollar amount by using independent data on the hire rates of prime-age males (cf. FE, II, pp. 81–82).[32] The full significance of this

revenues from their age profile of slave prices and expected survival rates, or else defend their whole approach by maintaining that slaveholders gave no consideration whatsoever to risk.

[30] Cf. FE, I, pp. 73–78, 82–83, for these inferences. The estimation method, discussed in FE, II, pp. 80–81, involves using relative prices for adjoining ages and year-to-year survival frequencies to infer an underlying age profile in net revenues. The authors employ an iterative procedure in order to jointly find the uniform discount rate required to set the present value of the inferred remaining stream of average anticipated (i.e., survival adjusted) net revenues equal to the price of a slave at any given age. This internal rate is found to be 10 percent, or so we have reason to believe from the figure cited—in a different connection—in FE, II, p. 78.

[31] In other words, part of the rise in the price of a young slave as he aged was due to a reduction in risk. Not all was due to the rise in the net earnings of a slave with age. Therefore the true net earnings of young slaves relative to prime-age hands must have been larger than Fogel and Engerman estimated.

[32] The argument developed here extends to their inferences about females' earnings as well. Fogel and Engerman state (FE, I, p. 83) that "on average, net income from childbearing was only about 10 percent of the total net income

particular bias will shortly become clear.

Let us return to the question whether we should be interested in the discounted version of the "rate of exploitation" or in the undiscounted version which, by Fogel and Engerman's own reckoning, is five times larger. This problem is not addressed in the text of *Time on the Cross*, but a line in Appendix B classifies the choice between the two as "a moral rather than an economic question." The issue posed there (FE, II, p. 125) is whether the owner of human capital is entitled to receive interest on his investment, or whether a man is entitled to the fruits of his own labor.[33] Nevertheless, the authors proceed immediately to justify giving their exclusive attention to the *discounted* sum of expected net revenues not upon moral grounds, but on account of its power to explain a historical *curiosum,* namely, the alleged difference between the behavior of Jamaican and mainland planters in regard to slave childrearing. Fogel and Engerman assert that if child rearing was discouraged in Jamaica—a "fact" about whose validity they previously expressed some serious doubts—this was because "the accumulated expropriation" of Jamaican slaves "never becomes posi-

---

earned by women during their childbearing years." They go on to argue from this that manipulation of the sexual lives of slaves in order to *further* raise fertility could not have substantially affected the overall net income derived from the ownership of females. But inasmuch as the derivation of these net income (revenue) figures abstracts from the differentially greater risk associated with the yield via the (sale of) birthrights of the offspring—compared with the risk associated with net revenues from participation in field work—the 10 percent figure cited is clearly a *lower* bound estimate of the magnitude in question. Whether or not the latter is relevant for the slaveholder's decision-making, as the authors' discussion would suggest, and whether or not their argument on this point is germane to the thesis that there was little interference by masters in the sexual lives of the slaves because it would not have been very profitable to do this, are important questions. But they raise issues quite distinct from those being considered in this chapter.

[33] The (discounted) measure corresponding to the first "moral" position is termed a "Robinsonian" measure (FE, II, p. 87) to distinguish it from the second, "Marxian" measure of exploitation—although there appears to be no precedent in either the early or the recent writings of Joan Robinson to support the ethical propriety of considering *only the present value* of an expected future difference between the marginal productivity of labor and the real wage.

tive." [34] Since the accumulated expropriations expected over an average life is simply another expression for "the value of a birthright," this statement (on their reasoning) says no more than that the average price of a newborn slave in Jamaica was negative. People cannot be expected to encourage the production of commodities (slaves) with negative prices.

The question then is what one gains by articulating this proposition in terms of expropriation rather than slave prices. According to Fogel and Engerman's way of putting things, the negative price for newborn infants meant that Jamaican slaves were exploiting their owners! They did so because their mortality rate was so high that the slaveowners incurred the costs of rearing children who were so inconsiderate as to die before earning enough to yield an overall 11 percent (opportunity cost) rate of return on the slaveholder's investment. Had American Negro slaves been placed in a regime in which they too died younger, would we find it instructive to say that their rate of expropriation was lower? No more than we would think it illuminating to say that they were "exploited less" had they happened to be transferred into the hands of an especially risk averse class of planters whose behavior in the purchase market would tend to establish a lower price (birthright value) on an asset that might well perish long before average experience suggested it should. One may rightly wonder whether "exploitation" and "expropriation"—ethically loaded terms referring to the unjust use of another man's labor—are really the appropriate words to employ as labels for a quantitative measure which looks at "justice" entirely from a slaveowner's vantage point. The same doubt extends to the authors' preference for the discounted version of the exploitation rate.

For the benefit of the general reader, Fogel and Engerman (FE, I, pp. 155–56) explain their finding of a low rate of exploitation in just these terms: "a substantial part of the income taken from those slaves who survived into the later years was not an act of expropriation, but a payment required to

[34] FE, II, Section 4.11.2.1, pp. 120–22, for Fogel and Engerman's skeptical questions about the "traditional interpretation" of the slave experience in Jamaica, and elsewhere in the Caribbean and South America.

cover the expenses" of rearing children who failed to live until
they could amortize themselves. To these "just" expenses, which
include the interest foregone, the authors' measure of expropriation would also add the interest cost (at 10 percent per
annum) on the childrearing "loan" extended to those slaves who
did survive. After all, "free men" as *Time on the Cross* (FE, I, p.
155) tells us, "must also bear the cost of rearing the young,
including those who fail to survive, as well as of supporting the
sick and the aged."

Free people, however, ordinarily are not required to borrow
money for the expenses of their childhood. They are supported
by their parents and more generally by their parents' generation. And when they become adults they do not repay their
parents with compound interest for the pecuniary cost of their
own early years—much less for the upbringing of brothers and
sisters prematurely deceased. In turn, they support children of
their own. Thus, the way such intergenerational transfers of
income are effected among the members of free societies does
not confront individuals with the costs of raising children and
supporting elderly dependents when they themselves are children, but rather allows them to assume these burdens contempo-
raneously with the income they earn in their adulthood. Viewed
from this reference point, it is the undiscounted version of the
rate of exploitation to which attention should be paid, inasmuch
as it represents the conceptually closer analogue to the proportion of income that parents in a free society must devote to the
maintenance of children (and elderly dependents). The analogy
is closer because (in the absence of discounting) a dollar spent on
childrearing will be given the same weight as a dollar of
earnings, which is just the way *contemporaneous* expenses and
earnings would be treated in calculating a discounted sum.[35] In

---

[35] The undiscounted version does not offer a perfect analogue, if only
because the earnings span of an individual's life, be he free man or slave,
typically begins before the economic burdens of childrearing are assumed,
and continue after they have ended. It would be desirable to weight
pre-parental earnings more heavily than the remote post-parental portion of
the earnings stream, but the information necessary to make this refined
computation has not been published in *Time on the Cross*. There are other,
possibly more serious errors in the undiscounted version of the exploitation
rate estimated by Fogel and Engerman, which will be noticed below.

other words, the essential objection to be made to Fogel and Engerman's use of discounting in this connection is not that they have failed properly to estimate the financing costs which the rearing of slaves entailed *for the master*. Rather it is that they have ignored the condition of freedom as the relevant alternative in reckoning how much of the individual slave's earnings were being taken from him.[36]

The undiscounted version of the rate of exploitation, it may be recalled, is put at 49 percent in Fogel and Engerman's Appendix B. Yet even this under-represents the truth. We have already noticed that the numerator of this ratio is calculated to equal the undiscounted sum of expropriations, i.e., expected future net revenues for a newborn infant, and have concluded that the authors' estimates understate this sum because they have ignored the effect of risk aversion on the prices of slaves. What of the denominator of the (undiscounted) exploitation rate? It is defined as the sum of undiscounted expected future *gross* revenues, and thus is calculated as the undiscounted sum of expropriations *plus* the undiscounted sum of expected future

[36] The question at issue at the moment is how to measure slave exploitation, not how to discount lifetime net revenue streams for durable assets. In exchanging the former question for the latter, the essential point gets lost. To keep the point in mind, an obvious analogy may be drawn with the situation created by gangsters who set up an "insurance" racket, selling people protection against fire by showing some of them the serious risks that one incurs by remaining uninsured with the right party. On the principle of analysis which Fogel and Engerman appear to have applied, there would be no "economic exploitation" worth mentioning if the "insurance rates" quoted were simply to reflect the likelihood of arson by one racketeer or another. A property owner finding himself in such a high risk situation couldn't hope to do better by buying insurance from a legitimate insurer, and thus could not legitimately complain about having to pay high premiums to someone else (the gangsters) in exchange for the same services. Utter fascination with pieces of analysis like this produces (to borrow Veblen's phrase) a "trained incapacity" in economists to notice the more obtrusive features of economic life—in the case at hand, the fact that an "insurance business" organized on the lines just described is an extortion racket, not a social activity founded on voluntary atomistic exchange. On the larger question of the relevance (or irrelevance) of modern economic welfare analysis in attempting an evaluation of slavery as an economic institution, see the brief discussion in the concluding part of this chapter.

maintenance cost over the slave's life. Consequently, if the latter sum has not been understated by Fogel and Engerman, we may unequivocally conclude that their 49 percent rate of exploitation is an underestimate.[37]

Now the facts of the matter suggest that if there is anything wrong with Fogel and Engerman's estimate of the average undiscounted value of life time maintenance expenditures on a slave, the error is one of *overstatement* rather than under-representation. In order to obtain an age-profile of the value of a typical slave's consumption stream, the authors first adjusted upward the familiar figures (based on plantation records) of average maintenance costs per slave. Then, as the illustrative passage from Appendix B (sect. 4.11.1) quoted earlier tells us, "Atwater's weights" were used to convert the average adjusted maintenance figure "into age and sex specific values." By consulting the source referred to in the U.S. Department of Agriculture publication cited (as [366]) by Fogel and Engerman, one learns that "Atwater's weights" are a set of "relative quantities of potential energy," i.e., *calories* "of nutrients required" by persons of varying ages.[38]

We may put aside the (unmentioned) fact that the data underlying the "required calories" estimates W. O. Atwater published in 1886 were the "standard rations" then being assumed by the Munich School of physiological chemists and have nothing whatsoever to do with the actual calorie consumption of Negro slaves in the American South, or with the actual or required consumption of other Americans for that matter. The simple point to be noted is that satisfying the relatively high calorie requirements of infants and children does not necessarily entail a commensurate relative expense. There is no reason to think that food (let alone other) expenditures would be proportional to calorie content over the course of human life cycle, and some substantial basis for thinking that calories are

---

[37] The undiscounted rate of exploitation $E°$, is calculated as $E° = [B°]/[B° + \sum \lambda_t M_t]$. $E°$ is understated unless $\sum \lambda_t M_t$ has been understated by the same proportional amount as is $B°$ (where λ_t is the probability of a slave living in age T, M_t is the maintenance cost of a slave of age t, and $B°$ is the birthright calculated in the absence of discounting).

[38] Cf. Massachusetts Bureau of Statistics of Labor [1886], esp. pp. 262–67.

provided in relatively inexpensive forms (for the master) during childhood. Breast-feeding is an exemplary practice in this regard, for if the nursing mother is not given extra rations or excused from part of her normal work, the cost of feeding the baby will be borne by the mother (in the form of less adequate nourishment) rather than the master. On these and still other grounds[39] it appears that the use of "Atwater's weights" has led Fogel and Engerman to use too high a relative level for slave maintenance costs during the early years. And even in computing the undiscounted sum of planter's expected maintenance expenditures, the application of a declining survival rate to each successive age-specific expenditure estimate places heaviest weight upon the (overstated) initial portion of the lifetime "maintenance cost profile." Thus there are two quite distinct bases for regarding the 49 percent figure supplied by Fogel and Engerman's second volume as a *lower bound* estimate of the conceptually appropriate undiscounted "exploitation rate," just as the startlingly low 12 percent figure presented by their primary volume must be treated as a *lower bound* proportion for the sum of the discounted appropriations.

Since the circumstances of being enslaved denied the Negro people access to the interest-free mode of intergenerational financing commonly arranged by free peoples, it seems to us appropriate to concentrate on the undiscounted exploitation rate. For only the latter measure counts the entailed financing burdens as part of the economic expropriation to which their slavery rendered them subject. Fogel and Engerman chose to omit this consideration and to treat the interest foregone as a "just" expense incurred by the slaveholders who had to undertake the financing of the intergenerational transfers among "their people." In doing so they implicitly have dragged the discussion around to looking at slavery once again as Phillips did—from the paternal planters' viewpoint.

Time on the Cross concludes the text discussion (FE, I, p. 156)

[39] It appears that Fogel and Engerman use Atwater's estimates of the calorie requirements of children and youths relative to requirements for adults doing moderate work, rather than expressing them as (smaller) fractions of the estimated calories required by adults engaged in vigorous labor.

of the "exploitation" issue, by pointing out that "the 12 percent rate of expropriation falls well within the modern tax rates on workers," even those whose incomes are at the "poverty" level. Fogel and Engerman do not disabuse the casual reader of the distinct impression he has received that the slaves were in some sense less heavily "taxed" than are some free persons in America today, but they do point out that the contemporary poor receive offsetting transfer payments and governmental services. Having thus acknowledged that taxation in modern society is not an act of expropriation but a payment for public goods and services, they ask whether the slaves did not also receive some services "which offset the [modest amount of] income expropriated from them." In response the authors point out that the slaves "shared in the benefits" of the large-scale purchases of clothing made by the planter. More importantly, through their master's intervention slaves were "in effect, able to borrow at prime rates," thereby making considerable "savings on interest charges." The suggested parallel with modern arrangements is unmistakable. But we cannot think that Fogel and Engerman seriously mean to rehabilitate slavery as a kind of antebellum credit union, particularly when free people had no need of the sort of "credit facilities" that were being extended to the slaves.

Taking the evidence on the material treatment of slaves together, a distinct pattern can be seen. The slave diet was compared with an inappropriate standard which makes it look better than might appear on deeper consideration. The value of slave consumption was compared with the value of free farm income under a set of historically unrealistic assumptions which again represent the slaves to have been in a more favorable position than was the case. And the relationship between slave production and consumption is treated in a manner which both under-represents the revenues accruing to the slaveowners and implicitly adopts the masters' point of view on the justice of exacting compensation for the interest costs entailed in rearing a slave from infancy. All quantitative studies are subject to error in some degree. But the description of the comparative material conditions of American Negro slavery which emerges from *Time on the Cross* contains a preponderance of errors that run in one direction, imparting an upward bias of undetermined magnitude. In the instance of the rate of exploitation or expropriation, the distortion has been seen to be so large as to negate the usefulness of Fogel and Engerman's published "findings."

Methods and Evidence on the Relative Efficiency of Slave Agriculture

Fogel and Engerman's discussion of the system of agriculture based on Negro slavery contains two analytically distinct classes of assertions about productive efficiency. One has to do with the comparative resource utilization typical of different agrarian production organizations, the other concerns the comparative performance of the workers associated with those organizations.

The authors begin (FE, I, pp. 191–93) with statements about "the relative efficiency of slave agriculture," defining efficiency operationally as "the ratio of output to the average amount of the inputs" of labor, land and capital. Slave agriculture is discussed as an archetypal production organization to be compared with free family farming, thus: "southern slave farms were 28 percent more efficient than southern free farms," and "compared with northern farms . . . slave farms were 40 percent more efficient" (FE, I, p. 192). It would be of interest to know whether these reported differences in the average level of measured efficiency are statistically significant, but neither the text nor the relevant sections of Appendix B (FE, II, pp. 126–42) present the measures of farm-to-farm and plantation-to-plantation variance that would be needed in carrying out such significance tests.[40] In all likelihood, however, this is not the proper way to interpret the authors' actual "findings." [41] Rather

---

[40] A difference is "statistically significant" if it would not normally arise by chance from two different samplings of a single population.
[41] Appendix B (FE, II, p. 139, Tables B.23 and B.24) discloses wide variation in the relative efficiency indexes which are presented as *averages* for slave plantations belonging to different regions and different broad size-classes. For example, the measured total factor productivity of plantations holding 16–50 slaves in the New South is 70.5 percent greater than that of "plantations" in the 1–15 slave category in the Old South. Thus, within the

than taking their statements about the efficiency differences between slave and free farms literally, as statistical assertions about the representative individual production units, we should read them as relating to comparisons of the ratios of output to inputs for different collections, or *aggregations* of farms and plantations. It is at least clear that such an aggregate productivity comparison underlies their statement that "southern agriculture *as a whole* was about 35 percent more efficient than northern agriculture in 1860." [42]

From this aggregative empirical foundation, Fogel and Engerman (FE, I, pp. 209–10) go on to identify "the special quality of plantation labor" as being the source of the superior efficiency of slave agriculture, and to elaborate upon their basic contention that the typical black field-hand, far from being lazy, inept, or uncooperative, "was harder-working and *more efficient* than his

---

group of slave farms the difference from the mid-point to the extreme of this range is at least 35 percent, which is just as large as the relative productivity advantage that Fogel and Engerman report for their comparison of "all slave farms" and "northern farms." This suggests that the latter productivity differential in favor of the slave mode of farming is not statistically significant.
[42] FE, I, p. 192, emphasis added. Unfortunately, the text immediately goes on to restate this in the following way: "that is, on average, a southern farm using a given amount of labor, land, and capital could produce about 35 percent more output than a northern farm, or groups of farms, using the same quantities of these inputs." This is a formally correct restatement if we take the qualifying "on average" to refer to *weighted* averages of all the individual southern and northern farms, the weights corresponding to their contributions to the respective aggregate agricultural outputs of the two regions. Appendix B, Tables B.21 and B.22 (cf. FE, II, pp. 135–37), and the accompanying discussion make it clear that the relative efficiency index derives from an aggregate total factor productivity calculation for southern and northern agriculture. But in describing the derivation of parallel average productivity measures for the farms in different regions and size classes *within* the South (FE, II, pp. 138–40), Fogel and Engerman do not explicitly say whether the averages are weighted or unweighted. And as their southern production in this case comes not from the full Census of Agriculture for 1860, but instead from the Parker-Gallman sample, it also remains unclear whether the weighting—if weighting was implicitly or explicitly employed—followed the representation of farm types in all southern agriculture, or just in the 5230 farm sample drawn from counties that produced at least 1000 bales of cotton in 1860. For further details of this sample, cf. Parker [1970], esp. the articles by Gallman, Foust and Swan, and Wright.

white counterpart" (FE, I, p. 5, emphasis added). Superior "efficiency" is thus said to have characterized the work performance of the individual slaves, as well as the class of production organizations that utilized them.

While they are analytically distinct, it is important to notice that the two types of statements involving comparisons of efficiency are not empirically unconnected. *Time on the Cross* does not present any independent quantitative evidence of a microeconomic character to support the authors' propositions regarding the comparative personal efficiences of the typical slave and free worker in agriculture. Rather, it seeks first to impeach the credibility of the existing non-quantitative evidence: Fogel and Engerman reject as tainted by racism all contemporary statements, and more recent historical interpretations, which would suggest that slaves were less competent, and less diligent workers than free northern farm laborers. The fact that the slaves were black and the free workers were white obviously complicates the question of the weight to be accorded to the testimony of white contemporary observers. But the race issue should not be allowed completely to obscure from view the long-standing, far more general predisposition to regard slaves as inferior workers. As David Brion Davis points out:[43]

> The white slaves of antiquity and the Middle Ages were often described in terms that fit the later stereotype of the Negro. Throughout history it has been said that slaves, though occasionally as loyal and faithful as good dogs, were for the most part lazy, irresponsible, cunning, rebellious, untrustworthy and sexually promiscuous.

Moreover, it is one thing to argue as Fogel and Engerman do, against a presumption of inferior work performance by black slaves, but it is quite another thing to establish their superiority to free whites as workers. Discounting the contrary qualitative evidence will not suffice for the latter purpose.

Fogel and Engerman implicitly acknowledge the need for positive evidence here by seeking it at an altogether different, much higher level of aggregation. They have arrived at the conclusion that black slaves must have been superior quality workers inferentially, by the process of eliminating some other

[43] Davis [1966], pp. 59–60.

conceivable explanations for the measured factor productivity advantage of slave-using agriculture as a whole. Differential economies of scale, technical knowledge, and managerial ability figure principally among the alternatives thus considered for elimination.

For example, their cross-section analysis of the variation of factor productivity with differences in the size of the slave workforce employed on southern farms in 1860 leads Fogel and Engerman to conclude that although there were significant positive scale effects, these could not account completely for the efficiency advantage of the slave-using sector as a whole.[44] They point out, further, that such economies of scale "were achieved only with slave labor"—presumably because "at the crux of the superior efficiency of large-scale operations on plantations" lay the organization of field slaves into "highly disciplined, interdependent teams capable of maintaining a steady and intense rhythm of work" (FE, I, pp. 193, 204). In much the same vein, Fogel and Engerman argue that if the managers of plantations possessed any superior technological knowledge and entrepreneurial skills, these consisted primarily of the organizational know-how required in creating "a highly disciplined, highly specialized, and well-coordinated labor force" (FE, I, pp. 199–203).

This line of argument, however, does not lead *Time on the*

---

[44] Indeed, the mystery concerning the *physical* source of the measured productivity advantage of the southern slave-using agricultural sector is actually deeper than Fogel and Engerman acknowledge, since there is reason to doubt that technological economies of scale were as important quantitatively as the authors assert. In Chapter 7, below, Gavin Wright points out that the positive association which did exist between plantation size and the proportion of acreage devoted to cotton (rather than corn and other food crops) would have given rise to the spurious appearance of cross-section scale economies whenever yields (per acre) of cotton were abnormally high while yields of other crops were not. The year 1860, to which the cross-section evidence studied by Fogel and Engerman refers, happened to be a record harvest year for cotton cultivation. For the purposes of the following discussion, Fogel and Engerman's "findings" in regard to economies of scale are disregarded entirely, and we shall consider the extent to which the whole of the relative productivity advantage found for the slave-plantation sector can be accounted for by errors in the measurement of inputs and outputs.

Cross into full agreement with studies of modern plantation agriculture which give most emphasis to the role that organization and managerial ability play in ensuring success in competition with independent family farming.[45] Instead, the authors insist that what counted in the antebellum South was the *combination* of superior management and the "superior quality" of black labor. The latter, unlike free white labor, would be "driven" in gang work. On further consideration, Fogel and Engerman suggest that the fruits of this special combination of capabilities might just as well be entirely inputed to labor as to management:

> In a certain sense, all, or nearly all, of the advantage is attributable to the high quality of slave labor, for the main thrust of management was directed at improving the quality of labor. [FE, I, p. 210]

But even putting it that way, the extent to which this effort succeeded because of the "responsiveness" of the plantation workers is left unclear.

Were it not for the need to explain the apparent superior productivity showing of plantations, there would be less reason to view the allegedly greater capacity of Negro slaves for being "driven" in gang labor as indicative of some general superiority of the quality of the labor services they provided. An overall quality advantage ought to mean that black slave workers would also perform more effectively than free workers (white or black) when employed within the regime of independent family farming. Yet, when Fogel and Engerman speak of "the superiority of slave labor in the plantation context" (FE, I, p. 205), it is the specific context that matters. They are referring to the advantages slaveowners derived from the special way black workers responded to the non-pecuniary motivation set up by the "rhythm" of a repetitive gross motor activity such as hoeing, and to the rivalrous interaction of the hoe gang and plough

---

[45] In the essay entitled "Plantations," in *The International Encyclopaedia of the Social Sciences* [1968], W. O. Jones maintains that such economic advantage as the modern plantation possesses derives from "its ability to mobilize unskilled labor"; the plantation succeeds by substituting supervisory and administrative skills for skilled, adaptive labor, making most of the availability of a labor force whose principal skill is to follow orders."

gang.[46] And surely there is a legitimate question to be faced here: was this particular "quality" of the ante bellum Afro-American labor force not specific to hoe culture and organizationally similar production tasks? Can it then support more general inferences about the comparative personal efficiency of individual slave workers in the multiplicity of non-repetitive, discretionary farm chores called for by the regime of the family farm? Doubts on this score would become stronger if there were no reason to believe southern plantation agriculture was productively more efficient than northern farming.

Similarly dependent upon the "finding" that slave agriculture exhibited a pronounced physical efficiency advantage is the assertion by Fogel and Engerman that blacks must share in any of the credit awarded to "management" because on the majority of the large plantations in the cotton belt key supervisory and managerial functions were performed by overseers who were themselves *slaves* (FE, I, pp. 210–12). This startling conclusion emerges from the population tabulations the authors made using the observations recorded in the Parker-Gallman sample: they report the absence of an identifiable white overseer on 70 percent of the plantations holding over 100 slaves, coupled with the absence on 75 percent of these overseer-less plantations of a white adult male other than the owner who might have performed the duties of an overseer.

It has elsewhere been shown that Fogel and Engerman's mis-use of the sample data (drawn by Parker and Gallman) from the Census of Agriculture is responsible for creating this

---

[46] One should not be tempted into speaking of "the superiority of black labor in the context of slavery," for slavery clearly was neither a sufficient nor a necessary condition for eliciting a response to the intrinsic motivation of group competition and work rhythm. Both phenomena have been remarked upon by ethnographers and students of work organization among *free* non-industrial peoples. Rhythm is sometimes reported explicitly as an "incentive" in tillage labor, where a line of workers may reap or hoe in unison; in the Dahomean *dokpwe,* and the Haitian *combite* we are told, special drummers and songs are used. Gang competition as a work "incentive" is more widely observed and certainly not restricted to peoples of African stock. In rice planting among the Betsileo, for example, the women attempt to plant shoots faster than the men can prepare the field ahead of them. Cf. Udy [1959], pp. 114–15.

puzzling statistical artifact; they have simply ignored the facts
that the overseer was the only white male adult resident (and
thus confused with the "owner") on some plantations and that
on many other plantations overseers lived in separate households and consequently would not have been recorded by census
marshals as belonging to the resident owner's household.[47] But
in noting the flagrantly erroneous factual basis for the assertions made in *Time on the Cross* concerning the prevalence of
black overseers, one should not overlook the tenuous character
of the reasoning which carries Fogel and Engerman from the
putative absence of overseers who are white to the presence of
overseers who are black. Quite obviously, two unstated premises
underlie the authors' inference from the (erroneous) statistics
just cited: (1) it is assumed that a large plantation could not be
properly run without an overseer in addition to the resident
owner, and (2) it is supposed that because the large plantations
were so efficient, they must have been well run. Once the latter
presupposition is withdrawn, however, the logic of this piece of
inferential history unravels along with the rest of the fabric of
Fogel and Engerman's argument.

It now should be evident that a great deal hinges on the
validity of the relative indexes of aggregate factor productivity
which the authors have developed for slave and free farming
operations. This makes it necessary to look more skeptically into
the details of their construction—as described by Appendix B.
For it appears that in as many as three different respects the
procedures followed give rise to a systematic overstatement of
the relative efficiency of production on southern slave farms—at
least in the usual sense in which "efficiency" has been used in the
present discussion. In adumbrating these suspicions we concentrate on the simplest of the factor productivity comparisons,
that between southern and northern agriculture as a whole; but
the exercise will serve to indicate the nature of the problems
that also arise in regard to the productivity comparisons made

---

[47] For fuller discussion of the question of black overseers, and the significance of Fogel and Engerman's error on this point in relation to the
estimates of the occupational structure of the slave population, see Chapter
4, above.

among the different segments of the agricultural industry of the antebellum southern cotton belt.

The estimated relative factor productivity standing of southern agriculture will be biased upward to the extent that the ratio of southern factor inputs to northern factor inputs is understated. Inasmuch as this appears to be the case with respect to both the measures of labor and land, we take up these two major points in turn, considering first a number of deficiencies in the comparative treatment of the labor inputs. The third problem with Fogel and Engerman's measurement of relative productivity involves the definition of productivity itself.

On the Measurement of Labor Inputs

In reckoning the amount of labor services deployed by northern and southern agriculture, respectively, Fogel and Engerman count a southern man-year as equal to a northern man-year. This neglects the greater length of time which the climate of the more southerly latitudes afforded for field work. Most northern farming around 1860 was carried on in a region having 160 to 180 frost-free days, whereas the center of the southern farming region lay in a zone having 220 to 240, or roughly 60 *additional* frost-free days. This, however, substantially exaggerates the proportional difference between the duration of the southern and northern farm work year.[48] Leaving aside dairy-farming regions, a rather conservative estimate would suggest that on

---

[48] Cf. Higbee [1958], p. 27, for maps of frost-free periods based on the records for the years 1899–1938. According to the discussion of farm hours by Blodgett [1903], pp. 23–24, however, 3 to 4 months were lost for field work in the North, whereas perhaps 2 months were lost in the South—typically 6 weeks in the hot months when cultivation ceased as corn and cotton crops mature during the lull from active growth, and 2 more weeks in winter. (It is noted that the traditional week of freedom afforded slaves at Christmas coincided with the winter suspension of field work.) Putting the difference between the time lost in the North and in the South at 6 weeks, and taking the 6-day week as normal for slaves in the antebellum period, we can think of latitude putting 36 extra field work days at the disposal of the southern plantation. No extra allowance is considered for differences in field work time due to suspensions of activity enforced by rain, etc.

account of the difference in latitude alone the annual number of hours put in by a farm worker in the south was 10 percent greater than that worked by his counterpart in the North. The latter, modest figure makes allowance for the following considerations: (1) the days of field work "lost" in the North occur around the winter solstice, when daylight hours are shortest, (2) outside the "lost" winter months the greater average duration of daylight per day allows northern farmers more time for field work—particularly at the period of the grain harvest, and (3) during the slack winter quarter antebellum northern farm workers in wheat and corn regions may have put in as much as a daily average of 4 ½ hours on livestock care and chores, compared with 1 hour per day spent on chores in the Eastern and Delta cotton regions.[49] With regard to the last of these considerations we have hazarded a backward projection of what seem to be the relevant findings about regional differences in

[49] The 10 percent extra southern labor input figure is based upon the estimate of 36 extra field days discussed in the previous footnote. It was developed in the following steps: (1) The 36 extra field work days was translated into 367.2 hours, using 10.2 hours per day. The latter is the average amount of daylight in the latitude of Charleston, S.C., during the December-January period when the net loss of time occurs for the North (cf. *American Almanac* [1888]).

(2) Outside the winter months the length of the northern period of daylight is greater. In June-August, when the difference is greatest, farms in the latitude of New York City had approximately 54 extra hours of daylight compared with farms in the latitude of Charleston, S.C., according to the sunrise-sunset intervals published in the *American Almanac* for 1888.

(3) According to the W.P.A. National Research Project field survey conducted in 1936, average daily chore hours per worker in northern wheat- and corn-region farms exceeded those on southern Eastern and Delta cotton-region farms by 3.5 hours, during the winter quarter. It is therefore appropriate to subtract [3.5 × 36 =] 126 hours of chore work from the 313 [= 367 − 54] net additional hours afforded southern farms by the latitude difference. This gives a remainder of 187 extra hours, which represents 9 percent of the 2163 hours estimated as the annual per man input of labor in northern corn regions by the National Research Project Survey for 1936. Cf. Hopkins [1941], pp. 23–27. An alternative procedure, using the figures supplied by Hopkins and assuming that due to differences in weather as well as in climate (associated with latitude) indicates that the South enjoyed 60 extra days of field work and yields a 14.8 percent adjustment in the per worker input of labor time for the South relative to the North. On the strength of this we round the previous, conservative 9 percent figure upward, to 10 percent.

the length of the work year at a much later point in time, specifically during the 1930s. This may be permissible in a heuristic exercise intended to suggest the possible magnitude of the bias arising from neglecting the effects of latitude. But further research in *antebellum sources* will be needed before the question can be satisfactorily resolved.

A second oversight in reckoning the ratio of southern to northern labor services is rather more substantial. Fogel and Engerman neglect to consider that over the course of the whole year *slave* laborers put in more hours of work than did (southern or northern) free farm workers.[50] A rough and rather conservative indication of the quantitative dimension of this omission is provided by considering the difference between the number of hours worked annually by *black* members of the southern agricultural labor force when they were in bondage, *circa* 1860, and when they were free men, *circa* 1870. For this purpose we may make use of the estimates assembled by Roger Ransom and Richard Sutch, which count an hour of female or child labor effort as fractions of an hour of male labor effort.[51] On this basis the proportional increment in annual (male equivalent) hours

[50] Their text says that plantations' comparative ability to fully utilize potential labor arose, "not because slaves worked more hours per day or more days per week than free farmers. The best available evidence is that both slaves and free farmers averaged approximately 70–75 hours of work per week during the peak labor periods of planting, cultivating, and harvesting. Nor does it appear that slaves worked more days per year" (FE, I, p. 208). We are unable to find any citations supporting these assertions in the Appendix B Notes to Chapter 6. Moreover the statement about length of the average work day carried the significant qualifying phrase: "during the peak labor periods." For evidence and arguments contradicting Fogel and Engerman on this point, see below.

[51] See Ransom Sutch [1975], pp. 1–28. The fractional weighting of women's and children's labor-time differences gives a particularly conservative measure in this case, because the proportional decline in the hours worked by secondary family workers in the transition from slavery to freedom was more pronounced than the proportional decline in the case of males. For all members of the black work force the absolute reduction in estimated annual labor time runs in the range of 500–600 hours. These estimates are consistent with Charles Seagrave's estimates of declines of between 9 and 74 days worked per year by Louisiana class 1 field hands in the immediate post emancipation period 1864–67. Cf. Seagrave [1971], pp. 71–72.

per worker that corresponded to the difference between the condition of freedom and the condition of slavery can be put in the neighborhood of 16–22 percent. It is possible that this difference might overstate the size of the permanent reduction of effort which freedom brought to black agricultural workers. In 1870 the transient effects of the first "taste of freedom" to allocate one's time and the postwar disruption of southern agricultural organization had perhaps not disappeared completely. On the other hand, there are good grounds for thinking that confining attention to black workers' transition between slavery and freedom must understate the proportional difference between the annual labor input of slaves compared with free white members of the (northern or southern) antebellum farm labor force. Modern studies of family labor supply indicate that leisure is a *superior* good, particularly the leisure of secondary workers (women and youths); relative to the demand for other commodities, the family demand for leisure increases with increases in wealth. On average, in 1860 free farming families had greater non-human wealth than did the newly freed blacks of 1870. Therefore it is to be expected that, *certeris paribus*, the labor time supplied by the free antebellum farm family worker would be less than that estimated to have been supplied by black freedmen during the era of Reconstruction.

By multiplicitively combining the two "correction factors" just considered, one may arrive at a rough assessment of the effect of these omissions on the overall ratio of southern slave labor inputs to northern free labor inputs. The upshot is that the relative labor input index for slave agriculture should be 28 to 34 percent higher than Fogel and Engerman say it is, which alone would raise the *relative* total factor input index for slave agriculture by 15 to 18 percent. Consequently, the estimate of the total factor productivity differential for the southern slave farm sector compared with northern agriculture should be on this account cut from the 40 percent reported by Fogel and Engerman to something more like 18–21 percent.[52]

[52] The calculation is made as follows: Relative to free northern farming the southern slave farm sector labor input index is to be raised by (1.10) (1.16) =

This, however, probably does not exhaust the downward adjustment that would be necessary simply to rectify the net tendency of the errors they have introduced in measuring the relative inputs of labor. That is not to say that all the measurement errors operate in one direction. The authors point out in Appendix B (FE, II, p. 138) that because they have followed nineteenth-century Census practice in ignoring labor force participation by women on free family farms, their estimates of the labor input for northern agriculture (and for the southern free farm sector) must on this account be too low, relative to the figures for southern farming (and slave agriculture) as a whole. They suggest that on this account their total factor productivity estimates under-represent the efficiency advantage held by slave-using farms. But Fogel and Engerman do not notice that still another procedure of theirs for "refining" the southern labor input measure introduces what is probably a more than offsetting downward bias in the relative labor input index for southern agriculture vis-à-vis northern agriculture.[53] The aggregate southern labor force estimate appears to have been recalculated so that it is expressed in terms of equivalent (prime-age adult male) worker units, using for this purpose the age-profiles of relative gross earning which Fogel and Enger-

---

1.28 or (1.10) (1.22) = 1.34. Fogel and Engerman (FE, II, pp. 126–27) adopt the Cobb-Douglas form of aggregate production function and therefore compute the index of total factor inputs as a weighted *geometric* average of the labor, land and capital input indexes. Their weight for labor—as previously noted above—is 0.58, so the adjustment factor by which the relative total input index for slave agriculture (vis-à-vis northern agriculture) should be multiplied is $(1.28)^{.58} = 1.154$, or $(1.34)^{.58} = 1.185$. These ratios, divided into the ratio of southern slave factor productivity to northern agricultural factor productivity (which Fogel and Engerman report as 1.40) yield the partially "corrected" versions of the latter relative productivity ratios which are mentioned in the text below: 1.40/1.185 = 1.18, and 1.40/1.154 = 1.21.

[53] After these two procedures are described, at the beginning of the second paragraph in FE, II, p. 138, there follows this statement: "This adjustment in the southern labor input without a corresponding adjustment in the northern labor input biases the relative advantage of the South downward." On careful reading it becomes clear that this applies *only* to their adjustment for labor force participation by women and children in southern agriculture, and not to the "equivalent worker" adjustments.

man inferred from the "age-price" profiles for slaves. But the same adjustment could not at the time be carried out for the northern agricultural labor force. Thus the "refinement" must substantially reduce the level of the southern labor input relative to that measured for northern agriculture: quite apart from the accuracy of the "equivalent worker" weights, their effect is to count members of the southern labor force who were either younger than or older than the inferred age of peak gross earnings as being less than a full worker. Unfortunately we cannot determine by how much this further contributes to inflating the reported relative factor productivity standing of southern agriculture.

On the Measurement of Land Inputs

The second major source of upward bias in Fogel and Engerman's relative efficiency estimates for southern agriculture is their use of average land values to adjust acreage figures in reckoning the relative inputs of the services of land. This adjustment has the effect of raising the relative total factor productivity index for southern (vs. northern) agriculture by 25.6 percent.[54] In other words, it accounts for more than the apparent southern efficiency advantage remaining after the (preceding) attempts made here to partially correct for the bias introduced by Fogal and Engerman's treatment of the relative labor inputs.

Some weighting of the relative acreage figures clearly is needed to allow for the greater resource inputs represented by improved lands in comparison with unimproved lands, and perhaps also for natural variations in average soil fertility between the regions. But the authors' use of the simple ratio of the aggregate value of agricultural land in the South to that in the North, based on the 1860 census, deserves fuller discussion

[54] Cf. FE, II, pp. 132, 135, and Tables B.20 and B.21. The ratio of southern to northern land inputs is reduced by a factor of 0.40 (from 1.257 to .505) by the value-weighting of acreage. Since land gets a .25 weight in the geometric averaging of all inputs, the latter index is only reduced by the factor $(.40^{.25} =)$ 0.796 on this account. The effect on measured total input productivity is calculated as $1/(.796) = 1.256$.

than it receives in Appendix B (FE, II, p. 136). Implicitly, the theory of rent has been invoked to justify the supposition that greater soil fertility would merely permit landowners to extract the market value of the extra crop yield per acre as an incremental rent. It is further tacitly supposed that all such expected future rental earnings would be capitalized into the prices of the land—at a uniform discount rate—so that the latter would vary in strict proportion to the former. We have already had occasion to point out that this gambit, in effect, ignores the possible intervening influence of attitudes toward risk in determining the market value of the assets (lands) in question. But in the case at hand the authors' procedure also requires one to stipulate the existence of a perfectly competitive capital market (establishing a uniform *national* rate of discount), a perfectly competitive national land market, and perfect markets for all of the agricultural products that might be raised on northern and southern lands. It is a tall order.

Even if the lattermost of this string of implicit assumptions was warranted, it might reasonably be argued that the others collectively abstract from the existence of a set of historical circumstances that may well have caused the relative average prices of farm land in the antebellum South to understate their relative average crop yields, in comparison to the farm lands of the North.[55]

Moreover, the assumption that uniform national prices were received by all agricultural producers in 1860 is patently at

[55] Thus, were resident southern landowners preponderant in the market for southern rural land because they had better access to information than non-residents, and were they more risk-averse as a class than northern rural landowners (because those having access to mortgage finance tended to be the larger, wealthier planters, and the degree of risk aversion increases with wealth), it would follow that the market price established for the same future expected stream of land rental yields would be *lower* in the South than in the North. Note that higher southern mortgage rates, and/or shorter time horizons on the part of investors in southern land, would have parallel effects biasing Fogel and Engerman's index of the relative "quality" of southern land inputs in a downward direction. We are not prepared to assert that all these awkward conditions obtained, but the authors have neither discussed the possibility nor adduced any evidence to suggest that such was not the case historically.

variance with well-known facts. To see what comes of tacitly
ignoring this aspect of historical reality, we may proceed by way
of a heuristic example. Suppose that everywhere land was of the
same physical quality in terms of crop yield per acre—given that
the amounts of capital and labor applied per acre also were
everywhere identical. Imagine, further, that in a part of this
hypothetical territory—call it the North—the state subsidized
the transportation of crops to market. Then, for any level of
final market prices, the on-farm price received by the growers
would be higher in the subsidized region. Under the other
assumptions Fogel and Engerman have freely invoked, landowners in the North would be extracting a rent equal to the
transport subsidy on the (standard per acre) crop yield, leaving
farm operators there no worse off than those in the rest of the
country. The resulting higher average value of northern farm
lands—reflecting the capitalization of these differential rents—
would be accepted by Fogel and Engerman as indicative of
higher land "quality," and so would raise the per acre index of
total factor inputs calculated for the North in comparison with
the index they would calculate for the South. But because crop
yields per acre were taken at the outset to be everywhere
identical, the index of physical output per unit of total factor
input *as measured* would then turn out to be lower in the
(northern) region. This "finding" would not reflect anything
regarding the relative physical efficiency of resource utilization
within agriculture per se, but rather the existence of an
external condition represented in the example by the arbitrary
northern transportation subsidy.

At the close of the antebellum era the pattern of North-South
differences in the local prices of agricultural commodities—
largely reflecting the effects of regional differences in transportation costs—was not so far removed from the circumstances
just imagined. There are several alternative adjustments that
might have been attempted to prevent this situation from
imparting an upward bias to the relative factor productivity
measures computed for agriculture in the (higher transport
cost) South. But as long as one continues to use local average
land value as an index of land input "quality," an obvious thing
to do is to symmetrically weight the physical outputs so that a

given quantity of production counts for less if high transport costs—or other regional-specific conditions extrinsic to agriculture—cause farmers to be paid less for it.[56] Fogel and Engerman unfortunately have omitted making any such correction of their output measures; in justification they cite Richard Easterlin's computations for 1840 as showing "about the same relative agricultural output for the South vis-à-vis the North using either nationally uniform prices or regional prices applied to regional physical production" (FE, II, p. 134).

From the same study by Easterlin, however, it appears that in comparing aggregate agricultural production in the South Atlantic states with production in the Middle Atlantic and New England states for 1840, the effect of switching from national price-weights to regional price-weights lowers the relative output measure for the southern region by a factor of 0.899.[57]

[56] As an alternative to the strategy considered in the text discussion, Fogel and Engerman might have attempted to apply a common *national* set of relative average prices in weighting improved and unimproved acreage in the two regions. In the same spirit, it would be possible to compute two separate indexes of relative unit values for all the improved lands within each region, and then set the median values of the two indexes equal.

It should be clear that the procedures sketched here would, and probably should be employed to remove biases in the measurement of land inputs due to the effect of varying transportation conditions on land price levels *within* the South—and not only between the South and the North. It remains unclear to what extent the apparent factor productivity advantage reported for free and slave farms of all sizes in the New South, vis-à-vis corresponding farms in the Old South, actually derives from the lower level of land prices associated with inferior transport conditions in the former region. Cf. FE, II, p. 139, Table B.23, for these comparisons. Fogel and Engerman's text discussion of intra-South factor productivity differences (FE, I, pp. 192–95) does not mention their finding that these extend to free farms as well, but the latter suggests that the greater relative efficiency of New South plantations compared with those of the Old South cannot properly be taken as solely reflecting regional differences in slave plantation characteristics and management.

[57] See Easterlin [1975]. The comparison cited by Fogel and Engerman (FE, II, p. 134) is for the entire South against the entire North in 1840. This yields a (.938) correction factor which would not have quite as large an effect in reducing the relative southern output. (Still, 7 percent represents a fifth of the 35 percent relative efficiency advantage they find for all southern agriculture.) in 1840, however, the transport conditions in the Old Northwest and the

Had just this correction factor been applied by Fogel and Engerman, it would have cancelled out almost half of the substantial (26 percent) upward effect which their dubious land value adjustment imparts to the relative level of factor productivity presented for southern agriculture in comparison with northern farming as a whole.

On the Measurement of Agricultural Output

The third major problem raised by Fogel and Engerman's procedures basically is a conceptual one: it concerns the proper interpretation of their measures of agricultural output in the South relative to that in the North, and hence of their relative efficiency findings. Throughout the preceding discussion the concept of total input efficiency has been used in the same way that the authors employ it—a usage carrying strong *physical* or technical connotations. Indeed, it is precisely this physical interpretation upon which Fogel and Engerman rely in arguing that they can infer something about the "task" efficiency of slaves compared with free laborers on the basis of measures of the comparative rate at which a given bundle of labor, land, and capital inputs could be transformed into agricultural "output" by slave and free farms.

The products of northern and southern farming were not, however, physically identical. Wheat, corn and hogs, for example, were raised in the regions above and below the Mason-Dixon line, but in different proportions. Moreover, the North grew neither cotton, nor rice, nor cane sugar. To form an

---

trans-Mississippi west were much inferior to those prevailing in the southern Gulf Plains and Delta regions, and correspondingly the general level of local prices was higher in the latter than it was in the North Central census region. By 1860, on the other hand, these conditions had been dramatically transformed by the building of railroads and the fuller development of the northern water routes leading to the eastern seaboard. (Cf., for example, Fishlow [1965], pp. 187–200.) For this reason we think the comparison of northern and southern price structures in 1840 based on conditions prevailing along the eastern seaboard—which we have referred to in the text—is more apposite for the purpose of adjusting the 1860 regional agricultural output ratio.

aggregate measure of agricultural output for the two regions it is necessary somehow to render these physically disparate commodities commensurable, and for this purpose Fogel and Engerman adopt the economist's conventional method of weighting the items in the set of output quantities by standard (or uniform) relative prices. This means that the measures of relative aggregate output for northern and southern agriculture depend upon a relative set of exchange values of the various crops prevailing in 1860 and hence reflect *inter alia* the relative commodity preferences of the consumers who participated in the markets where these prices were established. In this aggregation process the initial concept of physical efficiency necessarily undergoes a subtle transmutation: "efficiency" comes to mean using less resources to produce a unit of whatever some standard group of consumers happens to *want*. There is an ineluctable element of arbitrariness about this— which economists recognize by referring to the measurement effects of using one set of price-weights, rather than some other, as "the index number problem." The problem arises in comparing two bundles of commodities which are not identical in composition, i.e., in the relative quantities of the various goods they contain. Placing relatively high valuations on goods which are more amply represented in one bundle (than in the other) makes the aggregate size of that particular bundle appear larger in comparison.

An extreme manifestation of this general problem occurs when one output bundle contains a collection of commodities that is totally missing from some other bundle to which the first is being compared. The easiest way to see what this implies for Fogel and Engerman's "findings" will be to suppose that we were considering two modes of agricultural production that were equally efficient in the physical or "technical" sense. This can be represented by stipulating that, given the same bundle of costly resources, the northern mode and the southern mode would both have the technical capacity to produce the full array of the combinations of "grain" and "cotton" described by the concave transformation curve in Figure 1. For the moment assume that northern and southern agriculturalists faced the same relative prices for cotton and grain, indicated by the slope of the line PP.[58] Were they free to adjust the composition of their output, both should produce the mix of cotton and grain indicated by the point S in Figure 1, as that will bring in the maximum *revenue* (price-weighted output) attainable along the common transformation curve. When both are at S, their respective aggregate products are identical, whether we measure both in terms of "grain equivalent" units along one axis or in terms of "cotton equivalent" units along the other axis. By assumption, the amount of resource input required to produce along the common transformation curve also is the same for northern- and southern-style agriculture; so the ratio between measured total output and measured total input for the South just matches the corresponding "efficiency" measure for the North.

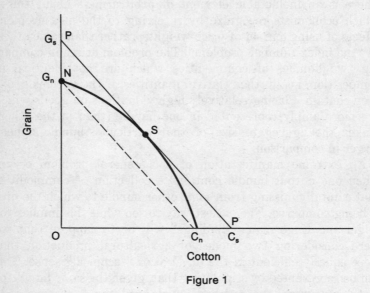

Figure 1

But now suppose that northern agriculturalists in reality were debarred by extraneous (climatic) conditions from raising any

[58] In other words, at the relative price shown by PP, all combinations of cotton and grain represented by different points on PP cost the same amount.

"cotton." Having to specialize in "grain" at point N, their output (evaluated at the prevailing commodity price ratio indicated by the dashed line parallel to PP) would be necessarily smaller than the output recorded for southern agriculture as C_s, or alternatively as G_s. In this extreme situation, which happens to mirror the historically relevant case, the supposed index of relative *technical* efficiency is subject to an upward bias of undetermined magnitude.[59] The cause is the index number problem created by the absence from the northern output set of a class of commodities that figure importantly among the outputs of southern agriculture. Rather than telling us about relative technical efficiency, Fogel and Engerman's findings really report on relative "revenue-earning efficiency" (which is to say, on relative profitability) under a particular set of product- and factor-price conditions. And the relative *revenue* efficiency of the sector which can freely adjust its output mix so as to maximize revenues must in general overstate its relative *technical* efficiency, in comparison with a sector that is confined to producing only some portion of the commodity array.

In the foregoing exposition the effect of climate might have been likened to that of a prohibitive tax levied on the marketing of cotton, sugar, and rice grown in the North, or, equivalently, to a subsidy paid the growers of those crops in the South. From our earlier consideration of the question of regional differences in land values, however, we should be prepared for the argument that competition among "cotton" growers would bid up the rental price of any inelastically supplied factor that was required to produce the (subsidized) crop. If one takes southern land as the sole region-specific input, it would then appear—always assuming perfectly competitive market conditions—that southern rents and, hence, land values would automatically

---

[59] Note that if a higher relative price for cotton ruled than that indicated by the slope of PP in Figure 1, S-producers would move towards greater specialization in growing cotton and the comparison of aggregate outputs evaluated at the new (steeper sloped) price-line would show an even greater advantage for southern agriculture. It should be apparent from the text discussion that Fogel and Engerman's "efficiency" measures for different regions and farm-types *within* the South are subject to the same distorting influences caused by crop-mix variations.

incorporate an appropriate upward adjustment which would prevent the difference between the regions' climatic endowments from reflecting itself in a misleadingly high relative measure of southern efficiency. On this line of reasoning—which the authors do not advance—it would seem that by using relative land *values* Fogel and Engerman actually have managed to allow for the awkward problem of region-specific crops in the southern agricultural output-mix.

But this is not the case. For in the antebellum South there was a factor of production in still more inelastic supply than land, and equally specific to the region: black slave labor. Would not the prices bid for the latter asset reflect the higher revenue which the South's climate made it possible to derive from crops produced with slave labor on a given acre of land, crops that always could be produced more profitably in the South using slaves than using free workers? Elsewhere in *Time on the Cross* it is maintained that such was indeed the case; the presumption that (expected) movements in the price of cotton should have been reflected in the movements of slave prices lies at the roots of Fogel and Engerman's entire discussion of the rational capitalistic character of antebellum slavery.[60] It cannot be abandoned lightly. But to the extent that the rent-creating effects of increases in the price of region-specific southern staples were reflected in the market for *slaves* rather than the land market, the use of average land values in computing the relative measure of land inputs cannot have captured the general effect of latitude on the length of the growing season and the differential ability of the South to raise crops which brought comparatively high revenues per acre.

The conclusion seems inescapable: Fogel and Engerman's factor productivity measures at best can speak to the issue of

---

[60] FE, I, pp. 95–96, especially, where they refer to an equation (eq. 3.10 in Appendix B, FE, II, p. 62) for predicting the course of slave prices on the basis of cotton prices and other information. The justification for this specification clearly has to be that there was enough land in crops other than cotton, in the short-run, and enough land clearable at constant costs per acre, in the long-run, to warrant supposing that slave prices would reflect expected (and actual) cotton price changes. Otherwise the latter would tend to be capitalized into movements in southern land prices.

the comparative "revenue-earning efficiency" of the southern agricultural system, not the comparison between the technical or "standard physical task" efficiency of agriculture using slaves and free family farming. Furthermore, as has been seen from the preceding discussion of the methods used to measure the land and labor inputs, their "findings" lean heavily toward exaggerating even the relative *revenue*-efficiency of southern agriculture. Their inferences about the relative personal efficiency of slave workers, correspondingly are overdrawn.

On Welfare-Efficiency and the Morality of Slavery

Some broader patterns begin to emerge from the welter of details sampled for discussion in the foregoing, admittedly incomplete methodological appraisal of *Time on the Cross*.

Although the authors present their empirical "findings" as objective economic statements uncontaminated by judgments about the "morality" of slavery, their cliometric investigations have been conducted within a conceptual framework whose ethical perspective seems peculiarly one-sided. The authors consider the diet of slaves as given and assess its caloric worth without asking whether blacks under freedom would have chosen to work so hard enough to require so much food energy, or whether the intake allowed them was adequate for *their* actual energy needs. The authors do not inquire how poor a free man—say, a freed black in the Reconstruction period—might have to have been before he chose to obtain such a level of food energy in the carbohydrate-intensive way the slaves were compelled to obtain theirs. Nor do the authors ask how impoverished a free family would have to have been in the nineteenth century before the husband, wife, and children "chose" to toil the number of hours expected of slave families. In reckoning what was being "expropriated" by the masters the authors start by accepting the fact that blacks as slaves were not financially responsible for their own offspring; thus they tacitly suppose that each generation would in any event have had to finance its own upbringing, paying interest charges for loans obtained against future earnings. And, finally, in measuring the comparative "efficiency" of the agricultural system based on slavery, the authors have in effect accepted the contemporary market valuations as measuring the social welfare benefits derived from the specific goods produced by slave labor—while failing to count the longer average hours worked, i.e., the additional leisure lost by slaves as among the social resource costs incurred for that worthwhile "output".

Thus, in quantifying the economic dimensions of the experience of slavery, Fogel and Engerman recurringly slip into a tacit acceptance of the *status quo* of black bondage as the appropriate point of departure for making their evaluations. The resulting work looks at the "economic performance" of the system of slavery mainly from the perspectives of the owners of the human capital and the consumers of the commodities that it produced; the condition of freedom is not correspondingly adopted as an alternative which might be systematically employed in quantifying the economic welfare burdens imposed upon the slave population.

In a brief, concluding exercise (FE, I, p. 244), Fogel and Engerman do present a measure of welfare costs to the blacks of the "non-pecuniary disadvantages" of laboring under the slave plantation's gang system; $75 per head, annually. But this estimate is conceptually inadequate and empirically unfounded. To derive it they argue that the difference between the post-Emancipation earnings of freedmen employed on labor gangs and the earnings of black sharecroppers provides a pecuniary measure of the blacks' distaste for the system in which they were compelled to work under slavery.[61] But beyond

[61] Despite gang wages 2.11 to 2.42 times as large as the earnings of share-croppers (on 4 Louisiana plantations during 1865–66), say Fogel and Engerman, "planters found it impossible to maintain the gang system once they were deprived of the right to apply force," and sharecropping became the predominant mode through which southern Negro labor was mobilized (FE, I, pp. 238–39; FE, II, p. 160). Yet, as the source they cite for these Louisiana earnings differentials makes clear, during the two years in question the weather was miserable and the sharecroppers took a particularly bad financial beating. Moreover, it is noted there that the high wages set in these Louisiana parishes by the Freedmen's Bureau *did succeed in recruiting black gang labor.* In May 1866 only 21 percent of the Negroes under the supervision of the Bureau in Louisiana were sharecroppers instead of working under various types of wage contracts. This "anomalous" preponderance of the

Fogel and Engerman's factual misconstruction of C. E. Seagrave's evidence on this point, it hardly seems adequate to represent the "non-pecuniary" disadvantages of being "driven" by *slave*-drivers as measurable in terms of the difference between the earnings obtained under two alternative systems of *free* labor. And to cap it off, the authors have reckoned the net economic burden imposed on the slaves by deducting—from this inappropriate measure of the gross burden—an allowance for the fictitious pecuniary advantage which slaves allegedly enjoyed in comparison with free agricultural workers (FE, I, pp. 244–45, particularly Table 3).

For reasons such as these it is unfortunately not possible to accept the sanguine belief that the quantitative methods applied in writing *Time on the Cross* truly have fulfilled the authors' expectations by providing "a more *accurate and complete* portrayal of slavery than was previously available." [62]

That the tacit ethical orientation of Fogel and Engerman's "cliometric" contributions should have defeated this aspiration to completeness as well as to accuracy, really is not so surprising. In an important respect the slant of their quantitative work reflects the economist's professional habits of mind, and the methodological pull of the tradition established by Conrad and Meyer's studiously *de-personalized* approach to the issue of slavery's profitability. Those two pioneers of the "new economic history" stressed that the analytical problems of determining the profitability of holding slaves were not different from those met in determining the returns from investments in machines or cattle. Trouble comes, however, from adhering to this bent when venturing beyond the quantification of profitability—a dimension of the institution's performance which certainly was of more immediate interest from the vantage point of some members of antebellum society (the masters) than from that of others (the slaves). In defining what is meant by the *social* "optimality" of resource allocation, or in devising criteria for

system of paying wages for gang labor seems to have persisted in the Louisiana sugar-growing regions (Seagrave [1971], pp. 41–42, 53–54).
[62] FE, II, p. 19 (emphasis added). Undoubtedly Fogel and Engerman are right in identifying the validity of this methodological claim as "the real question."

comparing the allocative "efficiency" of different economic
systems, the natural predisposition of economists is to consider
how affairs appear to the human agents who are capable of
acting so as to better satisfy their wants. Modern economic
welfare theory simply does not encourage one to view life also
from the standpoint of the lathes and the livestock.

Certainly *Time on the Cross* makes it perfectly clear that it is
not any insensitivity on the authors' part to the moral evil of
slavery which has led them to re-evaluate the economic performance of the institution by reference to standards that tend
to embrace the viewpoint of the owners of productive assets,
rather than that of the assets in question. The immorality of
slavery for Fogel and Engerman is unquestionable; it is a
fundamental ethical precept which can be, and is asserted
categorically—regardless of their supposed exoneration of slavery from the "economic indictments" falsely brought against it
by abolitionist propaganda.

> Even if slavery did produce, on the average, better material conditions
> than obtained for free Negro laborers, or white laborers for that matter,
> the *moral* indictment of slavery still prevails. [FE, II, p. 222]

Indeed, we are warned that the historian of slavery who persists
in the neoabolitionist penchant for "continually linking the issue
of morality with physical cruelty, with sexual abuses, or with
mistreatment in respect to food, clothing and shelter," runs the
grave risk of having "obfuscated rather than clarified the
profound immorality of the *system*." [63]

What is one to make of this effort to separate "economics"
from "morality"? [64] A dichotomy works two ways: the authors'

[63] FE, II, p. 222. Kenneth Stampp is charged with having thus "inadvertently
obfuscated" the true immorality of slavery, and with having failed "to stress
that proof of good treatment was insufficient to remove the moral brand" from
the institution.
[64] It is the thesis of Fogel and Engerman's Chapter 5 ("The Origins of the
Economic Indictment of Slavery," FE, I, esp., pp. 158–61) that the "moral
purity" of the eighteenth-century radical Quaker position against slavery
subsequently was diluted by the addition of an "economic indictment"
constructed to meet the propaganda needs of nineteenth-century abolitionists. But as an essay in intellectual history this seems quite incorrect. Cf. Davis
[1966], pp. 291–309, 316–17, on the elements of rational analysis in Quaker

insistence that economic matters should not be permitted to becloud issues of "pure morality" also suggest that no prior ethical judgments have contaminated the "purely economic" findings upon which *Time on the Cross* is based. But do the methods of welfare economics enable one to carry through an ethically neutral re-examination of the comparative social efficiency of the system of slavery? Is it possible to conduct the soft of "value-free" inquiry which Fogel and Engerman appear to envisage as establishing the economic facts concerning the consequences of this particular institutional arrangement, the objective historical truths about which moral judgments subsequently may be made?

The brief answer is that modern welfare theory is quite incapable of supporting such an undertaking. Not only does the central analytical concept of the "welfare efficiency" of a specific pattern of resource allocation have a distinct ethical content, but the ethical premises upon which it rests makes this a peculiarly inappropriate framework within which to comprehend systems based on varying degrees of personal involition.

The notion that questions concerning the allocative efficiency of alternative economic arrangements usefully can be separated from concerns with other aspects of those arrangements, such as the distribution of wealth, income, and ultimately of the human happiness that may be derived from them, is fundamental in modern economic welfare theory. But this notion rests on the idea that maximization is good—that a state of the world in which more of an inherently desired thing is available to be (potentially) shared by all is "better," in some widely shared sense of the word, than states in which there is less. For by moving to such a state at least some individual could be given more of what he desired (made "better off") without necessarily rendering anyone worse off. To such a change reasonable men

---

theology, reflected in a willingness to examine Biblical texts in the light of reason and human standards of justice, as well as for the inclusion in early Quaker tracts of arguments concerning slavery's social and economic consequences. Davis explicitly cites (p. 317) an American Quaker pamphlet of 1713 as anticipating Hinton Rowan Helper's (1857) warning that Negro bondage would promote economic divergences and political conflicts between rich slaveholders and poor whites.

freely would assent. Economists describe states where any individual's further gain must come at someone else's expense to be welfare-efficient, or Pareto-efficient; and a move toward such a position is said to be "Pareto-safe."

Pareto efficiency, then, is not an ethically neutral concept. It rests on the premise that each individual's desires (preferences among goods, and between goods and leisure, and goods today versus goods tomorrow) should be allowed to count. Thus Pareto-safe moves are ethically safe for the "scientific" economist to recommend only because maintaining the new position presumably would require no coercion. Indeed, it is because one presumes that all commodities "consumed" are voluntarily chosen, and all efforts and sacrifices made for the production of commodities are freely rendered, that the commodities ethically can be called "goods." But, once the presupposition of autonomous individual preferences is seriously questioned, it becomes unclear how truly voluntary "choice" is. The serious possibility that what individuals seem to want may be systematically shaped by what they have been allowed to have therefore undermines the ethical foundations of normative welfare analysis. If people who had been long enslaved eventually "chose" to continue in the security of their chains, should we unhesitatingly say that this test revealed bondage to be a "better" condition than freedom?

Welfare analysis based on the search for Pareto optimality not only subscribes to the complex ethical character of that criterion, but "counts" individual preferences only as these can be expressed through market behavior. Recommendations of Pareto-safe changes in the pattern of resource allocation therefore must implicitly accept the past and the existing distribution of income and wealth, the institutional working rules, and the larger social and political power structure. The criterion applies to consensual, "no injury" changes from whatever *status quo* has come to prevail as a result of the past economic and noneconomic processes.

But because the prior specification of property rights can, and usually does exercise a powerful role in determining whether a particular change is deemed Pareto-safe, the rule of unanimity itself carries a strong bias in favor of the *status quo*. A slave set free might not be able, given his prior lack of training, to earn sufficient income both to compensate his master for the loss of his services and improve his own economic welfare. The two parties could not agree on manumission. Yet if a prospective master were obliged fully to compensate a free man for the welfare loss entailed in entering perpetual bondage, it is unlikely that the two could agree to that change either. So in determining which, between slavery and freedom, is the more welfare-efficient economic system, the thing that may well matter most is whether the new economic historian will start from an ethical presumption of the human right to freedom, or accept a factual *status quo* which finds a people already "stolen" and held in bondage.

Modern welfare economics is grounded on the supposition that all market and non-market transactions of interest between individual actors are voluntary. Involuntary transactions, in which goods are wrested from unwilling "sellers" or forced upon unwilling "buyers," amount to theft and extortion, respectively. Such a theory is not helpful for deriving precise statements about the welfare consequences of changes which entail the introduction or further extension of involuntary transactions of the sort essential to slavery. As the ethical premise that each individual's preferences must count underlies the notion that the only "Pareto-safe" (welfare-efficiency justified) changes are those to which there would be unanimous assent, it is difficult to use this apparatus to assess the *comparative* economic welfare-efficiency of slave and free societies. For in imagining the change from one to the other you must acknowledge that the entailed redistribution of property rights violates the ethical premises for making formally justifiable statements about the resulting change in social welfare. When people are enslaved, *welfare necessarily is transferred* to their masters, and there is no ethically neutral way to compare the welfare-efficiency of the resulting institution with the set of outcomes characterizing an alternative institution, under which that particular interpersonal welfare transfer need not take place. Any such comparison would require weighing the slaves' losses against the masters' gains.

There would be no difficulty conducting an analysis of

economic welfare-efficiency that treated slaves as objects, mere instruments of production whose condition was excluded from the purview of welfare considerations except insofar as it impinged on the well-being of the actors whose preferences *did* count. Economic theory is thus well set up to guide us in making coherent statements about the welfare-efficiency of slavery from the standpoint of everyone but the slaves. If this were what *Time on the Cross* had set out to do, it would be both a less arresting and a less misleading book.

CHAPTER SIX

The Care and Feeding of Slaves

Richard Sutch

The nature of the treatment the slaves received is central to the new interpretation of the peculiar institution that is advanced in *Time on the Cross*. Fogel and Engerman's stated objective is to overturn "the economic indictment of slavery," their term for a list of five allegations of which the fifth holds "that slavery provided extremely harsh material conditions of life for the typical slave." The bill of indictment that they have drawn up is in large part artificial, for, as Fogel and Engerman acknowledge, three of the charges regarding the conditions and consequences of slavery have long been disputed by historians of the antebellum South, notably by Lewis C. Gray and Kenneth Stampp.[1] On the profitability of investment in slave plantations, on the economic vitality of the institution, and on the prosperity of the southern economy, the authors of *Time on the Cross* essentially summarize and reaffirm the views of previous writers. By contrast, their assertions regarding the treatment of the

[1] Lewis C. Gray (1933) and Kenneth Stampp (1956). See FE, I, pp. 226, 228–29, and II, pp. 169, 189 and 218. See also FE, I, Chapter 5 and the Epilogue. The other four propositions of the economic indictment, according to Fogel and Engerman are: "1, that slavery was generally an unprofitable investment, or depended on trade in slaves to be profitable, except on new, highly fertile land; 2, that slavery was economically moribund; 3, that slave labor, and agricultural production based on slave labor was economically inefficient; 4, that slavery caused the economy of the South to stagnate, or at least retarded its growth, during the antebellum era" (FE, I, p. 226).

slaves (like their views on the comparative efficiency of slave labor), constitute a major new interpretive theme.

What Fogel and Engerman conclude is that slavery was not harsh and cruel. "The belief that the typical slave was poorly fed is without foundation in fact," they say. "[T]he houses of slaves," they add, "compared well with the housing of free workers in the antebellum era." Furthermore, "it was generally the intent of planters to supply slaves with medical care of a relatively high quality." The latter "finding" helps them to explain why "U.S. slaves had much longer life expectations than free urban industrial workers in both the United States and Europe." In short, the view that slaves were comparatively ill-fed, ill-clothed, ill-housed, and cruelly treated is "an exaggeration of the severity of slavery." [2]

Fogel and Engerman reach these conclusions by arguing that slavery was a business run by "shrewd capitalistic business-men," so that as capitalists, the slaveowners were interested in profit. Fogel and Engerman maintain that the most profitable way to run a slave plantation was to ensure that the slave received good treatment, since good treatment would secure the slaves cooperation. In Fogel and Engerman's view the black slave was a willing, diligent worker, who identified his own interests with that of his owner. Harsh treatment would have resulted in resistance, sabotage, and attempted escape, thus costing more in the long run than it would save in day-to-day expenses. [3]

[2] FE, I, pp. 109, 116, 120, 126, and 262. This chapter deals only with food, shelter, clothing, and health care. I have discussed other aspects of slave treatment in Chapters 2, 3, and 4 of this volume written in collaboration with Herbert Gutman.

[3] See, in particular, FE, I, pp. 52, 83–84, 127, 130, 133–34, 147–51, 202–3, 231–32 and 239–42; and FE, II, pp. 155–58 and 221–22. It has already been suggested that *Time on the Cross* has stereotyped the American slave as a character from a novel by Horatio Alger (Chapter 2), a "bourgeois" (David and Temin [1975]), and as an "Uncle Tom" (Ransom, [1974]). Fogel and Engerman recognize this themselves, but dismiss as "myths" notions which would turn "those who struggled for self-improvement in the only way they could into 'Uncle Toms' " (FE, I, pp. 263–64). While Fogel and Engerman emphasize the benign implications of an economic system which recognizes property rights in human beings, they nevertheless reject slavery on "moral" grounds (FE, II, p. 222).

However, the logic of this argument need not be compelling. It turns on the *assumption* that harsh treatment would have incurred more costs than it saved, and *Time on the Cross* does not support this assumption with factual evidence or defend it with argument. Rather, Fogel and Engerman present explicit "new evidence" on the quality of slave treatment. They have estimated the diet of the typical slave and characterize it as varied and nutritious. They describe the typical slave cabin, and imply that it was relatively comfortable. They list the items of clothing typically provided for slaves and suggest that they were ample. They discuss the medical care provided slaves, review statistics on morbidity, infant mortality, and life expectancy, and they conclude that the quality of health care was quite good by the standards of the time.

It is this new evidence therefore that I will examine more closely. What follows is a page-by-page and, in some cases, a line-by-line dissection of several major issues raised in *Time on the Cross* concerning the material treatment of the slaves. For this purpose I have accepted the procedures adopted by Fogel and Engerman—although not always without question—and I have asked whether or not the procedures were carried out correctly. In each case I have found so many errors of computation or citation, the data so selective or weak, and the presentation of the results so distorted that I have been forced to conclude that in this important respect *Time on the Cross* is a failure. It not only fails to establish that American slaves received good treatment, but it also fails to provide an example of the power or usefulness of "cliometrics."

Food: Quantity and Variety

Food fulfills two purposes in the life of a free man. It provides the nourishment required by the human body, and, perhaps as important, it is also one of the primary sources of enjoyment in life. Beyond the necessary caloric and nutritional requirements, the free man selects a diet which provides variety, refinement of taste, and, occasionally, luxury. In fact, in the United States today, almost the entire expenditure of money for food can be said to be for its hedonic attributes rather than the nutritional necessities. George Stigler pointed out some time ago that a nutritionally adequate diet could be purchased for a mere $39.93 per *year* at the prices prevailing in August of 1939. It consisted almost entirely of dried navy beans, wheat flour, and cabbage.[4]

Any slaveowner, but particularly the capitalistic profit-max-imizing businessman envisioned by Fogel and Engerman, would find it in his own interest to provide a diet for his slaves with ample calories and, to the best of his knowledge, ample nutrients for good health. Economic incentive, then, if not human kindness, would rule out serious food deprivation as a characteristic of slave life. There is no question that the slave diet was sufficient to maintain the slave's body weight and general health. The rapid growth of the slave population between 1810 and 1860 and the relatively high life expectancy of slaves suggests a tolerable standard of health. Moreover, none of the contemporary observers who were critical of the slave diet described the slaves as malnourished.[5] The issue, then, is not whether the slaves were typically starved. They clearly were not. Rather, Fogel and Engerman join the debate with the historians who precede them over the issue of the variety and quality of the slave's diet.[6]

Economic considerations, it is usually argued, would rule out both variety and luxury from the slave diet. To provide diversity and refinement would cost money. Unless such expenditures were justified by increased output per slave, it would not be in the master's interest to provide them. This argument suggests that slaves received a monotonous and barely adequate diet, and

[4] Stigler [1945], p. 311. The retail cost of the same diet today would be approximately $253.00 per year. An even less expensive diet could undoubt-edly be found, since shifts in relative prices since 1939 have probably brought other foods into contention.

[5] For a summary of the views of contemporary observers who were critical of the slave diet, see Postell ([1951], pp. 48–49) and Phillips ([1929], pp. 213–14). Olmsted on occasions described slaves as "abundantly supplied" ([1860], p. 74), "well fed" ([1860], p. 202), and as having "plenty to eat" ([1856], p. 110). For population data, see U.S. Bureau of the Census [1918]. For estimates of life expectancy see my discussion below and FE, I, Fig. 36, p. 125.

[6] FE, I, pp. 111–15. Fogel and Engerman did place the calorie intake of an adult field hand significantly above that implied by the standard ration. The implications of this upward revision is discussed in the next section.

the evidence collected by historians seems to confirm this prediction. Writers from such diverse schools as U. B. Phillips, Charles Sydnor, Rosser Taylor, Lewis C. Gray, and Kenneth Stampp all agree that the standard food ration issued to an adult field hand consisted of 3½ pounds of "salt pork" or "bacon" and 1 peck of corn meal per week.[7] A diet of salt pork and corn meal would indeed be "wanting in variety," and despite the legendary skill of southern cooks, meals would be likely to be "coarse" and "crude." [8]

Fogel and Engerman contend that this "pork-corn ration" is a mistaken view of the actual slave diet, which arose from the "misinterpretation of the instructions of masters to their overseers" (FE, I, pp. 109–10). The pork and corn allowances mentioned in these instructions, they believe, were only a shorthand for the quantities of *meat* in general, and the quantities of all *grains and vegetables* which were to be served. According to *Time on the Cross*, substitutions of foods other than pork and corn were implicit in the instructions to overseers. In practice, the substitutions included beef or molasses in place of pork, and sweet potatoes, beans, or even wheat flour in place of corn.

There can be little doubt that such substitutions occasionally took place. The context surrounding the overseers' instructions about pork and corn often made that explicit. More doubtful, however, is Fogel and Engerman's claims that historians have misinterpreted those instructions. Not only have historians noted the possibility of a more varied diet, but they never relied exclusively upon overseers' instructions for their information about diet in the first place. The notion that the slave's diet was based *primarily* upon pork and corn is also supported by the observations of travelers such as Olmsted, by articles written by slaveowners on the "proper" care of Negroes which appeared in

---

[7] The references are Phillips ([1918], pp. 265–66, 277, and 279); Sydnor ([1933], pp. 31–32); Taylor [1924]; Gray ([1933], I, p. 563); and Stampp ([1956], pp. 282–89). The most recent detailed study by Sam Hilliard also confirmed this finding ([1972], pp. 104–5, 157, and 272).

[8] The quotations are from Olmsted ([1856], p. 700). They have been cited by Stampp ([1956], p. 285) and were quoted back to him by Fogel and Engerman (FE, II, p. 240).

such southern journals as *De Bow's Review*, by the autobiographies and recollections of ex-slaves, and by surveys of planters conducted by the U.S. Patent Office and the U.S. Department of Agriculture. It cannot be argued that an overseer's shorthand was employed in all of these sources.[9]

Fogel and Engerman's attack on the conventional view, however, is not actually based, even in part, upon a reinterpretation of masters' instructions to overseers, although they try to give that impression, for example, when they assert that:

> More careful reading of plantation documents shows that the slave diet included many foods in addition to corn and pork. Among the other plantation products which slaves consumed were beef, mutton, chickens, milk, turnips, peas, squashes, sweet potatoes, apples, plums, oranges, pumpkins, and peaches. . . . salt, sugar, and molasses. . . . fish, coffee, and whiskey. [FE, I, p. 111].

It is doubtless true that every one of these foods is mentioned somewhere in "plantation documents" although Fogel and Engerman do not provide citations.[10] Rather than such documentation, they relied instead upon the Agricultural Census of 1860 to estimate the *production* of food on slave plantations. As they put it:

> The fallacy in the position of those who argue that slaves were poorly fed stems from the failure to recognize the implications of the fact that the South in general, and big plantations in particular, produced large quantities of food in addition to pork and corn. If these other foods were not being consumed by slaves, where were they going? (FE, II, pp. 90–91]

They dismiss the possibility that much of the food produced

[9] For an example of a traveler's report, see Olmsted [1856], pp. 108, 432, 706, and quoting others on pp. 691, 693, and 697; and [1860], pp. 42, 50, 74–75, and 201. In *De Bow's Review* see Anonymous ([1847], p. 420); Anonymous ([1849], pp. 380 and 382); Agricola ([1851], p. 325); Mississippi Planter ([1851], p. 623); and Cocke ([1853], p. 177). For autobiographies and recollections of former slaves, see Blassingame [1972]. The U.S. Patent Office reports on surveys of planters ([1848], pp. 478, 493, and 500); ([1851], p. 325); and ([1852], p. 86), corresponded to later surveys by the Department of Agriculture, e.g. USDA ([1867], p. 416).

[10] The best discussion, which is also profusely documented, of the antebellum diet is Hilliard's [1972], particularly Chapters 3, 7, and 9. See also Postell ([1951], Chap. 3).

could have been consumed by whites for "whites formed less than 10 percent of the [sampled] population") or that any crops other than corn or small grains could have been fed to animals (such a practice would have been poor economics and questionable animal husbandry) (FE, II, pp. 91–92 and 95). They assume that no foodstuffs other than 30 percent of the beef and 15 percent of the pork production were sold off the slave plantations (FE, II, p. 94). With these problems out of the way, the production of food is estimated from the crop outputs and livestock inventories for a sample of slave plantations drawn from the manuscript schedules prepared by the enumerators of the census.[11] Fogel and Engerman then compute the slave diet as a residual from this estimate of food production. In other words, they assume that all of the food produced, after deducting allowances for grain fed to animals, food consumed by resident whites, and meat sold off the farm, was eaten by the slaves (FE, II, pp. 92–95).

The obvious danger inherent in this residual technique is that its accuracy depends upon identifying all of the alternative uses for the output and accurately estimating their magnitude. If some uses for the crop are overlooked or underestimated, the residual and hence the estimated slave diet will be exaggerated. Regrettably, Fogel and Engerman's treatment of these difficulties is not reassuring.

They do not explain how they arrived at, nor do they justify, their estimate that 30 percent of the beef and 15 percent of the pork were the only food products sold. Considering that 15 percent of the entire stock of cattle on the farms included in Fogel and Engerman's sample were located on just four farms in two Texas counties, their deduction of only 30 percent of the beef for off-farm sale may be too low.[12] Robert Gallman, using

---

[11] Fogel and Engerman based their computations upon a sample of farms from the cotton regions of the South collected by William Parker and Robert Gallman for use in an unrelated series of studies (Parker [1970]). This source is not cited in *Time on the Cross*. Its use has been confirmed by Stanley Engerman in private correspondence (July 15, 1974). For details on the Parker-Gallman sample, see Wright [1970] and Foust [1967].

[12] I have examined a copy of the original Parker-Gallman sample of farms. The four Texas farms mentioned were located in the counties of Falls and Grimes.

the identical sample of farms, found evidence which suggested that southern farms produced surplus food, particularly pork.

> [S]urplus meat production was equal to almost 30 percent of the total meat output of the sample farms. . . . The farms of the cotton South, far from being dependent on external sources of basic foods, were in a position to supply food to outsiders on an impressive scale.

This finding at least suggests the possibility that *Time on the Cross* underestimates off-farm sales of food.[13]

Fogel and Engerman apparently hoped to minimize this possibility by excluding *all* farms located in counties within 50 wagon miles of a city (size unspecified), the logic being that these farms would have had no outlet for their surpluses.[14] As it turns out, this exclusion of farms with access to urban markets did not have the intended effect of excluding all sales, and it severely constrained the geographical area upon which the results were based. The final sample used by Fogel and Engerman drew farms from only 44 of the 413 counties originally sampled by Parker and Gallman.[15] These 44 counties are disproportionately located in the back country, but their isolation did not have a depressing effect upon their production of foodstuffs. In fact, the included farms actually produced more, not less, food per resident slave than those excluded.

A critical step in using the residual method to estimate the diet of slaves is the estimation of the food consumed by whites. Since over one-half of the South's population was free, any errors committed in estimating the consumption of free persons would be magnified and transmitted to the residual. "Since" Fogel and Engerman have, they say, "no systematic information on the diets of these whites . . . ," they "resolved the issue by assuming that their consumption of particular foods was substantially in excess of national averages." They argue that this

---

Between them the four farms had a herd of 580 cattle. I am indebted to William Parker and Robert Gallman for making a copy of their data available to me and to Stanley Engerman and Robert Fogel for providing me with a list of the farms included in their sub-sample.

[13] Gallman [1970], p. 19.

[14] See FE, II, p. 94. I have been informed in a letter from Engerman (November 4, 1974) that all cities with a population greater than 2500 were considered.

[15] Letter from Stanley Engerman (July 15, 1974).

procedure will lead to an underestimation of slave consumption, but that the error introduced would be "less than 5 percent" (FE, I, p. 11).

That a "substantial" overestimation of white consumption led to only a "relatively small" (p. 11) underestimation of the slave diet is explained by a second restriction Fogel and Engerman place upon their sample. They exclude all farms with less than 51 slaves. This is done "to separate free from slave consumption" by minimizing the number of whites (FE, II, p. 94). While over one-half of the population of the slave states was white, Fogel and Engerman find that "less than 10 percent" (actually 8.0 percent) of the total population on farms with over 50 slaves was free (FE, II, p. 91).

This exclusion of farms with less than 51 slaves together with the restriction of the sample to back-country regions sharply reduced the sample size. William Parker and Robert Gallman originally collected a sample of 5229 farms from the cotton growing regions of the South.[16] Fogel and Engerman's subsample retains only 77 plantations, or less than 1.5 percent of the full sample. The subsample includes less than 10 percent of the total population surveyed in the original Parker-Gallman sample.

The restriction of the sample to large plantations also reintroduced the problem of off-farm sales, although Fogel and Engerman do not seem to be aware of that fact. In any case, they do not exclude the possibility that large slave plantations produced surplus food which they sold, not to urban markets, but to neighboring small farms. Gallman's study should have given them pause. He found that large farms produced substantially more grain per capita and had more grain remaining after other uses to feed their swine. They also produced more meat per capita than did small farms.[17] This finding, based on the same sample of farms as that used by Fogel and Engerman, certainly opens up the possibility that transactions between large and small farms took place. If indeed they did take place, then *Time on the Cross* exaggerates the availability of food for the slave population.

[16] Gallman [1970], p. 6.
[17] Gallman [1970], pp. 7, 11, 14, and 17.

If these off-farm sales did *not* take place, Gallman's results would still discredit Fogel and Engerman's attempt to estimate the "average daily diet" of the "typical slave" (FE, I, pp. 113 and 109). If the large plantations did not sell food to small plantations, then the slaves on large plantations must have been much more adequately fed than those on small farms. How else can Gallman's finding be interpreted?

Fogel and Engerman attempt to dismiss this second possibility by asserting that "Stampp believed that the diet of slaves was poorer on large than on small plantations" (FE, II, p. 240). The difficulty with this attempt is that Stampp did *not* make this assertion on the page cited by Fogel and Engerman.[18] What Stampp did say on that page was that the use of slave cooks and a common kitchen "resulted ordinarily in a better diet" than did the practice of allowing slaves to prepare their own food. He went on to suggest that the larger plantations would be more likely to have "special cooks and kitchens." [19] If anything, Stampp implied that slaves on large plantations were more adequately fed. Olmsted, for one, would have agreed. He observed that "wealthier slave owners" with a large body of slaves manifested a "greater ability to deal with their dependents indulgently and bountifully." [20]

Fogel and Engerman's device of "overfeeding" the whites in order to deliberately underestimate the typical slave diet is also seriously flawed in its application. The major issue under contention is not the quantity of food fed to the slaves, but rather the *variety* of foodstuffs in their diet. Yet they assume that whites ate the same foods as the slaves, with the exception of only beef and milk. It is by making the presumption that free residents on slave plantations "consumed twice as much beef as the national average [of 1879] and 1.5 times as much milk as the national average" that Fogel and Engerman achieve their "overestimate" of the free diet (FE, II, p. 95).[21] This presump-

[18] *Time on the Cross* (FE, II, p. 240) cites Stampp ([1956], p. 288). Stampp did comment on another page (284) that "there seemed to be no appreciable difference in the *quality or variety* of foods given slaves . . . in the practices of large and small slaveholders" (emphasis supplied).
[19] Stampp [1956], p. 288.
[20] Olmsted [1860], p. 65.
[21] Fogel and Engerman assert that "[t]his overfeeding resulted in an average intake per white of about 5,300 calories" (FE, II, p. 95). The data presented in

tion may overestimate the amount of beef and milk in the free diet, and it undoubtedly exaggerates the amount of pork and corn eaten by whites as well, but it also will certainly *underestimate* the amounts of lamb, wheat, Irish potatoes, and other foods consumed by whites.

The procedure obviously distorts the relative proportion of foods in the free diet, and this distortion is transmitted to the estimated slave diet. It is usually contended that free persons ate less pork and corn relative to other foods than did slaves. Fogel and Engerman assume they ate as much. If this exaggerated estimate of the pork and corn consumed by free persons is subtracted from the total food output, then the residual output will underestimate the pork and corn in the slave diet relative to the other foods. In other words, Fogel and Engerman produce the appearance of greater variety in the diet of the slave by creating an artificial parity between slave and free diets.

The "overfed" whites were the resident free whites of the large farms in Parker and Gallman's study. Yet, Fogel and Engerman surely underestimate the number of free persons residing upon the large farms. The Parker-Gallman sample was drawn from the enumerators' returns of the Agricultural Census. The name of the farm operator for each farm sampled was then located in the free population census of the same enumeration district (a region generally smaller than a county).[22] The entire population of the house in which the farm operator lived was then counted as the resident free population.[23] Only those whites living under the same roof as the

---

their Table B. 13 (FE, II, p. 97) shows that the 1860 slave diet with twice the beef and 1.5 times the milk of the 1879 free diet replacing the slave's allowances for these two foods would provide only 4638 calories per day. Fogel and Engerman apparently added to this number the 614 calories per day provided by "All Other Foods" which were part of the free diet of 1879 but were not included in the slave diet (p. 97). This would bring the total to 5252 calories per day or "about 5,300."

[22] If the name could not be located, either because the farm operator lived elsewhere or was omitted by error from the population census, the farm was eliminated from the sample (Wright [1970], p. 98). See also Gallman [1965] for more information on the Parker-Gallman sampling procedure.

[23] The slave population had to be obtained from a third set of census manuscripts by a similar matching procedure.

designated farm operator would be included in this count, while any who lived in separate houses would be omitted. The larger the plantation the greater the likelihood that the free population would be distributed in more than one house. Overseers, for example, frequently lived apart from the masters of the plantation. Hence it is uncertain how large a free white population was being fed by on-farm production.

Robert Fogel and Stanley Engerman attempt to make a virtue of their "overfeeding" of the resident free population. Yet, their failure to completely count that population or justify their estimates of *what* it was fed vitiates their contention that the consumption of slaves is biased downward by their procedure. The difficulties with the procedures which Fogel and Engerman adopt to isolate the slaves' diet from the aggregate production of foodstuffs are sufficiently great to convince me that their results would be unacceptable whatever they revealed. Not until further research has established the extent and composition of off-farm sales as well as the diet of whites on slave plantations can much reliability be hoped for from this residual technique.[24] Nevertheless, I feel it is important to pursue Fogel and Engerman's use of the census data in their attempt to estimate the slave diet one step further. I do this, not to perfect their diet estimates, but to review critically their use of historical sources and their application of statistical procedures.

Estimating Food Production: A View from 1900

The Census of 1860 did not collect information on food production. It collected data only on crop yields and livestock inventories. To estimate the output of food Fogel and Engerman apply conversion factors which they assume reflect the relationships between crop output and food output or between livestock numbers and meat production. For the most part the conversion

[24] I should also point out that Fogel and Engerman made no allowance for food losses due to spoilage, insect damage, or cooking. This neglect contributes to the exaggeration of both the bulk and variety of the slave diet.

ratios used in *Time on the Cross* are based upon national experience around the end of the nineteenth century. However, there is abundant evidence that antebellum slave plantations were neither as productive nor as efficient in the conversion of agricultural output into food as were the commercial food processing industries circa 1900. If I am correct, this anachronistic (and anachoristic) use of conversion ratios coupled with a large number of errors conspired to systematically *under*estimate the quantity of pork and corn meal produced and *over*estimate the quantities of other meats, grains, and milk. If this is so, then the slave diet was substantially less varied than Fogel and Engerman picture it.

To simplify my argument, I shall adopt Fogel and Engerman's residual procedure and employ the identical sample of farms despite my belief that this is not the way to produce a reliable estimate. In this section I shall address only the problems of converting census data to estimates of food production. To record the implications of the points I wish to make, I have compared in Table 1 (page 262) the diet estimated by Fogel and Engerman and the diet they might have estimated had they accepted the corrections I offer. I shall begin my detailed discussion with pork, then turn to other meats, milk, vegetables and miscellaneous grains before finally returning to discuss the corn allowance.

Pork: The Census of 1860 did not collect the quantity of meat produced on farms. Rather, it enumerated the number of livestock on hand June 1, 1860.[25] The estimates of meat production made by Fogel and Engerman are derived from estimates of the average live weight of animals when slaughtered, the ratio of dressed weight to live weight, and the

[25] The Census did, however, enumerate the *value* of animals slaughtered. It is surprising that Fogel and Engerman did not try to exploit these statistics in light of the complexities of converting livestock inventories into the annual production of meat. On the farms included in their sample an average of $10.34 worth of meat per slave was produced in 1859. At $6.00 a hundred weight (a typical wholesale price of pork in Cincinnati in the late 1850s [Berry (1943), Table 27, p. 571] this would be the value of 172 pounds of pork (net)—approximately the weight of meat which I ultimately estimate for the purposes of Table 1 (150 pounds of pork plus 29 pounds of beef).

fraction of the June 1 inventory which was slaughtered. In the case of swine, Fogel and Engerman estimated the live weight of hogs at 160 pounds and the dressed-to-live-weight ratio at 0.53, thereby calculating that only 84.8 pounds of meat (including bones and lard) were derived from each slaughter (FE, II, p. 95).

They take the 160 pound live-weight estimate from Gallman who was explicitly attempting to *underestimate* the meat supply and Fogel and Engerman paradoxically add the comment that "this figure may be too low, since weights contained in plantation records probably are slaughter, rather than live, weights" (FE, II, p. 95).[26] This statement is puzzling since Robert Gallman was quite conscious of this problem. He discussed it at length, and concluded that the weight estimates of Genovese and Jane Gallman based on plantation records probably do measure net (dressed) weight and not gross (live) weight. Genovese's estimate was 140 pounds and Jane Gallman's was 144 pounds. Robert Gallman accordingly suggested that the true *live* weight of an antebellum hog at slaughter was approximately 186–92 pounds.[27] His acceptance of 160 pounds introduced a deliberate downward bias into his self-sufficiency estimate.[28] This figure is indeed too low, but not for the reasons given in *Time on the Cross*.

Fogel and Engerman take the ratio of dressed to live weight to be 0.53 (FE, II, p. 95). Despite a number of citations, it is not clear how they obtain this ratio. It was previously used by Fogel in his work on railroads where it appeared without supporting citation.[29] In any case, there is overwhelming evidence that this

26 Gallman [1970], p. 19.
27 Gallman [1970], pp. 15–16. See also Genovese [1965], p. 115. Gallman uses a dressed- to live-weight ratio of 0.75 ([1970], p. 15). Fogel and Engerman use a ratio of 0.53 (FE, II, p. 95). Acceptance of this lower ratio should have required Fogel and Engerman to reestimate the live weight based on the Genovese-Gallman net weight estimate upward to the range of 264–72 pounds, a full one hundred pounds above the weight they assume.
28 Gallman [1970], p. 19.
29 Fogel [1964], p. 43. The other citations provided by *Time on the Cross* do not help. One of them is to a five-volume work but without a page reference (Holmes [1916]). The only discussion of the dressing yield of swine which I could find in this publication gives three estimates ranging from 76.2 to 78.0 percent (Holmes [1916], I, pp. 137 and 276). It is true that the ratio of total pork

ratio is too low. Berry, in his study of the antebellum Cincinnati market, put the ratio at 0.80, which is consistent with the price differential he observed between swine on the hoof and swine dressed.[30] The U.S. Commissioner of Patents collected information on the dressing yield of hogs in 1849. The responses from Virginia and North Carolina suggest a ratio of 0.8. Gallman cites Cincinnati market data on weights from 1870 to 1880 to support his use of a 0.75 ratio, Battalio and Kagel use a ratio of 0.76, and the ratio Hutchinson and Williamson use is 0.75. The currently accepted conversion factors of the USDA suggest that 22 percent of the live weight of a pig is skin (5 percent) and inedible waste (17 percent) and that the dressing yield is 76.1 percent. The effect of Fogel and Engerman's underestimate of the dressing yield is to understate the pork consumption of slaves.[31]

consumption in the United States in 1899 given in one of the other citations (USDA [1958], p. 284) to the estimated total live weight of hogs slaughtered that year given in another (Strauss and Bean [1940], p. 119) is 0.55 but this ratio cannot be the basis of Fogel and Engerman's calculation since the consumption figures are net of exports, increases in the inventory of meat, and military purchases (USDA [1958], p. 287). I might note that this source gives the monthly average dressing yields for the period January 1921 through December 1957 from federally inspected slaughters. The ratios range from 72.5 to 77.8 (p. 202).

[30] Berry [1943], p. 144. Berry cites an unpublished paper by H. E. White in which the ratio of the net price to gross price per hundred weight calculated from data for the years 1853–67 is 1.220588235 (Berry, [1943], p. 145), which—assuming no premium for the labor involved in slaughtering—implies a weight ratio of .82. A charge for slaughtering would increase the ratio.

[31] USPO ([1849], pp. 138 and 143); Gallman ([1970], p. 15); Battalio and Kagel ([1970], p. 37); and Hutchinson and Williamson ([1971], p. 603). Current USDA estimates from USDA, ERS [1965], pp. 5 and 9. Fogel and Engerman suggested at the MSSB-Rochester conference that their dressing yield was intended to be net of the lard content of hogs (Fogel and Engerman, 1974, p. 21). The modern yield of pork excluding lard is 57.9 percent of the live weight of the hog (USDA, ERS [1965], p. 9). This counterargument would be well taken if the 1879 pork consumption data used by Fogel and Engerman for comparison with the slave's diet or the nutritional content of the pork used to calculate the caloric and dietary value of the slave ration were for lean meat. Neither of these conditions, however, are met. To obtain the 86 pounds of pork annually consumed per capita by the U.S. population in 1879 Fogel and Engerman included 13.2 pounds of lard together with 50 pounds of lean pork

Some of the difficulties in estimating the net weight per hog slaughtered can be avoided by simply relying upon the great deal of *direct* evidence which has been collected upon this datum, thereby bypassing the problems associated with the Fogel-Engerman dressing yield. Eugene Genovese has examined plantation records for "almost 4,000 hogs" with the resulting estimate of a median slaughter (dressed) weight of 140 pounds. Jane Gallman has collected records on 2115 southern hogs "all slaughtered in the 1850's and early 1860's" and found an average dressed weight of 144 pounds. Hilliard has studied the records of 11,212 slaughters and reported an average dressed weight of 146 pounds.[32] Seventeen thousand hogs can't be wrong. A dressed-weight average of 85 pounds (the number used by Fogel and Engerman) is at least 40 percent below the mark. Accordingly, I have revised Fogel and Engerman's estimate of 88 pounds of pork per year per slave upward by an additional 70 percent based upon a revised net slaughter weight of 144 pounds.[33]

I have accepted Fogel and Engerman's slaughter-to-inventory ratio of 0.83 (FE, II, p. 95). This is higher than that used by other scholars, but in each case the other estimates were described as "too low" or "conservative." These alternative estimates of the slaughter ratio were derived from assumptions about the average surviving litter size, the average number of litters, and the average age at slaughter.[34] My own research

---

and 23 pounds of bacon and salt pork per capita (Bennett and Pierce [1961], p. 114). Stanley Engerman has informed me (letter of July 15, 1974) that the calorie and nutritional content of pork was taken from the 1963 edition of the USDA's *Composition of Foods* (Watt and Merrill [1963]). (Fogel and Engerman's citation of the 1950 edition of Watt and Merrill (FE, II, pp. 98 and 265) is an error.) This source gives the calories of swine meat *including* lard (Watt and Merrill [1963], Item 1659, pp. 47 and 103).

[32] Genovese ([1965], pp. 115 and 122–23), Gallman ([1970], pp. 15–16), Hilliard ([1972], p. 102). The 7718 animals killed from 1845 to 1861 in Hilliard's sample averaged a heftier 153 pounds ([1972], p. 261).

[33] A net slaughter weight of 144 pounds is also corroborated by correspondents of the Commissioner of Patents in 1848 (USPO [1848], pp. 470, 481, and 678–680) and in 1849 (USPO [1849], pp. 138, 140, and 143).

[34] Fogel and Engerman do not explain the derivation of their slaughter ratio. Gallman assumes 0.5 but says this is "probably a little too low" ([1970], pp. 14

suggests that the number of pigs saved per litter averaged between four and five. The number of litters must have exceeded one per sow, on the average, since the better-managed plantations arranged both spring and fall farrowings. Most critical, however, is the evidence that the antebellum slaughter age of swine ranged from 12 to 18 months, and averaged 16, rather than lying within the 20–36 month range assumed by the other authors. If I am correct in taking the average age at slaughter to be 16 months, a litter size of 4, and further in assuming that 20 percent of the sows had a fall as well as a spring litter, then the killings as a ratio to the June inventory would be 0.83, Fogel and Engerman's own estimate.[35]

Beef: If Fogel and Engerman err on the low side in estimating pork production, they offset this by exaggerating the amount of beef and mutton available for consumption. They put the live weight of southern cattle when slaughtered at 750 pounds and cite Gray as their source (FE, II, p. 96). However, Gray's figure was taken from a Richmond, Virginia, stockyard and was not

---

and 17). Battalio and Kagel use 0.45 ([1970], p. 36). Hutchinson and Williamson estimate the slaughter ratio at 0.67 based on "conservative" assumptions ([1971], pp. 603 and 611–12). Hilliard put the slaughter ratio between 0.43 and 0.75 although he favors the higher figure ([1972], pp. 104 and 260). For estimating slaughters from 1866 to 1898, Strauss and Bean used a slaughter ratio of 1.022 on the January first inventory based on U.S. data from 1899–1910 ([1940], p. 116). Since the ratio of inventories on January 1 are approximately 81 to 85 percent of the June first levels (Towne and Rasmussen [1960], p. 284; and USDA [1937], pp. 13, 21, and 26), a slaughter rate of 83 percent is consistent with turn-of-the-century experience. In the antebellum studies estimated litter size ranged from two (Gallman [1970], p. 14) to five (Battalio and Kagel [1970], p. 36). Except for Gallman, who assumed two litters per year, one annual farrowing per sow was taken as average. The age at slaughter ranged from 20 months (Gallman [1970], p. 14) to 36 months (Hilliard [1972], pp. 103–4; and Hutchinson and Williamson [1971], pp. 611–12).

[35] For evidence on the average age at slaughter, see USPO ([1840], pp. 120, 138, 140, 143, 296, and 297) and Ellsworth ([1840], pp. 194–95). A farmer could obtain an annual slaughter of 24 hogs from five breeding sows. The June inventory, taken by the census enumerators, would include the five sows, 20 pigs from the spring farrowing, and four shoats from the previous fall. I have knowingly neglected to consider boars. Hilliard cites plantation records suggesting a sow-boar ratio of at least 12 ([1972], p. 103) which would lower the slaughter ratio to only 0.82.

intended to represent a typical farm slaughter.[36] Fogel and
Engerman attempt to lend credence to their 750 pound live
weight by noting that "at this weight the average live weight of
northern cattle at slaughter exceeded that of southern cattle by
more than one third" (FE, II, p. 96). However, their weight
average for northern cattle was based upon Department of
Agriculture estimates for the years around 1899, not upon
northern estimates for the late antebellum period. Northern
cattle at that time, according to Bidwell and Falconer, weighed
approximately 650 pounds.[37]

Gallman put the *average* farm weight of antebellum southern
beef cattle at 500 pounds.[38] Battalio and Kagel take 450 pounds
as average, but they describe this weight as "small." Hutchinson
and Williamson offer several contemporary citations to support
the range of 500 to 600 pounds for the live weight of southern
cattle. The U.S. Patent Office *Report* for 1848 gives live weights
varying from 300 to 600 pounds.[39] I think 500 pounds would be a

[36] Gray [1933], II, p. 846.
[37] Bidwell and Falconer [1925], pp. 401–403. Strauss and Bean ([1940], p. 106)
were the authority cited by Towne and Rasmussen ([1960], pp. 281–83) who
are cited at FE, II, p. 96 as the authority for the weight of northern cattle
around 1899.
[38] Gallman [1970], p. 12. Fogel and Engerman erroneously reported Gallman's
figure as 550 pounds rather than 500 pounds (FE, II, p. 96). Gallman notes that
his estimated weight is inconsistent with the feeding standards for cattle he
adopted. "The feeding standards would have produced more beef than the
[500-pound] estimates allow for" (Gallman [1970], p. 12). This is because
Gallman deliberately biased his feeding standards upward (p. 11), *not*
because he biased the live weight of beef cattle downward.
[39] Gallman ([1970], p. 12), Battalio and Kagel ([1970], pp. 37 and 30),
Hutchinson and Williamson ([1971], p. 604), and USPO ([1848], pp. 474–75,
and 678–80). The manuscripts of the 1880 Manufacturing Census schedules
reported 70 slaughterhouses in the rural counties (that is, those without a city
of 4000 or more [Ransom and Sutch, 1971, Appendix C]) of South Carolina,
Georgia, Alabama, Mississippi, and Louisiana. In all they reported the
slaughter in 1879 of 14,396 "beeves" with an overall average gross weight of
469.5 pounds. Georgia was the only state to report an average live weight at
slaughter exceeding 500 pounds. Her 28 rural slaughterhouses averaged 535
pounds. In 1880 the Georgia Department of Agriculture surveyed stock
raisers in every county of that state. The average *net* weight of beef cattle as
sold was reported at 342 pounds (GaDA [1880], p. 10), implying a live weight
of 662 pounds. Since the farmers surveyed were considered to be the more

reasonable allowance for the weight of southern cattle. Therefore, I suggest that Fogel and Engerman's estimates of beef
consumption are 50 percent too large.[40]

Mutton: Fogel and Engerman give no information concerning
their estimates of mutton consumption and Gallman, Fogel and
Engerman's cited source (FE, II, p. 94), does not make mutton
estimates. I have been told in a letter from Stanley Engerman
that they used Towne and Rasmussen's estimate of the average
live weight of sheep for the United States. Towne and Rasmussen's estimate was in turn based upon Strauss and Bean's
estimate for 1900.[41] Fogel and Engerman, however, have little
justification for employing this procedure. They make no deduction for the loss in dressing the carcass, a weight loss typically
greater than 50 percent.[42] Their estimate of the average live
weight was taken from turn-of-the-century sources rather than
based on the pre-Civil War experience of the cotton South. They
applied a national average to large-scale slave plantations.

These shifts in time and geographic coverage are particularly
serious in the case of sheep. Towne and Rasmussen's 1900
national average was meant to reflect production of meat from
sheep raised for slaughter. But sheep were relatively scarce in
the cotton states, and those were primarily raised for wool, not
mutton. Gray suggests that "[t]here was a strong prejudice in
the South against mutton, a prejudice that must have been
widespread, judging from frequent references to it." [43] A

---

experienced and professional beef producers, it would seem difficult to
accept an average live weight of antebellum cattle above this one taken
twenty years after the start of the Civil War.

[40] I accept Gallman's dressing yield of 55 percent ([1970], p. 19) and slaughter
rates of 20 percent of the cattle and one sixth of the milk cows and working
oxen (p. 12), which seem to agree with other authorities (USDA, ERS [1965],
p. 6; Strauss and Bean [1940], p. 106; Towne and Rasmussen [1960], p. 283;
and Holmes [1916], I, p. 70] and which are the ones used by Fogel and
Engerman (letter from Engerman, July 15, 1974).

[41] Private correspondence with Stanley Engerman (November 4, 1974). See
also Towne and Rasmussen ([1960], pp. 285–86) and Strauss and Bean
([1940], pp. 121–22).

[42] Battalio and Kagel [1970], p. 37.

[43] Gray [1933], II, p. 832. Hilliard, however, attempts to throw doubt on this
statement ([1972], pp. 45–46).

planter from Washington County, Mississippi, wrote, "Few planters keep more sheep than enough to supply their own tables with . . . mutton." [44] In the absence of any evidence to the contrary, I assume that *slaves* ate only trivial amounts of lamb and mutton.

Milk: Fogel and Engerman's view concerning the milk consumption of slaves is also based on livestock inventories rather than a direct enumeration of production. They estimate milk output as the product of the number of "milch cows" enumerated by the census times and an estimate of milk yield per cow. The latter figure was obtained from the non-slave farms included in the Parker-Gallman sample. However, only butter production figures were collected by the Census of 1860. [45] The milk output per milch cow on the antebellum free labor farms was computed using the ratio of milk to butter as estimated by Bateman for the North, on the basis of post-Civil War data (FE, II, p. 96). [46] This rather round-about procedure yielded the conclusion that every slave—man, woman, and child—consumed 171 pounds of milk or 7.0 fluid ounces per day. [47]

This estimate of milk consumption based on the Census enumeration of southern milch cows seems to be fraught with difficulties. Hilliard has concluded that [48]

> there were no real "milch" cows in the South. The appellation would be more accurate if it were changed to read "lactating females" or simply "any cows" since that is about all it meant.

Most often lactating cows in the South were milked only during

[44] USPO [1849], p. 161.

[45] There is a small problem in dating the Fogel-Engerman consumption estimates. The Census upon which they are based was taken in mid-1860. The crop outputs refer to the previous crop year, 1859. Thus those consumption estimates based on the number of livestock refer presumably to 1860 while those based on crops refer to 1859. The case of milk production is confused, since the milk per cow estimate is based upon 1859 butter production but the 1860 stock of cows.

[46] Bateman [1968], p. 258.

[47] The weight of one gallon of milk is approximately 8.6 pounds (USBC [1960], p. 272). Fogel and Engerman describe their estimate of 7 fluid ounces as "about one glass per day" (FE, I, p. 113). They make no allowance for waste or animal feed.

[48] Hilliard [1970], p. 265.

a brief spring season, in some cases not at all.[49] By estimating milk output for all enumerated "milch cows" using yields applicable to the northern dairy industry, *Time on the Cross* undoubtedly exaggerates production.

Nor is it at all clear why Fogel and Engerman estimated the milk yields per cow based on the butter production of free, rather than slave, farms. It may be that slave farms produced less butter relative to fluid milk then did free farms as Fogel and Engerman suppose (FE, II, p. 96), but they offer no evidence for this.[50] Their assumption that the ratio of butter to milk output on *free* southern farms equaled Bateman's estimate of this yield for a later time and for a different region is likewise unsupported. Since the ratio of butter to milk output in 1889 in the five southern states was significantly *above* the average for the United States, there is at least a suggestion that Fogel and Engerman's assumption for 1859 is questionable.[51] Comments reported by southern farmers to the U.S. Commissioner of Patents in 1849 imply that cows were kept primarily for butter and that the surpluses beyond the needs of the "planter's" table were sold.[52]

There is little or no evidence upon which to base a firm estimate of milk production on the slave plantations studied by Fogel and Engerman. I assume that they produced milk in the same ratio to butter that was achieved by southern cows in 1889. This procedure gives 104.7 pounds of milk (about 12 gallons) and

---

[49] Hilliard [1972], pp. 120 and 124–26; Gray [1933], II, p. 846; Bateman [1968], pp. 268–69; and Agricola [1851], p. 326. Judged by butter production in 1859 the cows on farms included in the Fogel-Engerman sample were poor performers. They averaged only 17.1 pounds per year, while the milch cows of Vermont, New York, and Pennsylvania managed a more respectable 90.1 pounds per year (U.S. Census [1860], Agriculture, pp. 184 and 186).

[50] *Time on the Cross* cites Hilliard, but there is no support for this assumption on the page given (Hilliard [1972], p. 61).

[51] U.S. Census [1890], Agriculture, p. 275. The ratio of butter to milk production (in pounds) for the South Atlantic and South Central states was .0292. For the balance of the United States it was .0216. In Georgia it was .0317, nearly 50 percent higher than in the North and West. This tendency of southern cows to be greater producers of butterfat has persisted until recent times (USDA, AMS [1956], pp. 8, 12, 16, 20, and 24).

[52] USPO ([1849], p. 160) and USPO ([1852], pp. 82, 83, 90, 102, and 110).

3.1 pounds of butter per year per slave.[53]

Sweet Potatoes: Fogel and Engerman's estimates for the consumption of sweet potatoes are based on the assumption that none of this crop was fed to animals.[54] This assumption is clearly false. A Georgia correspondent of the Patent Office in 1848 wrote "the sweet potato is grown as a field crop for stock, as well as for the table", and other correspondents confirmed this use of the sweet potato. Benjamin Wailes's discussion of the sweet potato in Mississippi published in 1854 states that "some planters put in a large crop of sweet potatoes for [the purpose of

[53] The total butter output of the Fogel-Engerman sample farms was converted into an estimate of milk production by use of the ratio of 0.0292 pounds of butter per pound of milk noted in footnote 51. Subtracting the Fogel-Engerman estimate of 550.5 pounds of milk per capita for the consumption of whites (which, incidentally, is 21 pounds short of the figure which Fogel and Engerman should have obtained using their procedure and the consumption figures for dairy products other than butter given in Bennett and Pierce [1961, pp. 114–15]) and attributing the residual to the slaves (without making an allowance for animal feed) gives the numbers reported in Table 1, a quite gererous estimate in my opinion.

[54] Fogel and Engerman take "[f]eed and seed allowances for *grains* [only]" (FE, II, p. 95, emphasis supplied). They provide the following explanation: "The notion that stinginess would have led masters to have fed various grains, vegetables, and fruits to livestock rather than slaves is too farfetched to be plausible. Since most livestock were bound, eventually, for the stomachs of the slaves, masters would hardly have saved money by depriving slaves of sweet potatoes, peas, or fruits while feeding these foods to swine. Moreover, planters who pursued such a policy must have been ignorant . . . of rudimentary economics and animal husbandry" (FE, II, p. 91). Regardless of the plausibility of this argument for not deducting a *feed* allowance for crops other than grains, it cannot explain the failure to take an allowance for *seeding* the crops other than grains. (However, see footnote 78 below.) When I attempted to replicate Fogel and Engerman's results I discovered that their reported consumption of sweet potatoes (318 pounds per year) was 4.9 percent below the number I obtained (334.4 pounds per year). Had I taken Towne and Rasmussen's feed and seed deduction for sweet potatoes, as Fogel and Engerman did for grains, I would have to subtract 9 percent from my figure ([1960], p. 302; see also Strauss and Bean [1940], p. 54; and Gallman [1960], p. 52). However, since Fogel and Engerman's calorie-per-day figure for sweet potatoes is 16.2 percent too large given their reported consumption in pounds per day (see footnote i to Table 1), I assume that a typographical (or computational) error in *Time on the Cross* explains the difference between our estimates.

fattening hogs], and when corn is scarce give no other food." [55]
After an extensive review of antebellum swine-feeding practices, two cliometricians have concluded that "corn and *potatoes*
were the main swine feeds." [56]

Estimates based on annual inquiries mailed to crop reporters
during the period 1909 to 1914 suggest that 29.5 percent of the
sweet potato crop was fed to animals, used for seed, or wasted
on the farms in the five major cotton states.[57] An urban market
for sweet potatoes did not exist in the South before the Civil
War. However, by the twentieth century such a market had,
indeed, arisen, and thus the adoption of an early twentieth
century consumption figure would probably exaggerate antebellum consumption of sweet potatoes. Employing the 29.5 percent
deduction, I estimate that slaves ate 204 pounds of sweet
potatoes per year (see Table 1). Yet Hutchinson and Williamson
cite contemporary sources which suggest that only 100 pounds
per person was typical.[58] Three bushels (150 pounds) per
individual was reported by one correspondent of the Patent
Office.[59] Fogel and Engerman most surely overestimate consumption when they set it at over six bushels.

A final correction to the sweet potato consumption estimate
relates to the weight of a bushel of sweet potatoes. Fogel and
Engerman used 55 pounds to convert the Census output in

[55] USPO ([1848], pp. 501 and 503), USPO ([1849], pp. 159 and 261), USPO ([1852], p. 66), and Wailes ([1854], p. 193).
[56] Hutchinson and Williamson ([1971], p. 595 emphasis added; Table 3, pp. 599–600). Hutchinson and Williamson estimate the per-swine consumption of potatoes by state ([1971], Table 1, p. 596). However, they base these estimates on the assumption that humans ate only 2 bushels of potatoes per year—man, woman, and child; free and slave (p. 595)—basing this estimate in turn upon scattered contemporary observations. To use their estimates of swine consumption to obtain a residual left for slaves would beg the question at issue.
[57] USDA, AMS ([1958], pp. 25, 26, 30, 31, and 33). The USDA estimates for 1909–1914 suggest that 5.9 percent of the sweet potato crop was used for seed. Thus animal feed and waste consumed 23.6 percent. A 5 percent seed allowance is confirmed by contemporary antebellum sources [USPO, 1848, p. 454].
[58] Hutchinson and Williamson [1971], p. 595.
[59] USPO [1848], p. 482.

bushels into pounds, a figure obtained from the Chicago Board of Trade's *Annual Report* for 1890.[60] However, a pre-Civil War source gives 50 pounds per bushel.[61] The 50-pound weight is also given as the approximate net weight at shipping in the USDA's official conversion statistics. The Department notes that the weight at harvest would average 55 pounds, and attributes the 5-pound loss to curing or drying. Since the calorie and nutritional content of sweet potatoes is given "as purchased" rather than as harvested, it seems most appropriate to use 50 pounds as the conversion rate.[62]

I have reduced the sweet potato consumption to 64 percent of that given by Fogel and Engerman.

Irish Potatoes: The USDA has estimated that during the 1909–14 period, 18 percent of the white potato crop of the United States was fed to animals, used for seed, or wasted.[63] Since Fogel and Engerman make no deductions for these disappearances, I have reduced their Irish-potato estimate to 82 percent of the figure they report.

Peas: What many readers of *Time on the Cross* will take to have been garden peas were not (FE, I, p. 113). The Agricultural Census of 1859 collected and reported the aggregate production of "peas and beans" together. Although it is true that the bulk of this aggregate for the southern states were "peas," [64] the "peas" referred to are not garden peas *(Pisum sativum)* but cowpeas (*Vigna sinensis*, a type of bean),[65] and as their name implies, they were "cultivated principally as food for animals on the farms, or for plowing under as a green crop for manure." At

---

[60] Private correspondence with Stanley Engerman (November 4, 1974).
[61] Homans and Homans [1858], p. 1953.
[62] USDA, ERS [1965], pp. 52–53. The calorie and nutritional content of sweet potatoes are found in Watt and Merrill ([1963], pp. 4–5; and item 2246, p. 115).
[63] USDA, BAE [1949], pp. 55 and 170.
[64] U.S. Census [1860], Agriculture, p. lxxvi. In 1854, Wailes reported that "[t]he bean is not cultivated at all in Mississippi as a field crop" ([1854], p. 195). A similar statement from Alabama is given in the Patent Office Report for 1852 (USPO [1852], pp. 71 and 81).
[65] Piper [1912], p. 143. Fogel and Engerman apparently made this confusion themselves, since they used the energy and nutritional content of garden peas to convert the estimated slave consumption (letter from Engerman, July 15, 1974).

least so says the Introduction to the published report of the Agricultural Census.[66]

The cowpea can be eaten by humans, when it usually goes by the name "black-eyed pea," and, although references are rare, perhaps significant quantities were eaten by slaves.[67] On the other hand, Hutchinson and Williamson have shown that significant quantities were also eaten by southern pigs.[68] Moreover, the responses to a U.S. Patent Office questionnaire asking, in 1849, for what purpose cowpeas were cultivated included the following:

> Halifax, North Carolina: *Peas* are cultivated extensively in North Carolina as a food for man and cattle, and especially for hogs, and also as an improver of the soil. . . .
> Baldwin County, Georgia: *Peas* are raised by. almost every farmer . . . [and are fed to] hogs and cattle.
> Barbour County, Alabama: *Peas* are planted more for stock pastures than for a fertilizer.
> Washington, Mississippi: No varieties of the genus *Pisum* are grown, except in gardens. But the pea, or more properly the bean, known as the "cow" or "Carolina" pea, is grown to a great extent, as food for man and beast, and for the improvement of the land.
> Iberville Parish, Louisiana: The next crop in importance to corn, to the sugar planter, is the cow-pea, both as a restorative to exhausted cane land, and as provender to the numerous teams necessary to the cultivation of a sugar estate.[69]

[66] U.S. Census [1860], Agriculture, p. lxxv.
[67] Mention of cowpeas for slaves is made by Agricola ([1851], p. 325), Cocke ([1853], p. 178), and U. S. Patent Office ([1848], p. 478, and [1852], p. 81). See also Hilliard ([1972], p. 177). Agricola says: "[T]here is no vegetable of which negroes are more fond than of the common field pea, it is well to save enough of them in the fall to have them frequently during the spring and summer. They are very nutritious, and if cooked perfectly done, and well seasoned with red pepper, are quite healthy" (p. 325). After some experimentation with this suggestion, I can recommend the following modern adaptation: Fry one-quarter pound of lean bacon, chopped, until crisp in a large soup kettle. Add two large onions, chopped; two carrots, grated; and one garlic clove, crushed; and saute in the bacon fat until the onions are transparent. Add six cups of rich chicken stock and one pound of dried black-eyed peas, washed and picked over. Season with red pepper and salt to taste. Simmer for one to one-and-one-half hours. Serve in soup plates with corn bread and molasses. Delicious!
[68] Hutchinson and Williamson [1971], pp. 596–600.
[69] USPO ([1849], pp. 84–85). The responses are taken from the following pages: Halifax, North Carolina, p. 143; Baldwin County, Alabama, p. 145;

Fogel and Engerman are probably correct to suggest that slaves ate cowpeas; they are clearly incorrect to suggest that swine, cattle, and workstock did not.

I have found it very difficult to establish the fraction of the Census-reported production of peas and beans which was available to slaves. The problem lies in determining not only the amount of pulse fed to animals but also the quantity required for seeding the following year's crop. Because of the high cost of harvesting peas and beans only the portion needed for seed and as food for humans or for stock feed in future months would be harvested. The bulk of the crop would be fed to hogs by turning them loose in the fields or ploughed under to fertilize the soil. Since presumably only the crop actually gathered was weighed and reported to the census taker, the fraction of *that* yield required for seed would be much higher than the fraction of the potential yield. Wailes says "a large portion of planters [in Mississippi] save little more than is necessary for seed." [70]

The problem of estimating the seed requirements is also complicated by the fact that it was common—some say nearly universal—during the late antebellum period to plant the peas in the corn field between the rows of corn stalks. [71] Cultivated in this manner, the *potential* yield was apparently between 3 and 10 bushels per acre with 6 or 7 bushels probably typical. [72] One antebellum source suggests that one bushel of seed would be required per acre, but practices must have varied considerably, since an 1870 agricultural journal recommended 2 to 3 bushels per acre. [73] This suggests a seed requirement of between 20 and 40 percent. As late as 1916, however, the fraction of the U.S. crop of harvested cowpeas which was used for seed was 60

Barbour County, Alabama, p. 148; Washington, Mississippi, p. 158; Iberville Parish, Louisiana, p. 169.

[70] Wailes [1854], p. 195. See also Hilliard ([1972], pp. 177–78) and the U. S. Patent Office ([1849], pp. 143 and 159). In 1916 the fraction of the potential cowpea crop which was harvested was little more than one-third (USDA, BCE, [1916], p. 19).

[71] See USPO ([1848], pp. 495 and 502; [1849], pp. 145, 148, 158, and 172; and [1852], pp. 61, 63, 75, 90, and 94), Gray ([1933], II, p. 824), and Hilliard ([1972], pp. 177–178).

[72] USPO ([1848], pp. 495 and 502; and [1849], pp. 145 and 172).

[73] USPO [1848], p. 495. *Rural Carolinian* [1870], I, p. 210.

percent. In South Carolina the average was 78 percent, and in Mississippi it was 68, while Alabama and Georgia reported 43 and 44 percent so used.[74] Based on these sources, I have assumed—conservatively, I think—that 40 percent of the 1859 harvest went to seed the crop of 1860.[75]

The division of the remaining crop between animals and humans presumably favored the livestock, since the 1860 Census reported that the crop was harvested "principally" for animals. In 1916, 45 percent of the national harvest (net of seed) went to stock and 55 percent to humans. In South Carolina, Georgia, and Louisiana, however, 58 percent of the net crop went to animals and 42 percent to the table.[76] As a guess, then, I have assumed that 42 percent of the antebellum crop (net of seed) was fed to slaves and the free population living on slave plantations. Taken together with the seed requirements this assumption suggests that only 25.2 percent of the crop was actually available for humans.

The quantity of cowpeas consumed by slaves is also exaggerated in *Time on the Cross* by Fogel and Engerman's use of the 60-pound bushel which was and is standard for dried beans rather than the 50-pound bushel which is standard for cowpeas.[77]

Since Fogel and Engerman apparently took only 60 percent of the reported bushels of peas and beans when making their calculations, I have reduced their pounds-per-year estimate to 35 percent of its original level. I wish to emphasize that my revision is based on guess work. But at the same time I suggest that it is much closer to the truth than Fogel and Engerman's estimate. My final estimate allots each slave regardless of age 35 pounds of cowpeas per year (see Table 1).[78] Hutchinson and

[74] USDA, BCE [1916], p. 19.
[75] Other authorities have based their seed requirements on the assumption of a full harvest of cowpeas sown alone (Gallman [1970], p. 10; Battalio and Kagel [1970], p. 28; and Hutchinson and Williamson [1971], p. 594).
[76] USDA, BCE [1916], p. 19.
[77] Langworth and Hunt [1913], p. 9.
[78] Although Fogel and Engerman did not mention a seed deduction for cowpeas and they denied setting aside a feed allowance (see footnote 54 above), Fogel and Engerman nevertheless used the 40 percent reduction for

Williamson have estimated cowpea consumption at one-fourth bushel (12.5 pounds) per year. Diet studies of Negro farmers in Alabama in the late 1890s suggested that this food was "little used out of its immediate season [early fall]." This comment, the scarcity of references to cowpeas in the slave's diet, and the disapproving comment which accompanied one such antebellum reference suggest that even 35 pounds a year may be an excessive estimate.[79] In 1928–30 the per capital consumption of cowpeas has been estimated to have been only one-half pound per year.[80]

Wheat: Time on the Cross reports that slaves ate on average 34 pounds of wheat "flour" per year (FE, II, Table B. 13, p. 97). The authors deducted 14.5 percent of the output for seed and animal feed. This is probably conservative, since contemporary reports of seed requirements alone suggest a range of 9.6 to 25 percent. Gallman took the seed requirements for wheat to be 12.5 percent. Fogel and Engerman make no allowance for losses in milling wheat into flour (letter from Engerman, July 15, 1974), despite the fact that approximately 25 percent of the weight is typically lost in the modern manufacturing of white flour.[81] The almost complete absence of contemporary references to wheat in the slaves' diet does not allow a determination of whether wheat was served as white flour or whole grain, therefore I have accepted the Fogel-Engerman consumption estimate but changed its designation from "flour" to "wheat." [82]

seed adopted by Towne and Rasmussen ([1960], p. 304) and Gallman ([1960], p. 52). My attempt to reproduce Fogel and Engerman's figures using the Parker-Gallman sample suggests that they made a deduction of that magnitude. Reinflating their consumption figure and then correcting their bushel weight by multiplying by 5/6 gives a *production* per slave of 140.3 pounds a year. Since I estimate human consumption at 25.2 percent, Table 1 gives 35 pounds per year as the average allotment per slave.

[79] Hutchinson and Williamson [1971], p. 595. The diet studies were reported by Atwater and Woods ([1897], p. 10). See USPO ([1852], p. 81) for a disparaging view of the value of cowpeas.

[80] USDA, BAE [1949], pp. 83 and 173.

[81] Fogel and Engerman's deduction is based on Towne and Rasmussen [1960], p. 294. The other estimates are from USPO [1848], pp. 647–48), Gallman ([1970], p. 10), and USDA, ERS ([1965], p. 29).

[82] Agricola recommended that "a small patch of wheat" be sowed for the slaves as a "little luxur[y]" ([1851], p. 325). This is the only explicit reference

Miscellaneous Grains: The small grains included in Fogel and Engerman's "miscellaneous" category include rye, barley, and oats.[83] Allowances for animal feed and seed made were 26, 30, and 72 percent respectively for each of these crops.[84] The balance, they assumed, was fed to slaves and the resident whites. Actually, however, what rye and barley were harvested were undoubtedly converted into alcoholic beverages or animal feed.[85] In any case, only 4.14 pounds of rye and 0.48 pounds of barley per slave were harvested in 1859 on the Fogel-Engerman sample of large plantations. Over one half of the total rye production was produced on just four farms, and only 13 farms in all reported this grain. Only 2 farms in the entire sample reported barley. The appearance of either of these grains in the slaves' diet is dubious.[86] Oats were the only small grain grown to any extent in the South. However, oats were a feed and pasture grain fed almost exclusively to work animals.[87] I was unable to find a single reference to oats as a food for slaves. I feel justified in eliminating the miscellaneous grain category altogether.

Corn: I have left to last the consideration of the most important slave food: corn. In contrast to their treatment of foods other than pork, Fogel and Engerman *under*estimate the corn consumption of slaves. This is because they overestimate the quantity of corn fed to animals on the farm. Despite the fact that they adopt Towne and Rasmussen's deductions from wheat and other small grains for animal feed (FE, II, p. 95), Fogel and Engerman neglect the contribution of these feeds when computing the corn requirements for working stock and meat animals from corn.

To estimate the feeding allowances, Fogel and Engerman

---

to wheat as food for slaves which I have found. See also Hilliard ([1972], pp. 166–67, 170, and 230).

[83] The Census also reported the output of buckwheat and rice, but Fogel and Engerman excluded rice from their calculations (letter from Engerman, Nov. 4, 1974) and no farm in the Parker-Gallman sample reported the cultivation of buckwheat.

[84] Towne and Rasmussen [1960], pp. 294–98.

[85] See Hutchinson and Williamson ([1971], p. 595) and Hilliard ([1972], p. 168).

[86] See Wailes ([1854], p. 187) and Hilliard ([1972], pp. 50 and 168).

[87] Wailes ([1854], p. 187) and Hilliard ([1972], pp. 168–69).

employ Gallman's estimate of feed requirements for all animals other than swine.[88] Yet they failed to note that: "Without doubt [these] feeding standards," according to Gallman, "are far more abundant than the standards followed in the antebellum South." [89] Gallman assumed that each swine required 10 bushels of corn to produce 100 pounds of live pork, a figure deliberately chosen to be on the high side of contemporary, antebellum practice.[90] Fogel and Engerman reduce this requirement to 7 bushels per 100 pounds (FE, II, p. 95).[91] Since their live-weight estimate is 160 pounds at slaughter, they presumably assume 11.2 bushels per slaughtered hog or approximately 9.3 bushels per enumerated hog. This is considerably above the estimates of other scholars. Hilliard takes four bushels as the average consumption per swine, but admits that "other estimates vary up to eight bushels." Hutchinson and Williamson estimate the per-swine allotments of corn per year in the cotton states at well below 6 bushels. For South Carolina their estimate is 1.1 bushels in 1860; for Georgia, 4.0 bushels; Alabama, 5.7; and Mississippi is estimated at 5.4 bushels.[92]

For the purposes of my revision, I have ignored Fogel and Engerman's overfeeding of animals other than swine and confined myself to reducing the swine requirements from 9.3 to 7 bushels per year. Fogel and Engerman's data imply that there were 1.47 hogs per slave on their sample farms.[93] Thus my lowering of the corn fed to swine by 2.3 bushels per pig would

[88] Private correspondence with Stanley Engerman (July 15, 1974).
[89] Gallman [1970], pp. 10–11.
[90] Gallman [1970], pp. 13–14.
[91] Fogel and Engerman state that Gallman's estimates "were appropriate for hogs with live weights of about 220 pounds" and suggest that such estimates would not apply to the hogs of 1860. This statement is difficult to understand. The Gallman estimates were for each 100 pounds of live weight and such feeding ratios are relatively insensitive to the final weight of the pig (Henry [1898], pp. 551 and 553; and Morrison [1948], p. 93).
[92] Hilliard [1972], p. 158. Hutchinson and Williamson [1971], Table I, p. 596.
[93] They reported 88 pounds of pork per slave. Since they have derived only 84.8 pounds of pork per slaughtered hog, assumed a slaughter ratio of 0.83 and assumed 15 percent of the pork was sold off the farm, an inventory of 1.47 hogs per slave would be required. My own calculations based on the Parker-Gallam sample confirm this ratio.

free another 3.38 bushels (189 pounds) of corn for human consumption. If accepted, this recomputation would bring the corn consumption of slaves to 696 pounds per year. However, Fogel and Engerman make no deductions from the corn output for seed requirements. Gallman assumes a seed allowance of 5 percent, which I have accepted.[94] Fogel and Engerman also make no allowance for losses in milling the corn into corn meal. Ransom and Sutch report that the most commonly experienced milling loss was two pounds per bushel based on a sample of 305 flour and grist mills located in the cotton belt of the South and drawn from the 1880 Census of Manufacturing.[95] I have reduced my initial estimate of the corn consumption of slaves from 696 to 636 pounds per year to correct for these oversights.

The Revised Estimate of Calorie Intake

Table 1 summarizes the results of my revision of the Fogel-Engerman conversion factors. I wish to emphasize that these figures cannot be taken as an accurate estimate of the slave diet because of the weaknesses inherent in Fogel and Engerman's application of the residual technique, which I have accepted and followed only for the purposes of this argument. Moreover, I have strived to make my revisions of Fogel and Engerman's conversion factors conservative ones. I suspect that the average slave's diet had substantially fewer calories and was even less varied than these revised estimates suggest. Nevertheless, I am confident that my computations have yielded results much closer to the reality of slave experience than those of Fogel and Engerman. I should also stress that there was undoubtedly great variance in individual experience. The use of averages, a practice which I copy from Fogel and Engerman, will obscure these differences and threaten to be more misleading than helpful unless used with great caution.

[94] The statement that *Time on the Cross* makes no allowance for seed is based upon information in a letter from Engerman (July 15, 1974) and confirmed by my own replication of Fogel and Engerman's results using the Parker-Gallman sample. Gallman's seed allowance is taken from Gallman [1970], p. 10.

[95] Ranson and Sutch [1973], Table 4, p. 13.

Table 1:
Revision of the Per Capita Food Consumption of Slaves in 1859–1860

Food	Item Number[a]	Fogel and Engerman[b]			Revised[c]			Standard Ration[d]	
		Pounds per Year	Calories per Day	Percent of Energy Derived	Pounds per Year	Calories per Day	Percent of Energy Derived	Pounds per Year	Calories per Day
Pork	1665[e]	88	543[f]	13.0	150	685[e]	16.3	143	653
Corn	883	507	2265	54.1	636	2803	66.6	571	2516
Subtotal		595	2808	67.0	786	3488	82.9	714	3169
Beef	210	43	108[g]	2.6	29	96[e]	2.3		
Mutton	1177	2	5	0.1	--	--	0.0		
Milk	1320	171	144	4.2	105 }	88[h]	2.1		
Butter	505	3	30	4.2	3 }		2.1		
Sweet Potatoes	2246	318	424[i]	10.1	204	233	5.5		
Irish Potatoes	1785	22	19	0.5	18	14	0.3		
Cowpeas	903[j]	101	427[j]	10.2	35	149	3.5		
Wheat	2432	34	156[k]	3.7	34	138	3.3		
Miscellaneous Grains	[m]	14	64	1.5	--	--	0.0		
Subtotal		708	1377	32.9	439	718	17.1		
Total		1303	4185	100.0	1225	4206	100.0	714	3169

a Source for calorie conversion: Watt and Merrill [1963], Table 2. The item numbers are references to the products listed in this source. Fogel and Engerman's source for calories per pound is the same as mine, despite their erroneous citation of an older edition of that work (letter from Engerman, July 15, 1974, confirmed by telephone in late July).

b Source: FE, II, Table B.13, p. 97.

c Source: see text.

d The adult ration described in the text was divided by 1.28 to convert to the age and sex distribution reported by Fogel and Engerman. This conversion rate is the one they employ (FE, II, p. 98).

e Fogel and Engerman claim to use item number 1659, "Fat class fresh pork carcass." I have used number 1665, "Thin class," for the revised estimates. See text.

f This figure is apparently in error. Fogel and Engerman's source would give 477 calories per day.

g This figure is apparently in error. Fogel and Engerman's source would give 145 calories per day.

h The caloric value of whole milk (3.7 percent fat) (Watt and Merrill [1963], item 1321, p. 96) was used to convert the 108 pounds of milk products. Fogel and Engerman err when they assume all of the milk produced had full butterfat content. See text.

i This figure is apparently in error. Fogel and Engerman's source would give 365 calories per day.

j Fogel and Engerman erroneously use the value of garden peas (Watt and Merrill, [1963], item 1514, p. 43) rather than cowpeas. The correct figure is 430 calories per day.

k This figure is apparently in error. Fogel and Engerman's source would give 138 calories per day.

m Fogel and Engerman's source for the calorie content of "miscellaneous grains" is Bennett and Pierce ([1961], p. 116) which gives 1650 calories per pound.

Table 1 converts the food allowances to a calorie-per-day basis. Fogel and Engerman apparently made several errors when performing this conversion on their own figures. These errors are noted in the footnotes to the table. Once corrected, their calorie consumption per day adds up to 4082 instead of 4185. In addition, I question their use of the calorie content of whole milk for converting milk consumption since most contemporary comments suggest that slaves were given buttermilk, if they were given any dairy products at all.[96] Fogel and Engerman's procedure of evaluating all milk consumed by slaves as whole milk and additionally providing the slaves with butter implies that the milk consumed by whites had to have been skimmed of the cream necessary to make the butter fed to slaves. Yet, that would have required skimming twice as much milk as Fogel and Engerman allot to the whites. I have adopted an alternative procedure which converts the total weight of all dairy products at the value for whole milk. Had Fogel and Engerman employed this conversion factor, they would have obtained 142 calories per day from dairy products rather than the 174 which they reported.

Fogel and Engerman also exaggerate the calorie content of pork by employing the conversion for a "fat-class" pork carcass. The low slaughter weight of southern hogs argues that a substitution of the calorie content of the "thin-class" pork carcass would be more appropriate. Hilliard notes that " 'bacon' and 'pork' referred to more than simple pork sides, and must have included at least the shoulders and, on occasion, all the joints." [97] This justifies the use of the calorie content of the

[96] See Affleck ([1850], p. 435), Cocke ([1853], p. 177), Postell ([1951], p. 35), and Hilliard ([1972], p. 61). When computing the calorie content of the milk consumed by the free population in 1879, Bennett and Pierce use a lower caloric value per pound than that of whole milk because of the consumption of skim and buttermilk (FE, II, Table B.13, p. 97; and Bennett and Pierce [1961], pp. 116–17). It is not without significance that most contemporary references of milk fed to slaves specify buttermilk. Today, approximately 70 percent of American blacks exhibit an intolerance to lactose—a sugar—which is present in whole milk but not in buttermilk (Bayless and Rosenweig [1966] and Kretchmer [1972]). Most adult slaves would have become physically ill if they drank whole milk.

[97] Hilliard [1972], pp. 42–44 and 56–58.

entire animal, not just the side meat. These two adjustments, had they been made by Fogel and Engerman, would have reduced the number of calories per day in their estimated slave diet to 3976.

When converted to a calorie-per-day basis, my revision suggests that slaves received 82.9 percent of their daily energy allotment from pork and corn. By contrast, *Time on the Cross*'s estimated diet supplies one third of the slave's daily intake of calories from other foods. Fogel and Engerman used conversion factors from more modern times and for the entire country rather than parameters based upon the experience of slave plantations similar to those they were studying. This procedure, together with a number of errors and oversights produced an appearance of diversity in the slave diet which is not warranted by the data they chose to examine.

The fallacy in the position of those who argue that slaves were fed a varied diet stems, I might suggest, from the failure to recognize the implications of the fact that the South in general, and big plantations in particular, did not produce significant quantities of foods other than pork and corn. If these other foods were being consumed by slaves in significant quantities, where did they come from?

Calories and Work Energy

Time on the Cross, in my opinion, too quickly passes over the implications of the quantity of food eaten by slaves. The standard adult ration of one-half pound of pork and two pounds of corn meal per day, alone, contains 4056 calories.[98] The diet estimated in *Time on the Cross* would provide 4185 calories per day to every slave (FE, I, p. 112). According to Fogel and Engerman, this would imply an intake of 5357 calories per day for a male adult.[99] My revision of their diet markedly shifted its

[98] This figure is computed from a diet of one-half pound of raw pork from a "thin class" carcass (41 percent lean, 37 percent fat, 22 percent refuse such as bone) and 2 pounds of unbolted whole-ground corn meal per day. The energy value of the foods has been taken from the latest revision of the United States Department of Agriculture's *Composition of Foods* (Watt and Merrill [1963], item numbers 883 and 1665, pp. 85 and 103).
[99] This figure is obtained by multiplying the 4185-calories-per-day-per-slave

composition but did not significantly change its caloric content. It would provide an adult male 5384 calories per day.

Consumption of food at these rates would greatly exceed the measured consumption of modern hard-working laborers. The diet of the average coal miner in Scotland contains 3660 calories per day, that of a forestry worker 3670 calories. The slave ration exceeded the intake of Swiss peasants (3530 calories) and English Army cadets (3490 calories). According to my source, the "hardest workers in the world" are rickshaw pullers in Calcutta, and they consume 4880 calories per day.[100]

If one is to maintain seriously that adult slaves consumed over 5300 calories per day—and Fogel and Engerman believe that this level *under*estimates the true diet by 20 percent (FE, I, p. 113)—either slaves were prone to obesity (a possibility I think can be ruled out), or else they worked extremely hard. Of course, another possibility, already mentioned, is that Fogel and Engerman exaggerate the actual diet. Even so, the standard ration with over 4000 calories is also a relatively heavy diet; it certainly exceeds modern recommended levels of food consumption.

Comparisons of the slave's caloric intake with that of free workers or with modern recommendations can, however, be misleading. The calorie requirements of the human body depend upon the total energy expended as well as body weight and stature. Since we have reason to believe that the slave was required to exert more work effort than free workers, the question of the calorie requirements for slaves will depend upon how hard they were forced to work. Rather than tackle this difficult question directly, I shall turn it around. How much work could be expected of a field hand who is provided 4056 calories per day, the amount contained in the standard ration?

Consider an adult male weighing 65 kilograms (143 pounds) who sleeps 9 hours per day, who rests (sitting quietly) for 3 additional hours, and who spends 2 hours in eating, dressing,

estimate times 1.28, the conversion factor given by Fogel and Engerman to convert food intake per slave to food intake per adult male, 18–35 (FE, II, p. 98).
[100] Durnin and Passmore [1967], pp. 115 and 117.

and other light personal activity.[101] The fourteen hours thus
spent would require approximately 1200 calories.[102] This leaves a
balance of approximately 2860 calories from the standard slave
diet, or approximately 4.8 calories per minute, for the remaining
ten hours.

The Christensen grading system for work, displayed in Table
2, suggests that such an individual could be expected to perform
"light" to "moderate" work all day or perform some heavy tasks
provided that they were sufficiently balanced by lighter work.
Studies of energy expenditure at various tasks have categorized
such plantation-type activities as dragging logs, felling trees,
and digging ditches as "heavy" to "very heavy"; plowing using
traditional European technology, mowing with a scythe, hoeing,
clearing brush and scrub, and washing clothes by hand would be
classed as "moderate"; and jobs such as feeding hens, milking by
hand, walking (at 3 to 3½ miles per hour), cooking, and floor
sweeping would be classified as "light." [103]

Table 2:
The Christensen Grading System of Energy
Expenditure for Men

Grade	Kcal/Min/65Kg
Light	2.0–4.9
Moderate	5.0–7.4
Heavy	7.5–9.9
Very Heavy	10.0–12.4
Unduly Heavy	12.5+

Source: Durnin and Passmore [1967], p. 47.

[101] I have intentionally attempted to exaggerate the fraction of a slave's time
spent in sleep, rest, and light personal activities, so as to exaggerate the
energy remaining for work.
[102] Durnin and Passmore [1967], pp. 31, 39, and 46.
[103] Durnin and Passmore [1967], pp. 72, 69, 79, 80, 51, 66, 67, 72, 42, 51, and
68.

It would appear that a "lightly" to "moderately" worked slave could subsist on 4056 calories. If more work were extracted from him without an increase in the diet, the initial effect would be to leave less energy for other activities. David and Temin suggest in Chapter 5 that this strategy might have proved desirable from the point of view of the capitalistic planter who "could have effected a saving of supervisory and police costs—without entailing much loss in routine work performance" (see page 183).

Another possibility is that the slaves were fed even more calories than provided by the standard ration and forced to work at a level where they utilized more than 4.8 calories per minute. Had an adult male received 5384 calories per day, a third more than the standard ration, he would have been able to exert a work effort which consumed 7.0 calories per minute during the ten hours of work. This level of energy expenditure is described as "moderate" by Christensen.

I have used 5384 calories per day in this illustration because that figure is the result of adjusting the 4206 calories provided by my revised version of Fogel and Engerman's diet (see Table 1) to the adult male equivalent by using Fogel and Engerman's conversion parameter, 1.28 (FE, II, p. 98). This presumably corrects for the age-sex distribution of slaves and the differing food intakes of the various age-sex groups. Thus it would seem that a diet with 4206 calories per slave per day, while an upper limit, would be neither excessive nor generous, but merely adequate to provide sufficient energy to enable one to work like a slave.

The Nutritional Value of the Slave Ration

Fogel and Engerman's cliometric estimate of the slave ration distorts its variety and probably exaggerates its magnitude as well. Moreover, these distortions may be serious enough to mislead them concerning its nutritional quality. They characterize "the average daily diet of slaves" as "quite substantial" (FE, I, p. 113). When they analyze the nutritional content of their estimated diet, its provisions of protein, essential vitamins, and minerals appeared to Fogel and Engerman as "adequate" (FE,

I, p. 115). Despite their claim that they find this result "astounding," they do not pursue the subject further and simply dismiss the suggestions of other historians that slaves occasionally suffered from dietary deficiencies (FE, I, p. 113; FE, II, pp. 91–92, 99, 240).

Despite Fogel and Engerman's effort (and mine as well), the inadequacy of our knowledge about the slave diet precludes a detailed study of its nutritional quality. Not only are Fogel and Engerman's estimates of the typical ration hopelessly flawed, but they provide no information concerning its seasonal, geographic, and individual variations. Even if the *average* ration was healthy, sizable variation in the provisions across plantations could mean that significant numbers of slaves were fed unhealthy or inadequate diets. As far as I am aware, no historian has made sufficiently detailed studies upon which to estimate or even guess at the range of these variations.

Nevertheless, it is worthwhile to examine the nutritional quality of the two diets we have discussed: the standard pork-corn ration and the revised Fogel-Engerman ration listed in Table 1. I suspect that the true average ration provided American slaves in 1859 probably lay between these two extremes.[104] This analysis will therefore set limits upon the range of nutritional problems likely to have plagued the slave population.

Fogel and Engerman's exaggeration of the variety of the slave ration would, by itself, call for a re-examination of their finding that the slave's diet was nutritionally adequate. However, a number of flaws would mar their analysis even if their version of the ration were to be accepted. The most serious

---

[104] I see no point in studying the Fogel and Engerman diet published in *Time on the Cross* (FE, II, Table B.13, p. 97). For reasons given in the preceding section, I believe that even my revised version of that diet exaggerates both the volume and variety of the typical slave ration. Before accepting the notion that the slave diet was as varied as my revised figures suggest, I would wish to see some positive evidence that slaves ate significant quantities of beef, wheat, Irish potatoes, and dairy products. And some attempt would have to be made to reconcile the revised consumption estimates of sweet potatoes and cowpeas with the much lower per capita estimates made by Hutchinson and Williamson [1971], Hilliard [1972], and others.

problems arise from Fogel and Engerman's adoption of the 1964 recommended dietary allowances for healthy adult males as their standard for "adequate" nutrition (FE, I, p. 115; FE, II, p. 98). These allowances were recommended by the National Research Council for twentieth-century Americans "under usual environmental stress." [105] This means a relatively inactive life style, at least when compared with that of the slave. Yet a hard-working slave would need considerably more calories than a modern white-collar worker. Furthermore, the recommended intake of a number of the essential nutrients are a function of the calorie consumption. For example, the amount of niacin necessary to prevent pellagra is greater for an individual consuming 4000 calories per day than for one consuming 2500. Yet the modern standards used by Fogel and Engerman were calculated with reference to the calorie intake of a relatively sedentary modern adult, rather than the 5000 plus calorie diet which they claim was provided the adult slave. Fogel and Engerman's use of the adult male standard also neglects the important fact that for some nutrients the requirements of women (particularly pregnant women) and teenagers exceed those of the adult male.

Another inadequacy of Fogel and Engerman's treatment of the issue of nutritional quality is their lack of attention to the evidence accumulated by historians which suggests that the slaves' diet occasionally lacked essential nutrients for good health. Several writers have noted that many of the symptoms of slave illnesses recorded in plantation logs or described by medical practitioners of the time sound suspiciously as if they were caused by dietary deficiency. The symptoms of pellagra (niacin deficiency), in particular, have been frequently commented upon.[106] Fogel and Engerman do take note of the frequent reports of dirt eating among slaves, but they dismiss this curious phenomenon by implication as an innocent habit, like "smoking or drinking" (FE, I, p. 99).

Niacin/tryptophan: The most frequently voiced indictment of

[105] NAS, NRC [1964].
[106]Shryock ([1936], pp. 460 and 467), Postell ([1951], pp. 85–86), Stampp ([1956], p. 304), and Hilliard ([1972], p. 64).

the slave diet is that it was pellagra producing. Pellagra, which is caused by niacin (nicotinic acid) deprivation, has always been associated with diets which rely heavily upon corn.[107] For many years this association was puzzling since corn apparently contains ample niacin.[108] The puzzle was solved in 1962 when E. Kodicek demonstrated that the niacin in corn—and in many other cereals—existed in a bound form (niacytin) not available to the consumer.[109] Fogel and Engerman's computation of the niacin content of the slave ration does not make this distinction, and hence, exaggerates the amount of niacin actually available. To make matters worse, they neglect to note that niacin requirements depend upon the energy expenditure of the body and therefore are related to caloric intake. Since slaves consumed more calories than modern Americans, Fogel and Engerman set the recommended level of niacin too low.

When recomputed correctly, neither the standard ration nor the revised Fogel-Engerman ration appear to provide sufficient niacin to match modern recommendations. The FAO/WHO Expert Group of the United Nations established 6.6 milligrams of niacin per 1000 calories consumed as the recommended provision and put 5.5 milligrams per 1000 calories as the minimum level. These standards have, in turn, been accepted by the National Research Council.[110] The standard slave ration contains 4056 calories per day, thus the minimal intake of niacin with that diet should be 22.3 milligrams per day, the recommended level being 26.8 milligrams per day. Corn provides no nutritionally available niacin. Pork contains only 9.3 milligrams per pound. One-half pound, the standard daily ration, contains fewer than 4.7 milligrams. Clearly the pork-corn ration is niacin deficient.

Normally, a shortage of niacin would not be serious if the diet

[107] Roe [1973].

[108] Whole-ground unbolted corn meal contains 9.1 milligrams of niacin per pound according to Watt and Merrill ([1963], item 883, p. 85). Since intakes of less than 7.5 milligrams of niacin or equivalents per day have been associated with the occurrence of pellagra (UN, FAO [1967], pp. 45–47), it would seem that less than one pound of corn per day would prevent the disease.

[109] Kodicek [1962]; and UN, FAO [1967], pp. 49–50.

[110] UN, FAO [1967], p. 47; and NAS, NRS [1968].

consumed contained ample protein. In addition to naturally occurring niacin, this vitamin can be manufactured by the human body from tryptophan, one of the constituent amino acids of crude protein. Unfortunately for the slave forced to subsist on the standard ration, that diet has little protein to spare. The crude protein available from one-half pound of pork and two pounds of corn is 103.3 grams.[111] However, the utilization of this protein would be limited by a shortage of tryptophan, one of a number of essential amino acids. These essential amino acids must be present in a set pattern to be utilized by the body. Because of the amino-acid imbalance in the pork-corn diet, only 47.4 grams of the protein would be nutritionally available.[112]

An intake of 0.71 grams of usable protein per kilogram of body weight is "considered adequate for all but a very small fraction (2.5%) of the population." [113] A 65 kilogram (143 pound) man would need 46.2 grams of protein to match this standard. While the available protein in the standard ration is slightly above this recommended level, tryptophan is the limiting amino acid in the protein. There is no tryptophan to spare. The niacin deficiency cannot be made up from this source.[114]

[111] Watt and Merrill [1963], pp. 85 and 103.

[112] I calculated the amino-acid pattern of the standard ration using the values given in Church and Church ([1970], pp. 121 and 108). The amino-acid content of pork given in this source is for a medium carcass. Therefore I adjusted this figure upward to reflect the difference in the crude protein per pound between a medium and a thin carcass. When compared with the essential amino-acid pattern suggested by the National Research Council (NAS, NRC [1959], Table 5, p. 14) or the "whole-egg pattern" adopted by the FAO/WHO Committee on Protein (UN, FAO [1965], Table 6, p. 36, and p. 38), tryptophan proved to be the limiting amino acid. Based upon the ratio of 1600 milligrams of tryptophan per 100 grams of protein in the FAO's recommended pattern, the 734 milligrams of tryptophan per 100 grams of the slave ration allows utilization of only 45.87 percent of the crude protein.

[113] UN, FAO [1965], pp. 49 and 41–42.

[114] Even if the protein requirement is ignored, there is insufficient tryptophan in the pork-corn ration to make up the niacin deficiency. The FAO/WHO Expert Group of the United Nations has adopted the conversion ratio of 60 milligrams of tryptophan into 1 milligram of niacin (UN, FAO, [1967]). Corn is low in tryptophan with only 250 milligrams of the amino acid per pound (Church and Church (1970), p. 108), equivalent to 4.2 milligrams of niacin. A

A slave who subsisted upon nothing but pork and corn might be expected to suffer from niacin deficiency. Supplementation of this diet with sweet potatoes, molasses, cabbage, collard greens, turnips, and turnip greens would not improve the situation. All of these common ingredients of southern cuisine were included in the pellagra-producing diet fed volunteers at Mississippi's Rankin Prison Farm.[115] However, milk, lean beef, eggs, and cowpeas would all be rich sources of niacin. The issue then becomes whether or not the master provided these foods in sufficient quantities to prevent pellagra.

The 5384-calorie adult ration implied by my revision of Fogel and Engerman's slave diet would require even more niacin than the 4056-calorie standard ration to measure up to the FAO/WHO standards. The minimum requirement with this more ample diet becomes 29.6 milligrams per day and the recommended intake rises to 35.5 milligrams daily. The availability of the niacin in foods other than corn and meat is uncertain. Yet, even assuming that all of the niacin in foods other than corn is nutritionally available, the revised diet would provide only 23.4 milligrams per day. Unless the ration provided ample protein to allow the manufacture of additional niacin, this diet would prove niacin deficient.

Since 60 milligrams of tryptophan are required to produce 1 milligram of niacin, 726 milligrams of tryptophan would be needed to bring the body's supply of niacin up to the recommended level. In addition, a man weighing 65 kilograms would require 46.2 grams of usable protein containing 739 milligrams of tryptophan. Thus the revised diet would need to contain a total of 1465 milligrams of tryptophan. According to Church and Church, however, that diet actually would contain only 1277 milligrams, short of the United Nations recommendation by over 12 percent.[116]

---

pound of fresh pork contains 516 milligrams of tryptophan, the equivalent of 8.6 milligrams of niacin per pound. The standard ration included 0.5 pound of pork and 2 pounds of corn meal, which together provide only 17.4 milligrams of niacin equivalents per day. The minimum requirement is 22.3 milligrams per day.

[115] Goldberger and Wheeler [1920], p. 67.
[116] Church and Church [1970], pp. 100, 108, 109, 114, 121, 122, 131, and 134.

The niacin/tryptophan content of the revised diet is above the minimum level, however, and probably would prove sufficient for a healthy male adult. On the other hand, it must be emphasized that the revised diet is an upper limit to the average diet. One-third of the protein supplied by foods other than pork and corn in the revised diet comes from cowpeas. Yet 30 percent of the farms sampled by Fogel and Engerman did not report the cultivation of cowpeas. Moreover, protein requirements are increased by sweating and heavy work.[117] But the calculations reported above make no additional allowances for these factors. Children, adolescents, and pregnant or lactating women all require more protein than the adult male.[118] But the Fogel-Engerman diet provides less food for these persons than for adult males. There seems to be sufficient cause for concern.

There is also circumstantial evidence that at least some slaves suffered from pellagra. Antebellum southern medical journals reported periodic outbreaks of a fatal disease among slaves called "black tongue" or "erysipelatous fever," whose symptoms strongly suggest pellagra.[119] Niacin deficiency in animals is today still called "black tongue."

Riboflavin: Riboflavin deficiency might have been the cause of "sore mouth" frequently reported by slaves, since the standard ration would provide only 1.23 milligrams of this vitamin while 1.78 milligrams is considered minimal and 2.23 milligrams is recommended given the slaves' caloric intake.[120] The revised Fogel-Engerman diet would provide 2.09 milligrams, still below the recommended level. This deficiency becomes even more serious when riboflavin loss due to cooking is adjusted for. According to Fogel and Engerman these losses are on the order of 15 to 30 percent (FE, II, p. 99).

Calcium: The standard diet would provide only 192.5 milligrams of calcium, well below the 300 milligrams per day which

[117] UN, FAO [1965], pp. 26–27.
[118] UN, FAO [1965], pp. 49, 52–53.
[119] Puckett [1844], Peebles ([1858], p. 39), Swados ([1941], p. 471), and Roe ([1973], pp. 2–7).
[120] Postell [1951], p. 85 and UN, FAO [1967], p. 40. Riboflavin deficiency would also aggravate the pellagra problem since riboflavin is necessary to convert tryptophan into niacin (Raghuramulu, Rao, and Gopalan [1965]).

is "certain to be harmful," also below the 400–500 milligrams *minimum* "practical allowance" for adults suggested by an FAO/WHO Expert Committee, and substantially below the 800 milligrams *recommended* by the National Research Council.[121] The calcium provided by the revised Fogel-Engerman diet is only 591 milligrams per day still below the recommended levels, though above the range of the FAO's adult minimum. The most important sources of calcium in the revised diet are milk (37 percent), sweet potatoes (14 percent), and cowpeas (7 percent). Since each of these foods would be typically available only seasonally (sweet potatoes and cowpeas in the fall and winter, milk in the spring and summer), the chances are good that reasonable numbers of slaves suffered from calcium deficiency.[122]

Vitamin A: "[B]ecause of the large consumption of sweet potatoes," allege Fogel and Engerman, "[slaves'] intake of vitamin A was at the therapeutic level" (FE, I, p. 115). If this were so, it was thanks to sweet potatoes whose flesh was bright orange in color, since yellow-fleshed potatoes contain only one-twentieth the vitamin A of the varieties adopted by Fogel and Engerman as the standard for their calculations. Moreover, the white-fleshed sweet potatoes contain only a trace of this vitamin.[123]

According to B.L.C. Wailes's 1854 *Report on the Agriculture and Geology of Mississippi:*

Five varieties are cultivated with us. . . . First in quality, as in extent of cultivation, stands the Yam, which, if surpassed by some in average size,

[121] UN, FAO ([1962], pp. 8 and 30) and NAS, NRC ([1968], Appendix). It is additionally recommended that this allowance be increased to 1200 milligrams for pregnant women and to 1300 milligrams for lactating women. Increased calcium intakes are also recommended for children between ages of 6 and 18. The adult requirement reported in the text is the lowest for any age group (NAS, NRC [1968]).
[122] Postell's examination of the records of medical practitioners who treated slaves revealed that a large portion of their practice was extracting teeth ([1951], pp. 85 and 107). Swados quotes a physician who complained that there were "few negroes not subject to tooth ache" ([1941], p. 471). It is possible that this high incidence of dental problems was related to calcium deficiency.
[123] Watt and Merrill [1963], p. 115.

is approached by but one in delicacy of flavor. Its shape is oval or roundish, with a smooth exterior, and *yellowish tint*. . . . The next in place is the Spanish, or *White* potato. . . . The Bermuda potato has a deep crimson or purple skin; but *the interior is very white*. . . . The *Red* is the earliest variety introduced here. It was formerly very generally cultivated; it is . . . not now very much in use. . . . The Popular Root, which somewhat resembles the yam in outward appearance, but not generally so round, with a smooth skin, and *the color rather a deeper yellow* . . . is now generally banished.[124]

If this description of Mississippi's sweet potatoes can be generalized, then Fogel and Engerman obviously attribute too much to the southern sweet potato. If the correspondents of the U.S. Patent Office may be relied upon once again, then this description may be generalized. When the circular for 1848 asked for the kinds of sweet potatoes "most successful," the responses were:

Virginia: early white, yam, Spanish, and Carolina red

South Carolina: Spanish

Georgia: Yams, red Spanish

Alabama: Yams and Spanish

Mississippi: Yams and Bermudas[125]

The only other non-trivial source of vitamin A in the Fogel-Engerman diet is corn. The vitamin A content of corn, like that of sweet potatoes, is related to its color. Yellow varieties contain over 2000 International Units of the vitamin per pound; white varieties contain only a trace.[126] Unfortunately for the slave who was not fed the orange-fleshed sweet potato, the most popularly cultivated corn varieties in the antebellum South were white.[127]

[124] Wailes [1854], pp. 191–92 (emphasis supplied).
[125] USPO [1848], pp. 654–55. See also the U.S. Patent Office Report for 1849 (USPO [1849], p. 261). Incidentally, one of the correspondents from Virginia in 1848 said that the Spanish potato, a white variety with little vitamin A, was "most preferred for home consumption" (USPO [1848], p. 494).
[126] Watt and Merrill [1963], p. 85.
[127] Wailes ([1854], pp. 181–83), USPO ([1848], pp. 652–55, 480, and 494), USPO ([1849], pp. 117, 129, 134, 137, 140, 142, 147, 150, 153, 172, and 230),

Despite the claim that slaves were supplied vitamin A in therapeutic quantities, the prevalence of white varieties of both sweet potatoes and corn raises the possibility that vitamin A would be deficient in the diet of slaves who could not supplement it with fresh vegetables, particularly in the winter months. Postell has suggested that the very frequent complaints of "sore eyes" recorded by antebellum medical practitioners could have been caused by vitamin A deficiency.[128]

Thiamine: One particularly striking symptom frequently reported by slaves was a form of pica known as geophagia, the ingestion of dirt or clay. The practice was quite common and, in fact, still prevails today in certain parts of the South and in northern urban ghettos. In some modern forms it does not seem to be particularly serious, a fact used by Fogel and Engerman to dismiss the significance of the practice.[129] During the early nineteenth century, however, clay eating was frequently associated with other symptoms which together manifested the presence of an extremely debilitating and frequently fatal disease known at the time as *cachexia Africana*.[130]

---

and Weld ([1839], p. 32). In contrast see USPO ([1849], pp. 148 and 169). Incidentally, Weld argues that the white "gourd seed" corn commonly grown in the South weighed five or six ounces per quart less than flint corn and consequently the bushel measure weighed less than 56 pounds ([1839], p. 32). There is some confirmation of this in the report from North Carolina in the U.S. Patent Office Report for 1849. That source reports that a bushel of white corn would weigh 53 to 54 pounds (p. 143).

[128] Postell [1951], p. 85.

[129] Cooper ([1957], pp. 57–59 and 64), Twyman ([1971], p. 444), and Mustacchi ([1971], p. 229). Fogel and Engerman attempt to dismiss the significance of clay eating among slaves by relying upon Twyman whom they quote as asserting that "the practice does not necessarily arise from an insufficient diet or a vitamin or mineral deficiency" (FE, II, p. 99). They neglect to report Twyman's next two sentences: "Clay eating has been known to exist among persons whose nutritional intake was adequate even by modern standards. The question, however, is still being studied." (Twyman [1971], p. 447).

[130] There can be little question that *cachexia Africana* was a different ailment than modern geophagia. Carpenter's essay in the *New-Orleans' Medical and Surgical Journal* made the distinction between the two quite clear ([1844], p. 147). *Cachexia Africana* was also called "Negro Consumption," "the paper-gum disease" (Cartwright [1853], pp. 320–21), "mal d'estomac" (Carpenter [1844], p. 147), and "scorbutic degeneration" (Mustacchi [1971], p. 229) by

    Antebellum doctors described the disease as a common cause of death among slaves. Considered "second only to yellow fever" around New Orleans as a cause of slave mortality, it resulted in "many hundreds of Negro deaths yearly." [131] Carpenter describes dirt eating as "by no means a rare occurrence." Grier, another antebellum doctor, asserted that on "nearly every plantation persons will be found addicted to this habit. . . . Sometimes a dirt-eating mania will seem suddenly to take possession of the inhabitants of a place, and rage with almost epidemic violence." Dr. James Duncan said that the disease was "very common" in Saint Mary Parish, Louisiana. "Almost every large plantation," he wrote, "has three or four, and sometimes more of them." [132]

    In addition to the perverse craving for clay, victims exhibited "extreme sluggishness, great edema, pallor (particularly of the mucous membranes), great susceptibility to cold, diminished secretions, blood thin and watery, of a livid purple hue." [133] The prognosis was in most cases death. [134]

    A detailed clinical description of the disease and autopsy

---

contemporaries. It was occasionally misdiagnosed as "phthisis pulmonalis," "dyspepsia," "scrofula," or "heart disease" (Cartwright [1853], p. 320; Jarvis [1855], p. 47; Carpenter [1844], p. 148; and Cooper [1957], pp. 25–26).

[131] Mustacchi [1971], pp. 229–230. The mortality statistics for July 1849 through June 1850 compiled at the Seventh Census reported 94 cases of "dirt eating," all but 10 of the cases among slaves (U.S. Census [1850], Mortality, p. 28]. The great preponderance was in Louisiana (54 cases) (pp. 108–109). These statistics undoubtedly undercount the number of reported deaths since those cases diagnosed as cachexia (wasting of the body) were placed in the "unknown" category (Jarvis [1855], p. 46). The prevalence of Louisiana in the statistics may reflect a real phenomenon since that state was mentioned as particularly susceptible (Mustacchi [1971], p. 230). The mortality reports from North Carolina and Alabama and the assertion by Cartwright that "many of the negroes brought south for sales are in the incipient stage of the disease" ([1853], p. 321) suggest that it was a problem throughout the South.

[132] Carpenter ([1844], p. 148), Grier ([1853], p. 757), and Duncan ([1849], p. 194).

[133] Cooper [1957], p. 24. Also see Carpenter ([1844], pp. 149–66), Cragin [1835], Duncan ([1849], p. 194), Cartwright ([1853], p. 321), and Mustacchi [1971].

[134] Mustacchi [1971], Cragin [1836], Carpenter [1844], Duncan [1849], Affleck [1850], and Twyman ([1971], p. 441).

findings reported by an Italian doctor, Cesare Bressa, who had first-hand experience with the disease in Louisiana in the 1820s were recently discovered in Italy by Piero Mustacchi. These reports for the first time permit "a reasonable medical diagnosis . . . with some degree of confidence." [135] According to Dr. Mustacchi the dreaded *cachexia* was beriberi (wet type) complicated in some cases by hypochromic anemia and hookworm. [136]

Beriberi is caused by thiamine deficiency. Thiamine can not be stored by the body for any period of time, and since the onset of the disease leads to a loss of appetite, a relatively short period of thiamine deprivation can initiate a "vicious cycle" leading to an advanced case. Antebellum doctors frequently reported that an improved diet would produce a cure in cases of *cachexia* Africana, lending credence to the suggestion that dietary deficiency was the cause of the illness. [137]

Since pork and its products are considered excellent sources of thiamine, it might seem surprising that so many slaves would suffer beriberi. The explanation is that thiamine is rapidly destroyed by heat and alkaline solutions. In addition, prolonged dehydration, such as accompanies the smoking of "bacon," destroys this vitamin. Thus the southern practices of long-

[135] Mustacchi [1971], p. 230.
[136] Mustacchi [1971], p. 232. Dr. Bressa's description of the symptoms of "Dissolution Scorbutique," as he called it, are closely paralleled by those of Cartwright ([1853], p. 321), Duncan ([1849], p. 194), and Carpenter ([1844], pp. 149–66). Richard Shryock suggested that *cachexia Africana* could have been beriberi in 1930 (Shryock [1930], pp. 160–61). For some years, this disease was thought by doctors to have been caused by hookworm infestation. Hence this attribution by Shryock ([1930], pp. 160–61; and [1936], p. 469), Swados ([1941], p. 467) and Postell ([1951], p. 82). Although some slaves undoubtedly suffered from hookworms in addition to dirt eating, this cause has now been ruled out (Cooper [1957], p. 23; and Twyman [1971], pp. 442–43). Iron deficiency has also previously been thought to have been the cause because of its apparent association with modern cases of clay eating (Keith, Brown, and Rosenberg [1970], pp. 627–29).
[137] Carpenter ([1844], pp. 166–67), LeConte ([1845], p. 443), Duncan ([1849], p. 195), and Bressa cited by Mustacchi ([1971], p. 232). It might also be noted that iron or iron containing foods were occasionally pronounced of value in treating the illness (Grier [1853], p. 758; Duncan [1849], p. 195; and Mustacchi [1971], p. 232) suggesting the presence of an accompanying anemia.

curing pork with salt or pickling it in brine, and the cooking of the meat by boiling, probably destroyed much of the thiamine content.[138]

Fresh uncooked corn meal contains 1.72 milligrams of thiamine per pound. The Food and Agriculture Organization of the United Nations reports that a value of approximately 0.33 milligram thiamine per 1000 calories consumed would represent an absolute minimum, although they recommend at least 0.4 milligram per 1000 calories. The most recent recommendation of the National Academy of Sciences has raised this to 0.5 milligram per 1000 calories.[139] A diet of 4056 calories would require at least 1.34 milligrams of thiamine to prevent beriberi. If there was no thiamine loss in storage or cooking, only three-fourths of a pound of corn meal could provide this minimum. However, "prolonged dehydration," which might result from storing the corn, would destroy from "one third to one half" of its thiamine content. The process of cooking the meal into corn bread or corn mush might destroy another 30 percent.[140] Thus less than one-half of the thiamine would remain, bringing the ration required for minimum health to one and one-half pounds per day. Two pounds of corn meal would

[138] Watt and Merrill ([1963], p. 168) and UN, FAO ([1967], p. 37. The thiamine content of dry long-cure country-style ham has apparently not been determined (Watt and Merrill [1963], items 1765–67, p. 106). A modern light-cure destroys about one-fourth of the original thiamine, and the cooking process probably would destroy about one-half of that remaining (Wilson, Fisher, and Fuqua [1965], pp. 264–65).

[139] The thiamine content of corn meal is reported by Watt and Merrill ([1963], item 883, p. 85). The minimum and recommended allowance of thiamine is given in UN, FAO ([1967], p. 34) and NAS, NRC [1968]. Studies of European prisoners in a Japanese internment camp, Changi prison in Singapore, during World War II found that thiamine deficiency occurred at approximately 0.30 mg per 1000 calories and that the highest incidence of beriberi appeared among the heavy workers (Williams [1961], pp. 68–80, especially, p. 72; and Keys, Brozik, Henschel, Mickelsen, and Taylor [1950], II, Table 561, p. 1243).

[140] UN, FAO [1967], p. 37 and Wilson, Fisher, and Fuqua [1965], p. 263, 265. If the corn were presented as hominy, it would contain only one-third of the thiamine of foods prepared from whole-ground corn. Compare the thiamine content of unenriched corn grits (item 864) with that of corn meal (item 883) in Watt and Merrill ([1963], p. 85). Hominy is produced by treating corn with lye, this process preserved the corn against insects, mildew, and rancidification and was, therefore, not uncommonly resorted to (USPO [1849], p. 153).

provide less than 85 percent of the currently recommended intake.

The Slave Ration and the Slave Diet

The prevailing view of the slave ration as monotonous, crude, and nutritionally suspect has not been upset by Fogel and Engerman's cliometrics. After examining their procedures and their evidence in detail, I conclude that each of these pejoratives can be fairly applied to describe the board provided slaves by their masters. Of course, the emphasis in *Time on the Cross* on the nutritional quality of sweet potatoes and cowpeas is well taken. Yet, not until a more sound research methodology can be found to establish not just the average quantity but also the seasonal frequency, the geographical pattern, and the typicality of such foods will historians and economists be able to assess their importance.[141] Until that time the Fogel-Engerman thesis, which suggests that slavery provided a better diet for blacks than did freedom for most whites, remains unsupported.

On the other hand, since it would not have been in the economic interest of masters knowingly to deny their slaves a diet adequate for good health, my finding that the slave ration was nutritionally inadequate may seem implausible. Why did not the profit motive, even in the absence of humanitarian ones, ensure tolerable nutritional quality in the slave ration? One possible answer is offered by Kenneth Stampp, who argues that ignorance, rather than miserliness, was responsible for the improper balance of the slave ration. If some slaves suffered from pellagra, beriberi, or other nutritional deficiencies, it is possible that they were "the victims of ill-informed masters—of the primitive state of the science of dietetics." [142]

An alternative, and yet not contradictory, resolution of the seeming paradox is that the slave *diet* may have generally been nutritionally balanced even when the slave *ration* provided by the master was not. Many slaves undoubtedly escaped nutri-

[141] Thirty percent of the farms in the Fogel-Engerman sample did not report cowpeas or beans; ten percent did not report sweet potatoes.
[142] Stampp [1956], p. 282.

tional deficiencies through supplementing their rations by hunt-
ing, fishing, and gathering wild greens in their "spare" time. In
some cases, masters allowed slaves to cultivate their own garden
plots and raise poultry.[143] On occasion hungry slaves were
known to have resorted to pilferage from their master's
stores.[144] When such opportunities were available slaves could
provide for themselves a better, more nutritious diet than the
one supplied by their masters. That they did so, however, is to
the credit of the blacks, not to the institution of capitalistic
slavery or to the humanitarian impulses of the whites.

The outbreaks of nutritional diseases among slaves which I
have cited were, after all, evidenced only in scattered references. They may only reflect a few isolated incidents uncharac-
teristic of the slave regime as a whole. It is also entirely possible
that southern whites of the poorer classes faired only a little
better than slaves in avoiding nutritional deficiencies. Yet, these
possibilities do not change the fact that it was the profit motive
which drove most masters to feed their slaves as cheaply as
possible. To the extent that this economizing zeal led to
nutritional imbalance in the daily ration, it was imposed upon
slaves by their masters, not, as in the case of poor whites, by
poverty or low productivity. The antebellum South had the
agricultural and economic potential to provide an ample, varied,
and nutritious diet for its entire population. That she did not is
as much the fault of slavery as anything else.

Medical Care

Fogel and Engerman also struggle to see the bright side of the
slave's medical care. They refer to Bennett H. Barrow as a
slaveowner who "treated slaves as though they were sick even
when he thought they were pretending" (FE, I, p. 119). Yet, I
could find no evidence of this in Barrow's diary. Indeed, the
entry for October 13, 1839, reads: "Put Darcas in Jail last night

---

[143] On the other hand, it has been suggested that slaves were often too tired
after 12 to 14 hours of field work to tend their own gardens or even cook
foods which required more than a minimal time to prepare (Stampp [1956], p.
284; Agricola [1851], p. 329; Olmsted [1856], p. 108).
[144] Anonymous [1847], p. 420; and Agricola [1851], pp. 325–26.

for pretending to be sick, repeatedly" Barrow punished slaves who he thought were feigning illness, for example when Old Demps used the excuse of his poor eyesight to escape objectionable tasks, Barrow "gave him 25 cuts yesterday morning & ordered him to work Blind or not, to show the scoundrel." [145]

Fogel and Engerman are no more accurate in reporting to the readers of their book when they turn from literary to quantitative sources. For example, they do *not* compute the average number of days lost to illness of the slaves from data collected by Postell as they assert (FE, I, p. 126; II, p. 100). Instead they report Postell's computation of the unweighted average of the morbidity rates from 15 different plantations as 12 days per man year. The actual mean morbidity rate for the working slaves included in the Postell sample is 14 days per slave, approximately 5 percent of the work year.[146]

Moreover, Postell's data will bias the morbidity rate downward since the determination of whether a slave was too ill to work was made by the owner or overseer and not by the worker who was ill. To compare such statistics with the lost time due to illness of workers in 1968 is therefore misleading (FE, II, p. 101). Free workers decide their own rate of work absence and may receive, irrespective of their state of health, paid sick leave. In 1968 a paid sick leave of one day per month was common practice. It is therefore not surprising that the average number of days lost to "illness" in 1968 was 12.7 days per year.

Life Expectancy and Infant Mortality[147]

When Fogel and Engerman report the life expectancy of male slaves based on a life table prepared by Evans, they report the highest estimate available.[148] Even so, the life expectancy of

[145] Davis [1943], pp. 166, 439, 44, and 329.
[146] Postell [1951], pp. 148–50; and FE, I, p. 208.
[147] I am indebted to Paul David for a number of points relating to infant mortality, infant suffocation deaths, and the "sudden infant death syndrome," which have been incorporated into this section. This material appeared originally in David's unpublished paper, "Child Care in the Slave Quarters. . . ." [1975].
[148] Evans [1962], Table 16, p. 212. Zelnick [1966–67] gives 32 years; Farley puts the female life expectancy at 27.8 ([1970], p. 67), and female life

white males estimated by Evans was 13.7 percent greater than that for the slave males, and there is at least some grounds for thinking that southern whites lived longer than their northern brethren.[149] In other words, the most conservative estimate gives white males five more years of life expectancy at birth than male slaves. Is there any doubt that this difference is attributable to the quality of care afforded black slaves by white masters? *Time on the Cross* attempts to foster such doubts.

A more sensitive index of the general health and welfare of the slave population is the infant mortality rate. Fogel and Engerman offer statistics on infant mortality to support their broad statement that work on demographic data for 1850 and 1860 "has revealed little evidence to support the charge that masters neglected the care of [slave] infants." Fogel and Engerman claim that the infant death rate among the southern whites and black slaves was "virtually the same" in 1850 (FE, I, pp. 123–24). To arrive at this finding, Fogel and Engerman accept Evans's death rate estimates for slave infants (183 per 1000) (FE, I, p. 123; and FE, II, p. 100), but inexplicably reject Evans's figure for white infants (104 per 1000). Instead, they replace Evans's estimate with one of their own making (146 per 1000)[150] before contrasting slave with free mortality experience. This upward revision of the white infant death rate reduced the gap between slave and free infant mortality from 76 percent to 25 percent.

Evans took his figures for white infants directly from Jacobson and keyed his own estimates of slave infant mortality to them. I do not see how Fogel and Engerman can justify rejecting Jacobson's white-infant estimates without simultane-

---

expectancies are thought to exceed those of males at birth. Eblen puts the average length of life for a black female infant at 32.6 years ([1974], p. 308). Evans's figure, as reported by Fogel and Engerman, for male life expectancy is 36 years (FE, I, Fig. 36, p. 125).

[149] See Evans [1962], Table 16, p. 212 for estimates of life expectancy of slave males and white males. Yasuba argues that life expectancy was longer in the South than in the North ([1962], pp. 79–82).

[150] This is not apparent from the citations provided in *Time on the Cross* (FE, II, pp. 100–101) but was confirmed by Stanley Engerman in a letter to me dated November 4, 1974.

ously rejecting Evans's slave-infant estimates. It is particularly strange that Fogel and Engerman choose to increase Jacobson's estimates, since Yasuba has argued that, if anything, Jacobson's estimates were already too high.[151]

Moreover, Fogel and Engerman's use of Evans's figures for the slave infant mortality rate (183 per 1000) disregards evidence that the actual rate was higher than that. Some indications to this effect were present in the work of Postell and Steckel, both of whom were consulted by the authors of *Time on the Cross* on other demographic questions. A recent study of vital rates in the black population during the nineteenth century by Eblen places the rate of slave infant mortality at 209 per 1000, twice the rate estimated by Jacobson and cited by Evans for the free population in 1850.[152]

The proportionate gap between black and white infant death rates thus may have been in the neighborhood of 100 percent. When Fogel and Engerman "find" a considerably smaller differential, only 25 percent, they present this as a "paradox"

---

[151] Yasuba [1962], p. 97.

[152] Eblen [1974], Table 7, p. 310. Postell ([1951], pp. 148–50) is used by Fogel and Engerman as a source of information or morbidity, as was noted above; but Postell also provides some evidence regarding infant mortality rates on a group of plantations in the period 1817–61. For the 12 plantations for which Postell was able to compile year-by-year lists of births and deaths of slave infants, the weighted average rate of mortality per 1000 is 176.4 (This computation weights the plantation averages by the fraction of the total 805 live births for which each accounted). The plantation averages range from 120.7 per 1000 in the case of Ossabaw Island Plantation, Georgia, to 444.4 per 1000 on the Rosedew Plantation, Georgia. Steckel ([1973], p. 32) reports that his preliminary analysis of plantation records suggests that the slave infant mortality rate was 210 per 1000. He goes on to calculate that the white infant mortality rate could be put at 113 per 1000, if it were assumed that the Census of 1850 underreported the level of the white infant mortality rate to the same proportional extent as his preliminary figures suggest the slave infant mortality rate was understated. The figure of 113 per 1000 is close to Jacobson's estimate for the white infant mortality rate, which Yasuba regarded as an overstatement. I suspect that the underreporting of white infant mortality was actually less pronounced than was the under-reporting of slave infant mortality. Note that the figures from Postell and Steckel just cited refer to rural infant mortality among slaves, and among slaves on larger plantations. On both counts they would tend to under-represent the true rate for the whole slave infant population.

whose resolution calls for further adjustment (FE, I, pp. 123–24). Most of the difference between their slave infant mortality rate estimate of 183 per 1000 and their figure of 146 for the white population they attribute to "the fact that the South was less healthy than the North" (FE, I, p. 124). Yet their correction procedure, which purportedly makes use of the North-South differences in *white* infant mortality in 1860 (FE, I, pp. 123–24), actually employs the mortality experience of the entire population including slaves.[153] The South-North difference they choose to impute to the influence of geography might simply reflect the differential infant mortality experience between slavery and freedom which Fogel and Engerman seek to explain away. This is a distinct possibility, inasmuch as their assertion that the South was less healthy than the North disputes the opinion of at least one authority who maintains that the reverse was the case.[154]

The causes of the differential between slave and white infant mortality rates (on the order of 105 deaths per 1000 live births) remains to be studied thoroughly. But regardless of the results of such studies, it will not be a straightforward task to infer from them differences between the attitudes of Negro slaves and southern whites regarding the survival of their respective progeny, or the efforts they directed toward that end. The difficulties are well illustrated by the problem of interpreting the higher rate of slave infant deaths attributed to suffocation, a subject which Fogel and Engerman consider more closely than any other among the numerous causes of infant mortality. They explain that they take up this issue because among the apparently avertible causes of infant mortality, suffocation figured especially prominently in the statistics of infant slave deaths recorded by the 1850 Census. That fact, they say, has provided a basis for allegations of infanticide from "some historians" (unnamed), and of widespread child neglect on the part of slave mothers from yet "others" (also unnamed) (FE, I, pp. 124–25). Furthermore, the estimate of the difference between the infant suffocation death rate for slaves and that for

153 U.S. Census [1860], Statistics, p. 280.
154 Yasuba [1962], Chap. III, particularly pp. 80, 82, and 100.

whites presented in *Time on the Cross* (17 per 1000 and 2 per 1000 live births respectively) looms rather large when compared with the negligible difference (6 per 1000) they report between the overall infant mortality rates in the slave and southern white populations.

The estimates just cited actually under-represent the absolute difference between slave and southern white infant suffocation death rates. Nevertheless, when the correct rates are compared it is evident that the *excess* of the infant suffocation death rate for slaves above that for whites (18.2 per 1000 live births) was only a minor factor, accounting at most for one fifth of the overall difference between slave and southern white infant mortality rates in 1850.[155] The phenomenon of higher infant suffocation rates among slaves thus is not so quantitatively preponderant that understanding it would shape the decision as to whose behavior it was that caused black infants to die at a rate twice that which obtained among white infants.

Fogel and Engerman, however, pursue a quite different line of interpretation. They first argue that since less than two out of every one hundred slaves born died from this cause, these mortality statistics "leave plenty of room for slave mothers who gave their children tender care," even if one were compelled to view infant deaths due to suffocation as a reflection of maternal negligence (FE, I, p. 125). Next, they make the plausible suggestion that in the case of infant deaths among slaves, more than among whites, suffocation may have been reported as the

---

[155] Fogel and Engerman report that 9.3 percent of slave infant deaths are ascribed to suffocation by the U.S. Census of 1850, whereas the corresponding figure for the white population was 1.2 percent [FE, I, p. 124]. Applying *their* estimates of slave and southern white infant mortality, they compute the excess infant mortality due to suffocation among slaves as [(.093 × 183 − .012 × 177) = 14.89] roughly 15 per thousand live births. Substituting the estimates of overall infant mortality cited in the text above, we compute the rate of infant suffocation among slaves as [.093 × 209 =] 19.4 per thousand, that among whites as [.012 × 104 =] 1.2 per thousand, and the difference between them as 18.2 per thousand. The latter accounts for [18.2/(209−104)] roughly 17 percent of the absolute difference between slave and white rates of infant mortality, whereas on Fogel and Engerman's reckoning the suffocation rate difference appears two and a half times as large as the difference between overall infant mortality rates [14.89/(183−177)].

cause in the absence of other then-identifiable medical explanations, because overseers felt no reservations about expressing low opinions of slave women as mothers (FE, I, pp. 125–26). A final step is taken in Appendix B, where a possible "medical" explanation is advanced for the observed higher rate of infant suffocation among the slave population:

> Virtually all of the difference between the free and slave suffocation rates might be explained by what has recently been identified as the "sudden infant death" syndrome. One estimate placed the death rate from this disease today at 12.5 per thousand for Negro infants, and at 2.8 per thousand for all infants. [FE, II, p. 101].

That being all the information the authors provide concerning the sudden infant death syndrome (SIDS), it would not be surprising if their readers sustained an impression of SIDS as another genetically transmitted disease, like sickle-cell anemia, to which members of the Negro race are peculiarly subject. Such an impression certainly would serve to complete Fogel and Engerman's argument that even the seemingly awkward statistics relating to infant suffocation deaths offer no real support for invidious comparisons between the quality of the care received by the children of slaves and that received by southern white children in the antebellum period.

This entire line of this argument from start to finish, however, is grossly misleading. Whatever other inferences about child care one seeks to draw from a rate of infant suffocation death approaching 2 per hundred, it is hardly illuminating to present it as indicating a "rare occurrence" in the lives of slave mothers (FE, I, p. 137). Think what this statistic says about the probability that a randomly selected slave mother would have had at least one among her children perish during its first year of life from this cause: were we to suppose the occurrence of an infant suffocation was essentially independent of whether or not other babies born to the same woman had suffocated to death, the lifetime probability of a woman experiencing at least one such event then would be just the sum of the individual probabilities of death by suffocation (1.94 percent) for each of her babies. A representative slave woman who completed her reproductive life, surviving to her forty-fifth birthday, would have borne perhaps 10 live babies.[156] The probability that one or more of them would suffocate during infancy therefore was 19.4 percent. Imagine what this must have implied under any of the possible interpretations: something approaching one-fifth of the childbearing population either actually suffocated at least one infant, lost at least one through their own negligence or that of the youngsters or old folk in whose care they had been compelled to leave the child, or were wrongly regarded as having been in some way responsible for at least one infant death caused by an undiagnosed disease beyond their control. Whereas roughly 1 in every 5 slave women who completed a full career of childbearing would have lost an infant to causes described as "suffocation," had the white rate of infant suffocation (.0012 per live birth) prevailed among those same women, only 1 in 83 Negro slave mothers would have experienced this particular form of personal tragedy.

Fogel and Engerman certainly are justified in voicing the suspicion that "suffocation" constituted a residual heading under which unexplained (and at the time unexplicable) deaths of Negro infants were categorized—presumably with less hesitation about the social stigma thereby attached to the mother, or concern for guilt feelings thus engendered, than would apply when the unexplained death of a white infant was involved. Even today, when analysis of physiological and epidemiological evidence has led medical authorities to conclude that "crib deaths" as a rule do not result from suffocation, the position in which the dead child's body is found (face covered by a blanket, or head pressed into a corner of the crib) frequently leads uninformed parents, and sometimes also their physicians, to suppose at first that suffocation has been the mechanism of death.[157]

[156] A woman's reproductive period is conventionally defined as spanning the ages from 15 to 45, 30 years. Defined in this way, slave women in the Old South not infrequently exhibited fertility ratios exceeding 333 per thousand (Sutch [1975], p. 189). This figure implies 10 live children would be born on average to a woman surviving at age 45. This estimate is a conservative one, as it should be for the purposes of the illustration presented in the text.
[157] According to the medical authorities cited by Fogel and Engerman in reference to their discussion of SIDS, in approximately 15 percent of modern

In going beyond this, however, and implicating the sudden infant death syndrome as a plausible explanation for "virtually all of the difference between the free and slave suffocation rates," Fogel and Engerman perpetrate two rather serious errors. One is interpretative, the other statistical, but the two are closely related. The interpretive mistake lies in leaving their readers to surmise that Negroes have been observed to be more susceptible to SIDS than Caucasians. The statistical mistake consists of mis-reporting modern Negro-White differences in SIDS rates and suggesting that these are large enough conceivably to account for much of the historical difference between slave and free rates of infant suffocation—a difference that amounted to 15 such deaths per thousand live births, by their reckoning, or 18.2 per thousand by ours. Both mistakes would have been averted had Fogel and Engerman simply quoted the pertinent passage from the article by Bergman and Beckwith, the medical authorities they cite in this connection.[158]

> Most studies [of SIDS] have demonstrated a clear-cut seasonal distribution with preponderance during the late autumn, winter and spring. Temporal-spatial clustering of cases, suggesting "micro-epidemics," is observed.
>
> There is also an increased risk [of SIDS] among babies of low birth weight, those who are non-white, and those born to families in lower socio-economic classes. It remains to be established to what extent these variables are interdependent.
>
> In King County, Washington, the risk [of SIDS] for a Negro infant with a [low] birth weight of 1500 gm. living in a poor neighborhood exceeds one in eighty live births [12.5 per thousand], as contrasted to the overall county rate of one in 350 live births [2.8 per thousand].

Transparently, the figures cited by Fogel and Engerman do not compare the SIDS rate of typical Seattle, Washington, infants with that for Negro infants of the same birth weight, born to families of the same socio-economic position, and to

------

cases of sudden unexpected infant death a subsequent autopsy demonstrates the presence of lethal lesions not previously suspected. Thus, most sudden unexpected infant death nowadays qualifies as true SIDS: "The sudden death of an infant or young child which is unexpected by history, and for which a thorough postmortem examination fails to demonstrate an adequate explanation" (Bergman and Beckwith [1968], pp. 777–78).
[158] Bergman and Beckwith [1968], pp. 777–78.

women of the same maternal age who have had the same number of previous births. They do not even compare the entire Negro population with the Seattle population as a whole. Plainly, these figures were cited by Bergman and Beckwith to illustrate the *extreme* range of disparity in SIDS rates which the compounding of all apparently adverse factors may produce. The statistical study of Seattle, Washington, to which Bergman and Beckwith refer their readers, reported that for the Seattle nonwhite population as a whole the SIDS rate was 4.66 per thousand live births (not 12.5 per thousand), compared with a rate of 2.71 per thousand for the Caucasian population.[159] More recent statistical studies of modern American city populations have placed the *difference* between the SIDS rate for Negroes and Caucasians closer to 3 per thousand than to 2 per thousand,[160] but these modern Negro-White differential rates remain of an entirely lower order of magnitude, at most one-sixth the size of the historical difference which our estimates suggest existed between Negro and white infant suffocation rates in "slavery times."

Although the present state of knowledge concerning the mechanism of death in SIDS remains unsatisfactory, the evidence from epidemiology is quite extensive and is taken by medical authorities (including those cited by Fogel and Engerman) to be persuasive on at least one point: *genetically heritable mechanisms are not a factor in SIDS.*[161] Dr. Peter Frogatt, of The Queens University of Belfast, responded to an inquiry about the possible presence of "some kind of familial factor" in SIDS cases as follows:

[159] Peterson [1966]. The figure cited in the text refers to the nonwhite population, which in Seattle includes a significant number of Asians and American Indians as well as Negroes. Peterson's findings are discussed also in Bergman, Beckwith, and Ray ([1970], p. 9).

[160] A study subsequent to Peterson's [1966], conducted by Bergman, applied more rigorous criterion for the classification of SIDS cases and found that in King County, Washington during 1965–67 the "true SIDS" rate per 1000 live births was 5.01 for Nonwhites, 1.82 for whites. Valdes-Dapena has reported that in Philadelphia the SIDS rate per thousand live births is 4.32 for Negro infants, compared to 1.41 for white infants (Bergman, Beckwith, and Ray [1970], p. 47).

[161] Bergman and Beckwith ([1968], p. 779); and Bergman, Beckwith, and Ray ([1970], pp. 43–45, 76, 79).

On the ordinary standard measure of a single inheritance there is no evidence, consanguinity or important family aggregation in our data, nor do I think anyone has described this. I think most data can be explained in relation to environmental conditions.[162]

Indeed, a recent survey of studies of the epidemiology of SIDS in Europe and the United States during the 1960s finds remarkable uniformity in the impressions recorded concerning the higher incidence of cases in circumstances involving lower social class wage-earners, "poor living conditions," and "poor general care of the infant." [163]

Fogel and Engerman thus could be on the right track in suspecting a connection between the high rate of slave infant death reported as suffocation, and some unidentified disease similar in character to what commonly used to be called "crib death," and what today is more precisely identified as SIDS. But the true import of that connection is diametrically opposite to the interpretation suggested in *Time on the Cross*. The staggering difference between slave and white infant suffocation rates, no less than the overall excess of slave infant death rates over white infant death rates to which it contributed, would appear as reflections of extreme poverty, low birth weights, and poor postnatal care.

The Slave Cabin Versus the New York Tenement

Comments of observers suggest that the most typical slave houses of the late antebellum period were cabins about eighteen by twenty feet. [FE, I, p. 116]

Fogel and Engerman do not tell us who these "observers" were. Frederick Law Olmsted and Robert Russell are the only

---

[162] Bergman, Beckwith, and Ray [1970], p. 76.

[163] Bergman, Beckwith, and Ray [1970], pp. 9–11. Five of seven such studies involved European populations, three of them for Britain, and one each for Germany and Poland, where Negro-White differences in incidence could not conceivably have entered the picture in any significant way. Another study, treating epidemiological aspects of SIDS in Czechoslovakia, reports a disproportionately higher incidence of SIDS in larger families and speculates that "there could be a correlation of sudden death with the quality of care, as well as with the time devoted to care of the child" (Bergman, Beckwith, and Ray [1970], p. 62).

two travelers whose accounts they cite, and Weld's *American Slavery As It Is* is their only other primary source that could be considered to present the remarks of observers. My own review of these sources indicates that 18 by 20 would be much too large to be taken as "typical." [164]

Olmsted gives the actual dimensions of slave cabins at only four places which I could locate. Each of them is repeated in his summary volume, *The Cotton Kingdom*. They range from 10 by 10, a cabin of "the worst description," through 12 by 12 and 15 by 20, to the largest, houses 21 feet square on a Georgia rice plantation which favorably impressed Olmsted. Russell did mention a slave dwelling in Louisiana which measured 18 by 20, but he used this fact as evidence that the "negroes were well cared for" on the particular estate he was visiting. *American Slavery As It Is: Testimony of a Thousand Witnesses*, a tract of the American Anti-Slavery Society which pictured slave treatment as atrocious, cited one "witness" to the effect that the negro quarters varied from "8 by 10 to 10 by 12"; two others mentioned 10 by 12 feet; one witness recorded 12 by 12, and another 12.5 by 14. The largest cabin referred to by its dimensions was 14 by 14.[165]

Of the half-dozen state studies of slavery cited by Fogel and Engerman as supporting their description of the typical slave cabin (FE, II, p. 99), none would actually concur with their description.[166] Not one of the authors put 18 by 20 or larger as average. Flanders's study of Georgia asserted that "the size of the [slaves'] house was usually 15 x 15" and specifically cited first the case of a slaveholder who put an average of two occupants into rooms no less than 10 by 10 and of another who housed each family in a cabin 16 by 20.[167] Sydnor suggests that 16 by 18 would be a larger cabin than those found on many

[164] Olmsted [1856, 1857, 1860, and 1861], Russell [1857], and Weld [1839].

[165] Olmsted ([1861], pp. 290, 161, 42, 184), Russell ([1857], p. 264), and Weld ([1839], pp. 43, 106, 48, 99).

[166] I was unable to consult one of Fogel and Engerman's references, Abigail Curlee's unpublished 1932 Ph. D. dissertation (FE, II, pp. 99 and 252).

[167] Flanders [1933] pp. 152–53. Flanders also misquotes Olmsted's estimate of the cabin on the Georgia rice plantation, which I alluded to above ([1933], p. 152).

Mississippi plantations. None of the other cited works ventures an average or typical size.[168]

Taken together, Fogel and Engerman's sources would support a view of the typical slave cabin as approximately 15 feet square, with 16 by 18 an occasionally achieved ideal size, and larger accommodations the rare exception. On this basis it would be hard to accept 18 by 20 as anything but generous.[169]

The fact that numerous articles appeared in the southern agricultural press advising planters as to how to correct various evils with respect to slave housing suggests that standards were not too high. A slaveholding doctor advised in *De Bow's Review* that a "negro house should never be crowded. One sixteen or eighteen feet square is not too large for a man and woman and three or four small children." Another contributor warned against the "decaying logs of negro houses, open floors, leaky roofs, and crowded rooms." He suggested that 24 houses 16 by 18 feet would provide "comfortable quarters" for "upwards of 150" slaves. This would average 6.25 persons per cabin. The clear implication is that many Negro quarters did not measure up to this optimum.[170]

Fogel and Engerman also probably exaggerate the amount of living space available to each slave by underestimating the average number of slaves per cabin. They report even fewer persons per cabin than the correspondent of *De Bow's Review.*

[168] Sydnor [1933], pp. 39–40. Davis cites two illustrations in his study of slavery in Alabama: one, a recommendation that cabins be constructed with 16 by 18 feet in floor space; and, the other, a proposal by one planter—apparently never brought to completion—to replace his present "shanties" with apartments 15 by 18 feet ([1939], pp. 80–81). Sellers's study of Alabama and Joe Gray Taylor's study of Louisiana also cite recommendations that cabins be 16 by 18 (Sellers [1950], p. 85 and Taylor [1963], p. 113). Orville W. Taylor personally visited a former Arkansas slave cabin in 1953 which measured twenty-feet square (Taylor [1958], p. 146).

[169] See also U. B. Phillips ([1929], p. 281) and L. C. Gray ([1933], I, pp. 562–63). Postell attributes to Olmsted a description of a cabin which was 18 by 20 feet ([1951], pp. 45 and 178). But his citation is in error, and I was unable to locate such a description elsewhere in Olmsted's works.

[170] Anonymous ([1847], p. 419); Mississippi Planter ([1851], p. 623); and Agricola ([1853], p. 336).

Based on "systematic" data from the 1860 Census, *Time on the Cross* reports an average of only 5.2 persons per cabin (FE, I, p. 115). However this result is applicable only to plantations with over 50 slaves.[171] Why Fogel and Engerman restrict their analysis of the distribution of the number of slaves per house to large plantations is not exactly clear (FE, I, Fig. 35, p. 114, and p. 115). The manuscript census returns for 1860 were available to Fogel and Engerman and they provide information upon slave dwellings on all sizes of farms. Joe Gray Taylor used these census documents to make a comparison between large and small slaveholdings in Louisiana. He concluded that "slaves on large plantations were likely to be better housed than others." [172]

If Fogel and Engerman exaggerate the spaciousness of the typical slave dwelling by 50 percent and underestimate the average occupancy, they err even more seriously when comparing the slave cabin with the housing of New York City's workers in 1893. They assert that New York tenements typical of "most" urban workers provided "just thirty-five" square feet of "sleeping space" per person (FE, I, p. 116). Their source (cited at FE, II, p. 99) is a U.S. Bureau of Labor Special Report entitled *The Slums of Baltimore, Chicago, New York, and Philadelphia.* Contrary to their assertion, this study did not attempt to ascertain the living conditions faced by "most of New York City's workers" (FE, I, p. 116), but rather only of individuals living in certan neighborhoods of the four cities, neighborhoods "concerning which there can be no difference of opinion as to whether or not they are slum districts." The report says:

> The districts selected by no means contain the whole slum population of the cities included in the investigation. . . . [They] are among the worst in

[171] Fogel and Engerman drew their data, not from the census, but from Menn ([1964], cited at FE, II, p. 99). Menn considered only slaveholdings with 50 or more slaves ([1964], p. iii).

[172] Taylor [1963], p. 114. It should be noted that since the Census data reported only the total number of slave houses and the number of slaves per owner, Fogel and Engerman's distribution (FE, I,, Fig. 35, p. 114) is a distribution of the average number of persons per house on each plantation (weighted by the size of slaveholding) rather than the distribution of persons per slave house. This pre-averaging at the plantation level will reduce the variance in the reported distribution.

the cities, and may be denominated as the centers of the slum population.[173]

Only 1.8 percent of New York City's population was included in the districts surveyed.[174]

Had they consulted Kenneth Stampp's analysis of the anti-abolitionist literature, Fogel and Engerman might have avoided this comparison of the worst of the New York slums with a better-than-average-size slave cabin. "Proslavery writers," according to Stampp,[175]

> frequently contended that northern workers suffered greater privation than southern slaves. They demonstrated this by contrasting the hardships of the lowest paid, most heartlessly exploited factory hands with the comforts of the best-treated bondsmen. They found abundant evidence of widespread poverty among new immigrants and among unskilled or semi-skilled workers in the industrial towns of the Northeast, especially during the periods of economic depression.

The year 1893, Fogel and Engerman's standard for free workers, was in the middle of "one of the severest depressions prior to the 1930s." [176] Of course, the typical northern "free laborer" was neither a resident of a New York slum nor even an industrial worker. As Stampp notes when criticizing the comparisons made by proslavery authors, "he was a small farmer, a farm laborer, a journeyman or master artisan, or an employee of a small manufacturing enterprise, managed by its owner." [177]

Nor is it particularly accurate to assert that "much of rural America still lived in log cabins in the 1850's" (FE, I, p. 116). Martin's extensive review of the standard of housing in 1860 suggests that log cabins were common only as temporary dwellings on the frontier.[178] According to Martin the typical

[173] USBL [1894], p. 12; see also pp. 23–24.
[174] USBL [1894], pp. 12, 24, and 26. Fogel and Engerman also apparently failed to note that the median size of tenements in Baltimore and Philadelphia were substantially larger than in New York (which they report) or Chicago (USBL [1894], pp. 604–13).
[175] Stampp [1956], p. 281.
[176] Lebergott [1964], pp. 108 and 522.
[177] Stampp [1956], p. 281.
[178] Martin [1942], Chapter V, especially pp. 117–21 and 135–41. According to the New York State Census for 1855 only 6.35 percent of the dwelling houses

rural home was a one-and-a-half- or two-and-a-half-story frame house with five to seven rooms and an attic.[179]

Even if Fogel and Engerman were interested in comparing the worst of the free laborers' housing with that of the best treated bondsmen, their comparison is faulted, since the number of square feet reported per individual in the New York tenements included only the sleeping rooms of the apartments, not the entire living space. Fogel and Engerman, therefore, place the bedrooms of New York tenements for comparison against the entire home of the slave family. Since only 3.55 percent of the slum population surveyed lived in one-room tenements and nearly 60 percent had three or more rooms in their apartments, it is quite likely that the total size of New York slum tenements was substantially larger than the median 35 square feet per inhabitant reported by Fogel and Engerman.[180]

Even Fogel and Engerman's statistic of 35 square feet is suspect. The U.S. Bureau of Labor report did not actually record the *square* feet of sleeping space per individual but rather the number of *cubic* feet. Fogel and Engerman apparently assume an eleven-foot ceiling in order to compute the median square feet of floor space at "just thirty-five" (FE, I, p. 116). The published tabulations give the median number of cubic feet of sleeping space per person in the New York slums as "under 400."[181] If one assumes a ceiling of eight-foot height, the median number of square feet would rise to 50 per person.

The Labor Bureau's report contains the following statement:

> It is universally conceded that 600 cubic feet of air space per individual are desirable for adult persons, but in actual practice 400 are considered absolutely necessary.[182]

A slave cabin 15 by 15 with an 8-foot ceiling would provide only

---

in that state were made of logs (cited by Martin [1942], Table 2, p. 120). No plausible correction of this figure for urban populations could produce a sizable fraction of rural families with log houses.

[179] Martin [1942], p. 118.
[180] USBL [1894], pp. 101 and 87; and Table XXXIII, pp. 606–10.
[181] USBL [1894], p. 610.
[182] USBL [1894], p. 102.

346 cubic feet for each of the 5.2 slaves Fogel and Engerman report as the average number per dwelling on large plantations (FE, I, p. 115). If we assume two adults to each cabin and allow children only one-half the adult minimum air volume,[183] a 15 by 15 foot cabin could support a family of seven at the absolute maximum. A 16 by 18 foot floor would provide for two adults and three children at the more desirable 600-cubic-foot standard. These calculations suggest that the slave was housed at a level commensurate with absolute necessity but that resources were not "squandered" to improve his dwelling much beyond this.

Clothing

A similar conclusion can be reached concerning the clothing issued to slaves. There are no comprehensive census data or other extensive records of slave clothing forcing both the historian and the cliometrician to rely upon the observations of travelers, plantation record books, and the like. Fogel and Engerman do so indirectly. In this instance they cite the same state studies of slavery which they claimed supported their description of the slave cabin (FE, II, p. 100). Yet, here again, they distort the picture drawn by these scholars. They rely only upon the references to the most generous slaveowners to give their " 'typical' slave issue" (FE, I, p. 118) and ignore the references to the more parsimonious masters. For example, they suggest that the typical adult male slave received 4 pairs of pants and 4 shirts each year (FE, I, pp. 116 and 118). Postell and Joe Gray Taylor, it is true, refer to several articles in *De Bow's Review* which advised slaveowners to provide this issue, and Sydnor's book, *Slavery in Mississippi*, cites a letter in the *New York Tribune* to similar effect. Yet this letter was written to the *New York Tribune* to prove "that the condition of the slaves is better than that of free-laborers." [184] On the other hand, none of

183 This relationship between adult and child standards was suggested by the New York City's Health Department's Report for 1891 (cited in USBL [1894], p. 102).

184 Postell [1951], p. 39 and Taylor [1963], pp. 110–11. Sydnor ([1933], p. 27) is quoting Olmsted ([1856], p. 697) who in turn was quoting the letter to the

the other sources, nor the other examples cited by these authors, lend support to such a generous allowance. Two or three pairs of pants and shirts is the allowance most frequently mentioned.[185]

The Evidence and Its Implications

The evidence offered in *Time on the Cross* to support Fogel and Engerman's major conclusion, that slavery did not provide "extremely harsh material conditions of life for the typical slave," does not withstand scrutiny.

Fogel and Engerman claim that the ration provided slaves by their masters offered variety. I have argued that this finding was the product of an inadequate and biased procedure. I have also demonstrated that Fogel and Engerman's implementation of their own procedure was marred by computational errors and implausible assumptions which systematically exaggerated the variety of the ration.

Fogel and Engerman claim that the slave ration was nutritionally balanced. I have suggested that their analysis of the ration contains major errors which prevented their discovery of serious vitamin and mineral deficiencies.

Fogel and Engerman claim that the slaves enjoyed a relatively high quality of health care. I have charged that they misused and misinterpreted their sources and that the evidence does not support their case.

Fogel and Engerman claim that the slave was provided with better housing and clothing than the typical free worker. I have demonstrated that Fogel and Engerman reported the provisions of only the most generous slave masters and compared them with the conditions of the most impoverished free laborers.

Failing to make their case that slavery provided relatively generous and kind treatment to slaves, Fogel and Engerman are left only with their conjecture that capitalistic slavery *ought to*

Tribune. The characterization of the purpose of the letter which I quote in the text is Olmsted's, not Sydnor's.
[185] For example, see Flanders ([1933], pp. 160–161), Davis ([1939], pp. 84–85), and Sellers [1950]. Olmsted's observations also seem to agree ([1856], pp. 112 and 687–88; and [1860], p. 80).

have produced good treatment for the slave—a conclusion which is contradicted by the evidence. Are we then forced to conclude that slaveowners were not capitalists? Not necessarily. One historiographic tradition holds that they, like most business owners, were interested in increasing their profits, reducing their costs, and improving the economic efficiency of their business. Indeed, the standard economic analysis would suggest that the returns from slavery were maximized by using force to extract the maximum amount of work from the slaves while providing them only with sufficient food, shelter, clothing, and health care to keep them healthy and hardworking.

This combination of force and a low standard of living, of course, did produce resistance, sabotage, shirking, and even revolt. But the slaveowners need not have capitulated to these threats by reducing the harshness of enslavement. They might have responded by tightening control. Fogel and Engerman believe that the former course would have been more attractive to slaveowners in the long run, but they offer no evidence that slaveowners believed this. The fact that slave life does seem to have been harsh suggests that Fogel and Engerman are wrong on this point as well.

The authors of *Time on the Cross* convey the impression that it is important to establish their view of slave treatment because if slaves were poorly fed, cruelly treated, and ruthlessly exploited, it would imply to them that "black Americans were without culture, without achievement, and without development for their first two hundred and fifty years on American soil." They characterize the view that slavery provided harsh material conditions of life as "neoabolitionism" and refer to it, with evident scorn, as the "refurbished interpretation." They object that "while white America produced heroes of the struggle against tyranny who were honest, courageous, and industrious, the refurbished interpretation offered black rebels whose greatest achievements were such proficiency at stealing, shirking responsibilities, and feigning illness—and who were possessed of such sly capacity for lying—that they could trick their masters into believing that they were contented" (FE, I, pp. 259–60).

Having rejected Fogel and Engerman's attempt to overturn the "refurbished interpretation," must we accept their conten-

tion that with it comes the implication that enslaved blacks were
"without culture, without achievement, and without development," or their contention that it implies enslaved blacks were
thieves, liars, loafers, and bunglers? Of course not. The work of
numerous scholars—scholars who accept and helped fashion the
"refurbished interpretation"—have shown just the opposite.
The enslaved blacks had culture, achievement, and honest,
courageous heroes. That black America has succeeded less in her
"struggle against tyranny" than has white America in her
struggle is not due to inadequacies of black culture or black
leaders. Rather it is easily explained by the fact that for 350
years the tyranny against which black America has struggled
was the tyranny of white America.

CHAPTER SEVEN

Prosperity, Progress, and American Slavery

Gavin Wright

Time on the Cross portrays American slavery as profitable and productive, the slave economy as adaptable and efficient, the slave South as thriving, expanding, and optimistic. Rather than subject this research and these findings to a line-by-line critique, I propose to advocate as forcefully as I can an intellectual alternative to *Time on the Cross*, criticizing it only as it impinges on the propositions I wish to advance. The data and methods which I use do not differ in essential respects from those of Fogel and Engerman, but the historical portrait of the slave economy which emerges from my analysis is dramatically different. The alternative analysis holds that many of the historical relationships which *Time on the Cross* identifies as characteristics of slavery as a system of production, are better attributed to the one fundamental dynamic force in the southern economy: expansion of cotton demand. From the time of the cotton gin until World War II, the only periods of prosperity and progress for the South were periods of acceleration in world demand for this basic export crop. The greatest of these episodes happens to coincide with the late antebellum slave period.

The Economics of Slavery:
Some Alternative Hypotheses

Fogel and Engerman argue that slavery was highly profitable, productive, and efficient. They maintain that slavery was economically viable (FE, I, pp. 86–94) and was recognized as such by antebellum Southerners (FE, I, pp. 103–6), and that slaves would have become increasingly valuable over time (FE, I, pp. 94–97). They suggest that slavery contributed to a rapid rate of economic progress for the South (FE, I, pp. 247–55). They argue that the efficiency of slavery involved economies of scale, resulting from opportunities for division of labor, superior management, and the use of incentives—all at the expense of a basic nonpecuniary cost to the slave (FE, I, pp. 191–209). Finally, they argue that slaves were also efficient in industrial settings, but free workers were much closer substitutes for industrial slaves than for agricultural slaves, because of the nonpecuniary costs associated with gang labor on plantations.

In contrast, I will argue that the high regional growth rates, the apparent efficiency of slave labor, and the sanguinity of slaveowners, all rested on an inherently impermanent foundation: the extraordinary growth of world demand for cotton between 1820 and 1860. As the demand for cotton stagnated between 1860 and 1895, slave prices would have declined, and the growth rate of regional incomes would have been drastically reduced. I will argue that the evidence is consistent with the "null hypothesis" of no significant scale economies and no significant efficiency advantage associated with slave labor. Appearances to the contrary are explained by the degree of specialization in cotton and to reliance on the highly unusual census year 1859–60. Finally, I will argue that slavery affected resource allocation primarily by providing an elastic labor supply at the farm level, and that this effect acted to retard industrialization. To explain the absence of large-scale plantations based on wage labor, there is no need to appeal to nonpecuniary diseconomies, beyond the universal preference of rural workers for farm ownership. I will certainly not prove all of these propositions irrefutably, but I believe they are consistent with the evidence and that they provide a better overall characterization of the slave economy than the Fogel-Engerman alternative.

The student of southern history will readily observe that none of these assertions is genuinely original, though this particular analytical combination may be new. Taken as a whole, the analysis suggests that the flourishing American slavery described in *Time on the Cross* should be seen in perspective as the product of a special set of historical circumstances. In my view, the slave South was typical of many economies in history based essentially on extractive resource-intensive exports, which expand rapidly during a period of rising external demand, but which do not lay the institutional foundations for sustained growth once this era has passed. In terms of the broader political economy of slavery, the analysis amounts to a defense of the propositions that slavery did harbor serious internal contradictions and that American slave society was indeed approaching a crisis. The precise political shape of the crisis and its resolution are beyond the scope of the paper and beyond the professional expertise of an economist in any case. But the impending crisis was real, and the discussion of its implications should not be forestalled by enthrallment with a golden age—an age which could not have been resurrected by all the powers of post-1860 slaveholders.

"The Profitability of Slavery":
Was There Overspeculation in the Market for Slaves?

Communications are treacherous between cliometricians and the rest of the world. A reasonable man might think that the issue of the "profitability of slavery" had to do with tracking down the financial fortunes of slaveowners—but it doesn't. True, Fogel and Engerman do use the term "profits" with this common-sense meaning on pages 93–94 of Volume I. But the long debate surveyed in Volume II (pp. 64–79) concerns a quite different question: were slave prices appropriate in terms of (hypothetical) current and future earnings from slave labor? Ulrich Phillips thought they were not. Fogel and Engerman believe not only that Phillips was wrong, but that his belief is a classic case of an error based on a mis-specified implicit model. Phillips was no economist, but in my opinion he was more right than wrong on the substance of the matter.

In an analysis which has appeared more than once before,[1]

---

[1] Fogel and Engerman [1971], pp. 312–13. See also Fogel [1967].

Fogel and Engerman depict Phillips's argument as follows: he believed that the profitability of slavery was solely a function of the relative prices of cotton and slaves; "since the ratio of slave prices to cotton prices was much higher in 1860 than it had been in 1815, he drew the conclusion that by the eve of the Civil War, slavery had become unprofitable" (FE, II, p. 64). He explained this overvaluation in terms of speculation, economies of scale, and non-economic motives for holding slaves (FE, I p. 61). Because his implicit model assumes away changes in productivity and maintenance costs, Phillips's inference was incorrect; and the empirical evidence shows that his conclusion was erroneous.

But this simply is not an accurate portrayal of Phillips's views. Fogel and Engerman rely primarily on an early 1905 article rather than Phillips's more careful later works, but even in 1905 he clearly did not "implicitly assume . . . a linear equation with a zero intercept" (FE, II, p. 65). Instead, he *explicitly argued* that some part of the rise in the price ratio was attributable to "lessening of cost" in cotton marketing and transport, some part to better skills, some part to organizational improvements on the plantation.[2] Whatever errors Phillips may have made, the case does not illustrate anything about the dangers of implicit specification error in history. Furthermore, in his later works it is unmistakable that the "tendency to overcapitalize slave labor" was largely a *cyclical* or *periodic* phenomenon. And these periodic surges had little if anything to do with Phillips's broader views on planter motives and behavior (quite inadequately subsumed under the label "conspicuous consumption"), but represented actions of quite a different class of "sundry speculative buyers."[3] The assertion that slavery was

[2] Phillips [1905], p. 126. Page references are to the version reprinted in Genovese [1968]. The brief reference to the "advancement . . . toward the scale of maximum efficiency" appears in Phillips [1918], p. 394. This is clearly a way of referring to "productivity change," and is not offered as a factor in explaining the *over*valuation of slaves, as Fogel and Engerman seem to imply (FE, I, p. 61).

[3] "Slave prices . . . tended to remain on the lower levels and to return precipitately in sequel to each ascent. This reflects a disposition in the community to concern itself in the main only with routine earnings. . . . But when the market was thought to be going up, sundry speculative buyers

"unprofitable" at the end of the antebellum period was explicitly a claim that slave prices were at or near one of these speculative peaks in 1860: "But surely a peak was being shaped, whose farther side must have been a steep descent, whether in time of peace or war." [4]

In other words, when we cut through issues of terminology, style and rigor, there are two basic substantive propositions advanced by Phillips: that slave prices were characterized by wide speculative swings in excess of what was economiclly justifiable; and that the high prices of 1860 would not have been economically sustained. Empirical evidence relating to these propositions may be found in the "index of sanguinity" [5] (FE, I, pp. 103–6), the rates of return estimated by Evans from data on hire rates (FE, II, pp. 72–75), and the general estimates of average rates of return over 1820–60 (FE, I, pp. 70–71; II, pp. 65–79). In my view, it is difficult to imagine a set of results more fully in support of Phillips. The "index of sanguinity" shows at least three jagged peaks in a period of thirty years, well above or below the line of "normal" expectations. In particular, fully three-fourths of the price rise in the Lower South between 1846–50 and 1856–60 is attributable to "sanguinity" rather than "real" changes, and the rate of return based on these prices was 20 to 25 percent below the normal rate for the entire period. Fogel and Engerman cannot have the argument both ways: if the average rate of return over 1820–60 is a "normal" one, then the rate of return for 1856–60 must be "subnormal." There is abundant evidence that the textiles industry was on the verge of a cyclical downturn in 1860,[6] and in light of what we know

would purchase greedily with a view to profit by resale" Phillips [1929], p. 179. The discussion is quite similar in Phillips [1918], pp. 370–75. In the latter reference, Phillips does suggest briefly (p. 394) that "social status" and the inhibitions of "conventional morality" on selling slaves may have led to overvaluation.

[4] Phillips [1929], p. 181. An equally explicit statement appears in Phillips [1918], p. 375.

[5] The "index of sanguinity" is essentially the ratio of slave prices (which reflect expectations for the future) to hire rates (which reflect only current earnings). The index is analogous to the price-earnings ratio commonly used to infer expectations in stock market analysis

[6] See the arguments and references in Wright [1973], p. 463.

about the drastic slowdown in the expansion of world cotton demand (on which see below), the conclusion seems inescapable that Phillips was right in holding that "slave prices did rise to immoderate heights" and that "a crash must have come."

But Fogel and Engerman come to opposite conclusions. They argue, first, that the estimate of an average 10 percent profit rate (based on purchase at market prices) undermines the case for "conspicuous consumption" and "precapitalist" behavior among planters (FE, I, pp. 70–73). But the evidence on the profit rate has limited relevance, if any, for the issues of conspicuous consumption and "the capitalist character of slavery." [7] Second, Fogel and Engerman argue that the saguinity evidence "should not be interpreted as supporting the claim that the price of slaves was determined by wild speculation. Pessimism and optimism were generally rooted in experience. . . . Such behavior is more characteristic of sober businessmen doing their best to perceive an uncertain future" (FE, I, p. 105). In order to find in Phillips's favor, Fogel and Engerman would apparently settle for nothing less than a drunken random walk of slave prices, bearing no relationship whatever to prices and profits. But even "reckless speculators" do not march off in a direction *opposite* to that indicated by "experience." No reasonable man could support such an argument, and Phillips certainly did not. (Note particularly the phrase "when the market was thought to be going up" in note 3.) Further, since *Time on the Cross* argues elsewhere that the large planters entered the slave market only rarely, the evidence would seem to indicate that Phillips was not amiss in attributing these flights and falls to quite a different group (who certainly deserve the name "speculators," at least in the most general sense). In other words, Phillips has been done in on these points mainly by terminological oneupmanship, and not by economic logic or any compelling statistical evidence. If

---

[7] This point is argued in Wright [1973]. pp. 459–60. It is developed more strongly in David and Temin [1975]. The discussion of the issue by Fogel and Engerman (FE, II, pp. 62–64) is particularly misleading. They dismiss the possibility of *horizontal* addition of demand curves on the grounds that there were no "separate markets" for slaves as " 'objets d'art,' freed from all productive responsibilities." But all that is required is the existence of separate groups of demanders, *some* of whom are solely profit-maximizers.

he could read *Time on the Cross*, and if he were not intimidated by the mathematical notation, I feel sure that he would feel essentially vindicated on the profitability issue.

There is one point on which I believe Phillips did harbor an economic misconception, though it is not one clearly identified by Fogel and Engerman, a misconception which explains why he evidently felt that rates of return based on market prices were even lower than they actually were "by the close of the 'fifties.'" It was not that he ignored "productivity change," or assumed it to be zero: he recognized that the market price of a productive factor would rise because of improvement in the quality of *that* factor,[8] and because of advances in plantation organization (i.e., "neutral" technological progress). But he apparently failed to realize that the market price of a factor could rise because of an increase in the quantity or quality of *other* complementary factors of production. This relationship is perceived very naturally by economists, though it is often a source of confusion in public discussions of the proper share of labor in the distribution of productivity gains. Phillips was of course well aware of the enormous expansion of acreage and of the high fertility of cotton land in the Southwest. But he never listed this as a basis for higher equilibrium slave prices. He was of course mistaken on the theoretical point, but I believe he was not far off in his underlying assumption that most of the observed increase in labor productivity was in fact due to the increase in the quantity and quality of cotton land.

Was the Cotton Boom Sustainable?

In Chapter 3 of *Time on the Cross*, Fogel and Engerman establish to my satisfaction that the 1850s were a period of enormous profits for slaveholding cotton planters, and that the demand for cotton grew rapidly to the very end of the decade (FE, I, pp. 89–94). Much of the actual profitability was realized

---

[8] He wrote, for example, that "these great appreciations were accompanied by no remotely proportionate increase of the slaves' industrial capacities" (Phillips [1918], p. 386). See also the quotation in FE, I, p. 61.

in the form of capital gains—an increase in the value of slaves—a fact which supports the further proposition that the expectations of slaveowners were unusually optimistic at the time of secession (FE, I, pp. 103–6). What is *not* established is that these expectations were justified by the prospective economic future, nor that the growth of cotton demand would have continued beyond 1860.

In fact, world cotton demand collapsed catastrophically in the 1860s, a collapse everlastingly obscured by the virtually simultaneous collapse of the American cotton *supply*. Demand grew at approximately 5 percent per year from 1830 to 1860; between 1866 and 1895 the rate was less than 1½ percent. Measured from the peak year of 1860, demand grew at little more than 1 percent per year to the end of the century.[9] Demand turned up again in the late 1890s, but never again did the extraordinary growth rates of the antebellum decades return. This decline is at the heart of my argument in much of the rest of this paper.

The only point at which Fogel and Engerman address the question of post-1860 cotton demand is in the section of Chapter 3 in which they project slave prices, in the absence of a Civil War, to 1890 (FE, I, pp. 95–97). They find that slave prices would have risen at approximately 1.4 percent per year. This result rests on "two solid facts": (1) that "demand for American cotton grew a little more rapidly than the supply. . . . Hence the real price of cotton was higher in 1890 than in 1860"; and (2) that "land devoted to cotton nearly doubled between 1860 and 1890" (FE, I, pp. 96–97).

How can we reconcile these results with the evidence on world cotton demand? A growth rate of 1.4 percent per year is, of course, well below the pre-1860 figure, and does provide evidence of slowing down. But the projected 1.4 percent growth in slave prices is indefensible: it is not based on *projected* experience at all, but on the *actual* postwar (1890) levels of cotton production, prices, nonwhite population, and interest rates. It is

[9] The term "shift of demand" involves the economist's concept of a demand *curve* (or schedule) relating price and the quantity demanded (inversely). In other words, the phrase refers to a shift in the quantity of cotton demanded *at a given price*. The assertions in this section are documented in Wright [1974].

difficult to believe that all of these variables would have been the same under a projected post-1860 slave regime. The *actual* cotton production figures, for example, are far below any reasonable extrapolation of antebellum supply: hence, cotton prices would surely have been lower than they actually were. And considering the high mortality of the war years and the lower black life expectancy thereafter, the 1890 *slave* population would surely have been greater than the actual 1890 nonwhite population.

But even using the postbellum figures on supply, price, and population, the rise in the real value of cotton output to 1890 is too small to make any significant contribution to the projected slave price increase. Almost all of the increase in the Fogel-Engerman projection is attributable to a third "fact," which is not quite so solid: the fall in interest rates between 1860 and 1890 at about 2 percent per year. To believe this result, in other words, we must take very seriously the interpretation of the railroad bond rate as the real opportunity cost of capital for southern farmers.[10] Even if we ignore the large regional and local interest rate differentials which persisted in the nineteenth century, we can hardly ignore the 25-year period of deflation in the general price level: at least some part of the very low interest rate might reasonably be attributed to deflationary expectations rather than a real fall in the marginal productivity of capital.[11] Adjusting only the 1890 interest rate for the rate of deflation of the 1880s would cut the rate of decline in the interest rate in half.[12]

The one component of the projection which might reasonably

[10] The "opportunity cost of capital" means the rate of interest which slaveholders could earn on funds placed in alternative investments. A fall in interest rates will, *ceteris paribus,* raise the market price of financial assets. Neoclassical economic theory holds that, in equilibrium, the interest rate will equal the "marginal productivity of capital."

[11] If the general price level is expected to fall, then observed interest rates will fall because loans will have to be repaid in more valuable dollars. In such a case, we say that "nominal" interest rates have fallen, even though "real" interest rates (i.e., corrected for deflationary expectations) may not have changed.

[12] Jeffrey Williamson argues that in real terms interest rates sharply *rose* between 1845–61 and 1867–1878. See Williamson [1974], pp. 109–10.

be assumed to be independent of the Civil War and its
aftermath is cotton demand. But 1890 is not exactly a representative year for computing demand change. My estimates of the
postbellum demand curve indicate that the census year 1890 is in
fact the most *unrepresentative* year available. Specifically, the
percentage demand residual (actual minus predicted price) is
higher for 1890 than for any other year in the estimating period
(1866–95).[13] This untypicality is not quite evident in the chart in
Time on the Cross (FE, I, p. 97). The reader can see that most of
the projected price increase comes after 1886, but he is not able
to see that a sharp decline is in the offing for the 1890s.

Using the Fogel-Engerman formula with what I believe to be
reasonable projected rates of change for output and prices, and
adjusting the interest rate for deflationary expectations, I have
had no difficulty generating projections of a slave price *decrease*
of more than 1 percent per year for periods of 20 to 40 years. In
the best of circumstances such projections are highly sensitive to
assumptions, and I would certainly not ask readers to place
great confidence in them. But no one who is otherwise attracted
by my analysis should feel deterred by the Fogel-Engerman
projection. I would note further that all of this discussion
concerns changes in *equilibrium* slave prices. In light of the
established pattern of *overadjustment* of slave prices in both
upward and downward directions (FE, I, p. 104), I believe it is
not implausible to assert that the plunge of slave prices during
the cotton market collapse of the 1860s would have been very
drastic indeed.

I believe Ramsdell was on strong ground in forecasting an era
of low cotton prices and falling slave values in the 1860s and
1870s. Of course, there had been a major slave price fall earlier,
but in contrast with the 1840s, the slaveholders of 1860 would
have had to wait more than a generation to see their capital loss
restored. Even if one is not willing to agree with Ramsdell that

[13] An "estimate" of a demand curve is an equation relating price, quantity and
other variables, derived from historical data in an effort to approximate the
"true" demand curve and its rate of shift over time. Once such an equation
has been estimated, we can judge whether any particular year is above or
below "normal" demand by comparing the actual (observed) price to the
price "predicted" by the equation. This difference is known as the "residual."

slavery would have died out peacefully, it is not going too far to say that the political and economic equilibrium of 1860 would have been severely disturbed.

Was Slave Agriculture More Efficient Than Free?

Time on the Cross calculates that "southern slave agriculture" was 35 percent more efficient than "the northern system of family farming." This figure is obtained by computation of a "geometric index of total factor productivity": the ratio of the value of output to an index of inputs of labor, capital, and land. All inter-economy comparisons of this type are fraught with practical and conceptual difficulties, and many economists view them with great skepticism. The major points raised by critics of Fogel and Engerman concern problems of aggregation, the use of uniform national prices, the length of the work year, the implied differences in rates of return on capital, and the use of land value as an input, to reflect differences in soil quality.[14] The last-mentioned point is the most significant for the calculation itself, since it accounts for most of the large efficiency advantage enjoyed by the South under the "refined" (as opposed to the "crude") index (FE, I, pp. 131–38). The use of land *value* is dubious because it imparts a conceptual circularity to the whole exercise: economic theory suggests that *any* neutral regional difference in efficiency will be capitalized in the price of land, perhaps the more so in the North, where labor was not also capitalized. Further, land prices are affected by locational influences such as proximity to cities and access to transportation, influences which do not contribute to "output" as measured by Fogel and Engerman and which tend to bias the ratio against the North. Some correction of the acreage total may be called for to reflect the higher fraction of improved land in the North; but even taking the extreme step of excluding all unimproved acreage does not yield nearly a 35 percent efficiency advantage for the South.

But the reader should be able to guess by now that my major

[14] David and Temin [1974], and Chapter 5, above; Paul Krugman, "The Relative Efficiency of Slavery" (unpublished paper).

concern is with none of these points, but instead with the role of cotton supply and demand in this calculation. David and Temin make the essential theoretical point that one cannot define "productive efficiency" in a meaningful way where the production of one commodity is entirely limited for reasons of geography to one of the regions involved.[15] It is true that in principle this difficulty affects all international comparisons. But I will allow that, for diversified industrial economies, one might be able to suspend one's disbelief sufficiently to imagine a kind of generalized jelly called "output," which can be compared among countries. But this can't be done persuasively when the major component of "output" is a geographically distinct primary product. Hence I agree with David and Temin that the regional index of total-factor-productivity is not a meaningful basis for drawing inferences about the relative hardworkingness of slave and free labor, nor the relative efficiencies of the "plantation-slavery-system" and the northern "family-farm-system."

Putting aside the empirical objections, however, one may still view these indices as generalized measures of the extraordinary economic success of the slave economy in the census year 1859–60. But even if we adopt this less far-reaching interpretation, it is relevant to take note of just how very unusual and unrepresentative the census year 1859–60 was. Econometric estimates of the cotton demand curve indicate that the actual price for the crop year 1859–60 was between 7.6 percent and 15.9 percent above the level "predicted" on the basis of production and trend. (See Appendix A.) This is another way of saying that *demand* was unusually high in that year. Bear in mind that this "residual" is from a demand curve which includes a trend of

---

[15] See Chapter 5, above, pp. 216–18, 221–22. If one responds that such geographic differences should be "reflected in land prices," the proper retort is that in that case there should be no difference in measured regional efficiency. Unless, of course, there is some difference between the regions in the rate or process of capitalization. David and Temin go on to argue that southern land values will reflect geographic differences *less* fully than in the North, because of the capitalization of labor in the price of slaves, the supply of which was even less elastic than the supply of land.

approximately 5 percent per year. The corresponding residual
for supply ranges from 11.6 percent to 23.6 percent, depending
on the specification of the supply curve, on top of an annual
growth rate of almost 6 percent per year.

In short, in light of both the trends and the upward deviation
from the trends, there is no other year which would put the
South in a better light in terms of the Fogel-Engerman version
of "efficiency." Note that this is not the same as saying that the
cotton price was exceptionally high, historically speaking. Because *both* supply and demand shifted dramatically, the price
was only slightly above average. But that doesn't mean that the
crop *year* was not highly unusual in every relevant sense. The
atypicality may be seen graphically in the sharp peaks in both
supply and demand in Figure 28 (FE, I, p. 92) in 1860. It is just
this peak year which provides the one observation for comparison of total-factor-productivity between regions.

Production estimates for northern crops are not available on
an annual basis, but the annual data which are available show
plainly that neither supply nor demand conditions for the North
during 1859–60 were in any way comparable to those in the
South. Far from being above the trend, exports of wheat, flour
and corn were well below both previous and subsequent levels in
absolute terms.[16] Figures on internal shipments show no unusual
level of activity for the census year.[17] Northern farm prices
were no better than "moderate" compared to the average for
the 1850s, though they were higher than earlier census years. In
any case it is not safe to take national price averages as
indicators of the state of demand for northern crops. Compared
to cotton, prices of food crops varied much more widely among
major markets, increasingly so in 1859–60. On the general
prosperity of western agriculture, T. S. Berry refers to the
period 1860–61 as a "low-water mark." [18] One of the best general
indicators of agricultural prosperity is the value of public land

[16] See U.S. Census (1860), *Agriculture*, pp. cxl–cxli.
[17] See, for example, Berry [1943], pp. 168, 172; U.S. Census [1860], *Agriculture*, cxliv–clii; North [1961], pp. 251–54. The census-year production is
presumably reflected primarily in the 1859 annual figures, which are especially low.
[18] Cf. Berry [1943], p. 530.

sales, which stood at a peak for the South in 1859, while the Northwest approached a trough.[19]

It is the level of demand which is chiefly relevant for the southern regional efficiency index. Because of the dominance of world cotton markets by American cotton, short-run fluctuations in *supply* were generally accompanied by roughly proportional inverse changes in price: the enormous census year crop would have depressed the price, had it not been for the exceptional demand. In a situation where the demand elasticity is close to unity, it is *only* demand that can expand the aggregate value of cotton production.[20] Comparisons within the South are also affected by cotton demand—obviously so, since it is only in the great staple crops that Fogel and Engerman claim to have found a productivity advantage to slave labor—but here supply-side fluctuations may be more crucial. In the context of high cotton demand, I believe that much of the intra-South pattern of "efficiency" can be explained by the deviations of *supply* from its trend.

The bumper crop of the census year was especially good in the "New South." A cotton supply curve estimated for the leading New South cotton states alone (but excluding Texas) shows a spectacular 40-year average annual growth rate of 7 percent per year.[21] Even from this supply curve, the census year 1859–60 shows a positive residual between 35.2 and 43.5 percent. Small wonder that Fogel and Engerman find a substantial "total-factor-productivity" advantage for the New over the Old South (FE, I, pp. 194–96; II, pp. 138–40). Other reviewers have

[19] North [1961], p. 256. Berry ([1943], p. 528) notes the increasing price divergence among markets in 1859 and 1860. It is true that Berry's series on "Western States Terms of Trade" shows a peak in 1859 (North [1961], p. 255), but these high prices prevailed for the first half of the year only (Berry [1943], p. 505) and did not apply to the census year crop.

[20] The "elasticity of demand" is the ratio (along a demand curve) of the percentage fall in price to the percentage rise in quantity demanded. If this ratio is "unity" (i.e., 1.0), then the price change exactly compensates for the quantity change, leaving total revenue unaffected.

[21] The main states are Alabama, Arkansas, Louisiana and Mississippi. Unfortunately, since the states were grouped for the purpose of using land-sales data, the series also includes Florida, but this is a trivial share of the total cotton output covered. See Wright [1971].

commented on how unreasonable it would be to infer from the Fogel-Engerman results that New South slaves worked harder than Old South slaves.[22] Attention to the peculiarities of the census year resolves this problem, but it also casts further doubt on the wisdom of drawing such inferences in general.

Were There Economies of Scale on Slave Plantations?

The reader whom I have persuaded to this point may still wonder how any of these arguments undermine the evidence on economies of scale.[23] Obviously an unusually good cotton year will exaggerate the apparent efficiency of the South as a whole, but why should purely random effects have been concentrated in the large slave plantations? Certainly small free southern farms were not geographically debarred from cotton growing.

But in fact small southern farms did specialize much more in non-cotton crops and in livestock than the large plantations. This relationship may be illustrated crudely by measuring the share of cotton output in the cotton-corn total, for the size and regional groupings used by Fogel and Engerman (see Table 1). Appendix B presents evidence that uniformly, in each of the size and regional categories (as well as in the aggregate), the two-crop value of output per worker is strongly and positively correlated with the share of cotton in total output.[24] All but one of the coefficients are between .963 and 1.78, which is to say that a one percentage-point increase in cotton share implies an increase in output per worker between 1 and 2 percent. The labor productivity analysis of Appendix B indicates (a) that the

---

[22] Lichtman [1974], p. 24.

[23] Strictly, "economies of scale" refer to a more-than-proportionate increase in output when all inputs are proportionately increased. *Time on the Cross* does not always clearly separate the hypothesis of scale economies from the hypothesis that slave labor possessed an "efficiency advantage" over free labor. Presumably, such an "advantage" would hold true at any level of "scale."

[24] Output per worker will, *ceteris paribus,* be proportional to total factor productivity if the production function is Cobb-Douglas, as Fogel and Engerman assume.

crop-mix effect[25] alone will generate a pseudo-efficiency index very similar to the Fogel-Engerman total-factor-productivity figures,[26] and (b) that when the crop mix is held constant, there is no productivity advantage for slaves and there are no scale economies for slave plantations. In other words, the Fogel-Engerman "efficiency" index is largely a measure of who happened to be growing cotton during the most extraordinary cotton year of the nineteenth century.

Table 1:
Value of Cotton/(Value of Cotton + Value of Corn)

	Slaves per Farm			
Region	0	1–15	16–50	51 & over
Cotton South	.300	.401	.556	.661
Old South	.269	.373	.492	.605
New South	.312	.422	.599	.698

Source: Parker-Gallman sample, 1860. The figures are unweighted averages of the farm ratios in each class, valuing cotton at 10¢ per pound, corn at 80¢ per bushel.

The application of the Fogel-Engerman procedures to earlier antebellum years would produce a reduced measure of the "efficiency advantage" of slavery within the South, but I would conjecture that the advantage would not completely disappear. If this conjecture is correct, the question arises: Why did small and slaveless farms grow so much corn, when cotton apparently offered higher returns? The implicit hypothesis of *Time on the Cross* is that all farms were trying to maximize cash or

[25] The term "crop mix" is used here as a short-hand expression for "the share of cotton in the total value of crop production."
[26] The only instance where the crop-mix effect is not in the same direction as the Fogel-Engerman efficiency index is the case of farms with more than 50 slaves in the New South. Ironically, this is the one case where Fogel and Engerman believe that measurement error has contaminated their results (FE, II, pp. 140–41). A corrected measure, they believe, would show this to be the most efficient class.

cash-equivalent profits, and if some farmers grew disproportionate amounts of corn, either they were poor entrepreneurs or
cotton was too difficult a crop for them. Under this standard
economist's assumption, it would make sense to measure all
output by its market value.

But there is an alternative motivational possibility, one which
was widely preached in the nineteenth century and widely
practiced in the antebellum South: wise farmers should strive to
achieve self-sufficiency in foods first, and only then venture into
risky cash crops. Such a "safety-first" strategy implies, under
reasonable assumptions, that small farms will have to allocate a
larger share of their acreage and time to nomarket production,
even if large plantations are also self-sufficient in foods. The
basic underlying motivation is the desire to stay out of debt and
protect the security of the family's sustenance and property. It
is a reasonable strategy economically because—when one takes
into account the *combined* risks of cotton yields, cotton prices,
and the exchange of cotton for corn—growing cotton was a very
much riskier way to feed one's family than growing corn for
on-farm consumption. Indeed, about a fourth of the farms in the
Parker-Gallman sample did not grow cotton at all, and many
others grew only small amounts, apparently treating it as a
"surplus" crop in the sense described here.[27]

Hence I don't believe that the specialization in corn by small
farmers reflected inefficiency, but only smallness and risk
aversion. I believe that this hypothesis provides a *better* overall
explanation of the evidence, because it also explains why there
was virtually no tendency for these small, allegedly inefficient
farms to disappear. One cannot accept the Fogel-Engerman
"total-factor-productivity" results without also acknowledging
that the South experienced an enormous "deadweight loss"
from the existence of so many farms and plantations so far from
the optimal scale.[28]

Fogel and Engerman do present a "survivor" table taken

[27] For details on this assertion and the safety-first argument, see Kunreuther
and Wright [1974]; Wright and Kunreuther [1975].
[28] Economists use the term "deadweight loss" to refer to the net loss to the
economy from an inefficient allocation of resources.

from Gray (FE, II, p. 144), which they interpret as favorable to their conclusions.[29] But the changes in slaveholding shares found in that table are truly minute in light of the huge differentials in total-factor-productivity. When Fogel and Engerman write that "plantations between 200 and 1,000 slaves increased their share by 14 percent" (FE, II, p. 145) this means that the share rose from 1.9 percent to 2.1 percent of the total. Further, when one looks into the method which Gray used to estimate these shares, it becomes clear that these differences could not possibly be statistically significant.[30]

It is perhaps more in the spirit of the "survivor" approach to compare changes in the share of *output* over time. Appendix C presents some findings on trends in output shares by farm size between 1850 and 1860. The results indicate that slaveless farms *increased* their output share relative to slave farms, and the largest losers are plantations above 50 slaves—which Fogel and Engerman believe to be far more efficient than small farms. The fall is of dramatic proportions if one excludes the Alluvial region, where the largest size classes did actually gain. Note once again that Fogel and Engerman believe that their New South efficiency index is contaminated for the "over 50 slaves" category, which they actually judge to be universally "most efficient" (FE, II, p. 140).

In my view, the "survivor" evidence is very troublesome for the hypothesis of economies of scale. But the same evidence makes sense if viewed in terms of constant returns with differing access to financial capital and differing behavior toward risk. Indeed, one might well argue that under this theory the plantations were in fact more "efficient" because they were

[29] A "survivor" table shows the changing distribution of farms by size. The presumption behind such a table is that farms of the "optimum" size have a better chance of "survival," and hence the distribution of farm sizes should tend to converge toward this optimum over time.

[30] Gray [1933], pp. 529–44, especially the note to Table 10. The statistical uncertainty is especially acute for the large size classes. Gray assumed that the average slaveholding equalled the midpoint of the class (with a proportionate adjustment at the end of the calculation to reproduce the total accurately). For a size class like "100 and under 200," his estimated share could be off by as much as 50 percent.

in better position to risk cotton-growing and hence, on average, earned higher returns. But in my argument the advantage is essentially a *financial* one, which does not confirm the *productive* advantages attributed by Fogel and Engerman to organization, management, and incentives. Their interpretation of the advantage in terms of physical productivity is crucial to the whole analogy between the slave plantation and the modern industrial factory, and undergirds much of the broader argument of *Time on the Cross.*

If there are constant returns to scale, but farm and slaveholding size are constrained by access to cash (and by time), one would expect an upward drift of scale over time, though the creation of new farms may keep the median size down. One would not predict any tendency toward the disappearance of small farms, because the very purpose of their conservative behavior is to maintain their independence and security. Because they behave conservatively, one would neither expect small farms to disappear *nor* to grow very fast. In a time of rapidly rising slave prices, one would expect slaveownership to become out of reach for an increasing fraction of the southern population, even while the absolute number of slaveholders was rising. All of these trends were in fact observed in the late antebellum South.[31]

Why Were There No Wage-Labor Plantations?

In their section entitled "The Economic Significance of Property Rights in Man," Fogel and Engerman bolster their analysis of economies of scale by noting that large-scale plantation agriculture was achieved *only* with slave labor, never with free:

> . . . small free southern farmers were not bunglers. Nor were they lacking in enterprise. If there had been no special advantage to slave labor, one would expect at least some of these enterprising individuals to have based their plantations on free labor. The fact that economies of scale were achieved exclusively with slave labor clearly indicates that in large-scale production some special advantage attached to the use of slaves. [FE, I, p. 234]

[31] See Wright [1970].

Since I have rejected the evidence of economies of scale, it is incumbent on me to offer an alternative explanation for the fact that large-scale agriculture is observed only with slave labor, and for the further result (due to Goldin) that urban demand for slaves was much more elastic than the agricultural demand, suggesting greater substitutability between free and slave workers in urban industries.

My explanation is simple: there was no supply of agricultural wage labor forthcoming at wage levels which farmers could afford to pay. If we reject economies of scale, then there is nothing paradoxical about the absence of large-scale free-labor farms, because they were not observed *anywhere* in nineteenth-century American agriculture. To explain this absence, one need not postulate any special aversion to gang labor, but only a preference for the status of farmownership, and opportunities to obtain this status. Whether this preference—universally noted in the nineteenth century—should be called "nonpecuniary" is open to debate: perhaps farmers valued independence for its own sake, but they also valued the economic security which landownership provided, and they also enjoyed the earnings of the land and the prospect of realizing large capital gains from an increase in land values. For reasons such as these, farms throughout the United States were essentially limited to the family labor force, only occasionally making use of the uncertain and unreliable hired labor. A recent paper by Heywood Fleisig explains many of the observed differences between free and slave agriculture by postulating a *constraint* on the labor supply of farms in the free states. In other words, the "economic significance of property rights in man" was to provide an *elastic* supply of labor at the farm level, *allowing* an expansion under constant returns to scale which was not possible in the free states.[32]

---

[32] See Fleisig [forthcoming]. An "elastic supply of labor at the farm level" means that individual farmowners can hire as much labor as they choose (or purchase as many slaves) at the going rate (or price). This situation was clearly true under slavery, but the assumption of the Fleisig paper is that the opposite was true in non-slave regions: typically, farmowners had no access to a "labor market" of permanent wage laborers. On the universality of the sharp break between family and non-family labor, see Parker [1972], esp. pp. 393–98.

Fogel and Engerman argue instead that gang labor on plantations involved substantial nonpecuniary disadvantages for free men.[33] Some such aversion is certainly not implausible, but the evidence for very large nonpecuniary diseconomies (which the Fogel-Engerman explanation requires) is weak. Only scant attention is directed to the troublesome question of why, if the nonpecuniary cost of being treated like a slave is so great (perhaps 50 percent of wages, it is suggested), *no* such attitude is observed in cities. They write:

> Interestingly enough, there is no evidence that slaves possessed any special advantage or disadvantage for large-scale production in urban industries. . . . The nonpecuniary disadvantage of accepting the monotonous and intense routine of factories appears to have been offset by nonpecuniary benefits which both black and white workers attached to life in the cities. [FE, I, pp. 234–35, 238]

The claim is that free white workers allowed themselves to be treated like slaves in return for the privilege of living in cities. No direct evidence is offered in support of this momentous and (to me) implausible claim; it is entirely inferred from the coexistence of free and slave labor in "urban industries" but not in large-scale agriculture. Is it true, for example, that free-labor factories which were *not* in cities were forced to pay a 50 percent wage premium? The need for this layering of large conjectural nonpecuniary preferences is all ultimately traceable back to the finding of economies of scale in agriculture, a result which seems to bring no end of empirical and analytical difficulties. To my mind, a simpler and more straightforward analysis argues only that rural workers preferred farmownership and were not available for hire as wage laborers on a permanent or reliable basis. Those unskilled laborers without a farm or a reasonable hope of obtaining one (a category which might well include immigrants without farming skills) preferred industrial work because the wages were higher.

[33] "Nonpecuniary" motives are those directed at ends other than money. Note, however, that Fogel and Engerman treat "household" production (including food produced and consumed on the farm) as though it were "pecuniary" income, even though this production never entered into market exchange.

Two types of evidence are offered in support of the large nonpecuniary cost which whites and blacks attached to gang labor on plantations: (1) planters were not able to bribe small farmers to combine their farms and work in gangs on a large-scale plantation, despite the existence of a potential productivity gain of 50 percent, and despite the evidence that slave families earned a higher pecuniary income than the families of free farm laborers (FE, I, p. 236; II, p. 158); and (2) following emancipation, freedmen showed a clear preference for the independence of tenancy over wage labor in gangs, despite wage offers equal to two or three times their annual earnings as sharecroppers (FE, I, pp. 237–38; II, pp. 160–61). Both of these inferences are faulty. As David and Temin have argued,[34] the comparison between a slave and free worker involves a difference in *family* income, where in the slave case the wife is a field hand but in the free case she is not. Hence it is not clear that there was a difference in pecuniary income between hypothetical free and slave *workers*. More relevant for the present discussion is the fact that most free rural Southerners were not "farm laborers," but were also realizing all of the other on-farm returns which Fogel and Engerman impute to land and capital. Ever since the pathbreaking research of Frank Owsley [1949] and his students, it has been known that the great majority of southern heads of families owned their land in antebellum times. Even if there were a class of landless farm laborers available to the highest bidder, the fact of widespread landownership relates closely to my main reason for rejecting the Fogel-Engerman inference; it is misleading to compare realized pecuniary incomes between small farms and large slave plantations (especially in 1859–60), because most small farmers were intentionally sacrificing expected pecuniary income for security—precisely for the purpose of protecting their ownership of land and other property.

As for the evidence on postbellum wage rates and sharecropper earnings, it is difficult to have any confidence in inferences drawn from the Seagrave data on which Fogel and Engerman rely. The data pertain to Louisiana only (by all indications a

[34] See Chapter 5 above, pp. 184–86.

high wage state) between 1865 and 1867, years which encompass
both crop failures and a catastrophic decline in the cotton price.
In an environment of rapidly deteriorating economic prospects,
it is hardly surprising that wage contracts should be struck at
rates which look high compared to realized earnings at the
season's end (which is what the sharecropper income figures
reflect). Indeed this history helps to explain why sharecropping
looked so attractive in the late 1860s to *planters*. There is no
evidence of such large differentials for later postbellum years
when southern agriculture settled into a more stable institutional pattern, and earnings were not plummeting freakishly.
One recent calculation for the year 1900 actually *reverses* the
income-differential between tenancy and wage-labor which Fogel and Engerman describe.[35] Obviously, the post-emancipation
decline of large-scale agriculture and the rise of tenancy pose no
problem for the Fleisig-Domar hypothesis outlined earlier in this
section.

The Cotton Boom and
the Growth of Southern Income

Perhaps the most important implications of the analysis proposed here concern the explanation for the course of southern
regional progress before and after the Civil War. Several
scholars have questioned the sustainability of the high growth
rates observed between 1840 and 1860, on the grounds that these
rates were very largely a function of the redistribution of
population from east to west.[36] In *Time on the Cross*, Fogel and
Engerman respond to this criticism by noting that differences in
sectoral or subregional growth rates are a perfectly normal feature of economic growth, and that recent studies of twentieth-

---

[35] The calculation may be found in a forthcoming book by Robert Higgs,
Competition and Coercion. Higgs informs me in correspondence that "there
is no doubt whatever that share croppers *on the average* earned higher
incomes than wage hands . . . Quite direct documentation can be found in
many of the USDA farm management studies made just before and after
World War I" (letter of Aug. 16, 1974).
[36] Parker [1970], p. 119, Woodman [1972].

century experience also attribute a substantial share of productivity growth to intersectoral shifts. Their discussion may be somewhat misleading in that it fails to distinguish between the general phenomena of sectoral unevenness and responsiveness to change, and the particular phenomenon of a once-for-all contribution to growth from the closing of a disequilibrium "gap" between sectors or regions. Just as sectoral shifts have often been a part of economic development, so also have rapid growth rates often petered out when based on a nonrenewable resource or "gap." The citation to the research of Edward Denison seems particularly misplaced, since one of the central themes of *Why Growth Rates Differ* is precisely the argument that some very high growth rates recently observed should be discounted somewhat, because they rest on the transfer of labor from traditional to modern sectors, and hence cannot be sustained indefinitely. Thus, despite their verbal skills and powers of persuasion, I do not think that Fogel and Engerman have entirely disposed of their critics' objections that the growth achievement of the South is less substantial than the overall growth rate implies.

But the issue of impermanence runs deeper than the question of migration. The fundamental underpinning of most of this growth is, again, the rapid but essentially temporary growth in world demand for cotton. The reason that regional migration makes such a large contribution to growth between 1840 and 1860 is that per capita income in the West South Central region is more than twice as great as in the South Atlantic and East South Central regions. These high income levels do not represent a more "advanced" state of economic development in the west, but reflect primarily the superior soil and climate of the region in terms of cotton. Hence the source of growth was not really migration as such but cotton demand. Correspondingly, the income decline of this western region from 1860 to 1880 exceeded that of the two eastern regions by a wide margin.

In addition to the rapid average growth of cotton demand during the late antebellum period, the measured growth rate of per capita income between 1840 and 1860 is probably increased by the particular *state* of demand during the two census years involved. Econometric estimates of the cotton demand curve indicate, as noted above, that demand was above its trend value in 1859–60 (i.e., that the price of cotton was above the level predicted on the basis of production and trend) by 7.6 to 15.9 percent. On a comparable basis, the cotton price for the census year 1839–40 was between 4.0 and 11.5 percent *below* its predicted value. Hence, it appears that over and above the rapid average growth of cotton demand, the choice of endpoints imposed by the census data makes 1.7 percent a trough-to-peak figure, giving an extra upward "tilt" to the southern growth path.[37]

There is no getting around the fact that incomes earned in cotton were fundamentally governed by demand. But trends in productivity in cotton growing are not irrelevant to regional income growth, because resources released from cotton can be used to produce other outputs. Much of the loss of income to 1880 resulted from lower production of non-cotton crops because a larger fraction of southern resources went into cotton-growing. The possibilities for crop substitution were actually quite limited—most of the region had no other cash crop—but the trends in cotton productivity bear close examination anyway, because they at least were subject to the influence of Southerners, which was not true of demand and may not have been true of the choice of crops.

Fogel and Engerman state that improvements in the efficiency of *management*, especially labor management, were "the most important technological advance within the agricultural sector of the South after 1800" (FE, I, p. 199). They point to the "substantial increase in the average size of slaveholdings" during this period (FE, I, p. 200), a development which, in conjunction with their total-factor-productivity estimates, clearly implies significant productivity growth overtime.[38] In

[37] The same cannot be said for the northern figures. As North ([1961], p. 255) states, "the years from 1858 to 1861 present no picture of booming expansion."

[38] Fogel and Engerman do acknowledge briefly that the "changing *structure of demand*" (my italics) explains the migration of slave labor among states, and they note also that the expansion of scale "coincided" with a "shift from the production of grain and tobacco to cotton, sugar, and rice" (FE, I, pp. 199–200). But the bulk of their discussion deals with the development of managerial skills and techniques, and while it is not specific on the point, it

this way *Time on the Cross* conveys the impression of rapid technical progress and major gains in efficiency; but remarkably, the book contains little discussion and virtually no evidence on the rate or sources of productivity growth over time.[39] In fact, there is very little evidence of substantial productivity growth under slavery—other than that associated with the increase in the quantity and quality of cotton land.

The one specific piece of evidence presented by Fogel and Engerman to support a claim of efficiency improvement over time is the slow downward long-run trend in the price of cotton, at 0.71 percent per year (FE, I, p. 91; II, p. 86). But there is only casual effort to list the reasons for this rather modest decline. As they note, the list would have to *include* such factors as the "reduction in transportation and other marketing costs, and the relocation of cotton production in the more fertile lands of the New South" (FE, I, p. 93). Surely there is little basis here for a claim of major improvements in productive efficiency over time. To the contrary, it is difficult to see how there could be much room left for the contributions of "scale expansion" and "advancement in the realm of management," when the more obvious developments in location and transport are taken account of.

In an earlier publication, Fogel and Engerman did refer to the productivity estimates of Foust and Swan from the 1850 census, which imply that output per worker grew at 2.9 percent per year in the 1850s.[40] The authors calculated that this growth was too rapid to be explained by an expansion of acreage and must imply an increase in efficiency.[41] Unfortunately, the calculation by which this conclusion was reached was erroneous.[42] Further-

---

strongly implies that management was becoming increasingly efficient. That they do have in mind an increase in efficiency is acknowledged explicitly at several points (FE, I, p. 93; II, p. 86).

[39] The only exception is a reference to a 1947 U.S. Department of Agriculture study (Miscellaneous Publications No. 630), which offers a completely unsubstantiated figure of 0.79 percent per year for the period 1800–1840 (FE, II, p. 86). For what it is worth, *all* of the productivity gain in this estimate is due to a fall in manhours per acre.

[40] Foust and Swan [1970], pp. 44–45.

[41] Fogel and Engerman [1971], p. 315.

[42] From estimates of factor shares and population growth, Fogel and Engerman computed the implied rate of growth of cotton acreage under the

more, the Foust-Swan productivity figures contain a puzzling anomaly: *all* of the growth is concentrated in the "Alluvial" and "Other New South" regions; the "Old South" showed virtually no gain. This anomaly, and perhaps the entire increase, may be explained in terms of random fluctuations in yields around their normal levels, interpreted as deviations from the long-run supply function. As noted above, cotton supply was well above its predicted level in the census year 1860, especially in the New South; by contrast, in the census year 1850 New South output was at or slightly below its predicted level, while aggregate output was between 5.8 and 19.7 percent below. In other words, Old South yields must have been below normal in 1849–50, and at or below normal in 1859–60; New South yields were normal or below in the first year, far above normal in the second. Hence, it appears that virtually all of this alleged productivity growth is attributable to the accidental characteristics of the census years, which may even cover up *declining* productivity in the Old South.

I am led to the conclusion that the expansion of cotton demand was the only fundamental dynamic force driving the slave economy. For this reason, the various international comparisons of income levels presented in Chapter 6 (FE, I, pp. 250–57) are of limited relevance. They do help to put in perspective the notion of general southern poverty; but they prove too much to bear significantly on these issues. Similar tables would show that the South ranked fairly well by world standards even *after* the disastrous two decades of 1860–80, and indeed one can show that the United States and Britain were

---

assumption of constant efficiency. They found that, if there were no change in efficiency, 2.9 percent productivity growth implies that land must have increased by 3.4 times between 1850 and 1860 ($\frac{*}{T}$ = 12.1 percent, not 15.1 percent as the footnote reports). They argue that this is an unreasonably large increase in cotton acreage. Apparently, however, they erroneously *added* the 1860 acreage estimate to the 1850 figure to obtain their estimate of 19,000,000 required acres, when they should have subtracted the two. The actual implied expansion of cotton land is 10,100,000 acres, which is almost exactly equal to the increase in improved acreage in the seven states during these ten years (10,080,000 acres). This is with no allowance for improvement in average land quality, nor for the random yield fluctuations discussed in the text.

both rich by world standards *before* their major periods of industrialization and growth. But whatever one feels about such comparisons, critics of Fogel and Engerman would be poorly advised to use materials from the 1860 census to refute them, a year which puts the South in the best possible light. Rather than claiming "backwardness" for 1860 or indeed for the antebellum period generally, critics should instead focus on the *dependent* character of southern growth, and on the region's failure to use its earnings to develop the institutions and acquire the skills needed for sustained growth in the modern era.[43]

Did Slavery Retard the Growth of Cities and Industry?

Because the prosperity of Southern agriculture depended on demand, the prospects for a hypothetical slave economy after 1860 would have depended crucially on the ability of the system to transfer resources into non-agricultural economic activities. Fogel and Engerman do acknowledge, however briefly, that their analysis does imply that slavery probably did bias the allocation of resources against the urban industrial sectors (FE, I, pp. 255–57). This much is in keeping with "traditional" beliefs (though the issue is complicated by the low elasticity of demand for cotton). The alternative analysis proposed here implies such a bias even more clearly. The labor constraint on free family farms sharply limits the *absolute* profit which the farmer can hope for. An entrepreneur who wants to make as much money as possible must, in this setting, turn to non-agricultural pursuits. In the slave states, however, there was no limit to the personal fortunes which slaveowners could accumulate in farming. Given that the supplies of entrepreneurs and investible funds are limited, the availability of the plantation alternative must retard the growth of industry.

Of course, there are many other lines of argument by which economic and political features of slavery have been thought to

---

[43] This is essentially the position argued by North ([1961], especially Chap. 10). For a recent review of the literature on cases of this sort, see Caves [1971].

retard industrialization. Most of these are by no means disposed of in *Time on the Cross*. The confidence of Fogel and Engerman on the efficiency of resource allocation under slavery is primarily based on the findings of Claudia Goldin that the rural demand for slaves was much less elastic than the urban demand, and that when this differential is allowed for, one finds that the demand for slaves in cities was rising. I have no difficulty accepting these two results: the inelasticity of rural demand is clearly implied by the Fleisig hypothesis defended here, since slaves were virtually the only form of "hired" labor available to planters. The second finding pertains, of course, to *cities* rather than *industry*, and in any case relates to *changes* in the urban slave population rather than *levels*. There is no showing that the level of urban slavery or the level of urbanization under slavery was "correct" or "efficient" by any independent standard. Almost all southern cities experienced a marked upward shift in black population shares between 1860 and 1870 (at a time when cotton prices were high), a development which certainly suggests a presumption in favor of the traditional view on this question.[44]

In my view, the only flaw in Goldin's argument of any consequence is the failure to acknowledge the *political* significance of the high substitutability between free and slave workers in cities. She notes that those cities which experienced large "influxes of white immigrant labor" were also those which show the largest losses in slave population—and such influxes are presented as *exogenous* disturbances or shifts in the demand function, *in addition* to the general argument in terms of technical substitutability.[45] How should we interpret the finding that an influx of free white workers shifts downward the demand for slaves in that city? I see this result as support for the "traditional" argument that there was a hostility between slavery and both immigration and urbanization. To put the point differently, *Time on the Cross* does not acknowledge or discuss any possible interdependence between the levels of white

[44] Farley [1968], p. 247.
[45] "Exogenous" means "produced from without," i.e., originating outside the system under discussion.

immigration to cities and the success of white workers in making city life unpleasant for slaves and their owners—or their failure at such efforts. Such political struggles have been widely documented, and mention of them even crops up elsewhere in *Time on the Cross*: "The white artisans of Charleston were well-organized and extremely active politically. There was hardly a year during which they did not petition the city council for some new restriction against slave artisans" (FE, II, pp. 39–41).

The discouragement of immigrant wage laborers from coming South may be the main way in which slavery retarded urbanization and industrialization. In the North, immigrants were attracted into cities and into the industrial labor force much more easily than native-born farmers. Even the most successful southern manufacturers generally had to recruit labor vigorously in the North, and found the presence of slaves in the labor force made such hiring especially difficult.[46] In turn, the slowness in the growth of cities and population may have further discouraged the development of manufacturing by retarding the growth of markets. The Parker-Genovese thesis, which stresses the role of population density and market size for medium-scale manufactured goods, is still very much alive.[47] Any of these biases against the development of non-agricultural economic activity have, in my view, considerable long-run significance for Southern economic development, in light of the insecure foundation provided by world cotton demand.

In terms of the broader issue of viability, I do think that the question of slavery in the cities posed a real threat to the stable political economy of slavery. This threat is perhaps not "purely economic," but the roots of it may be plainly seen in the urban elasticities of demand for slaves, for those who care to read the results this way. As cotton demand declined, slaveowners would have made efforts to reverse the flow of the 1850s and turn slaves into industrial workers. This flow would have exacerbated the conflict with urban workers, a conflict which was an important factor in bringing down slave regimes elsewhere.

[46] See, for example, the account in Dew [1966], pp. 28–31.
[47] Parker [1970]; Genovese [1965], Chap. 7. For a more recent discussion, see Bateman and Weiss [1975], pp. 189–201.

Historians of industrial slavery have noted that instances of slave-free worker hostility were most common during periods of depression and job scarcity.[48] But the antebellum South never did experience very much of this friction because there never was any major shift of resources out of agriculture. But in the post-1860 world, the South and the slave system would have been faced with a choice between a stagnant agriculture and political turbulence in the cities. One of the main political pillars of support for slavery among non-slaveholding urban Southerners was the belief that maintaining slavery as an institution would *reduce* the competition for jobs in cities. At other times and in other contexts, slaveowners displayed an extraordinary political sensitivity to threats against slavery, and I have considerable trouble believing that they could have accepted with equanimity a serious abolition movement in the cities—a movement which might well have emerged if workers ceased to believe that maintaining slavery was in their economic interest.

Conclusion: The Internal Contradictions of Slavery

My research on the southern economy over the past several years has quite unexpectedly led me to an appreciation of the essential correctness of the insights of many of the traditional interpreters of the slave South. I have argued that Phillips was right in asserting that slaves were overpriced in 1860; that Ramsdell was right in maintaining that slaveowners faced an impending era of low cotton prices and capital losses on slaves; and that Genovese and Wade and others were right in suggesting a long-run incompatibility between slavery and modern urban-industrial society. These writers frequently fell into error when they claimed to observe the effects of these internal contradictions before 1861; but the contradictions were there nonetheless. I have not said, and I do not mean to say, that slavery would have "died out" in the absence of a Civil War. This is much too difficult a question, and I would be skeptical of anyone's claim to address it with rigor. I don't find it impossible

[48] Starobin (1970), p. 137.

to imagine that slavery might have weathered the rough period of 1860–1900 to emerge rejuvenated during 1900–14. The national consensus on white supremacy which prevailed before World War I might have been a consensus on slavery as well. The institution might only have been abolished (with generous compensation) by the New Deal administration in the 1930s—leaving the freedmen to fend for themselves in a world of surplus labor. I don't find this scenario totally implausible; because it is not so very different from what actually happened. In this hypothetical story, as in the actual history, only by breaking away from dependence on cotton could large and lasting economic gains be achieved for the black population and for the South.

APPENDIX A. Residuals from Cotton Supply and Demand Curves

1. Demand curves. For the purpose of this paper, only the simplest demand-curve estimates (including only price, quantity, and trend) are used, because the reasons for the deviations from trend are not relevant for the argument. These estimates are reported in Wright, "Cotton Competition and the Post-Bellum Recovery of the American South." Using ordinary-least-squares,

$$\ln P_c = 8.21 - 0.94 \ln Q + 0.052\, t$$

where t = time and t = 1 for the crop year 1820–21; output is lagged one crop year; and the notation "ln" indicates natural logarithms—which means that residuals may be read as *percentage* deviations. For this function, the residual for 1839–40 is −4.0 percent, the residual for 1859–60 is +15.9 percent.

Another version was estimated using the Cochrane-Orcutt method to correct for serial correlation in the residuals:

$$\ln P_c = 8.05 - 0.91 \ln Q + 0.049\, t$$

For this function, the residual for 1839–40 is −11.5 percent, the residual for 1859–60 is +7.6 percent.

2. Supply curves. The aggregate supply curves are reported in Wright, "The Economics of Cotton in the Antebellum South" (unpublished Ph.D dissertation, Yale University, 1969). The following are the major alternatives and the associated residuals (note that in this case t = 1 for the crop year 1819–20):

$$\ln Q = 5.07 + 0.05 \ln P_{-1}\ 0.059\, t$$

Residuals: 1849–50, −10.1%; 1859–60, +11.6%

$$\ln Q = -10.51 + 0.19 \ln P_{-1} + 1.51 \ln L_{-2}$$

where L = cumulative land sales, lagged two years

Residuals: 1849–50, $-.19.7\%$; 1859–60, $+18.7\%$

$$\ln Q = -2.70 + 0.14 \ln P_{-1} + 0.030 \, t + 0.74 \ln L_{-2}$$
Residuals: 1849–50, -5.8%; 1859–60, $+23.6-$

The five-state supply curves are reported in Wright, "An Econometric Study of Cotton Supply and Demand."

$$\ln Q(5) = 4.51 - 0.15 \ln P_{-1} + 0.070 \, t$$
Residuals: 1849–50, $+0.6\%$; 1859–60, $+35.2\%$

$$\ln Q(5) = -6.51 + 0.13 \ln P_{-1} + 1.21 \ln L_{-2}$$
Residuals: 1849–50, -5.8%; 1859–60, $+43.5\%$

$$\ln Q(5) = -2.13 + 0.09 \ln P_{-1} + 0.030 \, t + 0.71 \ln L_{-2}$$
Residuals: 1849–50, -5.9%; 1859–60, $+34.1\%$

APPENDIX B. *Evidence on Cotton-Corn Crop Mix and Productivity*

To test the effects of the crop-mix on measured "productivity" per worker, the natural log of "productivity" was used as the dependent variable in a regression, the independent variables being the share of cotton in the cotton-corn total (by value), as explained in Table 1; an index of soil quality; and, wherever a breakdown by slaveholding classes was not used, improved acreage. The labor force is defined as free males aged 15 to 60, slave males and females aged 15 to 60. Farm data are from the Parker-Gallman sample.

The coefficients of improved acreage show no indication of positive scale effects in the region-wide regressions. We can also use the size-class regressions to test for scale effects: the constant term represents the log of labor productivity on an "all-corn" farm of average soil quality. It is clear from the first column that slaveless farms were significantly more productive in corn. To get a "standardized crop mix" index of productivity, multiply the second coefficient by the desired cotton share and add to the constant. To give maximum weight to cotton, let us examine these sums for a hypothetical "all-cotton" farm:

	Whole South	*Old South*	*New South*
0 Slaves	6.03	6.07	6.01
1–15 Slaves	5.88	5.71	5.94
16–50 Slaves	5.98	5.71	6.05
Over 50 Slaves	5.81	5.83	5.80

Sample	Constant	Cotton Share	Soil Quality	Imp. Acr.	R^2
Whole South	4.80	1.08	0.006	−.00010	.151
	(267.1)	(27.7)	(5.89)	(2.05)	
0 Slaves	4.92	1.11	0.021		.160
	(205.0)	(19.28)	(8.66)		
1–15 Slaves	4.70	1.18	0.005		.165
	(148.5)	(18.0)	(3.42)		
16–50 Slaves	4.26	1.72	0.007		.300
	(68.5)	(16.7)	(3.84)		
Over 50 Slaves	4.03	1.78	0.007		.343
	(25.4)	(7.70)	(2.77)		
Old South	4.58	1.16	−0.0007	−0.00012	.155
	(156.7)	(17.4)	(0.33)	(1.71)	
0 Slaves	4.72	1.35	0.015		.212
	(110.1)	(12.5)	(3.75)		
1–15 Slaves	4.52	1.19	−0.0063		.183
	(102.8)	(12.3)	(2.15)		
16–50 Slaves	4.08	1.63	0.0029		.251
	(44.6)	(9.6)	(0.65)		
Over 50 Slaves	3.35	2.48	−0.012		.514
	(16.0)	(7.6)	(1.23)		
New South	4.93	0.96	0.005	0.00008	.143
	(222.6)	(20.62)	(4.42)	(1.18)	
0 Slaves	5.02	0.99	0.023		.137
	(174.2)	(14.66)	(7.56)		
1–15 Slaves	4.85	1.09	0.007		.148
	(111.2)	(12.67)	(3.56)		
16–50 slaves	4.59	1.46	0.002		.253
	(56.6)	(11.76)	(1.52)		
Over 50 Slaves	4.84	0.96	0.003		.152
	(24.8)	(3.62)	(1.18)		

With only one exception, it is the *slaveless* farms which are most productive in cotton-growing as well! In the Old South, the superiority of free farms over small slave farms is statistically significant. None of the other differences are statistically significant.

The following hypothetical table of "total-factor-productivity" was constructed under the assumption that there are no differences in factor proportions or efficiency, but that the "cotton share coefficient" is 1.0, i.e., that a 1 percentage point rise in the cotton share produced a 1 percent rise in productivity. This is approximately the value suggested by the labor-productivity regressions. I set the Cotton South, zero-slave TFP equal to 109.3 to achieve comparability with Fogel and Engerman (FE, II, p. 139). Only cotton and corn output is considered.

Hypothetical Total Factor Productivities

	Old South	New South	Entire Cotton South
0 Slaves	105.9	110.6	109.3
1–15 Slaves	117.3	122.6	120.3
16–50 Slaves	130.3	142.0	137.3
Over 50 Slaves	142.6	152.8	148.8

This table is illustrative only, intended simply to give some plausibility to the claim that total-factor-productivity differentials of roughly the same magnitude and direction might be generated entirely by crop-mix effects.

APPENDIX C. Survivor Tables from the Parker-Gallman and Foust-Swan Samples

Because the data described here were collected independently and for a variety of purposes, they are unfortunately not precisely comparable in categories or coverage to the data in *Time on the Cross*. They are presented nonetheless for the impressions they convey. The nine largest regions in the Parker-Gallman universe were included (see Wright," 'Economic Democracy,' for description of the regions) to achieve comparability with the smaller Foust-Swan sample for 1850. The regions were aggregated, using the shares of cotton output in the respective years as weights.

Share of Cotton Output by Improved Acreage Size Class (%)

	0–199	200–399	400–599	600–799	800–999	1000–1249	1250 & over
1850	28.4	20.8	14.0	11.1	11.6	7.6	6.5
1860	28.4	23.7	15.1	9.3	5.8	7.1	10.6

Share of Cotton Output by Slaveholding Class (%)

	0	1–15	16–50	51 and over
1850	.067	.227	.351	.356
1860	.086	.205	.381	.330

Excluding Alluvial Region

	0	1–15	16–50	51 and over
1850	.070	.235	.345	.350
1860	.100	.236	.421	.243

PART THREE

A Judgment

CHAPTER EIGHT

"Time on the Cross" and the Burden of Quantitative History

The authors of this volume have sought to judge *Time on the Cross* on its own merits, according to the standards of the discipline from which it claims to derive. Toward this end we have attempted, collaboratively, to reproduce every important statistical manipulation, check every significant citation, re-examine every striking quotation, rethink every critical chain of inference, and question every major conclusion in Fogel and Engerman's book. To our surprise and dismay, we have found that *Time on the Cross* is full of errors. The book embraces errors of mathematics, disregards standard principles of statistical inference, mis-cites sources, takes quotations out of context, distorts the views and findings of other historians and economists, and relies upon dubious and largely unexplicated models of market behavior, economic dynamics, socialization, sexual behavior, fertility determination, and genetics (to name some).

No work of scholarship, and certainly no work which undertakes to cover so broad a canvas, is unblemished by some errors. *Time on the Cross*, however, is simply shot through with egregious errors. Even more dismaying is the consistent tendency in the mistakes we have uncovered: all seem to work in favor of the particular "radical reinterpretation" of the institution of slavery that has been put forth by Fogel and Engerman. When the faults are corrected and the evidence is re-examined, every striking assertion made in *Time on the Cross* is cast into doubt. The effect in many instances is to restore and reinforce more orthodox conclusions hitherto shared by conventional and quantitatively oriented students of the peculiar institution.

Although these mistakes in technical procedure and the factual errors resulting from them are serious and numerous enough to undermine the particular historical interpretation advanced in *Time on the Cross*, it would be unfortunate if preoccupation with these "lower level" errors of execution obscured the more basic methodological deficiencies of the book. A proper appreciation of the behavioral sciences' strengths and limitations is essential for fruitful communication between historians who work in the humanistic tradition and those who are trained in the social sciences. Perhaps communication will be furthered if historians of both methodological persuasions can come to some understanding of the respects in which *Time on the Cross* transgresses the limits of the behavioral sciences by mechanically applying inappropriate models, and by seeking to wring from appropriate models various behavioral and attitudinal inferences that are quite unwarranted.

Problems of Inference

In *Time on the Cross* inferences are drawn about the personalities and behavior of the masters and the slaves. These inferences ignore much literary evidence provided by diaries, correspondence, accounts written by travelers and visitors in the Cotton Kingdom, and the testimony of former slaves. They proceed, instead, from quantitative information about the workings of the system of plantation slavery. In correction, we have been obliged to draw attention to the point that underlying motivations and modes of individual behavior cannot be uniquely inferred from an analysis of the outcomes of a social process, or of a market process for that matter. The tools of behavioral science, and particularly of modern economics, have been designed to permit robust predictions about a social system's performance to be derived from postulates describing the objectives and actions of individual agents. Unfortunately, such tools cannot be readily turned to answer to the needs of the historian who seeks to reveal the personalities of historical actors, to re-create the world as contemporaries perceived it, to understand human events within the objective and subjective contexts in which they transpired.

Fogel and Engerman insist that aspects of the actual functioning of the slave economy are "explained" consistently on the assumption that each and every slaveowner regarded slaves solely as productive instruments, and used them for a single, transcendent purpose: the maximization of pecuniary gain. But we have shown that the evidence which quantitative economic historians have presented concerning the profitability of investment in slaveownership also is consistent with the view that only a comparatively small segment of the antebellum planter class functioned as rational profit-maximizing capitalists.

The same line of reasoning demonstrates that it is not possible to determine uniquely the true states of belief representative of a social class merely from an analysis of the outcomes of market processes which possibly involved only a small minority of that class, and a temporally changing minority at that. Contrary assertions in *Time on the Cross* notwithstanding, the expectations of the slaveholding class with regard to the durability of the peculiar institution (sanguine or otherwise) simply cannot be read from the movements of the ratio between the prices established in the markets where slaves were hired and the prices prevailing in markets where comparable slaves were being bought and sold. In a similar vein, the implications of the observed pattern of variations in the monetary values placed upon slaves of different ages are not unambiguous. Certainly, the mere existence of that pattern does not require Fogel and Engerman's inference that planters typically valued slaves in accordance with the way their physical productivity rose and diminished in relation to the cost of maintaining them during the course of their lives. The same pattern could equally have reflected systematic variations of the subjective evaluations of risk which a minority of planters attached to the acquisition of slaves of various ages.

We have raised similar logical objections to the facile inferences made concerning Negro slaves' attitudes and actions in their roles as workers, spouses, and parents. The mere existence of an occupational hierarchy among the slave labor force does not imply that its members by and large were success-oriented workers who were responding to strong positive incentives created by opportunities for upward occupational mobility. At the opposite pole, evidence that it was unnecessary to whip every slave every day hardly warrants the inference that plantation management did not largely rely upon threats of physical punishment as the means of enforcing labor discipline. Indeed, negative incentives differ from positive ones precisely in that when they are most efficacious they seldom need to be implemented.

Even if southern slave agriculture were more productive than the agriculture of free northern farms (in the sense of achieving greater physical efficiency in utilizing the array of resources of which it disposed) it still need not imply that plantation slave workers typically possessed special qualities which rendered *them* more efficient than their free white counterparts. And surely the magnitude of the nonpecuniary (psychic) "disadvantages" of being worked under the lash as a member of a slave gang cannot be inferred accurately from the size of any post-Emancipation differences between the earnings of Negroes engaged as daily wage laborers and those of share-croppers.

Black mothers and fathers in bondage certainly may have cherished their own children. Without promptings from masters, mistresses or members of the slave community, they may have devoted to their offspring all the selfless care that one might wish. That such was the case, however, is not established by demonstrating that among fertile slave women the period of lactation typically lasted a full year. Nor is the latter "fact" strictly deducible from the information Fogel and Engerman present on the average length of the intervals separating successive births to slave women on a few plantations.

Fogel and Engerman infer the ages until which the daughters of slave parents were "closely guarded from sexual contacts with men," merely from a knowledge of the ages at which slave women were delivered of their first child. Yet this ignores the potential effects that diet-linked variations in the age of menarche (and more generally in the fecundity of young women) may have had upon the frequency with which sexual intercourse resulted in pregnancies.

Time on the Cross, then, is replete with tenuous behavioral and attitudinal inferences drawn from indirect, quantitative evidence. Time and again, a single pattern of personal behavior has been arbitrarily inferred where the data would admit many other equally plausible readings. But regardless of the interpretations one justifiably might place upon evidence of this kind, we have found that much of the ostensibly factual material presented in the book is simply wrong. Obviously, it cannot be all wrong, for (as Kenneth Stampp points out) many of the "revelations" made in *Time on the Cross* consist of refutations of propositions which professional historians had discarded long ago. And, of course, not all new empirical findings which the book reports have been overturned. Nevertheless, a quick recapitulation does suggest that the number of factual props underpinning Fogel and Engerman's argument which have now collapsed is sufficiently large to warrant that the structure of the book be pronounced distinctly unsafe for continued occupancy. Subsequent efforts to shore up a supporting element of the argument here and there may bring to light new historical material, and would be welcome contributions on that account. But such limited and selective repair work cannot restore to the book a general aspect of soundness and credibility.

The Evidence on Southern Agriculture and the Nature of the Slave Labor Force

Time on the Cross says that southern slave agriculture was substantially more efficient than northern free farming. We have shown that Fogel and Engerman actually compare the overall *revenue*-efficiency of the northern and southern agricultural sectors, not their physical productivities. Moreover, in those calculations virtually all of the South's apparent advantage is created by questionable measurement procedures which understate the amount of labor and the amount of land inputs used in that region relative to the amounts used in the North.

Time on the Cross says that within the South itself the larger slave-using plantations were physically more productive because they benefited from technological economies of scale, as well as from the superior quality of the work force they employed. We

344 *"Time on the Cross" and*

found that during the year to which Fogel and Engerman's evidence relates, larger southern farms (because they had a greater proportion of their acreage under cotton) benefited more than smaller ones from unusually high cotton yields: the observed pattern of apparent productivity differences can be accounted for by the effect which the bumper cotton crop of 1859 therefore had upon the comparative revenues earned by large and small plantations. We maintain that there is no compelling case for the claim that cotton plantations benefited from significant technological economies of scale. Nor is it appropriate to infer that black slaves were more productive than free laborers in the sense of being able to accomplish any given task more rapidly.

Time on the Cross says that a large fraction of slaves were skilled artisans and supervisory workers, and further, that a very large fraction of the overseers of large plantations actually were slaves. We have shown that these assertions have been based on faulty procedures and incorrect assumptions. When these are corrected, the first of the fractions is considerably reduced, and the second all but vanishes.

The Evidence on the Material Treatment of Slaves

Time on the Cross says that over the course of a typical field hand's lifetime the slave received about 90 percent of the income he produced. We have shown that Fogel and Engerman's findings justify no such statement, and that in truth their figures suggest that masters typically took for themselves rather more than one-half of the total of all revenues produced by a slave throughout the course of his life.

Time on the Cross says that the income retained by an average slave worker exceeded that of free agricultural workers. We have shown that Fogel and Engerman actually compared labor earnings not of workers, but of the average members of free families and slave families, thereby neglecting the fact that members of free farm families typically did not work as much or as hard as slaves. Furthermore, by comparing only current labor earnings, Fogel and Engerman omitted from consideration the income that free American farmers received as owners of wealth created by their previous labors, or conveyed to them by inheritance or windfall capital gains.

Time on the Cross says that the food ration provided for slaves by their masters offered variety as well as adequate food energy. We have argued that this assertion rests on an inadequate and biased quantitative procedure. We also have demonstrated that the implementation of this flawed procedure was marred by computational errors and implausible assumptions that systematically exaggerated the variety of the slaves' rations.

Time on the Cross says that the slaves' rations were nutritionally balanced and healthy even by modern standards. We have indicated that Fogel and Engerman's treatment of this complex question contains major errors that prevented them from uncovering serious vitamin and mineral deficiencies even in the slave ration they analyzed.

Time on the Cross says that the typical plantation slave was provided with better housing and clothing than the typical free worker in nineteenth-century America. We have pointed out that Fogel and Engerman reported the provisions furnished by only the most generous slave masters, and then compared these with the conditions of the most impoverished elements of the free working class.

Time on the Cross says that the infant mortality rates for slaves and southern whites were virtually the same. We have found that the available demographic information points to a slave infant mortality rate that was twice the average white infant mortality rate, and that the rate of infant mortality among southern whites may well have been still lower than the average for the entire white population.

Time on the Cross says the gap between the rate of infant suffocation deaths in the slave population and the corresponding rate in the white population signified little about the effects of slavery on the quality of child care, because a gap of that magnitude could be accounted for by the difference between the frequencies with which the sudden infant death syndrome appears today in the Negro and Caucasian populations. We have found that the modern gap between Negro and Caucasian infant death rates from this cause amounts to a trivially small

portion of the historical difference in infant suffocation death
rates, and that present medical knowledge does not support the
allusions Fogel and Engerman make in this connection.

The Evidence on Social Conditions of Slaves

Time on the Cross says that slave masters preferred not to
resort to physical punishment but chose instead to rely upon
positive incentives in managing "their Negroes." We have found
this claim to be based upon a distortion of evidence (which in
any case relates largely to a single plantation), so that when this
small body of evidence is examined properly it refutes Fogel and
Engerman's assertions about the limited reliance upon whippings and other negative incentives.

Time on the Cross says that slaveowners only rarely resorted
to the sale of slaves. We have revealed that this assertion is
based upon a study of slave trading in a single Maryland
county, that the estimated frequency of sales contains a
computational error, and we have shown that the resulting
figures are presented in a way that is itself grossly misleading.

Time on the Cross says that slave families were broken only
infrequently by sale, and assumes slave families never were
broken by the migration of plantations. We have demonstrated
that both points are without empirical foundation, and that the
figures adduced to support it are riddled with computational
errors.

Time on the Cross says that slaves were neither bred for sale,
nor forced into early marriages. We have offered evidence to
indicate otherwise. Fogel and Engerman report that the average age of slave women at the birth of their first child was high,
but we have found that their figures actually refer to the birth
of the first *surviving* child. Examination of the appropriate
figures suggests that sexual activity was not postponed long
after the time that young slave women began menstruating.

Time on the Cross says that most marriages among slaves
were contracted between partners quite close in age. We have
shown that the sources of information mentioned by Fogel and
Engerman could not disclose the age difference between partners at the time of espousal, whereas other sources indicate that

slave husbands often were more than a decade older than their wives.

Time on the Cross says that sexual exploitation of slave women leading to miscegenation was comparatively rare. We have shown that the evidence adduced on this point was selectively presented in terms that make it appear to support this claim.

Time on the Cross says that slave prostitution was nonexistent. We have shown that Fogel and Engerman followed a research approach which could not have discovered slave prostitutes, however many may have existed.

Time on the Cross says that modern conventional historians of the South have embraced many pernicious myths which have obscured the "true nature" of the Afro-American experience of slavery. *Time on the Cross* claims that by exposing such myths it has established the basis for a radical reinterpretation of slavery. We have shown that the evidence and arguments which are offered to support these claims are unsatisfactory. Indeed, they are so unsatisfactory that in retrospect it is the novel views of history and historiography propounded in *Time on the Cross* which appear to be largely mythical.

Toward a Reconstruction

We have been obliged to follow closely in the tracks of Fogel and Engerman's book, rather than freely exploring different theoretical approaches, venturing onto fresh empirical ground, or developing alternative interpretive themes. This is unfortunate although it is virtually inevitable in an undertaking of this nature. It is doubly unfortunate, in view of the largely negative nature of our judgment about the presentation of the Afro-American experience of slavery in *Time on the Cross*.

Rejecting the conclusions announced in that book, however, will not plunge the study of slavery and the South into a state of intellectual chaos. Quite the contrary. This volume serves another, rather more positive purpose than that of refuting the "radical reinterpretation" proposed by Fogel and Engerman. The discussion in the foregoing chapters has sought to clarify some key issues, and to provide more reliable quantitative answers to many questions which are bound to be addressed in subsequent efforts to reconstruct the social and economic history of the antebellum South.

On this occasion we have not attempted formally to present an all-encompassing alternative view of the terms of life in antebellum society, and of its relationship to the economy of the region. Indeed, we have not even attempted here to array all the elements which would have to find their way into such an account. Even less have we worked out the details of their arrangement in such an alternative view. It should be evident that the class of concepts, and the particular set of historical methods with whose use the preceding chapters have been preoccupied are capable of illuminating only some portions of the whole picture. Much help will be needed from other quarters.

Still, an attempt at sketching in the outlines of an alternative story, however quickly and tentatively, may prove of some use. It is a means of bringing into focus the positive aspects of the work presented here, and of indicating some directions in which future research by conventional *and* quantitative historians might fruitfully proceed.

A first step toward any understanding of the nature of the Afro-American experience of slavery must surely be to recognize that the institution of slavery itself, the larger economic context in which it was set, and the behavior of the people caught up within it, were all *changing*—rather than being fixed and immutable features of the socio-economic landscape. We have not been dealing in these pages with the whole sweep of the peculiar institution's history, but only with the brief and final phases of a long and complex development. The rich array of detailed quantitative evidence discussed in the preceding pages (and the yet-unmined statistical deposits from which these samples have been extracted) understandably encourages economic historians to attempt a detailed reconstruction of the plantation system and its place in the workings of the southern economy. But this data largely concerns southern society and the institution of slavery in the era when King Cotton reigned supreme; the unwary historian risks having this abundance of information rivet attention too exclusively upon the few decades before the Civil War, when the cotton economy was moving to unprecedented heights of prosperity.

The general prosperity of the late antebellum era of southern history, and its basis in the prosperity of plantation slavery, are facts beyond serious dispute. Their historical significance, however, is another matter. Consideration of the sources and of the nature of this movement suggests that the prosperity of the period was not only unprecedented but evanescent. The southern economy, at this time, was absorbing the benefits of strong and rapidly growing demands for raw cotton in international markets—demands connected with the process of industrialization elsewhere. Yet full advantage was not being taken of these fortuitous circumstances to lay more permanent foundations for prosperity—foundations that at a future date might have sustained a cumulative process of economic transformation and growth in the South itself.

Perhaps the similar features of antebellum economic growth in America's North and South would appear more worthy of comment were these regions to be viewed from a culturally and economically remote vantage point, such as that which a comparison with the contemporary sugar-growing regions of Brazil's Northeast might afford. But rather than joining the authors of *Time on the Cross* in stressing surface similarities in the aggregate growth records of the northern and southern sections of the United States during the 1840s and 1850s, it seems better to emphasize the ultimately more significant differences between southern extensive growth, on the one hand, and the process of agricultural diversification and urbanization which was taking place in the industrializing North. If one seeks to understand what was happening in the American South at that time, drawing parallels between South and North is less instructive than drawing them between the experience of the South and that of Egypt during the transitory cotton boom which was set in motion there when, during the 1860s, cotton exports from America were temporarily stopped.

The source of southern agricultural prosperity before the Civil War was not any comparative "efficiency" of slave plantations in competition with the free, owner-operated farmsteads characteristic of northern agriculture. Rather it lay in the exploitation of the region's absolute and comparative advantage in the production of cotton and other staple crops which were being grown commercially only in a few places in the world. Calculations of the South's aggregate factor productivity advantage vis-à-vis northern farming (such as appear in *Time on the Cross*) hardly measure relative productivity at all. Inasmuch as the South's staple crop was not grown in the North, it is scarcely possible to determine on the basis of actual performance which of these regions was technologically and organizationally more efficient in producing cotton. And while grain crops and livestock were grown on both sides of the Mason-Dixon line, the quantity of output per unit of input in the South was no larger in this kind of production than that in the North. The *economic* efficiency of southern plantation agriculture (as distinct from its physical production efficiency) consisted in a geographically determined capacity to secure purchasing power from industrializing regions by specializing in the production of an easily exportable crop that was not readily grown elsewhere.

Within the southern agricultural sector, the profitability of cultivating cotton redounded disproportionately to the commercial advantage of the larger plantations. This was less because their size permitted the realization of technological or organizational economies of scale akin to those being explored in northern industrial establishments. Nor was it largely traceable to the pecuniary advantages obtained from bulk-purchasing through the agency of the cotton factors who handled the business of the plantations. Rather, it appears that the main advantage of the larger plantations lay in the fact that their sheer size enabled them to devote only a small part of their acreage and manpower to providing for the basic consumption needs of their resident workforce. Their owners thus ran less risk than did smaller farmers when they committed the major part of their resources to the production of high-average-revenue crops for an uncertain and fluctuating market. Lesser farmers who specialized to the same extent faced a greater chance of being wiped out completely by an unanticipated adverse movement of the relative price of their cash crop.

For the region as a whole, specialization in primary export production brought prosperity in the short run, so long as the world demand for cotton remained buoyant. But it did so at the sacrifice of longer run gains. The South failed to develop alternative ways of generating income which would have helped it to cope with a fall in the rate of growth of the demand for cotton. And when, after the Civil War, the demand for cotton failed to resume its antebellum rate of growth, southern agriculture experienced serious economic difficulties. The southern economy thus grew in the antebellum era, but it did not *develop* in the sense that the economy of the North did.

This contrast appeared in many forms, but it revealed itself most clearly in the relationship between regional growth and migration. Economic progress was being achieved in the North despite the relative transfer of population from the richer seaboard section to the poorer, newly settled regions west of the Appalachian Mountains. The overall growth of per capita income in the North as a whole was therefore less than the growth in each northern sub-region. Precisely the opposite situation prevailed in the South. Per capita income there was growing, in part, *because* people were moving from the exhausted lands of the Seaboard South to the fertile soils of the Gulf Plains and the Mississippi Delta. The resulting economic progress within the sub-regions of the South was slower than the overall rate of growth achieved by the region as a whole (and indeed slower than that in the sub-regions of the North). Population migrations may be viewed as a form of resource reallocation in response to new economic opportunities. Such resource reallocations are generally regarded as an integral aspect of the process of economic modernization. But growth by flight from exhausted land cannot be continued, as can the reallocation of the labor force in response to changing industrial opportunities created by technological progress. Eventually, in the former (southern) case, there is nowhere new to go.

In the foregoing view, the relative revenue-earning advantage enjoyed by plantation agriculture in the South derived from the state of the market for cotton, not from any supposed advantages of slavery as a system of production, nor from any *superiority* in the quality—which is to say the personal efficiency—of the individual slave workers which it deployed. That the black slaves as a people were compelled to labor hard and long—harder and longer than the free white Americans—is an old and bitter story. It cannot be sweetened by confusing greater work effort with greater efficiency.

Once it is recognized that the source of the South's antebellum prosperity lay in the ephemeral conditions of the international market for cotton and other staples, it no longer seems so tempting to depict the southern economy (and the production units which it comprised) as operating like a smoothly turning, frictionless machine. The American South was the dominant supplier of cotton to the world market at the time, and this conveyed some degree of monopoly power which made profitability compatible with inefficiencies and wastage. Indeed, the unresolved conflicts and tensions within the peculiar southern labor system were themselves a potential source of economic inefficiencies which could persist under the reign of King Cotton.

The applications of conventional economic analysis which have illuminated some aspects of the institution of slavery have unfortunately also contributed to a misleading representation of the relationship in which slaves and their masters were joined. Conrad and Meyer's [1958] path-breaking analysis of investment in slaves as productive instruments subsequently led economic historians toward a depersonalized portrayal of the black bondsman as an unthinking agent who was devoid of volition and totally responsive to his owner's commands—a mere machine. Fogel and Engerman in *Time on the Cross* simply replace the total ownership nexus with an employer-employee relation. They suppose that masters, in order to make best use of their property, must have sought to elicit the voluntary cooperation of slave workers—in the fashion of that modern ideal, the perfect personnel manager. To do this, they suggest, a master would, in a sense, be obliged to act altruistically toward his slaves, incorporating consideration for their welfare and happiness into his own utilitarian calculus. This novel conceptualization neatly eradicates the aspect of conflict inherent in the lordship-bondage relation, thereby performing the impossible feat of absorbing the historical experience of slavery into the consensus view of America's past. But, considered as an exercise in labor economics or in industrial psychology it is neither theoretically nor factually satisfactory.

Future economic historians will find it far more illuminating to explore the implications of modern analyses dealing with the strategy of conflict and bargaining. In these alternative conceptualizations, it may be seen that by use of threat, bluff, and dissemblance (combined with appeals to personal loyalty, custom, and community sentiment) masters and slaves each sought to disguise the full degree of their mutual interdependence, and thus to alter the terms of the existing relationship, each to their own advantage. Such "game theoretic" behavior, however, is often fraught with dangers to one or both of the parties involved. Bluffs are called. Deceptions are punished. And in the jockeying for advantage, in the violating and the necessary policing of tacit understandings, valuable psychic and material resources are consumed. Such problems are not absent in the arrangements surrounding voluntary labor contracts. But they are likely to be greatly aggravated under slavery. One may take it as a testimony to the prosperity which was created by the South's advantages as a supplier of raw cotton (and some indication of the degree to which the incomes of slaveowners depended upon the expropriation of their workers' labor) that a system of production characterized by such great potentialities for wasteful conflict could long be sustained.

While the antebellum cotton boom was in progress, it engendered new attitudes, and elicited new capitalistic responses from white men stricken with "the cotton fever." It is more reasonable to expect that we may learn something about the aspirations and motives of such free individuals from the study of their behavior, than it is to draw such inferences about slaves whose range of action was so much more narrowly constrained. But it is nonetheless necessary to try accurately to delineate the range of different behavioral patterns among free men, rather than to assume that they all were cast in the same mold. The cotton boom in one sense induced, and in another sense exposed social divisions within the southern planter class: new men in new enterprises emerged in new regions, making a more vivid contrast to the established slaveowning families and to the estates of what became known as the "Old South." Moreover, the social ethos of the planter class—the attitudes and behavior of its members in matters concerning their human chattel—

were being reshaped by the fact that the slaves whom they owned were tending to appreciate greatly in value. On the one hand, the resulting capital gains allowed some planters to live beyond their current incomes—dissaving by selling off slaves or otherwise removing them from their estates—and yet not becoming any less wealthy within their own lifetimes. On the other hand, individual slaves had become more valuable pieces of property, whose management now called for more care and forethought than purely commercial consideration would previously have justified. A new rationale could thus be found to sustain some older, paternalistic attitudes and patterns of planter conduct.

The portrayal of slaveowners as "capitalistic" because they had no aversion to money-making is thus overly simplified: it obscures divisions within the planter class itself and obliterates real distinctions between the attitudes and conduct of wealthy people in the northern and southern sections of antebellum America. But the opposing view of the society of slaveowners—which characterizes them as uniformly pre-bourgeois and patriarchal, exalting family, personal honor, courtesy, and the genteel virtues, and thereby rejecting profit-seeking and the drive for accumulation—seems no less distorted. It ignores the effects of wealth and long-standing prestige upon social behavior and imputes those qualities to the effects of slaveownership *per se*. It reflects too exclusive an attention to the society of the older, long settled regions, while dismissing the barbarities and acquisitive fervor manifested in the frontier areas as transient phenomena, not indicative of some immutably "true" characteristics of a social and economic structure based on slavery.

The particular course of historical development just described was predicated upon two fundamental economic conditions. First, the availability of fertile land in the Gulf Plains and Delta regions combined with a strong external demand for cotton to establish a mounting demand for slave labor. But equally important was the second condition, namely, that the closing of the external slave trade in 1808 eliminated the possibility of a rapid adjustment of total United States supply of slave labor to meet the growth of demand for labor. The adjustment was made in another way: through the rise in the prices of existing stocks of slaves. This market adjustment had differential effects within the slaveholding class. New men in new regions might have wished to be able quickly to build up a labor force by importing slaves at the lower prices which prevailed in the Atlantic slave trade—prices which would have been little affected by the modest comparative size of the current demand for slaves on the North American mainland. Old slaveholding families, with already large estates on the Eastern seaboard may have resented the threat posed by the competition of cotton production in the fertile regions of the interior, but that competition was made less fierce (and the consequent effect upon the value of old landed estates was ameliorated if not entirely offset) by the rising valuation placed upon slave property holdings. Perhaps the dominance of such economic interests underlay the anomalous situation in the antebellum South. There, the opening up of the interior proceeded without initiating a reopening of the external slave trade, and thus little movement of population from abroad.

Whatever the reason for it, the fact that access to slave manpower from abroad remained closed carried a number of far-reaching implications. For one thing, the onset of the cotton boom did not enlarge the numbers and influence of recent captives from Africa within the slave communities, nor did it increase the proportions of blacks to whites in the population of the South as a whole. Patterns of Afro-American cultural adaptation therefore continued to evolve on the North American mainland in ways which diverged further and further from those in the contemporary slave societies of the Caribbean and Brazil.

A second implication of the high and rising prices of slaves was this: maintenance of minimum levels of material care and living arrangements compatible with the growth of the slave population by natural increase became economically more attractive. Taking a long view of human history, slaves in antebellum America appear to have been maintained at a comparatively high standard of living. And, as Phillip Curtin [1969] has shown, the demographic experience of the Negro slaves brought to the North American mainland was far better than that of the Negro slave populations of the Caribbean and

South America. But setting aside excursions into the comparative history of slavery, and viewing the Afro-American experience (as *Time on the Cross* has done) in its contemporary American context, neither the demographic nor the economic circumstances of the slaves' lives were in any way enviable. The share of their production which they were allowed to consume was nowhere near that of free Americans. Their food rations were far more monotonous, being largely composed of a few traditional staples. Although it was high in caloric content (apparently reflecting the high energy output which masters and overseers expected to extract from the average slave), the typical slave diet was at the same time nutritionally deficient in important respects. Similarly, the clothing, housing and other amenities of life which were provided typically for the slaves were adequate to sustain life but otherwise meager, even in comparison with the poorest of the urban slum-dwellers of the North.

That the slaves did not enjoy the standard of living of contemporaneous free Americans, and yet were neither being starved to death, nor worked to death in their youth, is no real paradox. We are dealing here with a society whose free citizens enjoyed an average standard of living far above the bare subsistence level. Long before the United States became an industrial nation, the level of per capita real income in America was higher than that in all but a few countries of the world. Furthermore, we are considering the material treatment which was accorded to a valuable form of property during a prosperous era, in which the mere preservation of that property seemed (to its owners) to be the key to the private accumulation of great wealth.

Yet a third consequence of the shutting off of the external sources of slave manpower was that a great internal migration was instigated by the profitability of meeting the buoyant demand for cotton by employing slave labor on the fertile interior lands of the American South. Labor demands in the newly opened regions could not be satisfied by fresh importations of slaves, such as had occurred in Brazil, for example. So they were met by the relocation of men, women, and children drawn from the slave plantations of the Old South. This nineteenth century population redistribution was part of the larger westward movement in which many desperate and eager people (from the Old World and the New) chose to participate. For enslaved black Americans, participation was not a matter of *their* choice. The process of geographical resource reallocation, which left worn lands behind and kept average agricultural productivity and slave values rising in the antebellum South, meant something a great deal different for the slaves caught up in it. It revived and continued to recapitulate the shock and horror of forced separations from family and friends, the frightening uprooting from familiar environments and understood social contexts, all of which had been well known by their forebears who had left Africa in chains.

Alas, this revival of old sorrows was the other side of the coin that vouchsafed to Afro-American slaves the modicum of care which very valuable property commands in an acquisitive society.

BIBLIOGRAPHICAL REFERENCES

The numbers following the brief citation form and date—those which appear within brackets [ ] preceded by the letters FE—correspond to the number assigned the particular reference in the Bibliography published in Volume II of Time on the Cross. Items for which no such number is supplied here do not appear in Fogel and Engerman's bibliography.

Affleck, 1850
Thomas Affleck, "On the Hygiene of Cotton Plantations and the Management of Negro Slaves," *Southern Medical Reports*, Vol. II (1850), pp. 429–36.

Agricola, 1851
Agricola [Pseudonym], "Management of Negroes," *De Bow's Review*, Vol. X [II, 3rd s.] (March 1851), pp. 325–28.

Aitken, 1971
Hugh G. J. Aitken, ed., *Did Slavery Pay? Readings in the Economics of Black Slavery in the United States*, Boston: Houghton Mifflin Co., 1971.

American Almanac, 1888
Ainsworth R. Spofford, ed., *American Almanac and Treasury of Facts, Statistical, Financial, and Political*, New York: American News Co., 1888.

American Anti-Slavery Society, 1841
American Anti-Slavery Society, *Slavery and the Internal Slave Trade in the U.S. of N.A.*, London: T. Ward and Co., 1841.

Andrews, 1836
Ethan Allen Andrews, *Slavery and the Domestic Slave Trade in the United States*, Boston: Light and Sterns, 1836.

Anonymous, 1847
[Anonymous], "The Negro," *De Bow's Review*, Vol. III (May 1847), pp. 419–20.

Anonymous, 1849
[Anonymous], "Negro Slavery at the South, Part II," *De Bow's Review*, Vol. VII [I, ns] (November 1849), pp. 379–89.

Arrow, 1965
Kenneth J. Arrow, *Aspects of the Theory of Risk-Bearing*, Yrjo Jahnsson Lectures, Helsinki: The Academic Bookstore, 1965.

Atwater and Woods, 1897
W. O. Atwater and Cha[rle]s D. Woods, U.S. Department of Agriculture, Office of Experiment Stations, "Dietary Studies with Reference to the Food of the Negro in Alabama in 1895 and 1896," *U.S.D.A. Experiment Stations Bulletin*, Number 38, Washington: GPO, 1897.

Bancroft, 1931 [FE 11]
Frederic Bancroft, *Slave-Trading in the Old South*, Baltimore: J. H. Furst Co., 1931.

Bassett, 1899 [FE 12]
John Spencer Basset, *Slavery in the State of North Carolina* (Johns Hopkins University Studies in Historical and Political Science, Series XVII, No. 7–8), Baltimore: Johns Hopkins Press, 1899.

Bateman, 1968 [FE 13]
Fred Bateman, "Improvement in American Dairy Farming, 1850–1910: A Quantitative Analysis," *Journal of Economic History*, Vol. XXVIII (June 1968), pp. 255–73.

Bateman and Weiss, 1975
Fred Bateman and Thomas Weiss, "Comparative Regional Development in Antebellum Manufacturing," *Journal of Economic History*, Vol. XXXV (March 1975), pp. 182–208.

Battalio and Kagel, 1970 [FE 14]
Raymond C. Battalio and John Kagel, "The Structure of Antebellum Southern Agriculture: South Carolina, A Case Study," *Agricultural History*, Vol. XLIV (January 1970), pp. 25–37.

Bayless and Rosenweig, 1966
Theodore M. Bayless and Norton S. Rosenweig, "A Racial Difference in Incidence of Lactase Deficiency: A Survey of Milk Intolerance and Lactase Deficiency in Healthy Adult Males," *Journal of the American Medical Association*, CXCVII (September 19, 1965), pp. 968–72.

Becker, 1962
Gary S. Becker, "Irrational Behavior and Economic Theory," *Journal of Political Economy*, Vol. LXX (February 1962), pp. 1–13.

Bennett and Peirce, 1961 [FE 18]
Merrill K. Bennett and Rosamond H. Peirce, "Change in the American National Diet, 1879–1959," *Food Research Institute Studies*, Vol. II (May 1961), pp. 95–119.

Bennett and Peirce, 1962
Merrill K. Bennett and Rosamond H. Peirce, "Approximate Levels of Food
Consumption Before 1909," unpublished memorandum, Food Research Institute,
Stanford University, April 16, 1962.

Benson, 1972
Lee Benson, *Toward the Scientific Study of History*, New York: J. B. Lippincott,
1972.

Bergman and Beckwith, 1968 [FE 19]
Abraham B. Bergman and J. Bruce Beckwith, "Sudden Death Syndrome of
Infancy," in Morris Green and Robert J. Haggerty, eds., *Ambulatory Pediatrics*,
Philadelphia: W. B. Saunders, 1968, pp. 777–80.

Bergman, Beckwith, and Ray, 1970
Abraham B. Bergman, J. Bruce Beckwith, and C. George Ray, *Sudden Infant
Death Syndrome*, Seattle: University of Washington Press, 1970.

Berry, 1943
Thomas Senior Berry, *Western Prices Before 1861: A Study of the Cincinnati
Market*, Cambridge: Harvard University Press, 1943.

Bertelson, 1967
David Bertelson, *The Lazy South*, New York: Oxford University Press, 1967.

Bidwell and Falconer, 1925 [FE 20]
Percy Wells Bidwell and John I. Falconer, *History of Agriculture in the
Northern United States, 1620–1860*, Washington: Carnegie Institution, 1925.

Blassingame, 1972 [FE 21]
John W. Blassingame, *The Slave Community: Plantation Life in the Antebellum
South*, New York: Oxford University Press, 1972.

Blassingame, 1974
John W. Blassingame, "The Mathematics of Slavery," *Atlantic Monthly*, Vol.
234 (August 1974), pp. 78–82.

Bloch, 1953
Marc Bloch, *The Historian's Craft*, New York: Alfred A. Knopf, 1953.

Blodgett, 1903
J. H. Blodgett, "Wages of Farm Labor in the United States," *U.S. Department
of Agriculture Bureau of Statistics, Miscellaneous Series*—Bulletin No. 26
(Washington: GPO, 1903).

Bridenbaugh, 1963
Carl Bridenbaugh, "The Great Mutation," *American Historical Review*, Vol.
LXVIII (January 1963), pp. 315–33.

Butlin, 1971 [FE 31]
N. G. Butlin, *Ante-bellum Slavery—Critique of a Debate*, Canberra: Department
of Economic History, Australian National University, 1971.

Cairnes, 1862 [FE 33]
J. E. Cairnes, *The Slave Power: Its Character, Career, and Probable Designs: Being an Attempt To Explain the Real Issues Involved in the American Contest,* Introduction by Harold D. Woodman, New York: Harper & Row, 1969.

Calderhead, 1972 [FE 34]
William Calderhead, "How Extensive Was the Border State Slave Trade?: A New Look," *Civil War History,* Vol. XVIII (March 1972), pp. 42–55.

Calhoun, 1917–19
Arthur W. Calhoun, *A Social History of the American Family from Colonial Times to the Present,* Cleveland: Arthur H. Clark Co., 3 vols., 1917–19.

Carpenter, 1844
W. M. Carpenter, "Observations on the Cachexia Africana, or the Habit and Effects of Dirt-Eating in the Negro Race," *New-Orleans Medical Journal,* Vol. I (August/October 1844), pp. 146–68.

Carr, 1962
Edward H. Carr, *What Is History?,* New York: Alfred A. Knopf, 1962.

Cartwright, 1852
Sam[ue]l A. Cartwright, "Philosophy of the Negro Constitution," *New-Orleans Medical and Surgical Journal,* Vol. IX (July 1852), pp. 195–208.

Cartwright, 1853
[Samuel A.] Cartwright, "Diseases and Peculiarities of the Negro," in J. D. B. De Bow, ed., *The Industrial Resources, Etc., of the Southern and Western States,* Vol. II, New Orleans: Merchants' Exchange, 1853.

Caves, 1971
Richard Caves, "Export-Led Growth and the New Economic History," in *Trade, Balance of Payments and Growth: Papers in Honor of C. P. Kindleberger,* Amsterdam: North Holland Publishing Co., 1971.

Church and Church, 1970
Charles Frederick Church and Helen Nichols Church, *Food Values of Portions Commonly Used: Bowes and Church,* Eleventh Edition, Philadelphia: J. B. Lippincott, 1970.

Coale and Demeny, 1966 [FE 45]
Ansley J. Coale and Paul Demeny, *Regional Model Life Tables and Stable Populations,* Princeton: Princeton University Press, 1966.

Coale and Rives, 1973
Ansley J. Coale and Norfleet W. Rives, Jr., "Statistical Reconstruction of the Black Population of the United States 1880–1970: Estimates of True Numbers by Age and Sex, Birth Rates, and Total Fertility," *Population Index,* Vol. 39 (January 1973), pp. 3–36.

Coale and Tye, 1961
Ansley J. Coale and C. Y. Tye, "The Significance of Age-Patterns of Fertility in

High Fertility Populations," *Milbank Memorial Fund Quarterly*, Vol. 39 (October 1961), pp. 631–46.

Cocke, 1853
[Phillip] St. Geo[rge] Cocke, "Management of Negroes," *De Bow's Review*, Vol. XIV (February 1853), pp. 177–78.

Collins, 1904 [FE 50]
Winfield Collins, *The Domestic Slave Trade of the Southern States*, New York: Broadway Publishing Company, 1904.

Coltman, 1969
C. H. Coltman, Jr., "Pagophagiz and Iron Lack," *Journal of the American Medical Association*, Vol. 207 (1969), pp. 513–16.

Conrad and Meyer, 1958 [FE 53]
Alfred H. Conrad and John R. Meyer, "The Economics of Slavery in the Ante-Bellum South," *Journal of Political Economy*, Vol. 66 (April 1958), pp. 95–130.

Cooper, 1957
Marcia Cooper, *Pica: A Survey of the Historical Literature as Well as Reports from the Fields of Veterinary Medicine and Anthropology, the Present Study of Pica in Young Children, and a Discussion of its Pediatric and Psychological Implications*, Springfield: Charles C. Thomas, 1957.

Cragin, 1836
F. W. Cragin, "Observations on Cachexia Africana or Dirt-Eating," *American Journal of the Medical Sciences*, Vol. XVII (February 1836), pp. 356–64.

Curtin, 1969 [FE 65]
Philip D. Curtin, *The Atlantic Slave Trade: A Census*, Madison: University of Wisconsin Press, 1969.

Curtin, 1975 [FE 66]
Philip D. Curtin, "Measuring the Atlantic Slave Trade," in Stanley L. Engerman and Eugene D. Genovese, eds., *Race and Slavery in the Western Hemisphere: Quantitative Studies*, Princeton: Princeton University Press, 1975, pp. 107–28.

David, 1975
Paul A. David, "Child Care in the Slave Quarters: Critical Notes on Some Uses of Demography in *Time on the Cross*," Research Memorandum, Stanford Center for Research in Economic Growth, July 1975.

David and Temin, 1974
Paul A. David and Peter Temin, "Slavery: The Progressive Institution?" *Journal of Economic History*, Vol. XXXIV (September 1974), pp. 739–83.

David and Temin, 1975
Paul A. David and Peter Temin, "Capitalist Masters, Bourgeois Slaves," *Journal of Interdisciplinary History*, Vol. V (Winter 1974/75), pp. 445–57.

Davis, 1939 [FE 68]
Charles S. Davis, *The Cotton Kingdom in Alabama*, Montgomery: Alabama
State Department of Archives and History, 1939.

Davis, 1966 [FE 71]
David Brion Davis, *The Problem of Slavery in Western Culture*, Ithaca: Cornell
University Press, 1966.

Davis, 1974
David Brion Davis, "Slavery and the Post-World War II Historians," *Daedalus*
(Spring 1974), pp. 1–16.

Davis, 1943 [FE 72]
Edwin Adams Davis, ed., *Plantation Life in the Florida Parishes of Louisiana
1836–1844, as Reflected in the Diary of Bennet H. Barrow*, New York: Columbia
University Press, 1943.

Denison, 1967 [FE 75]
Edward Denison, *Why Growth Rates Differ*, Washington: Brookings Institution,
1967.

Dew, 1832
Thomas R. Dew, *A Review of the Debate in the Virginia Legislature of 1831 and
1832*, Richmond: T. H. White, 1832.

Dew, 1966
C. B. Dew, *Ironmaker to the Confederacy*, New Haven: Yale University Press,
1966.

Dickens, 1928
Dorothy Dickens, "A Nutrition Investigation of Negro Tenants in the Yazoo
Mississippi Delta," *Mississippi Agricultural Experiment Station (A. & M.
College) Bulletin*, Number 254 (August 1928).

Douglass, 1855 [FE 81]
Frederick Douglass, *My Bondage and My Freedom*, New York: Miller, Orton and
Mulligan, 1855.

Duncan, 1849
James B. Duncan, "Report on the Topography, Climate and Diseases of the
Parish of St. Mary, La.," *Southern Medical Reports*, Vol. I (1849), pp. 190–96.

Durnin and Passmore, 1967
J. V. G. A. Durnin and R. Passmore, *Energy, Work and Leisure*, London:
Heinemann Educational Books, 1967.

Easterlin, 1960 [FE 93]
Richard A. Easterlin, "Interregional Differences in Per Capita Income, Population, and Total Income, 1840–1950," *Trends in the American Economy in the
Nineteenth Century*, National Bureau of Economic Research, Studies in Income
and Wealth, Vol. XXIV, Princeton: Princeton University Press, 1960, pp. 73–140.

Easterlin, 1961 [FE 94]
Richard A. Easterlin, "Regional Income Trends, 1840–1850," in Seymour Harris, ed., American Economic History, New York: 1961, pp. 525–47.

Easterlin, 1975 [FE 95]
Richard A. Easterlin, "Farm Production and Income in Old and New Areas at Mid-Century," in D. C. Klingaman and R. K. Vedder, eds., *Essays in Nineteenth Century Economic History: The Old Northwest*, Athens, Ohio: Ohio University Press, 1975.

Eblen, 1974
Jack Ericson Eblen, "New Estimates of the Vital Rates of the United States Black Population During the Nineteenth Century," *Demography*, Vol. II (May 1974), pp. 301–19.

Edwards, Thorndike, and Dill, 1935
H. T. Edwards, A. Thorndike, Jr., and D. B. Dill, "The Energy Requirements in Strenuous Muscular Exercise," *New England Journal of Medicine*, Vol. 213 (1935), pp. 532–35.

Elkins, 1959 [FE 101]
Stanley M. Elkins, *Slavery, A Problem in American Institutional and Intellectual Life*, Chicago: University of Chicago Press, 1959.

Elliott, 1860
E. N. Elliott, ed., *Cotton Is King; and Pro-Slavery Arguments: Comprising the Writings of Hammond, Harper, Christy, Strongfellow, Hodge, Bledsoe, and Cartwright, on This Important Subject*, Augusta, Georgia: Pritchard, Abbott and Loomis, 1860.

Ellsworth, 1840
Henry W. Ellsworth, *The American Swine Breeder, A Practical Treatise on the Selection, Rearing and Fattening of Swine*, Boston: Weeks, Jordan and Company, 1840.

Engerman, 1966
Stanley L. Engerman, "The Economic Impact of the Civil War," *Explorations in Entrepreneurial History*, Vol. 3, 2nd s. (Spring 1966), pp. 176–199.

Engerman, 1970 [FE 102]
Stanley L. Engerman, "The Antebellum South: What Probably Was and What Should Have Been," *Agricultural History*, Vol. XLIV (January 1970), pp. 127–42.

Engerman, 1972 [FE 103]
Stanley L. Engerman, "The Slave Trade and British Capital Formation in the Eighteenth Century: A Comment on the Williams Thesis," *Business History Review*, Vol. XLVI (Winter 1972), pp. 420–43.

Engerman, 1973
Stanley L. Engerman, "Some Considerations Relating to Property Rights in Man," *Journal of Economic History*, Vol. XXXIII (March 1973), pp. 43–65.

Engerman, 1975
Stanley L. Engerman, "A Critique of Sutch on 'The Breeding of Slaves,'" in
Stanley L. Engerman and Eugene D. Genovese, eds., *Race and Slavery in the
Western Hemisphere: Quantitative Studies*, Princeton: Princeton University
Press, 1975, pp. 527–30.

Engerman and Genovese, 1975
Stanley L. Engerman and Eugene D. Genovese, eds., *Race and Slavery in the
Western Hemisphere*, Princeton: Princeton University Press, 1975.

Erickson, 1975
Charlotte Erickson, "Quantitative History," *American Historical Review*, Vol.
LXXX (April 1975), pp. 351–65.

Evans, 1962 [FE 105]
Robert Evans, Jr., "The Economics of American Negro Slavery," in Universities-
National Bureau Committee for Economic Research, *Aspects of Labor Econom-
ics*, Princeton: Princeton University Press, 1962, pp. 185–243.

Eve, 1849
[Paul F. Eve] "Early Pregnancy and Infantile Menstruation," *Southern Medical
and Surgical Journal*, Vol. V ns (1849), pp. 610–15.

Farley, 1968
Reynolds Farley, "The Urbanization of Negroes in the United States," *Journal
of Social History*, Vol. I (Spring 1968), pp. 241–58.

Farley, 1970
Reynolds Farley, *Growth of the Black Population: A Study of Demographic
Trends*, Chicago: Markham Publishing, 1970.

Fishlow, 1965 [FE 109]
Albert Fishlow, "Antebellum Interregional Trade Reconsidered," in R. L.
Andreano, ed., *New Views on American Economic Development*, Cambridge:
Schenkman Publishing Company, 1965.

Fitzhugh, 1857
George Fitzhugh, *Cannibals All! or, Slaves Without Masters*, Richmond: A.
Morris, 1857.

Flanders, 1933 [FE 112]
Ralph Betts Flanders, *Plantation Slavery in Georgia*, Chapel Hill: University of
North Carolina Press, 1933.

Fleisig, forthcoming
Heywood Fleisig, "Slavery, the Supply of Agricultural Labor, and the Industrialization of the South," *Journal of Economic History* (forthcoming).

Fleming, 1975
Thomas Fleming, "The 'Real' Uncle Tom," *Reader's Digest* (March 1975), pp.
124–28.

Fogel, 1964 [FE 113]
Robert William Fogel, *Railroads and American Economic Growth: Essays in Econometric History*, Baltimore: Johns Hopkins Press, 1964.

Fogel, 1967
Robert W. Fogel, "The Specification Problem in Economic History," *Journal of Economic History*, Vol. XXVII (September 1967), pp. 283–308.

Fogel, 1975
Robert W. Fogel, "The Limits of Quantitative Methods of History," *American Historical Review*, Vol. LXXX (April 1975), pp. 329–50.

Fogel and Engerman, 1971 [FE 117]
Robert William Fogel and Stanley L. Engerman, "The Economics of Slavery," in Robert William Fogel and Stanley L. Engerman, eds., *The Reinterpretation of American Economic History*, New York: Harper & Row, 1971, pp. 311–41.

Fogel and Engerman, 1971a [FE 118]
Robert William Fogel and Stanley L. Engerman, "The Relative Efficiency of Slavery: A Comparison of Northern and Southern Agriculture in 1860," *Explorations in Economic History*, Vol. 8 (Spring 1971), pp. 353–67.

Fogel and Engerman, 1972
Robert W. Fogel and Stanley Engerman, "The Market Evaluation of Human Capital: The Case of Slavery," unpublished paper, Cliometrics Conference, Madison, Wisconsin, April 1972.

FE I
Robert William Fogel and Stanley L. Engerman, *Time on the Cross: The Economics of American Negro Slavery*, Boston: Little, Brown and Company, 1974.

FE II
Robert William Fogel and Stanley L. Engerman, *Time on the Cross: Evidence and Methods—A Supplement*, Boston: Little, Brown and Company, 1974.

Fogel and Engerman, 1974
Robert W. Fogel and Stanley Engerman, "Further Evidence on the Nutritional Adequacy of the Slave Diet," unpublished paper, University of Rochester and the MSSB-Rochester Conference, October 23, 1974.

Foner and Genovese, 1969
Laura Foner and Eugene D. Genovese, eds., *Slavery in the New World*, Englewood Cliffs, N.J.: Prentice-Hall, 1969.

Foust, 1967 [FE 121]
James D. Foust, "The Yeoman Farmer and Westward Expansion of U.S. Cotton Production," unpublished Ph.D. dissertation, University of North Carolina, 1967.

Foust and Swan, 1970 [FE 122]
James D. Foust and Dale E. Swan, "Productivity and Profitability of Ante-

bellum Slave Labor: A Micro Approach," *Agricultural History*, Vol. XLIV (January 1970), pp. 39–62.

Frazier, 1948
E. F. Frazier, *The Negro Family in the United States* (revised and abridged edition), New York: Dryden Press, 1948.

Fredrickson, 1971
George M. Fredrickson, *The Black Image in the White Mind*, New York: Harper & Row, 1971.

Freedman's Inquiry Commission, 1863
Freedman's Inquiry Commission, Letters Received, Testimony of Harry McMillan and Robert Smalls, Office of the Adjutant General, Main Series, Reel 200; file 3, National Archives.

Gallman, 1960
Robert E. Gallman, "Commodity Output, 1839–1899," in Conference on Research in Income and Wealth, *Trends in the American Economy in the Nineteenth Century*, Studies in Income and Wealth, Vol. 24, Princeton: Princeton University Press, 1960, pp. 13–67.

Gallman, 1965
Robert E. Gallman, "Efficiency and Farm Interdependence in an Agricultural Export Region—Sampling Procedure and Tests of the Sample," unpublished paper, University of North Carolina, October 20, 1965.

Gallman, 1966 [FE 133]
Robert E. Gallman, "Gross National Product in the United States, 1834–1909," in *Conference on Research in Income and Wealth, Output, Employment, and Productivity in the United States After 1800*, Studies in Income and Wealth, Vol. 30, New York: Columbia University Press, 1966, pp. 3–76.

Gallman, 1969
Robert E. Gallman, "Trends in the Size Distribution of Wealth in the Nineteenth Century: Some Speculations," in *Six Papers on the Size Distribution of Income and Wealth*, New York: Columbia University Press (for National Bureau of Economic Research), 1969.

Gallman, 1970 [FE 135]
Robert E. Gallman, "Self-Sufficiency in the Cotton Economy of the Antebellum South," *Agricultural History*, Vol. XLIV (January 1970), pp. 5–23.

Genovese, 1965 [FE 139]
Eugene D. Genovese, *The Political Economy of Slavery: Studies in the Economy and Society of the Slave South*, New York: Pantheon, 1965.

Genovese, 1968
Eugene D. Genovese, ed., *Ulrich B. Phillips: The Slave Economy of the Old South*, Baton Rouge: Louisiana State University Press, 1968.

368   *Bibliographical References*

Genovese, 1974 [FE 141]
Eugene D. Genovese, *Roll, Jordan Roll: The World the Slaves Made*, New York: Pantheon Books, 1974.

GaDA, 1880
Georgia, Department of Agriculture, *A Manual on Cattle: For the Use of The Farmers of Georgia*, Atlanta: James P. Harrison, 1880.

Glass and Li, 1953 [FE 145]
Bentley Glass and C. C. Li, "The Dynamics of Racial Intermixture—an Analysis Based on the American Negro," *American Journal of Human Genetics*, Vol. V (March 1953), pp. 1–20.

Goldberger and Wheeler, 1920
Joseph Goldberger and G. A. Wheeler, "The Experimental Production of Pellagra in Human Subjects by Means of Diet," *Hygienic Laboratory Bulletin*, Number 120 (February 1920), pp. 7–116.

Goldin, 1972 [FE 146]
Claudia Dale Goldin, "The Economics of Urban Slavery: 1820 to 1860," unpublished Ph.D. dissertation, University of Chicago, 1972.

Goldin, 1974 [FE 148]
Claudia Dale Goldin, "A Model to Explain the Relative Decline of Urban Slavery: Empirical Results," in Stanley L. Engerman and Eugene D. Genovese, eds., *Race and Slavery in the Western Hemisphere: Quantitative Studies*, Princeton: Princeton University Press, 1974, pp. 427–50.

Grandy, 1844
Moses Grandy, *Narrative of the Life of Moses Grandy; Late a Slave in the United States of America*, Boston: O. Johnson, 1844.

Gray, 1933 [FE 154]
Lewis Cecil Gray, *History of Agriculture in the Southern United States to 1860*, 2 vols., Washington: Carnegie Institution, 1933.

Grier, 1853
S. L. Grier, "The Negro and His Diseases," *New-Orleans Medical and Surgical Journal*, Vol. X (May 1853), pp. 752–63.

Gutman, 1972 [FE 165]
Herbert G. Gutman, "Le Phénomène invisible: la composition de la famille et du foyer noirs après la Guerre de Sécession," *Annales: Economies, Societies, Civilisations*, Vol. 26 (Juillet-Octobre 1972): pp. 1197–1218.

Gutman, 1975
Herbert G. Gutman, "The World Two Cliometricians Made: A Review Essay of F + E = T/C," *Journal of Negro History*, January 1975, pp. 53–227 [Reprinted as *Slavery and the Numbers Game: A Critique of Time on the Cross*, Urbana: University of Illinois Press, 1975].

Haskell, 1974
Thomas L. Haskell, "Were Slaves More Efficient? Some Doubts about 'Time on the Cross'" *New York Review of Books*, Vol. 21, September 19, 1974, pp. 38–42.

Henry, 1898
N. A. Henry, *Feeds and Feeding: A Hand-Book for the Student and Stockman*, Madison: Henry, 1898.

Higbee, 1958
Edward C. Higbee, *American Agriculture: Geography, Resources, Conservation*, New York: Wiley, 1958.

Hilliard, 1972 [FE 180]
Sam Bowers Hilliard, *Hog Meat and Hoecake: Food Supply in the Old South, 1840–1860*, Carbondale: Southern Illinois University Press, 1972.

Holmes, 1916 [FE 183]
George K. Holmes, U.S. Department of Agriculture, Bureau of Crop Estimates, *Meat Situation in the United States*, 5 parts, Part I, "Statistics of Live Stock Meat Production and Consumption Prices, and International Trade for Many Countries," *U.S.D.A. Report*, Number 109, Washington: GPO, 1916.

Homans and Homans, 1858
J. Smith Homans and J. Smith Homans, Jr., *A Cyclopedia of Commerce and Commercial Navigation*, New York: Harper and Brothers, 1858.

Hopkins, 1941
John A. Hopkins, *Changing Technology and Employment in Agriculture*, U.S. Department of Agriculture Economics, Washington, GPO, May 1941.

Hutchinson and Williamson, 1971 [FE 187]
William K. Hutchinson and Samuel H. Williamson, "The Self-Sufficiency of the Antebellum South: Estimates of the Food Supply," *Journal of Economic History*, Vol. XXXI (September 1971), pp. 591–612.

Jacobson, 1957 [FE 189]
Paul H. Jacobson, "An Estimate of the Expectation of Life in the United States in 1850," *Milbank Memorial Fund Quarterly*, Vol. 35 (1957), pp. 197–201.

Jarvis, 1855
Edward Jarvis, Letter to J. D. B. De Bow, September 22, 1855, printed in *U.S. Census, 1850, Mortality*, pp. 45–49.

Jenkins, 1935
William S. Jenkins, *Pro-Slavery Thought in the Old South*, Chapel Hill: University of North Carolina Press, 1935.

Johnson, 1930 [FE 195]
Guiou Griffis Johnson, *A Social History of the Sea Islands: With Special Reference to St. Helena Island, South Carolina*, Chapel Hill: University of North Carolina Press, 1930.

Jones, 1965 [FE 197]
Bobby F. Jones, "A Cultural Middle Passage: Slave Marriage and Family in the Ante-Bellum South," unpublished Ph.D. dissertation, University of North Carolina, 1965.

Jones, 1968
W. O. Jones, "Plantation," *The International Encyclopedia of the Social Sciences*, New York: Macmillan, 1968.

Kaser, 1964 [FE 198]
David Kaser, "Nashville's Women of Pleasure in 1860," *Tennessee Historical Quarterly*, Vol. XXIII (December 1964), pp. 379–82.

Keith, Brown, and Rosenberg, 1970
Louis Keith, Eric R. Brown, and Cary Rosenberg, "Pica: The Unfinished Story; Background: Correlations with Anemia and Pregnancy," *Perspectives in Biology and Medicine*, Vol. 13 (Summer 1970), pp. 626–31.

Keyfitz, 1971
Nathan Keyfitz, "How Birth Control Affects Births," *Social Biology*, Vol. 18 (September 1971), pp. 109–21.

Keys, Brožek, Henschel, Mickelsen, and Taylor, 1950
Ancel Keys, Josef Brožek, Austin Henschel, Olaf Mickelsen, and Henry Longstreet Taylor, *The Biology of Human Starvation*, 2 vols., Minneapolis: University of Minnesota Press, 1950.

Kodicek, 1962
E. Kodicek, "Nicotinic Acid and the Pellagra Problem," *Bibliotheca "Nutritio et Dieta*,*"* Vol. 4 (1962), pp. 109–27.

Kretchmer, 1972
Norman Kretchmer, "Lactose and Lactase," *Scientific American*, Vol. 227 (October 1972), pp. 70–78.

Kunreuther and Wright, 1974
Howard Kunreuther and Gavin Wright, "Safety-First, Gambling and the Subsistence Farmer," *Fels Center Discussion Paper* Series No. 59, University of Pennsylvania (July 1974).

Langworth and Hunt, 1913
C. F. Langworth and Caroline L. Hunt, U.S. Department of Agriculture, "Use of Corn, Kafir, and Cowpeas in the Home," U.S.DA.A. *Farmers' Bulletin*, Number 559, Washington: GPO, 1913.

Lebergott, 1964 [FE 207]
Stanley Lebergott, *Manpower in Economic Growth: The American Record Since 1800*, New York: McGraw-Hill, 1964.

Lebergott, 1974
Stanley Lebergott, "Review of *Time on the Cross*," *American Political Science Review*, Vol. 69 (June 1975), pp. 697–700.

LeConte, 1845
John LeConte, "Observations on Geophagy," *Southern Medical and Surgical Journal*, Vol. I ns (August 1845), pp. 417–44.

Levy, 1960
Babett M. Levy, "Early Puritanism in the Southern and Island Colonies," *American Antiquarian Society Proceedings*, Vol. 70 (1960), pp. 60–348.

Lichtman, 1974
Allen J. Lichtman, "A Benign Institution," *The New Republic*, Vol. 171 (July 6 and July 13, 1974), pp. 22–24.

McColley, 1964
Robert McColley, *Slavery and Jeffersonian Virginia*, Urbana, Illinois: University of Illinois Press, 1964.

Martin, 1942 [FE 217]
Edgar W. Martin, *The Standard of Living in 1860: American Consumption Levels on the Eve of the Civil War*, Chicago: University of Chicago Press, 1942.

Massachusetts Bureau of Statistics of Labor, 1886
Massachusetts Bureau of Statistics of Labor, *17th Annual Report*, Part III, "Food Consumption" (March 1886).

Menn, 1964 [FE 224]
Joseph Karl Menn, *The Large Slaveholders of Louisiana, 1860*, New Orleans: Pelican Publishing, 1964.

Michelson, 1944
Nicholas Michelson, "Studies in the Physical Development of Negroes: [Part] IV. Onset of Puberty," *American Journal of Physical Anthropology* Vol. II, ns (June 1944), pp. 151–66.

Mills, 1937
C. A. Mills, "Geographic and Time Variations in Body Growth and Age at Menarche," *Human Biology*, Vol. 9 (February 1937), pp. 43–56.

Mississippi Planter, 1851
A Mississippi Planter [pseudonym], "Management of Negroes Upon Southern Estates," *De Bow's Review*, Vol. X [II, 3rd s.] (June 1851), pp. 621–25.

Morgan, 1967
Edmund S. Morgan, "The Puritan Ethic and the American Revolution," *William and Mary Quarterly*, Vol. XXIV, 3rd s (January 1967), pp. 3–43.

Morgan, 1971
Edmund S. Morgan, "The Labor Problem at Jamestown, 1607–18," *American Historical Review*, Vol. LXXVI (June 1971), pp. 595–612.

Morrison, 1948
Frank B. Morrison, *Feeds and Feeding: A Handbook for the Student and Stockman*, 21st edition, Ithaca: Morison, 1948.

Murray, 1914
Nat C. Murray, "Disposition of Feed Crops," *U.S.D.A. Agricultural Outlook*
[Farmers' Bulletin Number 629] (October 16, 1914), pp. 8–9.

Mustacchi, 1971
Piero Mustacchi, "Cesare Bressa (1785–1836) on Dirt Eating in Louisiana: A
Critical Analysis of His Unpublished Manuscript *De la Dissolution Scorbutique*,"
Journal of the American Medical Association, Vol. 218 (October 11, 1971), pp.
229–32.

NAS, NRC, 1959
National Academy of Sciences, National Research Council, Food and Nutrition
Board, *Evaluation of Protein Nutrition* (Publication Number 711), Washington:
NAS, 1959.

NAS, NRC, 1964 [FE 120]
National Academy of Sciences, National Research Council, Food and Nutrition
Board, *Recommended Dietary Allowances*, 6th revised edition (Publication 1146),
Washington: NAS, 1964.

NAS, NRC, 1968
National Academy of Sciences, National Research Council, Food and Nutrition
Board, *Recommended Dietary Allowances*, 7th revised edition (Publication
Number 1694), Washington: NAS, 1968.

North, 1961 [FE 243]
Douglass C. North, *The Economic Growth of the United States 1790–1860*,
Englewood Cliffs, N.J.: Prentice-Hall, 1961.

North, 1966
Douglass C. North, *Growth and Welfare in the American Past*, Englewood Cliffs,
N.J.: Prentice-Hall, 1966.

Olmsted, 1856 [FE 244]
Frederick Law Olmsted, *A Journey in the Seaboard Slave States with Remarks
on Their Economy*, New York: Dix & Edwards, 1856.

Olmsted, 1857 [FE 245]
Frederick Law Olmsted, *A Journey Through Texas*, New York: Dix, Edwards &
Co., 1857.

Olmsted, 1860 [FE 246]
Frederick Law Olmsted, *A Journey in the Back Country*, New York: Mason
Brothers, 1860.

Olmsted, 1861 [FE 247]
Frederick Law Olmsted, *The Cotton Kingdom*, edited, with an introduction by
Arthur M. Schlesinger, New York: Alfred A. Knopf, 1953. [First published: New
York, 1861, an abridgment of Olmsted (1856, 1857, 1860)]

Osofsky, 1969
Gilbert Osofsky, *Puttin' on Ole Massa: Slave Narratives of Henry Bibb, William Wells Brown, and Solomon Northup*, New York: Harper & Row, 1969.

Owsley, 1949 [FE 250]
Frank Owsley, *Plain Folk of the Old South*, Baton Rouge: Louisiana State University Press, 1949.

Parker, 1970
William N. Parker, ed., *The Structure of the Cotton Economy of the Antebellum South* (also printed as *Agricultural History*, Vol. XLIV), Berkeley: University of California Press, 1970.

Parker, 1970a [FE 253]
William N. Parker, "Slavery and Southern Economic Development," *Agricultural History*, Vol. XLIV (January 1970).

Parker, 1972
William N. Parker, "Agriculture," Chap. 11 in L. E. Davis, R. A. Easterlin, W. N. Parker, et al., *American Economic Growth: An Economist's History of the United States*, New York: Harper & Row, 1972.

Parker, 1974
William N. Parker, "Economists and History," *Reviews in American History*, Vol. II, December 1974, pp. 472–73.

Passell, 1974
Peter Passell, "An Economic Analysis of that Peculiarly Economic Institution," *New York Times Book Review*, Vol. 28, April 28, 1974, p. 4.

Peebles, 1858
Jesse Peebles, "A History of the Diseases of Craven's Creek, and Its Vicinity [Lowndes County, Mississippi] from 1848, Down to the Present Time," *The New-Orleans Medical and Surgical Journal*, Vol. XV (January 1858), pp. 33–39.

Peterson, 1966
D. R. Peterson, "Sudden Unexpected Death in Infants—An Epidemiologic Study," *American Journal of Epidemiology*, Vol. LXXXIV (1966), pp. 478–82.

Phillips, 1905 [FE 257]
Ulrich B. Phillips, "The Economic Cost of Slaveholding in the Cotton Belt," *Political Science Quarterly*, Vol. XX (June 1905), pp. 257–75.

Phillips, 1910 [FE 260]
Ulrich Bonnell Phillips, ed., *Plantation and Frontier Documents, 1649–1863*, Vols. I and II of John R. Commons, et al., *A Documentary History of American Industrial Society*, Cleveland: A. H. Clark Co., 1910.

Phillips, 1918 [FE 261]
Ulrich Bonnell Phillips, *American Negro Slavery: A Survey of the Supply, Employment and Control of Negro Labor as Determined by the Plantation Regime*, New York: D. Appleton and Company, 1918.

Phillips, 1929 [FE 263]
Ulrich Bonnell Phillips, *Life and Labor in the Old South*, Boston: Little, Brown and Company, 1963 (First Edition, 1929).

Piper, 1912
C. V. Piper, U.S. Department of Agriculture, Bureau of Plant Industry, "Agricultural Varieties of the Cowpea and Immediately Related Species," *USDA, BPI, Bulletin*, Number 229, Washington: GPO, 1912.

Postell, 1951 [FE 266]
William Dosite Postell, *The Health of Slaves on Southern Plantations*, Baton Rouge: Louisiana State University Press, 1951.

Puckett, 1844
W. R. Puckett, "Remarks on Erysipelatous Fever, or Black Tongue," *New-Orleans Medical Journal*, Vol. I (May 1844), p. 116.

Raghuramulu, Rao, and Gopalan, 1965
N. Raghuramulu, B. S. Narasinga Rao, and C. Gopalan, "Amino Acid Imbalance and Tryptophane—Niacin Metabolism," *Journal of Nutrition*, Vol. LXXXVI (May 1965).

Ransom, 1974
Roger L. Ransom, "Was It Really All That Great To Be a Slave? A Review of *Time on the Cross*," *Agricultural History*, Vol. XLVIII (October 1974), pp. 578–85.

Ransom and Sutch, 1971
Roger Ransom and Richard Sutch, "Economic Regions of the South in 1880," *Southern Economic History Project, Working Paper Series*, Number 3, Berkeley: Institute of Business and Economic Research, March 1971.

Ransom and Sutch, 1973
Roger L. Ransom and Richard Sutch, "Estimating Surplus Food Residuals on Cotton Farms in 1880," *Southern Economic History Project, Research Memorandum Series*, Number 3, Berkeley: Institute of Business and Economic Research, October 1973.

Ransom and Sutch, 1975
Roger L. Ransom and Richard Sutch, "The Impact of the Civil War and of Emancipation on Southern Agriculture," *Explorations in Economic History*, Vol. 12 (January 1975), pp. 1–28.

Roe, 1973
Daphne A. Roe, *A Plague of Corn: The Social History of Pellagra*, Ithaca: Cornell University Press, 1973.

Rural Carolinian, 1870
The Rural Carolinian, Vol. I (January 1870).

Russell, 1857 [FE 285]
Robert Russell, *North America: Its Agriculture and Climate*, Edinburgh: Adam and Charles Black, 1857.

Sanderson, 1974
Warren C. Sanderson, "Does the Theory of Demand Need the Maximum Principle?" in Paul A. David and Melvin W. Reder, eds., *Nations and Households in Economic Growth*, New York: Academic Press, 1974.

Sarayadar, 1964 [FE 287]
Edward Sarayadar, "A Note on the Profitability of Ante Bellum Slavery," *Southern Economic Journal*, Vol. XXX (April 1964), pp. 325–32.

Scarborough, 1966 [FE 289]
William Kauffman Scarborough, *The Overseer: Plantation Management in the Old South*, Baton Rouge: Louisiana State University Press, 1966.

Seagrave, 1971 [FE 292]
Charles E. Seagrave, "The Southern Negro Agricultural Worker: 1850–1870," unpublished Ph.D. dissertation, Stanford University, 1971.

Sellers, 1950 [FE 293]
James Benson Sellers, *Slavery in Alabama*, University: University of Alabama Press, 1950.

Sherman, 1946
Henry C. Sherman, *Chemistry of Food and Nutrition*, 7th edition, New York: The Macmillan Company, 1946.

Shorter, 1974
Edward Shorter, "Protein, Puberty and Premarital Sexuality: American Blacks v. French Peasants," unpublished paper presented at MSSB-University of Rochester Conference: "*Time on the Cross*: A First Appraisal," October 24, 25, and 26, 1974.

Shryock, 1930
Richard H. Shryock, "Medical Practice in the Old South," *South Atlantic Quarterly*, Vol. XXIX (April 1930), pp. 160–78.

Shryock, 1936
Richard H. Shryock, "Medical Sources and the Social Historian," *American Historical Review*, Vol. XLI (April 1936), pp. 458–73.

Smith, 1960
T. E. Smith, "The Cocos-Keeling Islands: A Demographic Laboratory," *Population Studies*, Vol. XIV (November 1960), pp. 94–130.

Soltow, 1971 [FE 300]
Lee Soltow, "Economic Inequality in the United States in the Period from 1790 to 1860," *Journal of Economic History*, Vol. XXXI (December 1971), pp. 822–39.

Southern Cultivator, 1870
The Southern Cultivator, Vol. XXVIII (June 1870).

Southern Medical and Surgical Journal, 1839
Southern Medical and Surgical Journal, Vol. III (May 1839), pp. 507–8.

Stampp, 1956 [FE 303]
Kenneth M. Stampp, *The Peculiar Institution: Slavery in the Ante-Bellum South*, New York: Alfred A. Knopf, 1956.

Starobin, 1970 [FE 304]
Robert Starobin, *Industrial Slavery in the Old South*, New York: Oxford University Press, 1970.

Starobin, 1971
Robert Starobin, "Privileged Bondsmen and the Process of Accommodation: The Role of Houseservants and Drivers as Seen in Their Own Letters," *Journal of Social History*, Vol. V (Fall 1971): pp. 59–65.

Steckel, 1973 [FE 307]
Richard Steckel, "The Economics of U.S. Slave and Southern Free-White Fertility," unpublished paper, University of Chicago, 1973.

Stigler, 1945
George J. Stigler, "The Cost of Subsistence," *Journal of Farm Economics*, Vol. XXVII (May 1945), pp. 303–314.

Strauss and Bean, 1940 [FE 315]
Frederick Strauss and Louis H. Bean, U.S. Department of Agriculture, "Gross Farm Income and Indices of Farm Production and Prices in the United States, 1867–1937," *Technical Bulletin*, Number 703, Washington: GPO, December 1940.

Sutch, 1965 [FE 316]
Richard Sutch, "The Profitability of Ante Bellum Slavery—Revisited," *Southern Economic Journal*, Vol. XXXI (April 1965), pp. 365–77 reprinted in Hugh G. J. Aitken, ed., *Did Slavery Pay? Reading in the Economics of Black Slavery in the United States*, Boston: Houghton Mifflin, 1971, pp. 221–41.

Sutch, 1975 [FE 317]
Richard Sutch, "The Breeding of Slaves for Sale and the Westward Expansion of Slavery, 1850–1860," in Stanley L. Engerman and Eugene D. Genovese, eds., *Race and Slavery in the Western Hemisphere: Quantitative Studies*, Princeton: Princeton University Press, 1975, pp. 173–210.

Sutch, 1975a
Richard Sutch, "The Treatment Received by American Slaves: A Critical Review of the Evidence Presented in *Time on the Cross*," *Explorations in Economic History*, Vol. 12 (October 1975), pp. 335–438.

Swados, 1941
Felice Swados, "Negro Health on the Ante Bellum Plantations," *Bulletin of the History of Medicine*, Vol. X (October 1941), pp. 460–72.

Sydnor, 1933 [FE 320]
Charles S. Sydnor, *Slavery in Mississippi*, New York: Appleton-Century, 1933.

Tanner, 1962
J. M. Tanner, *Growth at Adolescence*, 2nd edition, Oxford: Blackwell, 1962.

Tanner, 1968
J. M. Tanner, "Earlier Maturation in Man," *Scientific American*, Vol. 218 (January 1968), pp. 21–27.

Tanner, 1973
J. M. Tanner, "Growing Up," *Scientific American*, Vol. 229 (September 1973), pp. 34–43.

Taylor, 1963 [FE 324]
Joe Gray Taylor, *Negro Slavery in Louisiana*, Baton Rouge: Louisiana Historical Association, 1963.

Taylor, 1958 [FE 325]
Orville W. Taylor, *Negro Slavery in Arkansas*, Durham: Duke University Press, 1958.

Taylor, 1924
Rosser H. Taylor, "Feeding Slaves," *Journal of Negro History*, Vol. IX (April 1924), pp. 139–43.

Terris, 1964
Milton Terris, ed., *Goldberger on Pellagra*, Baton Rouge: Louisiana State University Press, 1964.

Towne and Rasmussen, 1960 [FE 329]
Marvin W. Towne and Wayne D. Rasmussen, "Farm Gross Product and Gross Investment in the Nineteenth Century," in Conference on Research in Income and Wealth, *Trends in the American Economy in the Nineteenth Century*, Studies in Income and Wealth, Vol. 24, Princeton: Princeton University Press, 1960, pp. 255–312.

Twyman, 1971 [FE 333]
Robert W. Twyman, "The Clay Eater: A New Look at an Old Southern Enigma," *Journal of Southern History*, Vol. XXXVII (August 1971), pp. 439–48.

Udy, 1959
Stanley H. Udy, Jr., *Organization of Work*, New Haven: HRAF Press, 1959.

UN, FAO, 1962
Food and Agricultural Organization of the United Nations, FAO/WHO Expert Group, "Calcium Requirements," *FAO Nutrition Meetings Report Series*, Number 30, Rome: FAO, 1962.

UN, FAO, 1965
Food and Agricultural Organization of the United Nations, FAO/WHO Expert Group, "Protein Requirements," *FAO Nutrition Meetings Report Series*, Number 37, Rome: FAO, 1965.

UN, FAO, 1967
Food and Agricultural Organization of the United Nations, FAO/WHO Expert Group, "Requirements of Vitamin A, Thiamine, Riboflavine and Niacin," *FAO Nutrition Meetings Report Series*, Number 41, Rome: FAO, 1967.

USBC, 1918
U.S. Bureau of the Census, *Negro Population: 1790–1915*, Washington: GPO, 1918.

USBC, 1960 [FE 343]
U.S. Bureau of the Census, *Historical Statistics of the United States, Colonial Time to 1957*, Washington: GPO, 1960.

USBL, 1894 [FE 344]
U.S. Bureau of Labor, "The Slums of Baltimore, Chicago, New York, and Philadelphia," *Seventh Special Report of the Commissioner of Labor*, Washington: GPO, 1894.

U.S. Census, 1830
U.S. Census Office, 5th Census, 1830, *Fifth Census; or, Enumeration of the Inhabitants of the United States, as Corrected at the Department of State*, Washington: Duff Green, 1832.

U.S. Census, 1840
U.S. Census Office, 6th Census, 1840, *Sixth Census or Enumeration of the Inhabitants of the United States, as Corrected at the Department of State*, Washington: Blair and Rives, 1841.

U.S. Census, 1850, Mortality
U.S. Census Office, 7th Census, 1850, *Mortality Statistics of the Seventh Census of the United States, 1850*, Washington: A. O. P. Nicholson, 1855.

U.S. Census, 1850, Population
U.S. Census Office, 7th Census, 1850, *The Seventh Census of the United States: 1850*, Washington: Robert Armstrong, 1853.

U.S. Census, 1860, Agriculture [FE 337]
U.S. Census Office, 8th Census, 1860, *Agriculture of the United States in 1860*, Washington: GPO, 1864.

U.S. Census, 1860, Population [FE 338]
U.S. Census Office, 8th Census, 1860, *Population of the United States in 1860*, Washington: GPO, 1864.

U.S. Census, 1860, Statistics [FE 340]
U.S. Census Office, 8th Census, 1860, *Statistics of the United States (Including Mortality, Property, &c.) in 1860*, Washington: GPO, 1866.

U.S. Census, 1880, Manufacturing
U.S. Census Office, 10th Census, 1880, *Report on the Manufactures of the United States*, Washington: GPO, 1883.

U.S. Census, 1890, Agriculture
U.S. Census Office, 11th Census, 1890, *Reports on the Statistics of Agriculture in the United States*, Washington: GPO, 1895.

USDA, 1867
U.S. Department of Agriculture, *Report of the Commissioner of Agriculture for the Year 1867*, Washington: GPO, 1868.

USDA, 1937
U.S. Department of Agriculture, *Livestock on Farms, January 1, 1867-1919: Revised Estimates: Number, Value per Head, Total Value, by States and Divisions*, Washington: USDA, 1937.

USDA, AMS, 1956
U.S. Department of Agriculture, Agricultural Marketing Service, Crop Reporting Board, "Milk: Farm Production, Disposition, and Income: Revised Estimates: 1950-54," *USDA Statistical Bulletin*, Number 175, Washington: GPO, April 1956.

USDA, AMS, 1958 [FE 347]
U.S. Department of Agriculture, Agricultural Marketing Service, "Livestock and Meat Statistics, 1957," *USDA Statistical Bulletin*, Number 230, Washington: GPO, July 1958.

USDA, AMS, 1958a
U.S. Department of Agriculture, Agricultural Marketing Service, Crop Reporting Board, "Sweetpotatoes: Estimates in Hundredweight, by States, 1868-1953; Acreage, Yield, Production, Price, Value, Farm Disposition," *USDA Statistical Bulletin*, Number 237, Washington: GPO, September 1958.

USDA, BAE, 1949 [FE 345]
U.S. Department of Agriculture, Bureau of Agricultural Economics, "Consumption of Food in the United States, 1909-48," *U.S.D.A. Miscellaneous Publication*, Number 691, Washington: GPO, August 1949.

USDA, BCE, 1916
U.S. Department of Agriculture, Bureau of Crop Estimates, *Monthly Crop Report*, Vol. 2 (February 29, 1916), pp. 18-19.

USDA, ERS, 1965
U.S. Department of Agriculture, Economic Research Service, "Conversion Factors and Weights and Measures for Agricultural Commodities and Their Products," *USDA Statistical Bulletin*, Number 362, Washington: GPO, June 1965.

U.S. National Center for Health Statistics, 1973
U.S. Public Health Service, National Center for Health Statistics, "Age at Menarche: United States," *Vital and Health Statistics Series 11*, Number 133, Rockwell: Health Resources Administration, November 1973.

USPO, 1848
U.S. Patent Office, *Annual Report of the Commissioner of Patents for the Year 1848*, Washington: Wendell and Van Benthuysen, 1849.

USPO, 1849
U.S. Patent Office, *Report of the Commissioner of Patents for the Year 1849*, Part

II: "Agriculture," Washington: Office of Printers to the [U.S.] House of Rep[resentative]s, 1850.

USPO, 1851
U.S. Patent Office, *Report of the Commissioner of Patents for the Year 1851*, Part II: "Agriculture," Washington: Robert Armstrong, 1852.

USPO, 1852
U.S. Patent Office, *Report of the Commissioner of Patents for the Year 1852*, Part II: "Agriculture," Washington: Robert Armstrong, 1853.

Wade, 1964
Richard C. Wade, *Slavery in the Cities: The South, 1820–1860*, New York: Oxford University Press, 1964.

Wailes, 1854
B. L. C. Wailes, *Report on the Agriculture and Geology of Mississippi: Embracing a Sketch of the Social and Natural History of the State* [Jackson]: Barksdale, 1854.

Watt and Merrill, 1950 [FE 355]
Bernice K. Watt and Annabel L. Merrill, U.S. Department of Agriculture, "Composition of Foods: Raw, Processed, Prepared," *USDA Agricultural Handbook*, Number 8, Washington: GPO, June 1950.

Watt and Merrill, 1963
Bernice K. Watt and Annabel L. Merrill, U.S. Department of Agriculture, "Composition of Foods: Raw, Processed, Prepared," *USDA Agricultural Handbook*, Number 8, Revised edition, Washington: GPO, December 1963.

Weld, 1839 [FE 359]
[Theodore D. Weld], *American Slavery As It Is: Testimony of a Thousand Witnesses*, New York: American Anti-Slavery Society, 1839.

Wesley, 1927 [FE 360]
C. H. Wesley, *Negro Labor in the United States, 1850–1925*, New York: Vanguard Press, 1927.

Williams, 1961
Robert R. Williams, *Toward the Conquest of Beriberi*, Cambridge: Harvard University Press, 1961.

Williamson, 1974
Jeffery Williamson, *Late Nineteenth Century American Development*, New York: Cambridge University Press, 1974.

Wilson, Fisher, and Fugua, 1965
Eva D. Wilson, Katherine H. Fisher, and Mary E. Fugua, *Principles of Nutrition*, 2nd edition, New York: John Wiley and Sons, 1965.

Woodman, 1972
Harold D. Woodman, "Economic History and Economic Theory: The New

Economic History in America," *Journal of Inter-Disciplinary History,* Vol. III (Autumn 1972), pp. 323–50.

Woodward, 1951 [FE 385]
C. Vann Woodward, *Origins of the New South, 1877–1913,* Volume IX of Wendell Holmes Stephenson and E. Merton Coulter, eds., *A History of the South.* Baton Rouge: Louisiana State University Press, 1951.

Woodward, 1968
C. Vann Woodward, "Southern Ethic in a Puritan World," *William and Mary Quarterly,* 3rd s, Vol. XXV (July 1968), pp. 343–70.

Woodward, 1974
C. Vann Woodward, "History from Slave Sources," *American Historical Review,* Vol. 79 (April 1974), pp. 470–81.

Woodward, 1974a
C. Vann Woodward, "The Jolly Institution," *New York Review of Books,* Vol. XXI, 2 (May 2, 1974), pp. 3–6.

WPA Virginia, 1940
Works Progress Administration, Workers of the Writers Program, State of Virginia, *The Negro in Virginia,* New York, 1940.

Wright, 1970 [FE 388]
Gavin Wright, " 'Economic Democracy' and the Concentration of Agricultural Wealth in the Cotton South, 1850–1860," *Agricultural History,* Vol. XXXXIV (January 1970), pp. 63–94.

Wright, 1970a [FE 389]
Gavin Wright, "Note on the Manuscript Census Samples Used in These Studies," *Agricultural History,* Vol. XLIV (January 1970), pp. 95–100.

Wright, 1971
Gavin Wright, "An Econometric Study of Cotton Production and Trade, 1830–1860," *Review of Economics and Statistics,* Vol. LII (May 1971), pp. 111–20.

Wright, 1973 [FE 391]
Gavin Wright, "New and Old Views on the Economics of Slavery," *Journal of Economic History,* Vol. XXXIII (June 1973), pp. 452–66.

Wright, 1974
Gavin Wright, "Cotton Competition and the Post-Bellum Recovery of the American South," *Journal of Economic History,* Vol. XXXIV (September 1974), pp. 610–35.

Wright, 1975
Gavin Wright, "Slavery and the Cotton Boom," *Explorations in Economic History,* Vol. 12 (October 1975), pp. 439–51.

Wright and Kunreuther, 1975
Gavin Wright and Howard Kunreuther, "Cotton, Corn and Risk in the

Nineteenth Century," *Journal of Economic History*, Vol. XXV (September 1975), pp. 526–51.

Yasuba, 1962
Yasukichi Yasuba, *Birth Rates of the White Population in the United States, 1800–1860, an Economic Study*, Baltimore: Johns Hopkins Press, 1962.

Zelnick, 1966–67
Melvin Zelnick, "Fertility of the American Negro in 1830 and 1850," *Population Studies*, Vol. 20 (1966–67), pp. 77–83.

INDEX

CONCORDANCE* to
Time on the Cross
Volume I, The Economics
of American Negro Slavery

TOTC	RWS	TOTC	RWS
3–4	4	53	105, 110, 114, 114 n. 30
4	3		
4–5	95	53–54	20
4–6	12	55	20
5	55, 186, 203–4	61	305, 305 n. 2, 308 n. 8
5–6	187	70	42 n. 11, 160 n. 40
6	5	70–71	306
7–8	3	70–73	307
8	4	71	42
8–9	4	72	159, 189 n. 25
9–11	5, 6	72:F15	159
10	175	73	34, 189
11	239	73–78	194 n. 30
11–12	176	75	20
25:F6	151	78	21, 43, 135, 137, 155
38	26 n. 32	78–79	44 n. 16
39	26 n. 32, 77, 80, 81 n. 33	79	21, 44
		80–81	161 n. 42
40	19, 26, 26 n. 32, 28, 74, 76	82–83	155, 194 n. 30
		83	44, 44 n. 16, 135, 156, 194 n. 31
40–41	45, 76		
41	20, 26	83–84	157, 232 n. 3
43	26	83–86	155
46:F12	99 n. 3	84	135, 136, 137 n. 1, 156
48	100, 160		
49	100, 100 n. 5, 112–13, 116, 120, 121, 123:T2(n.c,d)	84–85	98
		86–94	303
		89–94	308
49–50	130	91	327
50	130	92	314
50–51	115	93	326 n. 38, 327
50:F14	116	93–94	304
51	132	94–97	303
52	43 n. 13, 232 n. 3	95–96	222 n. 60

* For the convenience of students and others who wish to locate quickly the places in this volume (RWS) where a particular passage in *Time on the Cross* (TOTC) is discussed, this concordance organizes in consecutive order our page citations to FE I and II. Tables are indicated by T, followed by the table number, figures by F, followed by their number. Footnote numbers follow (n.).

TOTC	RWS
95–97	309
96–97	309
97	311
99	270
102	75, 149
103–6	42 n. 12, 303, 306, 309
104	311
104–6	149
105	307
108	34, 38
108–9	6
109	34, 232 n. 2, 240
111	236
111–15	234 n. 6
112	265
113	240, 250 n. 47, 254, 266, 268
113–15	179
114:F35	295, 295 n. 172
115	268–69, 270, 275, 295, 298
115–16	25
116	232 n. 2, 292, 295, 296, 297
119	282
120	232 n. 2
123	51 n. 28, 284
123–24	284, 286
124	49, 286, 287 n. 155
124–25	286
124–44	46
125	234 n. 5, 287
125–26	288
125:F36	283 n. 148
126	21, 232 n. 2, 283
126–28	125
126–30	43 n. 13
126–44	136
127	94, 232 n. 3
128	95, 98
129	95
129–35	136
130	232 n. 3
131–38	313
132	149
133	21, 22, 150, 151
133–34	232 n. 3
134	26 n. 32, 30, 43 n. 13
134–35	153

TOTC	RWS
135	43 n. 13, 137, 153, 154 n. 30
136	49
136–39	49
137	49, 116, 139, 288
138	136
138–39	154 n.30
138:F37	140 n.6
139	22, 146
140:F39	147:T2
143	48 n.23
144	48
145	58, 59 n.4, 60, 61, 61 n.8, 62, 64:T1
146	55
146–47	43 n.13
147	38 n.6, 55, 74, 91, 94
147–51	232 n.3
148	23, 55, 70, 71, 73
148–49	69
148–52	23
149	74
150	34, 45 n.18, 75, 80 n.32
152	74 n.27
153	86, 186, 187
155	197
155–56	196
156	200–201
158–61	226 n.64
170	16 n.24
180–81	16 n.24
191–93	202
191–209	303
192	202, 203 n.42
192–93	181
192–95	217 n.56
193	205
194–96	315
199	326
199–200	326 n.38
199–203	205
200	84, 326
200–201	83
201	84
202–3	232 n.3
204	205
205	34, 92, 206
208	211 n.50, 283 n.146

Concordance 397

TOTC	RWS
209–10	203
210	34, 81 n.33, 206
210–12	83, 207
211	84, 86
212	84, 86, 90
215	14, 27, 90
216–17	14 n.21
223	90, 173 n.4
226	12, 231 n.1
228–29	231 n.1
230	90
231	55, 90
231–32	34, 90, 232 n.3
232	34, 40, 55, 67
234	321
234–35	322
236	323
237	55
237–38	323

TOTC	RWS
238	322
238–39	224 n.61
239	184
239–42	232 n.3
241–42	24
244	224
244–45	225
247–55	303
247–57	172 n.3
250–57	328
255–57	329
258	36
258–64	5
259–60	300
262	232 n.2
263	34
263–64	25, 232 n.3
264	37

Volume II, Evidence and Methods

TOTC	RWS
4	176
16	174
19	225 n.62
24	77, 113
37	61, 77, 78, 79, 79 n.31
38	122 n.34, 123: T2(n.a)
38–39	81
39	82 n.36, 83, 83 n.37
39–40	81 n.33, 83
39–41	331
40	79, 80, 83
40:TB.5	81:T4, 89:T6
41	84
42	26
43–48	99 n.3
44	99 n.3
45	99 n.3
46	108 n.21
48–49	117
49	115, 121:T2(n.a), 124

TOTC	RWS
49–51	122 n.34
50	122 n.34
51	115, 116, 123: T2(n.a), 124
51–52	122
52	105, 120, 121, 122, 123:T2(n.b,d), 125, 125 n.35
53	101, 101 n.6, 101 n.8
58–59	188
62	222 n.60
62–64	307 n.7
64	305
64–79	39 n.7, 304
65	305
65–79	306
72–75	306
78	160 n.40, 194 n.31
79	189, 189 n.25
80	158, 159, 190 n.26
80–81	194 n.30
81–82	194
83	188

TOTC	RWS
83–84	158
86	326 n.38, 327
87	195 n.33
90–91	236
91	239, 252 n.54
91–92	237, 269
92–95	237
94	180, 182, 237, 238 n.14, 239, 249
95	180, 237, 240, 240 n.21, 244, 244 n.27, 246, 252 n.54, 259, 260
96	247, 248, 248 n.37, 248 n.38, 251
97	240 n.21
97:TB.13	258, 262–63:T1(n.b), 264 n.96, 269 n.104
98	181 n.13, 245 n.30, 262–63:T1(n.d), 265 n.99, 268, 270
99	269, 274, 277 n.129, 293, 293 n.166, 295, 295 n.171
100	283, 284
100–101	284 n.150
101	283, 288
101–2	149 n.21
101–11	149
102	149 n.23
103:TB.14	149 n.23
105	150 n.24
109–10	235
110–13	151
111:TB.17	151
112	151
113	153 n.26
113–14	43 n.13, 153
114	49 n.25, 144
115	126, 127
115–16	128, 129:T3
116	59 n.4, 127
117	75
117–18	45 n.18, 74, 80 n.32
118	24 n.31

TOTC	RWS
118:TB.18	75
119–20	189 n.24
120	176
120–22	196 n.34
124	186, 187
125	188 n.22, 195
126–27	212 n.52
126–42	202
132	214 n.54
133	186 n.21
134	217, 217 n.57
135	214 n.54
135–37	203 n.42
136	215
138	213, 213 n.53
138–40	203 n.42, 315
139	217 n.56, 336
139:TB.23, TB.24	202 n.41
140	319
140–41	317 n.26
143	186 n.21
144	181, 319
145	319
151	84 n.40
151–52	83, 84 n.40
152	84 n.40
155–58	232 n.3
158	185, 323
159–60	185 n.19
160	224 n.61
160–61	323
169	231 n.1
189	231 n.1
218	231 n.1
221–22	232 n.3
222	226 n.63, 232 n.3
234–35	173 n.4
240	235 n.8, 240, 240 n.18, 269
250	128 n.27
252	59 n.4, 293 n.166
257	128 n.37
262	74
265	245 n.30